Beyond Constitu
The Pluralist Structure of
Postnational Law

Nico Krisch

OXFORD
UNIVERSITY PRESS

OXFORD
UNIVERSITY PRESS

Great Clarendon Street, Oxford, OX2 6DP,
United Kingdom

Oxford University Press is a department of the University of Oxford.
It furthers the University's objective of excellence in research, scholarship,
and education by publishing worldwide. Oxford is a registered trade mark of
Oxford University Press in the UK and in certain other countries

© Nico Krisch, 2010

The moral rights of the authors have been asserted

First edition 2010
First published in paperback 2012
Impression: 1

All rights reserved. No part of this publication may be reproduced, stored in
a retrieval system, or transmitted, in any form or by any means, without the
prior permission in writing of Oxford University Press, or as expressly permitted
by law, by licence or under terms agreed with the appropriate reprographics
rights organization. Enquiries concerning reproduction outside the scope of the
above should be sent to the Rights Department, Oxford University Press, at the
address above

You must not circulate this work in any other form
and you must impose this same condition on any acquirer

Crown copyright material is reproduced under Class Licence
Number C01P0000148 with the permission of OPSI
and the Queen's Printer for Scotland

British Library Cataloguing in Publication Data
Data available

Library of Congress Cataloging in Publication Data
Data available

ISBN 978–0–19–922831–7
ISBN 978–0–19–965996–8 (pbk.)

Printed in Great Britain by
CPI Group (UK) Ltd., Croydon, CR0 4YY

OXFORD CONSTITUTIONAL THEORY

Series Editors:
Martin Loughlin, John P. McCormick, and Neil Walker

Beyond Constitutionalism: The Pluralist Structure of Postnational Law

OXFORD CONSTITUTIONAL THEORY

Series Editors:

Martin Loughlin, John P. McCormick, and Neil Walker

One consequence of the increase in interest in constitutions and constitutional law in recent years is a growing innovative literature in constitutional theory. The aim of *Oxford Constitutional Theory* is to provide a showcase for the best of these theoretical reflections and a forum for further innovation in the field.

The new series will seek to establish itself as the primary point of reference for scholarly work in the subject by commissioning different types of study. The majority of the works published in the series will be monographs that advance new understandings of the subject. Well-conceived edited collections that bring a variety of perspectives and disciplinary approaches to bear on specific themes in constitutional thought will also be included. Further, in recognition of the facts that there is a great deal of pioneering literature originally written in languages other than English and with regard to non-anglophone constitutional traditions, the series will also seek to publish English language translations of leading monographs in constitutional theory.

Acknowledgements

This book has been long in the making. It has progressed in fits and starts, through phases of stagnation, interruption, and distraction, and through a process in which, for long, my ideas kept changing direction every time they seemed settled. Some of these changes were due to the different intellectual environments I have worked in over the last ten years—the idea to write a book on postnational law, pluralism, and constitutionalism came up while I was at NYU Law School and took shape during my years at Merton College, Oxford; most chapters were written while I taught at the London School of Economics and finished now that I work at the Hertie School of Governance in Berlin. All these contexts have provided me with different stimuli, but they have all proved to be enormously enriching, and I wish to thank my colleagues at all of them—as well as the institutions themselves—for the outstanding support I enjoyed. I also thank the Max Planck Society for the Advancement of Science for its generous financial support in the early stages of the project.

Many people have helped me directly, especially by reading and commenting on parts of the book as it was emerging. For this, I owe much gratitude to Aida Torres Pérez, Alec Stone Sweet, Alejandro Chehtman, Alejandro Sáiz Arnaiz, Alexander Somek, Andrew Lang, Anne Peters, Anne Thies, Anthea Roberts, Benedict Kingsbury, Carol Harlow, Caterina García, Cathryn Costello, Chandran Kukathas, Christian Walter, Christoph Möllers, Craig Scott, Eran Shamir-Borer, Ewan Macdonald, Greg Shaffer, Jo Murkens, Jochen Frowein, Joseph Weiler, Julia Black, Luzius Wildhaber, Marisa Iglesias, Mark Kayser, Martin Loughlin, Mattias Kumm, Michael Zürn, Neil Walker, Nicolas Lamp, Oriol Casanovas, Pavlos Eleftheriadis, Richard Stewart, Stephen Weatherill, Tom Poole, and Wibren van der Burg. I also wish to thank participants in workshops, conferences, and colloquia at the European University Institute, the Hertie School of Governance, the LSE Law Department, NYU Law School, Oxford University's Law Faculty, Princeton University's Woodrow Wilson School, the Law School at Queen's University, Belfast, the University of Bielefeld, Westminster University, Yale Law School, and the Law Faculty at Universitat Pompeu Fabra. The last has also proved to be a most welcoming environment during my stays in Barcelona. Aram Khaghaghordyan, Corey Barber, and Dana Trif have provided very valuable research assistance in the final stages of the book, and Natasha Knight, Lucy Page, and Joy Ruskin-Tompkins have steered the book through the production process at OUP with admirable effectiveness.

Most of all, though, I wish to thank Neus Torbisco Casals for her unflinching support throughout the project, despite the fact that it meant much more work for her and less time for us together. I owe apologies to our daughter, Clara—she tried to sabotage my work whenever she could but eventually (and grudgingly) accepted that I spent many evenings and weekends with my computer rather than with her. I cannot really make up for that, but I promise that the next book project will have to wait some time.

★ ★ ★

Some of the chapters are based on other publications of mine, and I gratefully acknowledge those publications as well as the permission to use the material in this book. Parts of Chapters 2 and 3 are to appear as 'The Case for Pluralism in Postnational Law' in G de Búrca & J H H Weiler (eds), *The Worlds of European Constitutionalism*, Cambridge: Cambridge University Press, forthcoming. An earlier version of Chapter 4 was published as 'The Open Architecture of European Human Rights Law', *Modern Law Review* 71 (2008), 183–216. A previous version of Chapter 6 appeared as 'Pluralism in Postnational Risk Regulation: The Dispute over GMOs and Trade', *Transnational Legal Theory* 1 (2010), 1–29. These papers were also published, in yet earlier versions, in the *LSE Law, Economics and Society Working Paper Series* (as nos 17/2009, 11/2007, and 12/2009 respectively).

Nico Krisch
June 2010

Summary Contents

Detailed Contents

Cases

Council of Europe

World Trade Organization

United Nations

Documents

World Health Organization and Food and Agriculture Organization

Codex Alimentarius Commission

World Trade Organization

International Agreements

Others

PART I

VISIONS OF POSTNATIONAL LAW

❧ 1 ❧
Postnational Law in Search of a Structure

I. CLIMAX AND CRISIS

In the twenty years since the end of the Cold War, the modern framework
of law and politics has plunged from one of its greatest successes into one
of its most serious crises. In the early 1990s, constitutionalism, the cornerstone of Western political imagination for two centuries, seemed to emerge
unrivalled when its main competitor disappeared from the scene, and it
became the model for political change not only in Central and Eastern
Europe but in many other parts of the world as well. At the same time,
international law turned into a beacon of hope, unleashed by the demise
of deadlock and disagreement and suddenly able to redeem its promise of
a better, more just world. The international sphere seemed to move from
anarchy to order, with new institutions and courts structuring the emerging landscape and common values providing a principled framework for
it. The spread of constitutional democracy at the domestic level seemed to
be reinforced and secured by an increasingly robust and fair international
legal order.

Two decades later, both constitutionalism and international law have
come under heavy pressure and are unlikely to survive in their classical
form. In both cases, this has to do with their own success and the success
of the respective other. Constitutionalism is struggling because international law and global governance have become increasingly effective, thus
removing key issues from the reach of national constitutions and domestic
political processes. International law, on the other hand, experiences problems because its thin, consent-oriented legitimacy base no longer appears
adequate to the task. Now that international law has grown in importance, it
is seen as overly formalistic and undemocratic, and a thicker, more substantive foundation seems called for. Constitutionalism stands ready to fill this
gap, but to many, it appears as unsuited for this expansion and also as too
emblematic of a particular political tradition.

As constitutionalism and international law are moving closer together,
both undergo radical change, risk their identity, and may well shift into a

twilight.[1] The classical distinction between the domestic and international spheres that had sustained them is increasingly blurred, with a multitude of formal and informal connections taking the place of what once were relatively clear rules and categories. In this sense, law has become 'postnational'—the national sphere retains importance, but it is no longer the paradigmatic anchor of the whole order. In Europe, this process began earlier under the influence of European integration, but many held out the hope that old frameworks could be revived once the integration process had gone far enough. Globalization and the rise of global governance have shattered this hope—they have undermined old distinctions, created deeper connections, yet without serious prospects to recreate the statist paradigm on a larger scale.

Law and politics have been transformed, but we do not quite know yet how—we do not have a settled understanding of what structures are currently taking shape, or in what directions the changes go or should go. We experience, as Neil Walker has phrased it, a 'disorder of orders', with countless analytical and normative proposals competing for influence.[2] Many are inspired by domestic analogues, such as administrative law or indeed constitutionalism. This is only too natural: if much of what used to be domestic has now moved into the global sphere, extending domestic concepts is an obvious move to salvage historical achievements. Yet other proposals take the opposite path: they seek to use the opportunity to break free from traditional frameworks that have perhaps captured our imagination for too long. As usual, a great transformation comes with freedom, opportunities, and anxiety.

This is the landscape in which this book is situated. It is a rugged landscape, one in which it is far from clear whether and how the forms and values that have shaped our political imagination for the last few centuries can be recast and made to work. We do not know yet whether in the postnational setting we can recreate the sense of collective political agency so characteristic of Western politics since the late eighteenth century; whether we can envision democratic theories with real purchase in the complex structures of global governance; whether the idea of a 'public' power will be as central to the postnational sphere as it has been in the domestic; or whether Western governance scripts should at all be the focus of our imagination for global structures.

---

[1] See M Loughlin & P Dobner (eds), *The Twilight of Constitutionalism?*, Oxford: Oxford University Press, 2010.

[2] N Walker, 'Beyond Boundary Disputes and Basic Grids: Mapping the Global Disorder of Normative Orders', *International Journal of Constitutional Law* 6 (2008), 373–96.

This book does not pretend to have conclusive answers to these big, open questions or to present a comprehensive proposal for the future development of postnational politics and law. If anything, it aims to clarify the challenge we are facing and some of the key choices that lie ahead. It begins in this chapter by outlining why it might be justified to conceive of today's law as 'postnational'—a notion that may be accepted more readily in politics but still meets with significant resistance in the legal arena. The remainder of the book explores the shape and trajectories of the order that is beginning to replace the classical, 'Westphalian' configuration. It focuses on two central structural visions for postnational law: constitutionalism and pluralism. Both capture elements of the way the legal order beyond the state has developed over the last decades, but observers disagree as to which has been more influential. This book seeks to shed light on this question, yet more importantly, it seeks to help us better understand how these antagonistic visions relate to the circumstances of postnational politics—circumstances which, because of the degree of societal diversity and contestation, are markedly different from those we typically find in domestic politics. What forms and structures we need to realize key political values in this context, is the question driving the inquiry in this and the following chapters.

II. POSTNATIONAL POLITICS—POSTNATIONAL LAW?

The term 'postnational' had been in use for some time before Jürgen Habermas made it prominent in the late 1990s. It was employed chiefly to analyse changes in the practice of citizenship and membership—it pointed to a process by which membership rights had become decoupled from a strong form of belonging to a national polity.[3] With Habermas and other authors picking the term up, it took on a broader meaning, denoting now a more general decoupling of political processes from the nation-state; a development that demoted the state from the centre of the political universe to one among a number of actors in a wider setting, populated also by international institutions, multinational companies and transnational non-governmental organizations (NGOs).[4] The diagnosis was, in Michael Zürn's words, that

> [t]he national constellation, that is the convergence of resources, recognition and the realization of governance goals in one political organization—the nation state—, seems to be in a process of transformation into a post-national

---

[3] See, eg, Y N Soysal, *Limits of Citizenship: Migrants and Postnational Membership in Europe*, Chicago, IL: University of Chicago Press, 1994.

[4] See J Habermas, *Die postnationale Konstellation*, Frankfurt am Main: Suhrkamp Verlag, 1998.

constellation. The nation state is no longer the only site of authority and the normativity that accompanies it.[5]

Throughout the first decade of the twenty-first century, this usage became more commonly accepted.[6] The diagnosis behind it—the fact that the centre of gravity had shifted away from the nation-state in its classical configuration—was in any event hardly contested any more.[7] The boundary between domestic and international politics had become a 'frontier', in James Rosenau's influential expression: 'a new and wide political space ... continuously shifting widening, and narrowing, simultaneously undergoing erosion with respect to many issues and reinforcement with respect to others'.[8] In other areas, postnationalism was subject to greater dispute. For example, while Ulf Hedetoft and Mette Hjort introduced their 2002 volume on 'The Postnational Self' by pointing out that 'hybrid identities, several homes, and multiple attachments are a fact of life in most nation-states',[9] the contributors varied in their assessment of the degree and direction of the actual shifts in individual identities.

1. Law at the Domestic–International Frontier

In law, diagnosing a 'postnational turn' faces yet higher hurdles. It is one thing to state that the centre of political authority and feelings of belonging have changed, another to claim that this has effected a shift in the structure of the legal order. Law's formality resists the simple reflection of shifts in its environment; the law insists on its own power to determine whether a fact is legally relevant and how.[10] Political deterritorialization and pluralization

---

[5] M Zürn, 'The State in the Postnational Constellation—Societal Denationalization and Multi-Level Governance', *ARENA Working Papers*, WP 99/35, <http://www.arena.uio.no/publications/working-papers1999/papers/wp99_35.htm>.

[6] See, eg, the *Wikipedia* entry on 'Postnationalism', <http://en.wikipedia.org/wiki/Postnationalism>: 'the process or trend by which nation states and national identities lose their importance relative to supranational and global entities'.

[7] For an early influential statement, see S Strange, *The Retreat of the State: The Diffusion of Power in the World Economy*, Cambridge: Cambridge University Press, 1996.

[8] J N Rosenau, *Along the Domestic-Foreign Frontier: Exploring Governance in a Turbulent World*, Cambridge: Cambridge University Press, 1997, 4.

[9] U Hedetoft & M Hjort, 'Introduction' in U Hedetoft & M Hjort (eds), *The Postnational Self: Belonging and Identity*, Minneapolis, MN: University of Minnesota Press, 2002, iii–xxxii at xvi.

[10] See, eg, N Luhmann, *Das Recht der Gesellschaft*, Frankfurt am Main: Suhrkamp Verlag, 1993, chs 1 and 2.

may thus contrast with law's aspiration for unity.[11] And indeed, the classical, formal separation between national and international law had long survived the factual pressures stemming from the increasing density of international law. The fact that there was a thick layer of law on the international level did not in and of itself challenge the distinct existence of domestic law, which regulated—through the national constitution or other domestic instruments—the extent to which external norms entered it.

In Europe, this came to be challenged by the rise of European Union law.[12] Through doctrines such as direct effect and supremacy, EU law claimed for itself the right to determine its impact in the domestic sphere, thus piercing the protective veil around national law. This impact could theoretically be traced back to delegations from member states, and domestic legal orders also continued to stipulate conditions for European law to have effect in them.[13] Yet the need for uniform interpretation and application largely reduced this insistence on domestic autonomy to a mere formality, relevant only in marginal cases, if at all. In the normal course of affairs, norms generated at the EU level trumped domestic law, and the two formed part of a more integrated legal order than the classical domestic/international dichotomy suggested[14]—albeit one in which European law was often 'indigenised' in its application in the national realm.[15] Unsurprisingly, EU law is often labelled as *sui generis*—it simply does not fit the established categories.[16]

[11] H Lindahl, 'A-Legality: Postnationalism and the Question of Legal Boundaries', *Modern Law Review* 73 (2010), 30–56.

[12] Throughout this book, I use 'European Union' and 'EU' also to refer to the European Communities as they existed before the 1992 'Treaty on European Union', in order to avoid confusion for readers less familiar with the development of Europe's formal and institutional structures. On the trajectory of European integration, see P P Craig & G de Búrca, *EU Law: Text, Cases, and Materials*, 4th edn, Oxford: Oxford University Press, 2008, ch 1.

[13] See, eg, the judgment of the German Federal Constitutional Court on the Maastricht Treaty, Bundesverfassungsgericht, Judgment of 12 October 1993, *Maastricht*, BVerfGE 89, 155.

[14] See E Stein, 'Lawyers, Judges, and the Making of a Transnational Constitution', *American Journal of International Law* 75 (1981), 1–27; J H H Weiler, 'The Transformation of Europe', *Yale Law Journal* 100 (1991), 2403–83.

[15] See J Jupille & J A Caporaso, 'Domesticating Discourses: European Law, English Judges, and Political Institutions', *European Political Science Review* 1 (2009), 205–28.

[16] See, eg, D Chalmers & A Tomkins, *European Union Public Law*, Cambridge: Cambridge University Press, 2007, 44–57.

Beyond the European Union, transformative processes had less of a formal pedigree. International law was increasingly dealing with domestic issues, but this fact did not at first appear to challenge classical structures.[17] Yet thicker linkages between layers of law are visible, for example, in human rights matters. In the European human rights regime—which I will analyse in greater detail in Chapter 4—national constitutions have increasingly been interpreted as linked with European human rights standards, creating a default position often difficult to rebut, while European rights bodies were careful to respond to domestic readings of certain rights.[18] Similar interactions have been observed well beyond Europe. International human rights norms and practices have became increasingly influential for domestic judges—sometimes even despite the fact that they were not binding for the country concerned, as in the much-noted *Baker* case in Canada.[19] This has led to a diagnosis of a 'creeping monism' in many common law countries, quite in contrast with their classical dualist stance.[20] Yet processes of adaptation and reinterpretation of national constitutions and law on the basis of regional or international human rights norms are widespread in other jurisdictions too—provoking the 'globalisation of state constitutions', as one commentator has noted.[21]

Another area in which the classical bifurcation between domestic and international law is under pressure is that of global regulatory governance. In the context of security governance, the UN Security Council began to target individuals and non-state groups in the 1990s, and at times it created

---

[17] See A-M Slaughter & W Burke-White, 'The Future of International Law is Domestic (or, The European Way of Law)', *Harvard International Law Journal* 47 (2006), 327–52 at 349–50, who emphasize the impact of international law on domestic politics but insist on the continuing divide between domestic and international law, 'at least conceptually'.

[18] See Chapter 4, I and II.

[19] Supreme Court of Canada, Judgment of 9 July 1999, *Baker v Minister of Citizenship and Immigration*, [1999] 2 SCR 817. For thoughtful discussions of this and related cases, see K Knop, 'Here and There: International Law in Domestic Courts', *NYU Journal of International Law and Politics* 32 (2000), 501–35; M Moran, 'Shifting Boundaries: The Authority of International Law' in J Nijman & A Nollkaemper (eds), *New Perspectives on the Divide Between National and International Law*, Oxford: Oxford University Press, 2007, 163–90 at 167–74.

[20] M Waters, 'Creeping Monism: The Judicial Trend toward Interpretive Incorporation of Human Rights Treaties', *Columbia Law Review* 107 (2007), 628–705.

[21] A Peters, 'The Globalization of State Constitutions', in Nijman & Nollkaemper, *New Perspectives*, 251–308.

immediate obligations for them, thus piercing the veil of the national legal order.[22] This has led to some resistance and countermoves, which will be the subject of more detailed investigation in Chapter 5. In spite of such tensions, Security Council resolutions are often granted particular weight in the domestic sphere. In many countries, they benefit from facilitated procedures, sometimes even from an automatic incorporation into national law. In this way, UN sanctions implementation often avoids participatory procedures and parliamentary oversight, which would have been applicable to other forms of regulation. And it often enjoys special weight when domestic courts conduct proportionality analyses of interferences with individual rights.[23]

In other areas of global governance, international norms may not insist on direct effect or enjoy formalized privileges in the domestic realm, but they have become an ever more integral part of overall law-making mechanisms— and have 'colonised' domestic law to an important extent.[24] As we will see in Chapter 6, world trade law has come to shape EU law and jurisprudence as a matter of course, despite the reluctance of the European Court of Justice formally to accept its direct effect in the legal order of the Union. This also helps related standards, such as those set by the Codex Alimentarius Commission on food safety matters, to influence the practice of domestic courts and regulators in significant ways.[25] In the area of financial regulation, non-binding global standards, usually set by the Basel Committee on Banking Supervision, are transformed into domestic regulations almost automatically—because they benefit from facilitated procedures (as in the EU), because states cannot afford not to implement them because of the costs involved, or because of an identity of domestic and global regulators which makes implementation a matter of course.[26] More broadly, we can observe an increasing number

---

[22] See J A Frowein & N Krisch, 'Introduction to Chapter VII' in B Simma et al (eds), *The Charter of the United Nations: A Commentary*, 2nd edn, Oxford: Oxford University Press, 2002, 701–16 at 714–16.

[23] See V Gowlland-Debbas, 'Concluding Remarks' in V Gowlland-Debbas (ed), *National Implementation of United Nations Sanctions: A Comparative Study*, The Hague: Martinus Nijhoff, 2004, 643–58 at 644–5.

[24] N Torbisco Casals, 'Beyond Unity and Coherence: The Challenge of Legal Pluralism in a Post-National World', *Revista Jurídica de la Universidad de Puerto Rico* 77 (2008), 531–51 at 543.

[25] See Chapter 6, II.2 and IV.

[26] See A van Aaken, 'Transnationales Kooperationsrecht nationaler Aufsichtsbehörden als Antwort auf die Herausforderung globalisierter Finanzmärkte' in C Möllers, A Vosskuhle & C Walter (eds), *Internationales Verwaltungsrecht*, Tübingen: Mohr Siebeck, 2007, 219–57. On the latter point,

of areas—from international security to civil aviation regulation—in which national judges have adopted subtle approaches to weigh the role of global norms, not granting them all-out authority but carefully calibrating their influence.[27] And on issues as diverse as counter-terrorism action, environmental protection and migration control, courts are making use of a panoply of domestic and international law to engage in cross-country dialogues with other courts about how to hold executives to account.[28]

Such processes testify to an increasing 'normalization' of international law and global standards in regional and national law, quite in contrast with—or at least circumventing—the classical picture of separate spheres.[29] This normalization is in part driven by the incentive structure in and through which global regimes operate: when they function as part of coordination games, they can set focal points individual states can only ignore at a high cost, especially at the risk of losing market access. In collaboration games, many regimes today operate with monitoring and enforcement mechanisms which raise the costs of non-compliance considerably.[30] The widely noted 'legalization' of world politics[31] formally remains mostly confined to the international level, but it creates pressures that lead to an ever-growing interwovenness of the different layers of law—national, regional, international.

This development is particularly pronounced in Europe, where the European Union has blurred the lines between the layers in an exceptional way. But the examples I have cited are by no means confined to this space. This would also be surprising—global governance may have an uneven impact across the world and its legal influence is subject to the forms and culture of national legal orders, but the factors that push for closer linkages

R B Stewart, 'The Global Regulatory Challenge to US Administrative Law', *NYU Journal of International Law and Politics* 37 (2005), 695–762 at 699–712.

[27] B Kingsbury, 'Weighing Global Regulatory Rules and Decisions in National Courts', *Acta Juridica* (2009), 90–119.

[28] E Benvenisti, 'Reclaiming Democracy: The Strategic Uses of Foreign and International Law by Domestic Courts', *American Journal of International Law* 102 (2008), 241–74.

[29] See also J Nijman & A Nollkaemper, 'Beyond the Divide' in Nijman & Nollkaemper, *New Perspectives*, 341–60 at 341–2, 350; Y Shany, *Regulating Jurisdictional Relations Between National and International Courts*, Oxford: Oxford University Press, 2007, chs 2 and 3.

[30] On the general regime structures, see A A Stein, 'Coordination and Collaboration: Regimes in an Anarchic World', *International Organization* 36 (1982), 299–324.

[31] J L Goldstein et al (eds), *Legalization and World Politics*, Cambridge, MA: MIT Press, 2001.

should have particular force in countries that are more dependent on international institutions than the rich states of the North. We require far more empirical work into the spread, shape and intensity of the links between domestic and international layers of law in different parts of the globe. Yet the initial survey above already shows that the categorical distinction between domestic and international layers of law has in many contexts given way to a greater interwovenness and a more nuanced assessment of the weight of norms from different origins.

2. Changing Practices and the Rise of Postnational Law

What consequences should we draw from this (admittedly sketchy) account? We could insist on formality and point to the fact that, despite all interlinkages, the divide between national and international layers of law continues to exist—after all, courts usually look first to their own legal orders to determine which norms apply.[32] The fact that both layers interact and perhaps even function in similar ways does not challenge this formalist view. It suggests taking the different layers into view together as an object of study, but not necessarily drawing them into one as a matter of legal theory.[33]

Yet keeping the layers strictly apart would hardly do justice to the more nuanced practice I have just outlined. We do not need an anthropological approach to take such practice seriously in legal theory; after all, positivist conceptions of law, such as the 'social fact' approach of H L A Hart, also place social practices at the centre. In Hart's view, for a rule of recognition to be in place it needs to be generally accepted by decision-makers and public officials.[34] It is certainly too early to claim that there is today a rule of recognition that includes domestic as well as regional and international spheres and binds them together in one integrated global legal order. We would need more empirical work to ground such a claim, and practices are probably too diverse at the moment to allow for a general conclusion in any

---

[32] See, eg, G Arangio-Ruiz, 'International Law and Interindividual Law' in Nijman & Nollkaemper, *New Perspectives*, 15–51.

[33] C A Whytock, 'Thinking Beyond the Domestic-International Divide: Toward a Unified Concept of Public Law', *Georgetown Journal of International Law* 36 (2004), 155–93 at 159–60; in a similar vein, P S Berman, 'From International Law to Law and Globalization', *Columbia Journal of Transnational Law* 43 (2005), 485–556; J Goldsmith & D Levinson, 'Law for States: International Law, Constitutional Law, Public Law', *Harvard Law Review* 122 (2009), 1791–868. See also the cautious stance in Slaughter & Burke-White, 'Future of International Law', 349–50; Nijman & Nollkaemper, 'Beyond the Divide'.

[34] H L A Hart, *The Concept of Law*, 2nd edn, Oxford: Oxford University Press, 1994.

case.[35] The ultimate reference points of the law are in flux, and courts and officials attach weight to sources from different spheres. Norms from all spheres do not enjoy the same weight—for many decision-makers, a clear norm from their own order will be more important than one originating from another context. Domestic judges will pay more attention to domestic norms; international judges to international ones (and among them, for example, World Trade Organization (WTO) panellists more to WTO law than to other international legal rules). However, norms of different origins will likely play a stronger role when solutions are not obvious—when, as is usually the case, a legal order leaves its own officials and judges interpretative space. Throughout this book, we will encounter various strategies of courts to fill this space by relating to other legal orders, and I will return to them in greater detail in Chapter 8.[36] Suffice it to note at this point that in this picture, external norms come in at the interstices of internal ones and may have persuasive rather than binding authority. It is a picture of gradated authority—one that leaves behind the binary scheme of binding/non-binding and instead associates norms with different weights, depending on the particular decision-making processes at issue.[37] Postnational law is not black and white; it comes in shades of grey.

We may thus not have arrived at one integrated legal order for the globe, but we have left behind the traditional dichotomy for a denser form of interaction in which national law—the anchor of the old order—only plays one part among others. As Nijman and Nollkaemper put it, '[n]o longer can we talk of *The* Divide; it rather becomes a more fluid set of continuities and discontinuities between national and international law'.[38] The resulting 'postnational law' is thus a frame comprised of different orders and their norms. It overcomes the categorical separation between the spheres, without however merging them fully or necessarily defining the degree of authority their different norms possess. How this frame is filled, and in particular what authority is assigned to the different layers and bodies of law, will have to be worked out in the further specification of postnational law's content.

---

[35] See also B Kingsbury, 'The Concept of "Law" in Global Administrative Law', *European Journal of International Law* 20 (2009), 23–57 at 29–30.

[36] See Chapter 8, III.

[37] See Knop, 'Here and There' at 535; Moran, 'Shifting Boundaries'; Nijman & Nollkaemper, 'Beyond the Divide', 354–5; Kingsbury, 'Weighing Regulatory Rules'. See also Shany, *Regulating Jurisdictional Relations*, ch 6, who emphasizes the flexibility of jurisdictional rules.

[38] Nijman & Nollkaemper, 'Beyond the Divide', 350.

3. Framing Law and Legitimacy

Besides providing a better fit with practice, such a conception of the legal order would have the advantage of aligning it more closely with the legitimacy questions postnational governance raises. From a positivist perspective, law may not be conceptually linked to morality. Yet law often provides a certain degree of legitimacy, and it is in any case a key instrument of social control. Throughout modern constitutionalism, it has thus been central to realizing visions of the right political order, and legal—especially constitutional—questions have typically been framed as questions of political theory too. This link becomes tenuous, though, if domestic and international law are treated separately while the political (and also legal) linkages between the layers continue to grow.

In the classical picture, national and international law were grounded in distinct forms of legitimacy—domestic law in thick concepts such as liberal democracy, communism, or theocracy; international law in the consent (or, as the case may be, acquiescence) of the individual states. The distinction of layers thus allowed for the coordination of very diverse, yet still thick domestic visions of political justice; as long as the two only intersected through consent, wide divergences could be managed.[39] However, the growing linkages between the layers render this model moot. As the domestic and international spheres come closer together, questions about their normative foundations come to the fore. International law, in particular, can no longer rest on its old basis when consent elements have been increasingly diluted through delegation to international institutions, decision-making in informal networks and enforcement through review mechanisms and formalized sanctions procedures. And domestic law cannot achieve its objectives if key parts of what it intends to regulate escape its reach. If this is so—and I will return to this point in the next section—legitimacy questions have to be framed for the entirety of the order, not just for one (domestic or international) part of it. In another context, this has led me and my co-authors to stipulate the emergence of a 'global administrative space' and 'global administrative law'.[40] Conceptualizing law as postnational allows us to link legal construction to legitimacy frames in an even more encompassing way. The move to 'postnational law' is thus also a response to the political

---

[39] See, eg, G de Búrca & O Gerstenberg, 'The Denationalization of Constitutional Law', *Harvard International Law Journal* 47 (2006), 243–62 at 244–6.

[40] B Kingsbury, N Krisch & R B Stewart, 'The Emergence of Global Administrative Law', *Law & Contemporary Problems* 68:3 (2005), 15–61.

enmeshment of all parts of the global order and to the ensuing shift in structures of legitimation.[41]

III. STRUCTURAL VISIONS

Postnational law is a relatively open frame that needs to be filled with content, but also with structure—with a determination of how the different layers of law and their various institutions relate to each other. The question of structure is at the heart of this book, and in the chapters that follow I will inquire in greater detail into different structural visions that compete for explaining and structuring the postnational space. We can situate this competition within three main strands of thinking that dominate the debate about structures—strands that reflect broader attitudes to the challenge of postnational governance.

1. Three Approaches: Containment, Transfer, Break

As suggested in the introduction, the rise of postnational governance provokes contrasting reactions. In some it causes anxieties, a sense of threat; in others, a sense of opportunity; and in many (of course) feelings somewhere in the middle. How these reactions are channelled into theoretical construction, however, depends on a second dimension, namely views about institutional possibilities—a focus on the continuity of traditional forms contrasts here with an emphasis on difference and disruption, the need to respond to the challenge with new institutional imageries.

The first broad approach to the structure of postnational law—*containment*—combines a vision of threat and a prospect of continuity. It largely rejects the changes brought about by postnational governance and seeks to limit their impact. It insists that both practically and normatively, the only hope for legitimate governance lies in the domestic constitutional framework and that governance structures should be conceived, and constructed, as ultimately flowing from and controlled by national political and constitutional processes. This stance is most commonly based on democratic arguments that emphasize the social and institutional preconditions for democratic processes which are difficult to replicate beyond the state. Sometimes these are framed in absolute terms, such as when a strong common *demos*, a somewhat homogeneous people, is seen as a prerequisite for democracy and the ability of a collective to give itself a constitution.[42] Many

---

[41] See, in a similar vein, de Búrca & Gerstenberg, 'Denationalization'; Whytock, 'Thinking Beyond', 191–3.

[42] See, eg, P Kirchhof, 'Der deutsche Staat im Prozeß der europäischen Integration' in J Isensee & P Kirchhof (eds), *Handbuch des Staatsrechts der*

approaches erect lower hurdles, but even so they require a degree of societal solidarity or a quality of common deliberation that usually obviates intense forms of cooperation beyond the state (or at least beyond highly integrated regional polities).[43]

Advocates of containment do not always focus on democracy alone; they also point to other obstacles for realizing key political values. For example, they see the idea of a constitution, and of constitutionalism, as largely utopian in the global realm—creating a framework for public power that redeems the promise of agency and self-government seems to them largely impossible in the absence of massive social and institutional change.[44] The consequence would be to tie international cooperation back to domestic processes and to re-establish the control of national parliaments and governments over the making and implementation of international norms—thus to return as closely as possible to the classical model of international law, even if this implies serious limits on transboundary cooperative efforts.

The second approach—*transfer*—likewise pursues continuity but harbours greater hope that such continuity can be achieved by transferring key domestic concepts and institutions to regional and global levels. Such hope is expressed most prominently in David Held's theory of cosmopolitan democracy,[45] but also, for example, in approaches such as that of Philip Pettit for whom the structure of domestic democracy—with an emphasis

---

Bundesrepublik Deutschland, vol VII, Heidelberg: C F Müller Verlag, 1992, 855–87; P Kirchhof, 'Die Identität der Verfassung', ibid, vol II, 3rd edn, Heidelberg: C F Müller Verlag, 2004, 261–316 at 288–93; E-W Böckenförde, 'Die Zukunft politischer Autonomie' in E-W Böckenförde, *Staat, Nation, Europa*, Frankfurt am Main: Suhrkamp Verlag, 1999, 103–26.

[43] See R A Dahl, 'Can International Organizations be Democratic? A Skeptic's View', in I Shapiro & C Hacker-Cordón (eds), *Democracy's Edges*, Cambridge: Cambridge University Press, 1999, 19–36; J Habermas, 'Hat die Konstitutionalisierung des Völkerrechts noch eine Chance?' in J Habermas, *Der gespaltene Westen*, Frankfurt am Main: Suhrkamp Verlag, 2004, 113–93, 137–42; I Maus, 'Verfassung oder Vertrag: Zur Verrechtlichung globaler Politik' in P Niesen & B Herborth (eds), *Anarchie der kommunikativen Freiheit*, Frankfurt am Main: Suhrkamp Verlag, 2007, 350–82.

[44] eg, D Grimm, 'The Constitution in the Process of Denationalization', *Constellations* 12 (2005), 447–63; also Maus, 'Verfassung oder Vertrag'. See also Habermas, 'Konstitutionalisierung', who regards a full (republican) constitutionalization as possible on the regional level but not in the global sphere.

[45] D Held, *Democracy and the Global Order: From the Modern State to Cosmopolitan Governance*, Cambridge: Polity Press, 1995; see also D Archibugi, *The Global Commonwealth of Citizens: Toward Cosmopolitan Democracy*, Princeton, NJ: Princeton University Press, 2008.

on contestation—is not as alien to the global order as in other theories that focus more on electoral authorization.[46] Others, who stress deliberation as key to democracy, also see chances for its realization beyond the state.[47] I will return to those theories in Chapter 8.

Other authors in the transfer category focus less on democracy as such, but more on broader frameworks: most prominent here are the widespread attempts to translate constitutionalism into the postnational arena.[48] As we will see in greater detail in the next chapter, these take a multitude of forms, ranging from a reinterpretation of the current international order in constitutional (hierarchical, value-oriented) terms, to calls for stronger legalization or a better realization of rights in postnational governance, broader attempts to conceive of global constitutionalism as 'compensating' for deficiencies in the domestic realm, or comprehensive reconceptualizations of constitutionalism in a cosmopolitan paradigm.[49] In this reading, transferring concepts means adapting them to the new circumstances while securing continuity with their core meaning.

The third strand of thinking—*break*—seeks to go beyond, rather than connect with, traditional forms in the postnational space. One element in this strand is a decoupling of legitimacy concerns from democracy as such, either through an emphasis on output over input legitimacy, through an exploration of non-electoral accountability mechanisms, or more broadly

---

[46]   P Pettit, 'Democracy, National and International', *The Monist* 89 (2006), 301–24; in a similar vein, A Kuper, *Democracy Beyond Borders: Justice and Representation in Global Institutions*, Oxford: Oxford University Press, 2004.

[47]   eg, J S Dryzek, *Deliberative Global Politics: Discourse and Democracy in a Divided World*, Cambridge: Polity Press, 2006; J Bohman, *Democracy across Borders*, Cambridge, MA: MIT Press, 2007.

[48]   See the survey in N Walker, 'Taking Constitutionalism Beyond the State', *Political Studies* 56 (2008), 519–43.

[49]   See, eg, B Fassbender, 'The United Nations Charter as Constitution of the International Community', *Columbia Journal of Transnational Law* 36 (1998), 529–619; E de Wet, 'The International Constitutional Order', *International & Comparative Law Quarterly* 55 (2006), 51–76; E-U Petersmann, 'Human Rights, Constitutionalism and the World Trade Organization: Challenges for World Trade Organization Jurisprudence and Civil Society', *Leiden Journal of International Law* 19 (2006), 633–67; A Peters, 'Compensatory Constitutionalism: The Function and Potential of Fundamental International Norms and Structures', *Leiden Journal of International Law* 19 (2006), 579–610; M Kumm, 'The Cosmopolitan Turn in Constitutionalism: On the Relationship between Constitutionalism in and beyond the State' in J L Dunoff & J P Trachtman (eds), *Ruling the World? Constitutionalism, International Law, and Global Governance*, Cambridge: Cambridge University Press, 2009, 258–324.

through a focus on accountability as a mix of relationships that does not necessarily find its anchor in democratic terms.[50] For some, the turn to global governance is seen as an opportunity to further projects which, like that of an 'agonistic democracy', have not been realized domestically.[51] On a more structural level, advocates of a 'break' eschew constitutionalism's emphasis on law and hierarchy and propose more pluralist models, which would leave greater space for politics in the heterarchical interplay of orders.[52] This often connects with a hope for change through activism and contestation, and some such theorizing is itself inspired by agonistic interpretations of politics, such as that of James Tully.[53] Other strands are rooted in the very different framework of Luhmannian systems-theory.[54] Chapter 3 will analyse the pluralist imagination and its promise in greater depth. It is probably the most pronounced attempt to break with traditional forms in the construction of postnational governance.

2. Containment's Bleak Prospects[55]

This book ultimately sides with the latter, pluralist vision and situates itself within the strand of thinking that favours a break with classical forms. As we will see in the following chapters, it shares with the advocates of containment the view that in postnational governance continuity with key political traditions is difficult, if not impossible. Like protagonists of the transfer approach, however, it sees the idea of returning to domestic constitutionalism as the main anchor of the political order as neither practically possible nor normatively desirable.

[50] See, eg, F Scharpf, *Governing in Europe: Effective and Democratic?*, Oxford: Oxford University Press, 1999; T Macdonald & K Macdonald, 'Non-Electoral Accountability in Global Politics: Strengthening Democratic Control within the Global Garment Industry', *European Journal of International Law* 17 (2006), 89–119; R W Grant & R O Keohane, 'Accountability and Abuses of Power in World Politics', *American Political Science Review* 99 (2005), 29–43. See also Kingsbury, Krisch & Stewart, 'Emergence of GAL', 42–51.

[51] C Mouffe, *On the Political*, Abingdon: Routledge, 2005, ch 5.

[52] For an overview, see R Michaels, 'Global Legal Pluralism', *Annual Review of Law & Social Science* 5 (2009), 243–62.

[53] eg, J Shaw, 'Postnational Constitutionalism in the European Union', *Journal of European Public Policy* 6 (1999), 579–97; N Walker, 'The Idea of Constitutional Pluralism', *Modern Law Review* 65 (2002), 317–59.

[54] eg, A Fischer-Lescano & G Teubner, *Regime-Kollisionen: Zur Fragmentierung des globalen Rechts*, Frankfurt am Main: Suhrkamp Verlag, 2006.

[55] This section is partly based on N Krisch, 'Global Administrative Law and the Constitutional Ambition' in Loughlin & Dobner, *Twilight*, 245–66.

Domestic Constitutionalism and its Limits

Domestic constitutionalism gains its teeth through the degree of control domestic political processes exercise over outcomes—through the extent to which they can decide on policies without being bound, or strongly influenced, by external action. In the classical picture, this was achieved through a buffer between the layers of law—international law and international institutions rested on state consent (expressed typically in treaties), and the obligations flowing from them, typically relatively vague, could be concretized and controlled through domestic implementation. Whatever substantive problems international law raised were dealt with through the channel of member states, and the central site for controlling transnational governance was the domestic constitutional setting.[56]

Today, constructing the accountability of postnational governance around delegation and control bears only limited promise.[57] This is largely because of the processes I have sketched above as lying at the core of the shift to postnational law. It is, first, because of the increasing legalization of international politics and the institutionalization of international law. When powers are delegated to international institutions, the initial delegation of powers is usually thin: the founding treaties of international institutions (as well as the European Union) generally contain only vague guidance as regards the scope of powers, especially informal powers,[58] and even this limited determination disappears when it comes to transnational government networks which typically operate without a formal basis altogether.[59] Moreover, delegation is entirely absent as regards outsiders (non-members) that may be affected by decisions,[60] or in the case of private regulators. The latter do not depend on any form of delegation but, even when they cooperate with

---

[56] Cf J H H Weiler, 'The Geology of International Law—Governance, Democracy and Legitimacy', *Zeitschrift für ausländisches öffentliches Recht und Völkerrecht* 64 (2004), 547–62 at 553–6.

[57] But see, eg, F Scharpf, 'Legitimacy in the Multilevel European Polity', *MPIfG Working Paper* 09/1 (2009), 10–12, <http://www.mpifg.de/pu/workpap/wp09–1.pdf>; E Schmidt-Aßmann, 'The Internationalization of Administrative Relations as a Challenge for Administrative Law Scholarship', *German Law Journal* 9 (2008), 2061–80.

[58] On the uncertainties surrounding the interpretation of powers of international institutions, see also J Klabbers, *An Introduction to International Institutional Law*, Cambridge: Cambridge University Press, 2002, 60–81.

[59] See A-M Slaughter, *A New World Order*, Princeton, NJ: Princeton University Press, 2004.

[60] The Basel Committee for Banking Supervision, for example, consists of only eleven members but its decisions are designed to apply far beyond this circle; see M

governments, are typically self-appointed.[61] Because of the need for flexibility in those institutions and the difficulty of creating and speedily adapting treaty mandates, more extensive formal bases and greater specificity will usually be hard to achieve.

Moreover, the level of control each member state can exercise over an international institution is usually low. This is in part because of the problem of multiple, diverse principals: delegation structures are relatively unproblematic and may allow for meaningful degrees of control and accountability if there is only one principal (or few principals), as is typically the case in domestic settings where central governments or parliaments delegate power to lower levels or independent institutions. The situation becomes more problematic when the number of principals increases: each of them can then retain only a smaller fraction of control, and mechanisms for holding agents to account become more cumbersome.[62] Greater control would only flow from veto rights, but these would risk stalemate in any institution with a significant number of members.

A more promising avenue for domestic control might then be the implementation of international decisions. Whether binding or non-binding, most norms and decisions in postnational governance depend on domestic implementation for their actual effectiveness; global regulatory action is typically not followed by its ultimate addressees (state officials, individuals, companies) unless it becomes part of the domestic legal and regulatory framework. In the classical vision of international law, this opens up space for states' sovereign choices as to their domestic policies—even if such choices contradict international rules, they remain decisive in the domestic realm (even though they might entail responsibility on the international level). This in turn allows domestic constitutionalism to take centre stage, by determining when and how international norms can enter domestic law, and by defining

S Barr & G P Miller, 'Global Administrative Law: The View from Basel', *European Journal of International Law* 17 (2006), 15–46 at 39–41.

[61] On the example of forestry regulation, see E Meidinger, 'The Administrative Law of Global Private-Public Regulation: The Case of Forestry', *European Journal of International Law* 17 (2006), 47–87.

[62] On international institutions, see A P Cortell & S Peterson, 'Dutiful Agents, Rogue Actors, or Both? Staffing, Voting, Rules and Slack in the WHO and WTO' in D G Hawkins et al (eds), *Delegation and Agency in International Organizations*, Cambridge: Cambridge University Press, 2006, 255–80; D A Lake & M D McCubbins, 'The Logic of Delegation to International Organizations', ibid, 341–68 at 361–7.

the substantive limits and procedural conditions for engagement with the international sphere.[63]

For this to be an effective tool of national control, however, it has to operate in a relatively permissive environment: if non-implementation is to remain a real (rather than merely formal) option, it must not be overly costly. In classical international law, this was certainly the case, as rules were often underspecified and non-compliance even with binding rules was rarely subject to meaningful sanctions. Yet today, as already mentioned, precision has increased and enforcement has gained teeth in many areas of postnational governance. The clearest example is the EU, with its doctrines of ultimate effect and supremacy as well as the possibility of sanctions against non-complying member states. But similar considerations apply on the global level too: if refusing compliance with WTO rules exposes a country to trade sanctions that cost millions (sometimes hundreds of millions) of dollars, it presents a conceivable option for only very few actors. And where international standards help solve coordination games in global markets, opting out is often not a real option as it entails exclusion from those markets, or at least significant hurdles for access.[64] Non-compliance—even with non-binding instruments—thus often comes at a prohibitive cost, and the prospect of domestic constitutionalism retaining control through implementation is accordingly limited. As pointed out above, this problem is exacerbated when global decision-making involves domestic regulators directly: if they are implicated in the setting of global standards (as they typically are in government networks), their commitment to compliance will often be too strong to allow for much flexibility at the implementation stage.[65]

Thus neither the delegatory relationship nor domestic implementation can guarantee significant national control over postnational governance beyond the creation stage. This significantly conditions the viability of the domestic constitutional route: except for particularly powerful states, or in contexts in which the costs of non-compliance are low, the prospect of domestic constitutionalism shaping global governance or controlling its impact is very limited. The only hope for advocates of containment would then be to turn

---

[63]   This is certainly the ambition of some constitutional courts; see, eg, Bundesverfassungsgericht, *Maastricht*; Judgment of 14 October 2004, *Görgülü*, BVerfGE 111, 307. See also M Kumm, 'Constitutional Democracy Encounters International Law: Terms of Engagement' in S Choudhry (ed), *The Migration of Constitutional Ideas*, Cambridge: Cambridge University Press, 2007, 256–93.

[64]   On the structure of coordination games in international standardization, see S D Krasner, 'Global Communications and National Power: Life on the Pareto Frontier', *World Politics* 43 (1991), 336–66.

[65]   See Stewart, 'Global Regulatory Challenge', 699–712.

the clock back and begin to withdraw from regional and international structures of cooperation.

Flaws of the Domestic Route

Such a return to the classical picture is not only unlikely but also ultimately undesirable. Domestic constitutionalism may have been a viable anchor for the international order for a long period of time, but today it risks being underinclusive and insufficiently effective.[66]

The first point is based on the lack of congruence of nation-state boundaries with the range of those affected by political decisions. In an interdependent world, political challenges as well as regulatory responses straddle national boundaries in most areas. Consequently, under any conception of democracy that relies (at least in part) on the degree to which individuals are affected by decisions, the range of those with a valid claim to participate in decision-making often goes well beyond the national community.[67] Domestic constitutionalism, which places the national community at the centre of the legal and political universe by giving it control over its commitments, cannot reflect this broader constituency—on transboundary issues, it remains underinclusive.[68]

Domestic constitutionalism not only fails to include but also fails to deliver. Realizing democracy not only poses demands on existing government structures, but also requires the creation of sufficient public power to implement self-legislation in society. Adjusting decision-making structures to the scope of the problems then becomes itself a democratic demand.[69] But here again, as we have seen, domestic constitutionalism is at a loss: it would require us to withdraw from, rather than extend, effective postnational decision-making structures in order to safeguard control by domestic political processes.

This signals the inadequacy of the domestic constitutionalist route even from the perspective of the national community, but it also points to a broader tension in the relationship of democratic thought with postnational structures. Democracy typically requires both a certain *quality* of the political process and a certain degree of *effectiveness* as to its outcomes. These two aspects were merged in the state setting, where processes of nation-building

---

[66] For a trenchant critique of state constitutionalism, see Kumm, 'Cosmopolitan Turn'.

[67] Held, *Democracy and the Global Order*, ch 10; I M Young, *Inclusion and Democracy*, Oxford: Oxford University Press, 2000, ch 7.

[68] M Poiares Maduro, 'Europe and the Constitution: What if This is as Good as it Gets?' in J H H Weiler & M Wind (eds), *European Constitutionalism Beyond the State*, Cambridge: Cambridge University Press, 2003, 74–102 at 81–6.

[69] See Held, *Democracy and the Global Order*, ch 11.

had produced communities cohesive enough for the demands of democratic practice and where central institutions were sufficiently strong to implement most democratic decisions.[70] Today, as problems increasingly require responses beyond the state, effectiveness and quality considerations pull in different directions and leave democratic theory in a quandary, forced to sacrifice either one or the other—or move into utopian territory to make both match again at a higher level, perhaps in something akin to a world state.

The difficulty of striking the right balance becomes evident, for example, in Jürgen Habermas's vision of global politics. Because of his insistence on relatively strong democracy, Habermas sees a potential for intense forms of cooperation only on the regional level (where robust democracy may be possible) and conceives of global politics merely in classical international (inter-regional) terms.[71] This may, however, lead to severe costs in the provision of global public goods and we may ask whether his approach (just as most modern political theory since the rise of the absolutist state) is not based too much on a preoccupation with *limiting* public power to invite translation to the postnational environment.[72] If we take a more Hobbesian, or possibly also republican, perspective, we may place stronger emphasis on *unleashing* public power and will perhaps rebalance the weight of effectiveness and procedural integrity for the postnational space. From this perspective, the *absence* of strong institutions would require as much justification as a departure from the ideal qualities of a democratic process.

It is not the place here to inquire further into how the balance between quality, effectiveness, and inclusiveness of democratic procedures should ultimately be struck or whether the tensions between them can be resolved at all. I will delve deeper into this issue in Chapters 3 and 8, and it will reappear throughout this book. Yet whatever solution one chooses, it is bound to depart from the 'pure' domestic constitutionalist route—if it is minimally responsive to the concerns about inclusiveness and effectiveness I have outlined above, the national community loses its key role—it may retain an important place in postnational politics and law, but one among others, not in the very centre. The 'containment' of the postnational turn, already improbable as a practical matter, turns out to be undesirable on normative terms too.

---

[70] Scharpf, *Governing in Europe*, 6–28.

[71] Habermas, 'Konstitutionalisierung'; J Habermas, 'Kommunikative Rationalität und grenzüberschreitende Politik: eine Replik' in Niesen & Herborth, *Anarchie*, 406–59 at 443–59.

[72] But see Maus, 'Verfassung oder Vertrag', 373, who criticizes Habermas for placing more weight on effectiveness than on procedural integrity.

IV. CONSTITUTIONALISM OR PLURALISM?
THE PLAN OF THE BOOK

Constructing postnational law is no minor challenge. In the age of post-national governance, the legal order has lost its anchor—national law and domestic constitutionalism are no longer at the centre of legal processes, and they do not present a promising option either. 'Containment' of the seismic shifts in law and politics is thus hardly viable. Both analytically and norma-tively, however, it is easier to describe where we come from than where we are going—the vocabulary of 'post'nationalism signals this departure from settled understandings as well as the uncertainty of its destination.

This book aims to make some progress towards elucidating this destina-tion. As I mentioned above, it focuses on structural issues—on the relation-ships between the different elements of the postnational order, rather than on the substance of the law these elements contain. It takes as its point of departure the framework I have sketched in the previous section and inves-tigates two contrasting structural visions, constitutionalism and pluralism. These are emblematic for the 'transfer' and 'break' attitudes to postnational law, and their precise meaning and implications will be the subject of fur-ther exploration in the following chapters. In a nutshell, postnational *constitu-tionalism* attempts to provide continuity with the domestic constitutionalist tradition by construing an overarching legal framework that determines the relationships of the different levels of law and the distribution of pow-ers among their institutions. It seeks to redeem the modern, revolutionary promise of a human-made constitution as an antidote to the forces of history, power and chance. *Pluralism*, in contrast, is a less orderly affair. It sees such an overarching framework as neither practically possible nor normatively desir-able and seeks to discern a model of order that relies less on unity and more on the heterarchical interaction of the various layers of law. Legally, the relation-ship of the parts of the overall order in pluralism remains open—governed by the potentially competing rules of the various sub-orders, each with its own ultimate point of reference and supremacy claim, the relationships between them are left to be determined ultimately through political, not rule-based processes. In this, pluralism eschews a central element of the Western politi-cal tradition—the hope to contain politics through the rule of law. Yet as we will see, the break this implies may be better suited to the radically diverse society characteristic of the postnational space. In this highly contested space, realizing public autonomy and creating order may require a departure from the classical imagination inspired by national social structures.

The book inquires into postnational constitutionalism, pluralism, and their respective virtues in three main steps. Part I, 'Visions of Postnational Law', focuses on the concepts as they have been put forward in the literature, places them into a theoretical context and presents an initial analysis of their suitability in postnational society. This has begun in the present chapter and continues in Chapter 2 with an examination of constitutionalism beyond the state—a notion with widely varying uses in scholarship as well as public discourse. The chapter asks what it means to translate a concept such as constitutionalism from the domestic to the postnational sphere and contrasts the different usages with competing strands of thought in the domestic tradition. Many of them, in fact, connect with a much weaker strand than the (foundational) one that has come to dominate Western political theory and practice over at least the last century. The chapter goes on to analyse what continuity with the foundational tradition might mean in the postnational context and what problems such continuity would face, given experiences in other highly diverse and contested settings. Chapter 3 focuses not on continuity and constitutionalism, but on break and pluralism. It asks, what does pluralism mean?, and what could be its normative basis in the postnational context? In the course of this inquiry it tries to disentangle the various, but often not fully convincing analytical and normative arguments put forward in support of pluralism in the literature, and seeks to develop an own normative framework in its defence—a framework that builds upon the public autonomy of individuals and their (ultimately democratic) right to determine which polity they want to be governed in and by.

Part II, 'Pluralism in Postnational Practice', seeks answers to some of the questions left open in the theoretical chapters through the study of three central areas of postnational governance. It aims to discern more clearly what analytical purchase constitutionalism and pluralism have on the processes in these areas and which of them might be more suitable to guide their further development. Chapter 4 focuses on the European human rights regime, which has often been characterized as a prime example of constitutionalization because of the ever tighter links between domestic and European layers of law in its frame. At closer look, however, the constitutionalist picture is challenged by processes of contestation, largely on the part of national courts that insist on the ultimate supremacy of their—national—constitutions. The resulting order is pluralist rather than constitutionalist, and the chapter seeks to gain a better understanding of its dominant trajectories and of the influence pluralism has had on the relatively smooth development of the regime.

Chapter 5 turns to the global level and studies the UN Security Council's sanctions practice and its embeddedness in international, regional and domestic layers of law. A security regime such as that of sanctions is a particular challenge for any vision of postnational law because of the widely assumed dominance of national interest (and consequent likelihood of national control) in this area. Yet the study of the sanctions regime reveals close links across layers of law—links that, however, do not necessarily lead to an integrated whole but trigger processes of resistance and normative distancing characteristic of a pluralist order. The chapter seeks to show how this difficult positioning is dealt with in different contexts, and how the pluralism of the resulting picture impacts on the stability and effectiveness of the regime.

The third case study, in Chapter 6, focuses on global risk regulation around the dispute over genetically modified organisms (GMOs) and trade. This area has been described as an example of 'when cooperation fails',[73] and it puts structural visions of postnational governance to a particular test. The chapter analyses how different actors have mobilized different regimes (of national, regional, and global origin) in pursuit of their own substantive preferences and how this has produced a tightly connected but again not fully integrated order. And it seeks to develop insights into the impact of this lack of integration—the pluralist rather than constitutionalist structure of the regime complex—on the success of cooperation on the matter.

Three case studies, taken from widely varying areas of regional and global governance with different sets of actors and rationalities, cannot provide the ground for robust conclusions on the relative virtues of pluralism and constitutionalism in the postnational sphere. Yet they indicate the prevalence of pluralist patterns in settings as diverse—and as important—as those of the European Union, the European Convention on Human Rights, the UN security regime, and global trade regulation. And they produce provisional insights into the dynamics of pluralist orders in all those contexts, thus providing a starting point for further empirical work as well as for theoretical engagement.

Part III, 'Pluralism's Virtues (and Vices)', attempts the latter. It draws on the case studies as well as existing analyses to take up issues that are often seen as particularly critical for pluralist orders. Chapter 7 focuses on stability and power. Both are usually regarded as problematic in pluralism: when relationships are not legally fixed but open to recurring contestation, friction rather than smooth cooperation appears as the likely outcome and might, not right, the probable driving force behind the resolution of conflicts. Chapter 8 responds to a different challenge: that from democracy and the rule of law. Democracy is an unsolved issue for any conception of postnational law and politics, but the rule of law poses particular problems for pluralism: leaving the relationship between legal sub-orders open seems to run counter to the very core of the rule-of-law ideal. And it leaves judges

---

[73] M A Pollack & G C Shaffer, *When Cooperation Fails: The International Law and Politics of Genetically Modified Foods*, Oxford: Oxford University Press, 2009.

and other decision-makers in a quandary as to how they should frame their links with other sub-orders—because it fails to posit an overarching frame, it seems to invite arbitrary choices.

As we will see throughout the book, such concerns are largely misplaced or at least exaggerated. Pluralist orders are not particularly unstable or prone to exploitation by the powerful—whether they are, depends on underlying societal circumstances that will affect any institutional structure. Pluralism's openness may bring with it certain risks, but it also has significant advantages over more rigidly constitutionalized structures, especially as regards the processes of adaptation and change so pervasive in postnational politics. It also has important strengths in democratic terms—not only because it gives contestation greater space but also because it reflects social indecision about which polity should govern transboundary issues. National, regional, and global polities often compete here, all with strong normative grounding and significant loyalties. Pluralism, unlike constitutionalism, does not need to decide hierarchies between them; it can grant them space for competition, mutual accommodation, and perhaps eventual settlement. Pluralism's institutional openness thus corresponds with the openness and fluidity of postnational society in a way constitutionalism, tailored to less heterogeneous societies, does not. As Chapter 9 suggests, this may have repercussions for the constitutional and legal theory of diverse societies well beyond the particular focus on the postnational space.

This book does not pretend to give final answers to questions about the structure of postnational law, democracy beyond the state, or the contest between constitutionalist and pluralist approaches. We are still trying to find our way through the maze, or 'mystery',[74] of global governance and lack many of the empirical and theoretical resources that would allow us to come up with solutions. What this book does, though, is to invite us to think in unconventional terms about the structure of postnational governance. It asks us to be honest about the (far-reaching and perhaps undesired) implications of the continuity with domestic models, above all constitutionalism, which many advocate. And it asks us to consider alternatives, such as pluralism, even if these do not accord with our political traditions or common expectations. Governing the postnational space, after all, requires both an analytical vocabulary and a normative compass attuned to the particular dynamics of a space much more fluid and diverse than the national. It is a challenge that should make use of as many imaginative resources as we can muster.

---

[74] D Kennedy, 'The Mystery of Global Governance' in Dunoff & Trachtman, *Ruling the World?*, 37–68.

2

The Promise and Perils of Postnational Constitutionalism

We tend to fill voids with what we know. When we are thrown into unfamiliar spaces, we try to chart them with the maps we possess, construct them with the tools we already have. Working with analogies, extending and adapting existing concepts, seems usually preferable to the creation of ideas and structures from scratch, not only because of the risks involved in the latter, but also because of our limits of imagination.

When we try to imagine the postnational space, it is not surprising then that we turn for guidance first to the well known, the space of the national. The postnational, no doubt, is unfamiliar territory; the shape of its institutions, of allegiances and loyalties, of influence and power, submission and resistance is different—sometimes radically different—from what we are familiar with. As we have seen in the introductory chapter, one of the certainties that has disappeared with the rise of the postnational is the distinction between national and international politics, and between national and international law. This distinction used to be central to our conceptualization of the political and legal order: it allowed us to layer our normative and institutional demands, with only thin requirements for the international level and relatively thick requirements for domestic institutions. With the demise of the distinction, it has become tempting to have recourse to domestic models of political order, to try to extend them to capture the extended scope of politics, to compensate for domestic losses. Otherwise, it seems, we will be unable to realize central political values in the new, modified political space we have come to inhabit.

One such model is constitutionalism, and it is central to our inquiry because it embodies, apart from substantive values such as rights and democracy, a structural vision. This vision is intimately bound up with the rule of law: it is directed at a political order comprehensively shaped by law, one in which politics, passions, and power are tamed by the particular rationality of the legal system. In its clearest expression, it is geared towards a constitution as a framework that determines how political actors can pursue their causes.

Constitutionalism in this reading represents a strong candidate for guiding our inquiry about the structure of postnational law, if only because of its thick domestic pedigree. Alternative, especially pluralist approaches would have to show why we need a break with key national traditions; why the structural implications of constitutionalism cannot carry over into the postnational realm. Yet some would argue that this contrast is overdrawn in the first place—that constitutionalism makes more limited demands, substantive rather than formal ones, that might even allow for a combination with pluralist ideas. In this reading, constitutionalism would simply reference a set of values—democracy, rights, the rule of law—and would be thin enough to be translated into the postnational sphere.

In this chapter, I seek to shed light on the notion and prospects of postnational constitutionalism by inquiring into the core content of constitutionalism as a political tradition and into what of this content should and can guide us in the construction of the new, postnational political space. I approach the issue in three main steps. In Section I, I trace the debate about constitutionalism in the postnational order, and I try to illuminate how we should approach the conflict between the different visions apparent here. This involves an inquiry into the idea of translation from one context into another: how tightly should our usage of a concept in the postnational realm be tied to that in its source context, the domestic one? In Section II, I apply the methodological insights of this inquiry and take a closer look at domestic origins by examining which notions of constitutionalism resonate there, focusing primarily on the contest between 'power-limiting' and 'foundational' conceptions since the eighteenth century. From history I move on to normative theory and seek to discern more clearly which elements of the contemporary practice of constitutionalism form essential pillars rather than merely secondary features. I then return, in Section III, to the postnational sphere and assess the implications there of foundational constitutionalism (the dominant domestic constitutionalist strand) and its problems in the highly divided, postnational society. I conclude by sketching some of the consequences of the findings for the value of alternative, especially pluralist approaches in the construction of postnational governance.

I. MODELS OF POSTNATIONAL ORDER

Constitutionalism made a relatively late appearance in postnational governance, both in Europe and—later still—on the global level.[1] For long, those new structures were dealt with through the classical prism of international

---

[1] For useful surveys, see N Walker, 'Taking Constitutionalism Beyond the State', *Political Studies* 56 (2008), 519–43; I Ley, 'Kant versus Locke:

order, intergovernmentalism, with some modifications but without a categorical challenge. As usual, old paradigms kept structuring our understanding of reality until they had become too obviously outdated and, for long, the gradual development of European integration and globalization helped to conceal the extent of the challenge.

1. The European Debate

In the European context, this changed slowly as the supranational character of the European Communities became more pronounced from the 1960s onwards, but it took until the early 1980s for constitutionalism to become a main theme in the analysis of the EC's transformation. Since then, however, it has become omnipresent, not only in theoretical discourse but also in practical politics, resulting not least in the drafting of an explicitly 'constitutional' treaty.[2] This project may have stalled, but constitution and constitutionalization have become indispensable terms of reference in the debate on the European project.[3]

Three main understandings of 'constitution' and 'constitutionalism' dominate this debate. The first equates constitutionalization with the increasing legalization of the European political order, the gradual submission of politics to a process of law. It found its earliest prominent reflection in the 1986 judgment of the European Court of Justice (ECJ) in *Les Verts*, with its famous statement that the EC was a 'community based on the rule of law' as its institutions could not avoid a review of their acts on the basis of the 'constitutional charter', the treaty establishing the EC.[4] It also underlay Eric Stein's much-noted 1981 article on the 'making of a constitution for Europe', in which he recounts the process by which the ECJ, over time, had expanded the legal determination of the European political order by insisting on direct

---

Europarechtlicher und völkerrechtlicher Konstitutionalismus im Vergleich', *Zeitschrift für ausländisches öffentliches Recht und Völkerrecht* 69 (2009), 317–45.

[2] Treaty establishing a Constitution for Europe, *Official Journal EU*, C 310/1, 16 December 2004.

[3] For analyses of the debate, see N Walker, 'European Constitutionalism in the State Constitutional Tradition', *Current Legal Problems* 59 (2006), 51–89 at 51–6; C Möllers, 'Verfassunggebende Gewalt—Verfassung—Konstitutionalisierung' in A von Bogdandy & J Bast (eds), *Europäisches Verfassungsrecht*, 2nd edn, Berlin: Springer Verlag, 2009, 227–78.

[4] ECJ, Judgment of 23 April 1986, 294/83, *Parti écologiste 'Les Verts' v European Parliament*, ECR 1986, 1339, para 23.

effect, supremacy, horizontal effects etc.[5] In this vein, many commentators in the 1990s believed that Europe already had a constitution.[6]

This understanding, however, was not alone in Stein's account. For him, the making of a transnational constitution was not only about increasing legalization, but also about the creation of a unitary, hierarchically ordered political structure in Europe—a structure he regarded as 'federal-type' already at that point.[7] This aspect connected his account with later, broader visions of what constitutionalizing Europe meant: with ideas of a European constitution as determining the overall structure, process, and basic values of the continent's political edifice, as expounded for example by Jürgen Habermas.[8] In this account, a constitution could become a focus for collective self-determination and enhance the legitimacy of the increasingly demanding political structure of the EU. It was precisely this association that the process towards the Treaty for a Constitution for Europe sought to evoke.[9] In the end, it may have contributed to its failure: critics were wary of the increased stability, autonomy, and legitimacy of a constitutionalized Union and of the threat this would have posed to member state sovereignty.[10]

A third main strand of constitutionalist thinking, a more discursive one, has arisen mainly since the late 1990s. Dissatisfied with classical models of constitutionalism and their potential for European governance arrangements, some authors have sought to construct alternative visions, based on the idea of a constitution as process rather than as a particular institutional form or structure. Jo Shaw, for instance, has put forward a view of 'postnational constitutionalism' based on citizens' dialogue and discourse and on contestation and recognition of difference rather than the entrenchment

---

[5] E Stein, 'Lawyers, Judges, and the Making of a Transnational Constitution', *American Journal of International Law* 75 (1981), 1–27.

[6] See, eg, G F Mancini, 'The Making of a Constitution for Europe', *Common Market Law Review* 26 (1989), 595–614; also the survey in J H H Weiler, *The Constitution of Europe*, Cambridge: Cambridge University Press, 1999, ch 6. Sometimes, this was explicitly linked to a contractual notion of constitution; see G Frankenberg, 'The Return of the Contract', *European Law Journal* 6 (2000), 257–76.

[7] Stein, 'Transnational Constitution', 1.

[8] J Habermas, 'Why Europe Needs a Constitution', *New Left Review* 11 (September–October 2001), 5–26.

[9] See J H H Weiler, 'On the Power of the Word: Europe's Constitutional Iconography', *International Journal of Constitutional Law* 3 (2005), 173–90.

[10] On underlying tensions in constitutionalist discourse around the constitutional treaty, see M Poiares Maduro, 'The importance of being called a constitution: Constitutional authority and the authority of constitutionalism', *International Journal of Constitutional Law* 3 (2005), 332–56.

of common values.[11] Other authors have taken this approach further, with notions of 'constitutional pluralism' and 'contrapunctual law' becoming increasingly prominent.[12] This vision of constitutionalism situates itself explicitly in a different tradition of thought than the previous ones, and I will return to its origins below.

2. Global Analogues

Unsurprisingly, it took constitutionalism much longer to gain prominence in the global context than it did in Europe.[13] The lack of a clear political centre or founding document, the variety of relatively disconnected regimes, the widespread weakness of law when faced with power politics—all these factors made it difficult credibly to interpret international politics in a constitutional vein. Early efforts to do so—such as the one by Alfred Verdross in 1926[14]—had only limited resonance; overall, the description of the international realm as 'anarchical'[15] secured the continued dominance of an intergovernmental framework in clear distance from domestic models.

This began to change in the 1990s, mainly for three reasons. One was the perception of a convergence of political ideas after the end of the Cold War, encapsulated in the notion of an 'international community' with common values and a stronger common normative framework.[16] The second factor was the increasing institutionalization of international law and politics as new institutions such as the World Trade Organization (WTO) appeared on the scene and old ones, such as the World Bank and the UN Security Council, were revitalized and strengthened;[17] along with this went a greater

[11] J Shaw, '"Postnational Constitutionalism" in the European Union', *Journal of European Public Policy* 6 (1999), 579–97.

[12] See, eg, N Walker, 'The Idea of Constitutional Pluralism', *Modern Law Review* 65 (2002), 317–59; and the contributions to J H H Weiler & M Wind (eds), *European Constitutionalism Beyond the State*, Cambridge: Cambridge University Press, 2003.

[13] For a historical account, see B Fassbender, 'The United Nations Charter as Constitution of the International Community', *Columbia Journal of Transnational Law* 36 (1998), 529–619 at 538–51.

[14] A Verdross, *Die Verfassung der Völkerrechtsgemeinschaft*, Vienna: Springer Verlag, 1926.

[15] H Bull, *The Anarchical Society: A Study of Order in World Politics*, London: Macmillan, 1977.

[16] See B Simma, 'From Bilateralism to Community Interest in International Law', *Recueil des Cours de l'Academie de Droit International* 250 (1994-VI), 217–384.

[17] See J E Alvarez, 'International Organizations: Then and Now', *American Journal of International Law* 100 (2006), 324–47.

prominence of legal mechanisms of dispute settlement in various contexts—the WTO, the law of the sea, the International Criminal Court—that led commentators to diagnose a progressive legalization of the international sphere.[18] Finally, economic globalization spurred an increasing awareness of the links between domestic and international politics and their various actors, pushing for an emphasis on transnational rather than classical inter-state structures.[19] Countertendencies, such as hegemonic action and the growing fragmentation of the system,[20] provided a challenge for constitutionalist thinking (though ultimately more of a trigger for reinforcing it).[21]

The main positions in the global constitutional debate show quite a few similarities with the European discussion; we can frame them—again, leaving out many nuances—as centring on checks, structure, and discourse.[22]

The first strand is characterized by an emphasis on *checks* in global politics. In part, this goes back to the diagnosis of an increasing convergence of values—values that now pose limits to classical international law because they have become enshrined in hierarchically superior norms, such as *ius cogens*, which states cannot deviate from by agreement. Much of the focus here is on human rights that operate as a check on politics in a similar form as in domestic constitutional settings. Yet constitutional checks are not only made out in substantive norms, but also in the mechanisms to enforce them. Here the legalization aspect, so prominent in the European debate, comes

[18] See J L Goldstein, M Kahler, RO Keohane, & A-M Slaughter (eds), *Legalization and World Politics*, Cambridge, MA: MIT Press, 2001.

[19] See, eg, M Zürn, *Regieren jenseits des Nationalstaats*, Frankfurt am Main: Suhrkamp Verlag, 1998.

[20] See N Krisch, 'International Law in Times of Hegemony: Unequal Power and the Shaping of the International Legal Order', *European Journal of International Law* 16 (2005), 369–408; A Fischer-Lescano & G Teubner, *Regime-Kollisionen: Zur Fragmentierung des globalen Rechts*, Frankfurt am Main: Suhrkamp Verlag, 2006.

[21] See J Klabbers, 'Setting the Scene' in J Klabbers, A Peters, & G Ulfstein, *The Constitutionalization of International Law*, Oxford: Oxford University Press, 2009, 1–44 at 18; J L Dunoff & J P Trachtman, 'A Functional Approach to International Constitutionalization' in J L Dunoff & J P Trachtman (eds), *Ruling the World? Constitutionalism, International Law, and Global Governance*, Cambridge: Cambridge University Press, 2009, 3–35 at 5–9. On the importance of US hegemony for the related phenomenon of a liberal transformation of international law, see N Krisch, 'Amerikanische Hegemonie und liberale Revolution im Völkerrecht', *Der Staat* 43 (2004), 267–97.

[22] See the survey in Klabbers, 'Setting the Scene'; and the contributions to R S J Macdonald (ed), *Towards World Constitutionalism*, Leiden: Martinus Nijhoff, 2005; Dunoff & Trachtman, *Ruling the World?*; and the special issue on global constitutionalism, *Indiana Journal of Global Legal Studies* 16:2 (2008).

in again, though it takes a different form in the decentralized global order. The focus is not exclusively on shaping and limiting central institutions, but also on keeping the most powerful players—states—in check and thereby strengthening elements of a broader rule of law. Judicial review—of states in settings such as the WTO Dispute Settlement, of international institutions such as the Security Council often in more aspirational form—is a key component here.[23]

Such checks typically operate on the level of particular regimes, not the whole global order, and constitutionalism is directed often at constitutionalization, at gradual progress in hedging in politics and institutions.[24] This circumscribed character is reflected also in the terminology used: authors speak of 'partial' constitutions or of processes of 'micro-constitutionalisation'.[25] And the regime-specific focus is brought out most clearly through conceptual multiplication: Gunter Teubner's 'societal constitutionalism', for example, gives rise to 'global digital constitutions', 'global health constitutions' etc.[26]

The second strand, less pronounced than in the European debate,[27] operates on a grander scale and focuses on *structural* issues. It sets its sights on the global order as a whole, seeking to identify and conceive structures that would redeem more comprehensive constitutional promises.[28] This may be based on redescriptions of the existing order: for example, Bardo Fassbender's portrayal of the UN Charter as a world constitution—as laying

---

[23] See, eg, E de Wet, 'The International Constitutional Order', *International & Comparative Law Quarterly* 55 (2006), 51–76; E-U Petersmann, '"Human Rights, Constitutionalism and the World Trade Organization": Challenges for World Trade Organization Jurisprudence and Civil Society', *Leiden Journal of International Law* 19 (2006), 633–67.

[24] See, eg, Klabbers, Peters, & Ulfstein, *Constitutionalization*; Dunoff & Trachtman, 'Functional Approach', 9–10.

[25] C Walter, 'International Law in a Process of Constitutionalization' in J Nijman & A Nollkaemper (eds), *New Perspectives on the Divide Between National and International Law*, Oxford: Oxford University Press, 2007, 191–215 at 195–8; A Peters, 'Compensatory Constitutionalism: The Function and Potential of Fundamental International Norms and Structures', *Leiden Journal of International Law* 19 (2006), 579–610 at 593–7.

[26] G Teubner, 'Globale Zivilverfassungen: Alternativen zur staatszentrierten Verfassungstheorie', *Zeitschrift für ausländisches öffentliches Recht und Völkerrecht* 63 (2003), 1–28; G Teubner, 'Fragmented Foundations: Societal Constitutionalism beyond the Nation State' in M Loughlin & P Dobner (eds), *The Twilight of Constitutionalism?*, Oxford: Oxford University Press, 2010, 327–41.

[27] See Ley, 'Kant *versus* Locke', 340–4.

[28] See, eg, Peters, 'Compensatory Constitutionalism'.

out fundamental rules, creating central institutions, and placing itself at the top of the global hierarchy of norms—uses the constitutional prism to make better sense of the ways in which the Charter already operates.[29] Christian Tomuschat sees the international legal order moving towards a structure that not only defines common values and processes but also the place of other institutions, namely the state, in the global order.[30] Other examples of this structural strand adopt a more openly prospective approach and develop models for restructuring global politics in a constitutional vein. This is common among political theorists—the global institutional visions of David Held, Iris Marion Young, or Jürgen Habermas build, for all their differences, on the domestic model of a constitution that shapes and delimits the powers of different organs and levels of government and frames conflicts between them.[31] Theirs is a quasi-federal project, popular also among lawyers,[32] in which powers are distributed among different levels of governance according to norms such as subsidiarity and inclusiveness. Unlike in Europe, even such holistic approaches do not aim at an overarching constitutional document, but their substance goes in a similar direction: towards a framework for politics based on reasoned principles and collective self-government, towering above our everyday, more mundane political struggles.

As in the European debate, a third, *discursive* strand of constitutionalism draws on quite different ideas of what a constitution is and ought to be. This is driven in part by authors who see their theories for Europe only

[29] Fassbender, 'UN Charter as Constitution'.

[30] C Tomuschat, 'International Law: Ensuring the Survival of Mankind on the Eve of a New Century', *Recueil des Cours de l'Académie de Droit International* 281 (1999), 9–438 at 72–90. For a discussion, see A von Bogdandy, 'Constitutionalism in International Law: Comments on a Proposal from Germany', *Harvard International Law Journal* 47 (2006), 223–42.

[31] D Held, *Democracy and the Global Order: From the Modern State to Cosmopolitan Governance*, Cambridge: Polity Press, 1995; I M Young, *Inclusion and Democracy*, Oxford: Oxford University Press, 2000, ch 7; J Habermas, '"Hat die Konstitutionalisierung" des Völkerrechts noch eine Chance?' in J Habermas, *Der gespaltene Westen*, Frankfurt am Main: Suhrkamp Verlag, 2004, 113–93; see also the specification in J Habermas, 'Kommunikative Rationalität und grenzüberschreitende Politik: eine Replik' in P Niesen & B Herborth (eds), *Anarchie der kommunikativen Freiheit: Jürgen Habermas und die Theorie der internationalen Politik*, Frankfurt am Main: Suhrkamp Verlag, 2007, 406–59 at 442–57.

[32] eg, M Kumm, 'The Legitimacy of International Law: A Constitutionalist Framework of Analysis', *European Journal of International Law* 15 (2004), 907–31; M Kumm, 'The Cosmopolitan Turn in Constitutionalism: On the Relationship between Constitutionalism in and beyond the State' in Dunoff & Trachtman, *Ruling the World?*, 258–324.

as a particular expression of broader trends. Ideas about constitutional pluralism, dialogue, and process are then applied well beyond the realm of European politics.[33] Structural elements have an even weaker place in other approaches which, like Martti Koskenniemi's, regard constitutionalism as primarily an attitude, a quest for universality and impartiality, a 'mindset'. Koskenniemi grounds this view in Kantian thought, though in a reading of Kant that downplays many of the more institutionalist aspects of his work.[34]

3. Problems of Translation

The constitutionalist debate on both the European and global levels is a deliberate attempt to connect those spheres to existing models of order—models that in the framework of the nation-state have proved successful and attractive over a long period of time. As outlined in the first chapter, this reflects an attempt to respond through 'transfer' to the changed circumstances of postnational governance that have undermined classical, intergovernmental models and call for new conceptualizations. Using domestic experiences is an obvious move, but not only have international lawyers and international relations scholars long been wary of domestic analogies,[35] the above sketch of the current debate also reflects continuing uncertainty as to whether and how such analogies can be constructed.

One central challenge then is to define more precisely what it means to transfer those notions to another context. Many authors have suggested understanding it as an effort in translation,[36] but few have specified the implications further. Among them, Neil Walker's approach best captures what lies beneath the surface in many other writings.[37] Walker emphasizes the need for understanding both the source and the destination environments and points to the importance of defining the translated term at a level of abstraction that respects the requirements of both contextual-historical

[33] Walker, 'Idea of Constitutional Pluralism'. See also N Tsagourias, 'Introduction—Constitutionalism: A Theoretical Roadmap' in N Tsagourias (ed), *Transnational Constitutionalism: International and European Models*, Cambridge: Cambridge University Press, 2007, 1–13.

[34] M Koskenniemi, 'Constitutionalism as Mindset: Reflections on Kantian Themes about Law and Globalization', *Theoretical Inquiries in Law* 8 (2007), 9–36.

[35] See the account of the debate in H Suganami, *The Domestic Analogy and World Order Proposals*, Cambridge: Cambridge University Press, 1989.

[36] See only Weiler, *Constitution of Europe*, 270.

[37] N Walker, 'Postnational Constitutionalism and the Problem of Translation' in Weiler & Wind, *European Constitutionalism*, 27–54.

fit and general comprehensibility. Unfortunately, though, the balance and context-sensitivity of this general approach fades away when applied to the concrete case of constitutionalism. Suddenly Walker claims that

> the value of the 'constitutionally signified' which provides the basis for translation is reduced to the extent that, for the sake of contextual 'fit', it is not of universal explanatory relevance across constitutional sites and does not speak to the deepest justificatory roots of constitutionalism's normative orientation.[38]

This already presupposes that constitutionalism's explanatory value and justificatory roots are indeed universal: that they are independent of its original context, namely state and nation, and that the transfer into another, supranational environment does not *a priori* pose significant problems. But this makes the argument circular: whether or not (and under which conditions) constitutionalism can be taken out of the state context should have been the result, not the starting point, of the translation effort—after all, we cannot be sure whether constitutionalism and the postnational sphere go together at all. As a result of this approach, Walker comes to define the concept in such an abstract way that the actual challenges of translation disappear; constitutionalism becomes a mere 'symbolic and normative frame of reference', and the elaboration of its content on the European level is only guided by the three elements of material well-being, social cohesion, and effective freedom. The fruit of the translation is then 'a mere framing of some of the common questions which should inform and validate constitutional analysis across all sites of authority';[39] at this level of generality, all the particular content of constitutionalism, all its connections to particular historical and social circumstances, are lost. Walker's later work acknowledges this problem more openly and develops a greater sensitivity for the origins of the concept; but here, too, constitutionalism is assumed to be open enough for an 'innovative understanding' that makes it applicable in the postnational context.[40]

The general problem with such an approach to translation becomes clearer if we take a closer look at another use of translation in a legal-political context, that of Lawrence Lessig. Lessig inquires into guidelines for interpreting the US Constitution, and he understands this interpretation effort as one in translation from the context of eighteenth-century America

---

[38] Walker, 'Postnational Constitutionalism', 42.

[39] ibid, 53.

[40] Walker, 'European Constitutionalism', 54; N Walker, 'Beyond the Holistic Constitution?' in Loughlin & Dobner, *Twilight*, 291–308 at 296.

into today's changed society.[41] As with Walker's approach, his interpretive results are quite far removed from the original context and meaning (and rightly so). But they are the result of a crucial choice Lessig makes—a choice about the ends of translation. As he explains, there is an important difference between translations that intend to carry meaning and guidance for the target context, and those that intend to let us travel back and understand the source context; he calls the first type *forward* and the second *backward* translation.[42] Interpreting the US Constitution, to him, requires 'forward translation'—unsurprisingly, as the constitution comes with a claim to validity for today's world and therefore requires not just understanding but *application* in changed circumstances.[43] Ronald Dworkin's theory of interpretation (which at times he also describes as translation[44]) is built on a similar intuition, namely that a two-step approach is required—that history, contextual 'fit', has to be complemented by an element of contemporary morality because, as participants and subjects to the validity claim of the law, we have to give it a meaning that can be justified overall.[45] Dworkin differs from Lessig by placing less emphasis on the 'humility' of the translator,[46] but both converge on the importance of the purpose of legal translation—application in today's world—for the methodological framework.

Yet when we translate constitutionalism into the postnational context, our goal is quite different, and so too has to be our method. Unlike in constitutional interpretation, constitutionalism in our context does not come with an established validity claim; it is merely an offer, and we can choose whether or not to accept it as a valid model—if we choose not to accept it, we may try to construct an entirely different type of order for postnational governance. Moreover, there is always the possibility that constitutionalism does not fit the target context: that it demands too much or is built on foundations that find too little resonance in the postnational order. In translation, this is a typical risk: it usually aims primarily at *understanding* terms from foreign languages and different contexts; and this can imply emphasizing their particularity, their interwovenness with practices that are and remain

---

[41] L Lessig, 'Fidelity and Constraint', *Fordham Law Review* 65 (1997), 1365–433; see also L Lessig, 'Fidelity in Translation', *Texas Law Review* 71 (1993), 1165–268.

[42] Lessig, 'Fidelity and Constraint', 1374–6.

[43] See also Lessig, 'Fidelity in Translation', 1189–214.

[44] R Dworkin, *Freedom's Law: The Moral Reading of the American Constitution*, Cambridge, MA: Harvard University Press, 1996, 8.

[45] See R Dworkin, *Law's Empire*, Cambridge, MA: Harvard University Press, 1986, chs 2, 6, and 7. For applications, see Dworkin, *Freedom's Law*.

[46] Lessig, 'Fidelity in Translation', 1251–61.

foreign. And unlike in constitutional interpretation, we do not need to *apply* constitutionalism to postnational governance; the two may simply remain strangers.

This suggests that the type of translation adequate to our task is closer to the model of *backward* interpretation Lessig proposes. We seek to establish whether or not, under what conditions, and on which terms, constitutionalism is useful as a framework for the postnational context. Understanding its meaning in the source context is not the whole enterprise, but it is its largest part—after all, the translation effort mainly seeks to establish whether in the postnational sphere we can connect to that particular domestic model of order and therefore benefit from the high degree of legitimacy it carries. For this purpose, we need to place emphasis on Lessig's first step of translation: on locating the original meaning in the source context of constitutionalism. This requires a detailed engagement with the history of the concept, with its different historical understandings and the varying degrees of appeal they have had over time. In a second step, we can then ask how this original meaning can be carried into our context; what the implications of central pillars of domestic constitutionalism would be in the postnational sphere.

But here we should be careful since the point of that second step is still largely to carry us back to the original context—if we want to connect to the legitimacy constitutionalism provides in domestic politics, we have to remain true to its central pillars. We may emphasize its aspirational value: in the postnational realm, constitutionalism might signify an objective, the end point of a potential process of transformation, and it might confront us with the imperfections of postnational reality when compared to the domestic ideal. Keeping the link with the domestic origins will then help us avoid the risks of a 'forward' translation: it prevents us from too easily adjusting the concept to what is possible in the circumstances of the target context.[47] For in the postnational realm, the conditions for realizing constitutionalism may not be fulfilled—perhaps not yet, perhaps they will never be. As in any translation, we have to retain the possibility of just being puzzled by the context-dependence, the potential lack of transferability of our object of translation. After all, it may turn out that constitutionalism is not made for the postnational context.

II. COMPETING CONSTITUTIONALISMS

Like most successful political concepts, constitutionalism comes in many guises, and pinning down its meaning is difficult not only in the postnational

---

[47] For a realization of this risk, see S Besson, 'Whose Constitution(s)? International Law, Constitutionalism, and Democracy' in Dunoff & Trachtman, *Ruling the World?*, 381–407.

sphere but also in its traditional source context, domestic politics. Already the term 'constitution' is used in so many ways that some authors regard it as 'increasingly polymorphic'[48] or as an 'essentially contested concept'[49]—sometimes it denotes a mere description of the state of society or of the operating rules of its political system; sometimes it is taken to refer to particular limits to governmental powers, especially bills of rights; and sometimes it stands for the existence of a written instrument specifying the shape and limits of public power.[50] 'Constitutionalism' hardly fares better: it has a more obvious normative component than 'constitution', but views diverge widely on what this normative component is. For some, it needs to be directed at a constitution in one of the more substantial meanings mentioned above; for others it signifies a movement towards ideals of freedom, democracy, and good governance; and sometimes it is also taken to represent an expansion of such goals from the political system into wider strata of society, including private law and the relations between individuals.[51]

Among those different interpretations, singling out the right one for all purposes is impossible. Some will fit better in some contexts, some in others, and the terms will derive their particular meanings from the discourses that shape them. In our case, the objective of the inquiry focuses the analysis in two ways. First, as the debate on postnational constitutionalism seeks to tap into the *legitimating* potential of its domestic counterpart, we are only interested in normatively rich conceptions, not in those of mere analytical or descriptive value. Some historically influential interpretations, for example, understand a constitution as the sum of the rules and institutions of a society's political system.[52] They fall outside our focus. The same holds true for contemporary approaches such as Niklas Luhmann's, which regards a constitution merely as the 'structural coupling' of law and politics.[53] However

---

[48] Walker, 'Constitutional Pluralism', 333.

[49] C Harvey, J Morison, & J Shaw, 'Voices, Spaces, and Processes in Constitutionalism', *Journal of Law and Society* 27 (2000), 1–3 at 3.

[50] See J Raz, 'On the Authority and Interpretation of Constitutions: Some Preliminaries' in L Alexander (ed), *Constitutionalism: Philosophical Foundations*, Cambridge: Cambridge University Press, 2001, 152–93 at 153–4; P P Craig, 'Constitutions, Constitutionalism, and the European Union', *European Law Journal* 7 (2001), 125–50 at 126–7.

[51] See Craig, 'Constitutions', 127–8.

[52] Raz, 'Authority and Interpretation of Constitutions', 153; D Grimm, 'Der Verfassungsbegriff in historischer Entwicklung' in D Grimm, *Die Zukunft der Verfassung*, Frankfurt am Main: Suhrkamp Verlag, 1994, 101–55 at 102–3.

[53] N Luhmann, *Das Recht der Gesellschaft*, Frankfurt am Main: Suhrkamp Verlag, 1993, 468–81.

much such a coupling might be an 'evolutionary achievement',[54] it lacks a normative core and can hardly account for the legitimating power constitution and constitutionalism exert in contemporary societies.

A similar consideration applies to conceptions of constitutionalism that historically have not been at the centre of the concept's societal impact. For example, James Tully's notion of a 'common constitutionalism' harks back to political practices that preceded the 'modern constitutionalism' that in his view has captured our political imagination far too long.[55] But while his alternative with its emphasis on diversity and accommodation rather than unity and hierarchy holds promise for the postnational space (I will return to it in the next chapter), it can hardly provide the link with the tradition of constitutionalism that has been central to domestic political legitimacy over the last two centuries.

1. Constitutions as Limitation and Foundation

Among normative visions of constitution and constitutionalism, the most enduring theme has been the limitation of public power. As Charles McIlwain puts it in his classical study of the concept:

> [T]he most ancient, the most persistent, and the most lasting of the essentials of true constitutionalism still remains what it has been almost from the beginning, the limitation of government by law.[56]

In contrast to earlier, more descriptive uses, this limitational interpretation became increasingly influential in seventeenth-century England, for example in the charges against Charles I in 1649 or against James II in 1688, or in Locke's 'fundamental constitutions' of Carolina in 1669.[57] After the successful challenge of royal prerogatives, constitutions were now regarded as rules the violation of which could have serious consequences—and the idea that government was subject to legal limits was given particularly clear expression in the Bill of Rights in 1689. It naturally faced difficulties in absolute monarchies but found increasing reflection where power was less concentrated. When rulers were weak or vulnerable, as in much of Germany at the time, the estates were often able to force them to agree on limitations

---

[54] N Luhmann, 'Verfassung als evolutionäre Errungenschaft', *Rechtshistorisches Journal* 9 (1990), 176–220.

[55] J Tully, *Strange Multiplicity: Constitutionalism in an Age of Diversity*, Cambridge: Cambridge University Press, 1995.

[56] C H McIlwain, *Constitutionalism: Ancient and Modern*, Ithaca, NY: Cornell University Press, 1940 (reprint: Clark: Lawbook Exchange, 2005), 24.

[57] Grimm, 'Verfassungsbegriff', 104–5.

to their power. These agreements were variously called fundamental laws, agreements of government (*Herrschaftsverträge*), or electoral capitulations (*Wahlkapitulationen*); they established limits to royal powers and could not be unilaterally terminated by the kings.[58]

Revolutions

A broader vision of what 'constitution' could mean arose only with the American and French revolutions in the eighteenth century.[59] The new understanding came to see constitutions not only as a limitation of government, but as its very foundation.[60] The main characteristic of the new type of constitution was not so much its written nature—as mentioned, written fundamental laws existed before. It was rather the comprehensive ambition, the claim to ground the entire system of government and not only to shape it in one way or another. Thomas Paine summed this ambition up when he noted that 'a constitution is a thing antecedent to a government, and a government is only the creature of a constitution'.[61] From then on, the justification of government increasingly depended on a formal constitution; governmental powers outside the constitutional framework—before taken for granted as based on divine right or other independent foundations—could no longer exist.

This comprehensive claim is clearly linked to the scope of revolutionary ambition it followed from, but neither in America nor in France did the revolutionaries set out with such far-reaching goals. Their initial arguments operated within the old scheme and relied on certain historically formed rights which they wanted to see reinterpreted and enforced against what

[58] See G Oestreich, 'Vom Herrschaftsvertrag zur Verfassungsurkunde' in R Vierhaus (ed), *Herrschaftsverträge, Wahlkapitulationen, Fundamentalgesetze*, Göttingen: Vandenhoeck & Ruprecht, 1977, 45–67; C Schmitt, *Verfassungslehre*, 9th edn, Berlin: Duncker & Humblot, [1928] 2003, 61–75; E-W Böckenförde, 'Geschichtliche Entwicklung und Bedeutungswandel der Verfassung' in E-W Böckenförde, *Staat, Verfassung, Demokratie*, Frankfurt am Main: Suhrkamp Verlag, 1991, 29–52 at 36–41.

[59] On the conceptual trajectory in the seventeenth and eighteenth centuries, see G Stourzh, 'Staatsformenlehre und Fundamentalgesetze in England und Nordamerika im 17. und 18. Jahrhundert' in Vierhaus, *Herrschaftsverträge*, 294–327.

[60] On the centrality of the contest between these two variants, see Möllers, 'Verfassunggebende Gewalt', 229–40; see also P Comanducci, 'Ordre ou norme? Quelques idées de constitution au XVIIIe siècle' in M Troper & L Jaume (eds), *1789 et l'invention de la Constitution*, Paris: LGDJ-Bruylant, 1994, 23–43.

[61] T Paine, *Rights of Man*, Mineola, NY: Dover Thrift Editions, 1999, 33.

was seen as a corrupted monarchical system.[62] Only over time, as this route proved unsuccessful, did the focus shift and calls for new foundations of government arise.[63] And even after American independence, it took a decade for this idea fully to take hold. The state constitutions of the 1770s were still seen as granted by state parliaments and often freely amended by them. It was only when suspicion against the legislatures grew that constitutions came to be seen as a higher body of law, deriving from the people in a more direct way and therefore also grounding (and limiting) parliamentary power. As a result, new state constitutions in the 1780s came to be enacted by special constitutional conventions, and the US Constitution in 1787 followed this model, largely in order to give it a foundation independent from—and above—state legislatures.[64]

This prepared the ground for developments in France, where the foundational vision was formulated most cogently by the Abbé de Sieyès: 'tout gouvernement commis doit avoir sa constitution'.[65] The 1791 constitution reflected this by emphasizing the delegated nature of public power—of the king, the legislature, and the judiciary—and by placing itself at the centre of the delegatory relationship. Without a basis in the constitution, no one could claim to speak on behalf of the nation; extraconstitutional powers no longer existed.[66] This was reinforced by the high procedural threshold established for constitutional amendments: while the power of the people to effect revision remained untouched, its delegatees—including the National Assembly—could not change constitutional provisions without going through a lengthy and burdensome process, culminating in a decision of a distinct 'Assembly of Revision'.[67]

Indecision

The American and French revolutions, however, did not settle the meaning of 'constitution' instantaneously. In 1830, an influential German dictionary noted that no term was more closely related to central political movements

---

[62] See G Wood, *The Creation of the American Republic, 1776–1787*, Chapel Hill, NC: University of North Carolina Press, ch 1; J M Roberts, *The French Revolution*, 2nd edn, Oxford: Oxford University Press, 1997, ch 1.

[63] See H Arendt, *On Revolution*, London: Penguin Books, [1963] 1990, 147–50.

[64] Wood, *Creation*, ch 8; J N Rakove, *Original Meanings: Politics and Ideas in the Making of the Constitution*, New York: Knopf, 1996, ch 5.

[65] E-J Sieyès, *Qu'est-ce que le Tiers Etat?*, Paris: Alexandre Correard, 1822, ch 5, 158. On Sieyès's thought and influence on the revolutionary constitutions, see P Pasquino, *Sieyès et l'invention de la constitution en France*, Paris: Odile Jacob, 1998.

[66] Constitution française (1791), Title III.

[67] ibid, Title VII.

and none sparked stronger disagreement.[68] Throughout the nineteenth century, the contest between different interpretations of the term remained at the core of political struggles all over Europe. France itself was a prime example of this contest. Its post-Napoleonic *chartes constitutionelles*, followed the revolutionary constitutions only in form: the *charte* of 1814 was a mere royal grant, based on the notion that 'in France, all authority lies in the king'—thus ultimately confirming the king's role above, not below the constitution.[69] The 1830 charter, while more contractual in character, still presupposed a pre-existing power of the monarch.[70] And ambivalence over the meaning of constitution continued to reign in the French republics. Here the people, though again recognized as the *pouvoir constituant*, was in practice largely replaced by parliament in the operation—and even revision—of most constitutions until the mid-twentieth century.[71]

Perhaps the most heated nineteenth-century battles over the constitutional idea were fought in Germany.[72] This was conditioned in part by the 1820 Vienna Final Act, which confirmed the supreme authority of the monarch and allowed constitutions only to regulate aspects of the *exercise* of that authority. The king was thus thought of as prior to the constitution, as above it, and the constitution was his act of grace. Most German constitutions of the time were thus unilaterally granted, but their scope and character remained subject to contestation. Liberals insisted that, even though initially based on a unilateral grant, they had become the new and sole foundation of public authority.[73] As a prominent liberal voice, Carl von Rotteck, put it in 1836, the monarch may have acted as *pouvoir constituant* in enacting a constitution, but through the constitution he had turned into a *pouvoir constitué* and could no longer undo his creation.[74] The conceptual contestation also found

---

[68] Quoted in Grimm, 'Verfassungsbegriff', 120–1.

[69] Preamble of the Charte constitutionnelle (1814). The quoted translation follows L Jaume, 'Constituent Power in France: The Revolution and its Consequences' in M Loughlin & N Walker (eds), *The Paradox of Constitutionalism: Constituent Power and Constitutional Form*, Oxford: Oxford University Press, 2007, 67–85 at 76.

[70] Charte constitutionnelle (1830); see Pasquino, *Sieyès*, 129–45.

[71] See Jaume, 'Constituent Power'.

[72] See D Grimm, *Deutsche Verfassungsgeschichte 1776–1866*, Frankfurt am Main: Suhrkamp Verlag, 1988; E-W Böckenförde, 'Der deutsche Typ der konstitutionellen Monarchie im 19. Jahrhundert' in E-W Böckenförde, *Recht, Staat, Freiheit*, Frankfurt am Main: Suhrkamp Verlag, 1991, 273–305.

[73] On the competing visions, see M Stolleis, *Geschichte des öffentlichen Rechts in Deutschland*, vol II, Munich: C H Beck, 1992, 102.

[74] Quoted in Grimm, 'Verfassungsbegriff', 132.

reflection in political disputes such as the Prussian constitutional conflict of the 1860s, in which the royal government's recourse to extraconstitutional powers met with serious resistance in parliament. The conflict's eventual resolution remained ambiguous—a reflection of the undecided character of nineteenth-century constitutions where the constitutional idea remained in abeyance between the limitational and foundational models.[75]

In Germany, the contest of constitutional visions was (provisionally) decided in favour of the foundational model in the Weimar Constitution in 1919[76] and then again in the *Grundgesetz* in 1949. Arguments about pre-constitutional powers reappeared, mainly based on the notion that the state preceded its constitutional form and thus retained certain preconstitutional competences; but in the course of the twentieth century such arguments became marginal, at least as regards their legal impact.[77]

Settlement

This shift reflects a much broader trend: if the nineteenth century was characterized by a competition between constitutional visions, the twentieth century saw a far-reaching convergence on the foundational model, reflected in the almost worldwide spread of written constitutions.[78] In several waves constitution-making swept the globe, and few states have defied the trend—key among them, of course, the United Kingdom. As in other states without a unified, written constitution (such as Israel and New Zealand), the political system of the United Kingdom relies on alternative sources of authority sufficiently strong to obviate the need for a constitutional document, or for reliance on the people as a *pouvoir constituant*.[79] In most states, though, such sources are unavailable, and reliance on a constitution has become crucial to legitimating the political

---

[75] See Grimm, *Verfassungsgeschichte*, 231–40; Böckenförde, 'Der deutsche Typ', 295–9. But see also Schmitt, *Verfassungslehre*, 54–6, who saw the outcome as confirming ultimate monarchical power.

[76] On the continuing dispute about the supremacy of the constitution, see R Wahl, 'Verfassungsstaatlichkeit im Konstitutionalismus und in der Weimarer Zeit' in R Wahl, *Verfassungsstaat, Europäisierung, Internationalisierung*, Frankfurt am Main: Suhrkamp Verlag, 2003, 331–7.

[77] See C Möllers, *Staat als Argument*, Munich: C H Beck, 1999, especially 72–6, 264–7.

[78] See, eg, J-E Lane, *Constitutions and Political Theory*, Manchester: Manchester University Press, 1996, 6.

[79] On the latter point, see M Loughlin, 'Constituent Power Subverted: From English Constitutional Argument to British Constitutional Practice' in Loughlin & Walker, *Paradox of Constitutionalism*, 27–48.

order. Constitutions have also become increasingly robust: most of them are now enforceable through mechanisms of judicial review (albeit with varying degrees of effectiveness).[80]

Written constitutions do not *necessarily* reflect a foundational vision, but most contemporary ones do so in fact. This can be gauged, for example, from the way they treat the most typical kind of extraconstitutional powers: emergency powers. For long, these seemed unamenable to constitutional definition; some thought they eluded legal regulation altogether.[81] But contemporary constitutionalism has extended its reach to them too. Most constitutions now contain provisions on the transfer of power between state organs in emergency situations, and typically they also regulate the extent to which fundamental rights can exceptionally be interfered with. Some only regulate certain aspects, or contain no explicit provisions at all. But even then, this is usually not taken to allow for a recourse to extraconstitutional powers that would set aside the constitutional framework.[82] Instead, it is assumed that the standard norms on the separation of powers and the protection of rights provide sufficient latitude for dealing with particular threats—because of the flexibility of the proportionality test in fundamental rights jurisprudence and because legislatures can grant the executive defined additional powers. This latter ('legislative') avenue, which keeps the constitutional settlement intact, seems to have become the most common way for tackling emergency situations in recent decades.[83] It has also come to dominate the US response to the terrorist attacks of 11 September 2001 once the Supreme Court had barred recourse to special, largely unfettered

---

[80] See T Ginsburg, 'The Global Spread of Constitutional Review' in K Whittington, R D Keleman, & G A Caldeira (eds), *The Oxford Handbook of Law and Politics*, Oxford: Oxford University Press, 2008, 81–98.

[81] C Schmitt, *Political Theology: Four Chapters on the Concept of Sovereignty* (G Schwab, trans), Chicago, IL: Chicago University Press, 2005, 6–7 and passim. For a discussion, see O Gross, 'The Normless and Exceptionless Exception: Carl Schmitt's Theory of Emergency Powers and the "Norm-Exception" Dichotomy', *Cardozo Law Review* 21 (2000), 1825–68.

[82] See European Commission for Democracy through Law (Venice Commission), *Emergency Powers*, Council of Europe Doc CDL-STD(1995)012, <http://www. venice.coe.int/docs/1995/CDL-STD(1995)012-e.asp>; see also O Gross & F Ni Aolain, *Law in Times of Crisis: Emergency Powers in Theory and Practice*, Cambridge: Cambridge University Press, 2006, ch 1. Switzerland appears to constitute an exception.

[83] J Ferejohn & P Pasquino, 'The Law of the Exception: A Typology of Emergency Powers', *International Journal of Constitutional Law* 2 (2004), 210–39 at 215–20.

executive powers[84]—even though a number of commentators had advocated a recourse to extralegal means.[85]

Twentieth-century constitutionalism has transcended boundaries also in other respects, for example as regards federal orders. In previous times, as sovereignty was often regarded as divided between levels of government, the scope of federal constitutional settlements was typically limited.[86] With sovereignty undecided, federal constitutions could provide no more than a partial framework, situated alongside constitutions on the state level—for lack of a clear hierarchy, conflicts between both could not be resolved by reference to either of the layers. Carl Schmitt even regarded this indecision as the hallmark of true federalism,[87] and conceptualizations of the European Union today have taken up this strand of thought.[88] But in domestic constitutional orders, this ambiguity has largely disappeared. In the US, this was due in part to the victory of the Union in the civil war; in Europe, accounts of composite orders changed as sovereignty was increasingly seen in a binary fashion—and the resulting entities as either confederal (ie, international) or federal (ie, statist) in character. Either way, sovereignty and with it the supremacy of the constitution belonged to one level, and one level alone.[89]

---

[84] See US Supreme Court, Judgment of 28 June 2004, *Hamdi v Rumsfeld* 542 US 507 (2004).

[85] See, eg, O Gross, 'Chaos and Rules: Should Responses to Violent Crises Always be Constitutional?', *Yale Law Journal* 112 (2003), 1011–34; M Tushnet, 'Emergencies and the Idea of Constitutionalism' in M Tushnet (ed), *The Constitution in Wartime: Beyond Alarmism and Complacency*, Durham, NC: Duke University Press, 2005, 39–54.

[86] See on the US, A R Amar, 'Of Sovereignty and Federalism', *Yale Law Journal* 96 (1987), 1425–520; R Schütze, 'Federalism as Constitutional Pluralism: "Letter from America"' in M Avbelj & J Komárek (eds), *Constitutional Pluralism in the European Union and Beyond*, Oxford: Hart Publishing, forthcoming, 2010. On Germany, see S Oeter, 'Souveränität und Demokratie als Probleme in der "Verfassungsentwicklung" der Europäischen Union', *Zeitschrift für ausländisches öffentliches Recht und Völkerrecht* 55 (1995), 659–707 at 664–76.

[87] Schmitt, *Verfassungslehre*, 371–5.

[88] See, eg, N MacCormick, 'Beyond the Sovereign State', *Modern Law Review* 56 (1993), 1–18; R Schütze, 'On "Federal" Ground: The European Union as an (Inter) national Phenomenon', *Common Market Law Review* 46 (2009), 1069–105. See also the discussion in Chapter 3, I and Chapter 5, II.3.

[89] See R Schütze, *From Dual to Cooperative Federalism: The Changing Structure of European Law*, Oxford: Oxford University Press, 2009, 15–40. For critiques and alternative conceptions, see ibid; O Beaud, *Théorie de la Fédération*, Paris: Presses Universitaires de France, 2007; C Schönberger, *Unionsbürger: Europas föderales Bürgerrecht in vergleichender Sicht*, Tübingen: Mohr Siebeck, 2005, 124–7.

This framework later became central also to the conceptualization of supranational integration, especially the European Union: for constitutional courts and domestic constitution-makers, sovereignty continued to reside on the national level, and it was for the national constitution that they claimed the ultimate say on the basis and limits of integrating processes.[90]

Over two centuries thus, foundational constitutionalism has come to dominate the domestic tradition of constitutionalism. As McIlwain put it in 1940:

> Whatever we may think of it theoretically, Paine's notion that the only true constitution is one consciously constructed, and that a nation's government is only the creature of this constitution, conforms probably more closely than any other to the actual development in the world since the opening of the nineteenth century.... Written constitutions creating, defining, and limiting governments since then have been the general rule in almost the whole of the constitutional world.[91]

2. Foundational Constitutionalism and the Modern Political Project

The emergence of foundational constitutionalism was in some sense a contingent event, and this might raise doubts as to whether it is indeed this tradition that should guide us when translating constitutionalism to the postnational level. It was born out of the very particular revolutionary projects of the late eighteenth century, and this link was not accidental: comprehensive constitutions were dependent on revolutions—an innovation of that scale could not have been introduced without a drastic break with the past.[92] And the revolutions were dependent on constitutions. They sought to establish new systems of government, a new basis of legitimacy, and also effect fundamental changes in society—in the French case the abolition of the feudal system, in the American the establishment of a more virtuous, less corrupted polity.[93] Constitutions were the perfect instruments for this: they symbolized the emergence of a new order that did not allow remnants of the past, and they promised to rebuild the political system entirely along the lines of the revolutionary ideals.[94]

---

[90] Schütze, 'On "Federal" Ground', 1092–9.

[91] McIlwain, *Constitutionalism*, 16.

[92] D Grimm, 'Entstehungs- und Wirkungsbedingungen des modernen Konstitutionalismus' in Grimm, *Zukunft der Verfassung*, 31–66 at 43–5.

[93] See Roberts, *French Revolution*, 24–9; Wood, *Creation*, chs 2 and 3.

[94] Arendt, *On Revolution*, 125–6; C Klein, 'Pourquoi écrit-on une constitution?' in M Troper & L Jaume, *1789 et l'invention de la Constitution*, 89–99 at 94–6.

Yet the spread of foundational constitutionalism over the last two centuries signals a much broader appeal that goes well beyond revolutionary situations. It signals an intimate connection, the modern political project as such, especially a link with Enlightenment thought, with the idea of a political and social order not based on history and tradition but shaped by humankind along rational lines. Power-limiting constitutionalism had been a step in this direction, but it left large parts of the old, traditional orders (and especially their foundations) untouched. Comprehensive constitutionalization brought these, too, under scrutiny and set out to construct a new, rational basis of the political system. The radicality of this shift was probably nowhere clearer than in Hegel's dictum about the French revolution that never before 'had it been perceived that man's existence centres in his head, i.e. in thought, inspired by which he builds up the world of reality'.[95]

Hegel's comments mirrored the perspective of constitution-makers. For Sieyès the contrast between old and new became clearest when the English constitution was taken into view. At the time frequently seen as a model, to Sieyès it appeared as a 'product of chance and circumstance rather than of enlightened reason [lumières]'.[96] The French nation, in contrast, was free of historical obligations and constitutional ties and could remake the political order at its will. In America, the constitutional debate was shaped more by historical experience than by abstract theorizing,[97] though, as Jack Rakove notes, '[eighteenth-century American] thought and the Constitution it produced were expressions of the Enlightenment' too.[98] This is on display most clearly in the *Federalist Papers*: in their very first paragraph, Alexander Hamilton framed the constitutional project as an attempt at 'establishing good government from reflection and choice' as against the old dependence on 'accident and force'.[99]

Enlightenment's human agency found its reflection in the political sphere in the insistence on popular sovereignty. In France, this was reinforced by the rise of the idea of the 'nation' throughout the eighteenth century: the nation as a unity transcended social and regional differences and made it possible to think of a collective, acting subject as the true author of a constitution. It did not have to rely on agreements with other actors, as had been the case

---

[95] G W F Hegel, *The Philosophy of History* (J Sibree, transl), Buffalo, NY: Prometheus Books, 1991, 447 (Part IV, Section III, ch III).

[96] Sieyès, *Tiers Etat*, ch IV, para VII, 146.

[97] See Wood, *Creation*, 3–10; Rakove, *Original Meanings*, 18–19.

[98] Rakove, *Original Meanings*, 18.

[99] A Hamilton, J Madison, & J Jay, *The Federalist Papers* (L Goldman, ed), Oxford: Oxford University Press, 2008, 11 (A Hamilton, *Federalist* no 1).

previously, for these other actors were no longer equals—they had become part of (and therefore subject to) the nation.[100] In America too, historical alternatives to popular sovereignty had been discredited in the eighteenth century, and 'the people' had come to be imagined as a unity, no longer as an aggregation of different groups.[101]

Popular sovereignty initially seemed antithetical to comprehensive constitutions that imposed constraints even on parliament, but this changed once awareness of the distance between the people and its representatives grew. This happened in America, as I have already mentioned, with a series of scandals in the 1780s. These entailed a shift towards constitution-making through special conventions, endowed with a higher legitimacy than the legislatures, and culminated in the federal constitution of 1787 which, precisely because of its ratification through popular conventions, could make the claim to derive from 'we the people' in a way that trumped resistance by state parliaments and became a higher law.[102]

In France, a similar move was associated with a shift from Rousseauian thought to the political ideas of Sieyès. Because Sieyès saw representation and delegation as key to political order, the link between the will of the people and its delegates—its representatives in the legislature and other holders of public power—became crucial, and the constitution came to provide this link.[103] The *pouvoir constituant* and the *pouvoirs constitués* were connected by the terms of delegation spelled out in the constitutional document.

A constitution thus became the necessary instrument to give the idea of a social contract effect.[104] It symbolized and took to new levels the possibility of man-made change. The constitution, being thought of as foundational and comprehensive, no longer knew any limits to what self-government and reason could achieve; it allowed for the radical realization of the idea of agency, so central to the modern imagination.

---

[100] Sieyès, *Tiers Etat*, especially chs I and V; see also Pasquino, *Sieyès*, ch III.

[101] See J P McCormick, 'People and Elites in Republican Constitutions, Traditional and Modern' in Loughlin & Walker, *Paradox of Constitutionalism*, 107–25 at 124.

[102] Rakove, *Original Meanings*, 94–113; Wood, *Creation*, 532–6. It also allowed for a claim of supremacy over state constitutions, which, however, did not prevent later dispute about the point; see Amar, 'Of Sovereignty and Federalism', especially 1450–5.

[103] See Sieyès, *Tiers Etat*, ch V; B Baczko, 'The Social Contract of the French: Sieyes and Rousseau', *Journal of Modern History* 60 (1988), S98–S125; N Urbinati, *Representative Democracy*, Chicago, IL: University of Chicago Press, 2006, ch 4.

[104] See Pasquino, *Sieyès*, ch II.

3. Foundational Constitutionalism's Contemporary Appeal

The historical attraction of foundational constitutionalism, its tight link with the modern political project, carries over into the contemporary world only in part. Ideals of agency and popular sovereignty remain central to political thought, and comprehensive constitutions also continue to be prime tools to translate moral ideals into institutional practice.[105] Yet other aspects have become more problematic, and especially the tension between constitutional constraint and democratic expression provides a continuing challenge.[106] On the other hand, under some influential conceptions of liberty, comprehensive constitutions hardly appear as more attractive than their power-limiting alternative;[107] at worst they help legitimize a public power better seen with sceptical eyes.

The contemporary appeal of foundational constitutions comes into clearer view through a focus on the interlinkages between liberal and republican approaches, or the rule of law and popular sovereignty. In their complementarities and tensions, both provide the reference points of most contemporary constitutional theory,[108] and the mutual dependence of their ideational bases has been at the heart of various strands of political thought. It is most explicit in Jürgen Habermas's conceptualization of a 'co-originality' of private and public autonomy. Because of this co-originality—their parallel emergence from the decline of earlier metaphysics as the sole post-traditional sources of law's legitimacy—none of them is intrinsically superior to the other; instead, they are mutually dependent. Popular sovereignty can be realized only through the medium of law which presupposes a system of rights; but rights depend for their formulation and interpretation on a legal basis that can only be created through the exercise of popular sovereignty.[109] As Habermas puts it:

> In the constitution-making acts of a legally binding interpretation of the system of rights, citizens make an originary use of a civic autonomy that thereby constitutes itself in a performatively self-referential manner.[110]

---

[105] See, eg, Dworkin, *Freedom's Law.*

[106] See, eg, J Waldron, *Law and Disagreement*, Oxford: Clarendon Press, 1999; R Bellamy, *Political Constitutionalism*, Cambridge: Cambridge University Press, 2007.

[107] See the discussions of constitutionalism in F A Hayek, *The Constitution of Liberty*, Abingdon: Routledge, [1960] 2006, chs 12 and 14; P Pettit, *Republicanism: A Theory of Freedom and Government*, Oxford: Oxford University Press, 1997, 276–8.

[108] F Michelman, 'Law's Republic', *Yale Law Journal* 97 (1998), 1493–537 at 1499–501.

[109] J Habermas, *Between Facts and Norms* (W Rehg, trans), Cambridge: Polity Press, 1996, ch 3.

[110] ibid, 128.

In this framework, a constitution becomes foundational in a particularly radical sense—it is the act in which private and public autonomy are not only exercised but in fact constituted. Popular sovereignty then no longer resides in a particular, pre-existing subject that could exercise an actual will; instead, it is dematerialized and has moved into the discursive processes of society that gain the attribute of popular sovereignty if they meet the necessary procedural conditions.[111] A constitution then has to both reflect and specify those conditions, and it is necessary for giving them a real existence.

Despite Habermas's claims to the contrary,[112] this position is in principle shared by other main strands of contemporary theory, both liberal and republican. In Philip Pettit's republican approach, for example, popular sovereignty is no longer distinct from rights and reason as 'there is no suggestion that the people in some collective incarnation, or via some collective representation, are voluntaristically supreme'. Instead, for Pettit, 'the democratic process is designed to let the requirements of reason materialize and impose themselves; it is not a process that gives any particular place to will'.[113] And public and private autonomy are also drawn together in core liberal conceptions, such as that of John Rawls. For Rawls, too, both forms of autonomy share—and have shared in much of liberal thought—the same moral roots and operate in parallel.[114] Both join forces when citizens select 'principles of justice to specify the scheme of (basic) liberties which best protect and further citizens' fundamental interests and which they then concede to one another',[115] and they are at the root of public power exercised by the state. As Rawls puts it,

> our exercise of political power is fully proper only when it is exercised in accordance with a constitution the essentials of which all citizens as free and equal may reasonably be expected to endorse in the light of principles and ideals acceptable to their common human reason.[116]

---

[111] ibid, 135–6, 298. See also J Habermas, 'Constitutional Democracy: A Paradoxical Union of Contradictory Principles?', *Political Theory* 29 (2001), 766–81.

[112] J Habermas, 'Reconciliation through the Public Use of Reason: Remarks on John Rawls's Political Liberalism', *Journal of Philosophy* 92 (1995), 109–31 at 127–8.

[113] Pettit, *Republicanism*, 201. See also, eg, Michelman, 'Law's Republic', 1526–7.

[114] J Rawls, 'Reply to Habermas' in J Rawls, *Political Liberalism*, New York: Columbia University Press, 1996, 372–434 at 416–19.

[115] ibid, 413.

[116] Rawls, *Political Liberalism*, 137.

Rawls claims to be agnostic about the precise shape a constitution should take,[117] but a comprehensive, foundational constitutional settlement is clearly key to realizing the two forms of autonomy jointly. Such a settlement can provide the focus for the specification of the principles of private autonomy in an exercise of popular sovereignty—a popular sovereignty that is itself proceduralized. In the dualist democracy Rawls favours, it can raise principled agreement above the level of daily politics and structure the field in which public reason is exercised.[118]

Other arguments may support foundational constitutionalism in contemporary political theory,[119] but its distinctive appeal emerges most vividly from the interlinkage of private and public autonomy that, as we have seen, characterizes key strands of contemporary political thought. If the two are connected and mutually dependent—when, to use a simplified formula, the formulation of rights depends on democratic processes, and democratic processes depend on rights—then a foundational constitution gains centrality as a focus for the self-referential formulation of the principles on both sides. A constitution that consists only of circumscribed limitations of existing governmental powers would not be able to reach far enough into the structuring of the political process to provide the basis for either rights or democracy. And it certainly would not provide for the very constitution of popular sovereignty that, in all the accounts discussed, no longer lies in the will of a pre-existing, material subject, but has either become dependent on stringent procedural conditions or has moved into society's discursive processes themselves.[120] Only a foundational, comprehensive constitution can provide the locus for an enterprise of that scope.

III. FOUNDATIONAL CONSTITUTIONALISM IN THE POSTNATIONAL ORDER

1. Constitutionalism's Implications

The implications of the discussion in the previous section are potentially far-reaching. They suggest that, if we want to tap into constitutionalism's

---

[117] ibid, 415–16.

[118] Rawls, *Political Liberalism*, 214, 231–40.

[119] See, eg, the emphasis on integration and constitutional patriotism in J Habermas, 'Citizenship and National Identity' in Habermas, *Between Facts and Norms*, 491–515 at 500; Rawls, *Political Liberalism*, 158–68; D Grimm, 'Integration by Constitution', *International Journal of Constitutional Law* 3 (2005), 193–208.

[120] See also A Kalyvas, 'Popular Sovereignty, Democracy, and the Constituent Power', *Constellations* 12 (2005), 223–44 at 234–9.

legitimate potential for the postnational sphere, we need to connect with the foundational tradition—the tradition that, because of its historical dominance and appeal, has come to shape the domestic constitutionalist imagination for the last two centuries.[121]

Yet foundational constitutionalism would pose high, perhaps radical demands on the existing structure and institutions of postnational governance, and it would go further than most proposals of postnational constitutionalism to date. We have seen above that in this literature the most prominent strands, as regards both the European and global contexts, emphasize elements of legalization, of institutional checks and normative limits to existing processes of law-making and -application.[122] These strands bear significant resemblance to the power-limiting approach to constitutionalism that has been prominent in the domestic context until the early twentieth century, and in some countries up until today. But they fall short of foundational constitutionalism in their circumscribed character and in their focus on limiting existing institutions and law-making processes rather than fully defining and organizing them. After all, establishing human rights limits for Security Council action or enforcing constraints on unilateral uses of force is a far cry from the aspiration radically to scrutinize and refound all exercises of public power, as the foundational vision demands. Likewise, the third group of approaches to postnational constitutionalism sketched in the first section—the 'discursive' ones—explicitly relies on alternative visions that only find limited expression in the contemporary practice of domestic constitutionalism. The distance from foundational constitutionalism here is deliberate: it involves a rejection of the modern hope to frame a society by means of an overarching legal structure or document, and instead relies on the discursive, societal processes by which power can be checked and channelled.

Closest to central tenets of foundational constitutionalism are then the more structural approaches to the postnational order—those that imagine a European constitution as comprehensively determining the structure, process, and values of the European polity, or envision a global order held together, in a quasi-federal style, not only by common principles and values but also by rules on the organization and delimitation of public power in this realm. But can they really redeem the promise of foundational constitutionalism? Or does the structure of the global sphere resist constitutionalization,

---

[121] See also Besson, 'Whose Constitution(s)?', 387.

[122] See text at nn 4 and 23 above.

perhaps because, as Dieter Grimm claims, the multiplicity of unconnected centres of governance simply does not represent a suitable object for it?[123]

Grimm's point may overstate the requirements even of a demanding conception of constitutionalism, but it certainly sharpens our sense for the extent of the challenge. For it reminds us that the existence of a centralized, monopolistic state apparatus facilitated the task of the modern constitution significantly: realizing both individual liberties and collective self-govern-ment could be achieved by focusing on that particular object, by (merely) redefining the conditions for its establishment and legitimate use.[124] The comprehensive ambition of the absolutist state thus paved the way for a comprehensive reach of the constitution. Achieving the same goals in the current polycentric setting of global governance would require a far greater institutional transformation. Similar to the polycentricity of medieval poli-ties, and to some extent still the structures of the early modern state, global governance today is characterized by forms of organic growth which are not steered by a definable centre but determined by the rationalities of social subsystems and the interests and position of particular actors.[125] Many of the institutions interact with one another in undefined—sometimes coop-erative, sometimes conflictive—ways, and it is unsurprising that 'fragmen-tation' has come to occupy a central place in our vocabulary for describing the postnational space.[126]

Reordering this space so as to redeem foundational aspirations may not involve a world state with a centralized government,[127] but it would, at the very least, require rules to define the relationships between the differ-ent forms of existing public power,[128] and it would have to extend to other

---

[123] See D Grimm, 'The Achievement of Constitutionalism and its Prospects in a Changed World' in Loughlin & Dobner, *Twilight*, 3–22 at 17–19; see also D Grimm, 'The Constitution in the Process of Denationalization', *Constellations* 12 (2005), 447–63.

[124] Grimm, 'Entstehungs- und Wirkungsbedingungen', 37–8.

[125] See the (somewhat exaggerated) account in Fischer-Lescano & Teubner, *Regime-Kollisionen*.

[126] See, eg, International Law Commission, 'Conclusions of the work of the Study Group on the Fragmentation of International Law: Difficulties arising from the Diversification and Expansion of International Law', *Report of the International Law Commission on its Fifty-eighth Session*, UN Doc A/61/10, 251; M Koskenniemi, 'The Fate of Public International Law: Between Technique and Politics', *Modern Law Review* 70 (2007), 1–30 at 4–9.

[127] But see A Wendt, 'Why a World State is Inevitable', *European Journal of International Relations* 9 (2003), 491–542.

[128] Grimm, 'Constitution and Denationalization', 460.

forms of power public institutions are unable to tame at present.[129] It would not content itself with 'constitutionalizing' particular regimes or institutions, such as the WTO or the UN. As laudable as it might be to infuse these regimes with human rights ideas—as long as a regime's relation with the outside, its position in the wider landscape of global governance, is left undefined, the constitutional promise is diluted.[130] The current 'multiplicity of unconnected centres of governance' may then represent not so much a bar to pursuing constitutionalism in the postnational sphere as an indicator of the extent of the challenge.

If this signals the size (and perhaps utopian character) of the constitutional ambition when it comes to *institutional* change, the challenge is hardly smaller as regards the transformation of postnational *society*. As we have seen, realizing foundational constitutionalism does not merely imply the creation of a unified set of rules about the exercise of public power, but this set of rules also has to explicate the conditions under which public power can be regarded as an exercise of public and private autonomy.[131] One of the main challenges behind this task is to clarify what self-government through a constitution could mean in a space such as the postnational in which there is no uncontested collective that could express its will in constitutional terms.[132] After all, one of the most prominent challenges of constitutionalism and democracy beyond the state is based on the alleged lack of a common 'demos'.[133] This challenge is overstated: the collective behind

[129] See the critique in D Kennedy, 'The Mystery of Global Governance' in Dunoff & Trachtman, *Ruling the World?*, 37–68 at 58.

[130] For a related argument in the trade context, see J L Dunoff, 'Constitutional Conceits: The WTO's "Constitution" and the Discipline of International Law', *European Journal of International Law* 17 (2006), 647–75 at 661–5.

[131] See above, Section II.3.

[132] On the related problems for constitutions' *Sinndimension*, their role as a repository of a collective self-understanding, see U Haltern, 'Internationales Verfassungsrecht? Anmerkungen zu einer kopernikanischen Wende', *Archiv des öffentlichen Rechts* 128 (2003), 511–57.

[133] See, eg, P Kirchhof, 'Die Identität der Verfassung' in J Isensee & P Kirchhof (eds), *Handbuch des Staatsrechts der Bundesrepublik Deutschland*, vol II, 3rd edn, Heidelberg: C F Müller Verlag, 2004, 261–316 at 288–93; E-W Böckenförde, 'Die Zukunft politischer Autonomie' in E-W Böckenförde, *Staat, Nation, Europa*, Frankfurt am Main: Suhrkamp Verlag, 1999, 103–26. For a trenchant critique, see J H H Weiler, 'The State "über alles": Demos, Telos and the German Maastricht Decision', *Jean Monnet Working Papers* 6/95.

constitution-making, the 'people', has typically been imagined anyway,[134] and the *pouvoir constituant* probably even more so than 'the nation' in general: constitutions are often part of processes in which a collective self constitutes itself.[135] And as we have seen in the previous section, they are best understood as reflecting an understanding in which the subject of popular sovereignty has become dematerialized and linked to a process that, because of its deliberative qualities, merits the attribution of constitution- and law-making powers.

This may alleviate concerns about a lacking, identifiable 'demos', but it may not reduce the broader challenge much: for however low one's requirements for a proceduralized popular sovereignty in the domestic realm may be, they will hardly be fulfilled in a postnational space where power and wealth differentials, language and culture barriers, and the lack of identification with a common project render meaningful communication and deliberation beyond a narrow elite very difficult.[136] This does not rule out postnational constitutionalism from the start—after all, modern constitutions have rarely been the result of ideal forms of collective self-government[137]—but it indicates the size of the challenge. Creating the conditions for a meaningful exercise of public autonomy in the postnational space may not have to follow domestic patterns and may be able to draw on inspirations from polycentric and contestatory models of democracy.[138] This may be easier in Europe than in the global context, but it remains a huge task.

---

[134] Cf B Anderson, *Imagined Communities: Reflections on the Origin and Spread of Nationalism*, London: Verso, 1983.

[135] See H Lindahl, 'Constituent Power and Reflexive Identity: Towards an Ontology of Collective Selfhood' in Loughlin & Walker, *Paradox of Constitutionalism*, 9–24; U K Preuß, 'Disconnecting Constitutions from Statehood: Is Global Constitutionalism a Viable Concept?' in Loughlin & Dobner, *Twilight*, 23–46 at 40–2.

[136] J Habermas, *Die postnationale Konstellation*, Frankfurt am Main: Suhrkamp Verlag, 1998, 160–7; but see also Habermas, 'Kommunikative Rationalität', 447–59, for a more optimistic take, also as regards processes of change in postnational society. See also Preuß, 'Disconnecting', 44–6, on the prospect of the international community constituting itself as a viable actor through constitutionalization.

[137] See J Elster, 'Deliberation and Constitution Making' in J Elster (ed), *Deliberative Democracy*, Cambridge: Cambridge University Press, 1998, 97–122.

[138] See, eg, J Dryzek, *Deliberative Global Politics*, Cambridge: Polity Press, 2006; J Bohman, *Democracy across Borders*, Cambridge, MA: MIT Press, 2007; P Rosanvallon, *Counter-Democracy: Politics in an Age of Distrust* (A Goldhammer, trans), Cambridge: Cambridge University Press, 2008.

Postnational constitutionalism thus has radical implications for the trans-formation of institutions and society beyond the nation-state; it has a dis-tinctly utopian flavour. This might make it less suited for projects that seek to formulate practically relevant proposals and achieve change in the short or mid-term. Here, a more limited ambition is more adequate, and under-takings such as that of a 'Global Administrative Law' have self-consciously adopted such a more circumscribed approach.[139] Problematic, though, is a tendency to start from current constraints and feasibility considerations to reformulate the constitutionalist project. Habermas, for example, discards hopes for the advent of foundational constitutionalism on the global level as unrealistic and settles for a form of power-limiting constitutionalism in which the legalization of global governance is linked with stronger legitima-tory, deliberative processes on the regional level.[140] He is explicit about the distinct intellectual tradition this invokes, yet even so, presenting a 'consti-tutionalist' project in these terms runs the risk of short-selling fundamental elements of domestic political practice and of legitimating what ought to be critiqued. For it suggests that the progressive legalization of postnational politics could be a continuation of the domestic tradition of constitutional-ism, duly translated into a new context, and that this tradition does not have further-reaching implications there. This risk is even more present in the great majority of proposals for global constitutionalism that gloss over the differences in domestic analogues entirely. They may well reflect progressive intentions, such as strengthening rule-of-law standards in Security Council decision-making. But they are forms of 'constitutionalism lite':[141] their lim-ited ambition is in stark contrast with the comprehensiveness typically asso-ciated with the use of the constitutionalist framework.[142] This association may eventually provide legitimacy for highly deficient structures, and it may dilute the critical edge inherent in the constitutional idea.

Some authors respond to such concerns by adopting a rhetoric of 'consti-tutionalization' rather than constitutionalism, highlighting the unfinished character, the element of process.[143] This might be adequate to highlight the

---

[139] N Krisch, 'Global Administrative Law and the Constitutional Ambition' in Loughlin & Dobner, *Twilight*, 245–66 at 255–8. On the GAL project in general, see B Kingsbury, N Krisch, & R B Stewart, 'The Emergence of Global Administrative Law', *Law & Contemporary Problems* 68:3 (2005), 15–61.

[140] Habermas, 'Konstitutionalisierung', 133–42; see also Habermas, 'Kommunikative Rationalität', 442–7.

[141] To borrow the term from J Klabbers, 'Constitutionalism Lite', *International Organizations Law Review* 1 (2004), 31–58.

[142] See also Grimm, 'Achievement of Constitutionalism', 21.

[143] See n 24 above.

distance from constitutionalist ideals and the many steps necessary on the way. Yet most such approaches do not reflect this at all. They instead present constitutionalization as directed at hedging in certain forms of public power through a number of procedural and substantive limits; in essence as working towards a power-limiting form of constitutionalism in the long run.[144] However pragmatic this might be, it represents a capitulation to contemporary circumstances when we should instead denounce the gap between our political ideals and what can be currently achieved. Only by naming that gap can we retain a sense for the challenge that constitutionalism, in its foundational reading, poses for the postnational space.

2. Foundational Constitutionalism in Postnational Society

Drawing on the domestic tradition of constitutionalism for the postnational order is ambitious, but it also comes with an ample promise—a promise to disregard the vagaries of the current, path-dependent, often accidental shape of global governance and to realize human agency in the construction of common institutions. It is this appeal David Held seeks to capture when he contrasts his well-ordered model of global politics with one in which the distribution of powers among institutions is left 'to powerful geopolitical interests (dominant states) or market based organizations to resolve'.[145] In good constitutionalist fashion, a principled construction of the global institutional order appears as an antidote to power, history, and chance.

That such a project might be somewhat utopian need not deter us, though it might extend the timeframe for its realization. Greater doubt arises from concerns about its adequacy in a postnational society that is—and is likely to remain—quite radically different from most domestic ones. Iris Young, for example, defends a principled framework for common global institutions, but she acknowledges that, as attractive as such a vision might be in the abstract, it stands in tension with the allegiances of individuals to their particular, mostly national, communities and their ensuing claims for self-determination.[146]

---

[144] See the analysis in M Loughlin, 'What is Constitutionalisation?' in Dobner & Loughlin, *Twilight*, 47–69.

[145] D Held, 'Democratic Accountability and Effectiveness from a Cosmopolitan Perspective', *Government & Opposition* 39 (2004), 365–91 at 382.

[146] Young, *Inclusion and Democracy*, 250–65. Young seeks to respond to this through a federal-style model that is 'jurisdictionally open'; I will return to this theme in the next chapter.

The divided character of the global polity appears indeed as the single greatest challenge to the globalization of constitutionalism. After all, international society is characterized by a high degree of diversity and contestation, and even the small signs of increasing convergence that we can observe are by no means unambiguous. Diversity may today not be as radical as it was in the 1970s, when Hedley Bull's vision of an anarchical society within a pluralist international order appeared plausible, given the deep-seated frictions between West and East and North and South.[147] Today, we can find indications of a stronger solidaristic, perhaps even cosmopolitan turn in greater agreement on fundamental principles and a higher degree of institutionalized policy- and law-making beyond the state.[148] Whether this warrants the diagnosis of an emerging 'international community', however, is questionable,[149] and it certainly is if we think of such a community as one that its members rank supreme over other communities of a regional, national, or subnational kind. Allegiance to national communities may have been complemented by those of a local, religious, ideological nature, some of which with a clear transnational, perhaps even cosmopolitan tinge, and this may have led to a world of multiple rather than exclusive loyalties, and to a variety of foundational discourses competing for dominance.[150] But cultural and political diversity remains strong and is often coupled with an insistence on ultimate authority on the national level—reflecting a vision of the international order as one of intergovernmental negotiation and exchange rather than an expression of a deeper common project.[151] Even in the European Union, where diversity is clearly weaker than in a global context, allegiance to national communities still trumps that to Europe by a large margin.[152] And identities seem to become more rather than less

---

[147] H Bull, *The Anarchical Society*, London: Macmillan, 1977.

[148] See A Hurrell, *On Global Order*, Oxford: Oxford University Press, 2007, chs 3 and 4.

[149] See A Paulus, *Die internationale Gemeinschaft im Völkerrecht*, Munich: C H Beck, 2001.

[150] M J Sandel, *Democracy's Discontent*, Cambridge, MA: Harvard University Press, 1996, 338–51; Dryzek, *Deliberative Global Politics*, ch 1; see also Bohman, *Democracy across Borders*, 28–36.

[151] See Hurrell, *On Global Order*, ch 5.

[152] See N Fligstein, *Euroclash: The EU, European Identity, and the Future of Europe*, Oxford: Oxford University Press, 2008, ch 5; J A Caporaso & M Kim, 'The Dual Nature of European Identity: Subjective Awareness and Coherence', *Journal of European Public Policy* 16 (2009), 19–42 at 23–30.

fragmented as European integration proceeds. As Peter Katzenstein and Jeffrey Checkel note:

> The number of unambiguously committed Europeans (10—15% of the total population) is simply too small for the emergence of a strong cultural European sense of belonging. The number of committed nationalists (40—50% of the total) is also too small for a hegemonic reassertion of nationalist sentiments. The remaining part of the population (35—40% of the total) holds to primarily national identifications that also permit an element of European identification.[153]

All this may not be fatal to the postnational constitutionalist project; after all, just as attempts have been undertaken to move from democracy to 'demoicracy',[154] we might come to imagine a constitutionalism on a plurinational basis.[155] But such an undertaking faces serious challenges based on critiques that have for long highlighted the difficulties of modern constitutionalism in diverse societies. James Tully's is perhaps the most prominent among them. For Tully, modern constitutionalism as it has emerged with the American and French revolutions—and has framed much of political thought ever since—cannot cope with serious social and cultural diversity because of its strong link to ideas of impartiality and uniformity.[156] Given its roots in the Enlightenment, it seeks to erect a regular, well-structured framework of government based on reason and distinct from the irregular, historically grown structures that characterized previous eras. In this uniformity, however, it fails to reflect the different customs and culturally grounded ideas of particular groups in society; and this even more so if these groups do not subscribe to the liberal vision of a 'modern', free individual, able and willing to transcend her history and culture and ready to engage with all others in unconditional deliberation over the course of the common polity. The impartiality sought through such mechanisms as Rawls's veil of ignorance or Habermas's adoption of the interlocutor's perspective only makes sense if individuals are ready to

---

[153] P J Katzenstein & J T Checkel, 'Conclusion—European Identity in Context' in J T Checkel & P J Katzenstein (eds), *European Identity*, Cambridge, Cambridge University Press, 2009, 213–27 at 215–16. For a very similar assessment, see Fligstein, *Euroclash*, 250.

[154] eg, Bohman, *Democracy across Borders*; K Nicolaïdis, 'We, the Peoples of Europe ...', *Foreign Affairs* 83:6 (2004), 97–110; see also U K Preuß, 'The Constitution of a European Democracy and the Role of the Nation State', *Ratio Juris* 12 (1999), 417–28.

[155] eg, S Tierney, *Constitutional Law and National Pluralism*, Oxford: Oxford University Press, 2004.

[156] Tully, *Strange Multiplicity*, chs 2 and 3.

leave particular allegiances behind; for all others, it means exclusion from the supposedly neutral frame.[157]

For Tully then, the integrationist, universalizing tendencies of foundational constitutionalism sit uneasily with the diverse identities of individuals in divided societies; the emphasis on common values and self-government by a shared, overarching collective stands in tension with their diverging allegiances. Historically, the tension may have been resolved by policies of nation-building which, over time, succeeded in overcoming linguistic and cultural divides. But these involved measures of forced assimilation that today would be regarded as grave violations of human rights, and such forcible integration would in any event be hardly conceivable in a European or international context. For constitutionalism to remain attractive as a model for the postnational polity, it has to find other ways to cope with that polity's deep diversity.

3. Constitutionalism vs Diversity?

Tully accuses modern constitutionalism of creating an 'empire of uniformity', but this downplays the many ways in which the constitutional project has come to respond to the challenge of divided societies. It may embody the quest for a reasoned, uniform order, and as we have seen, much of its appeal derives from this aspiration. Also today, many constitutional states pursue integrationist aims, build common institutions, and seek to 'privatize' diversity, relying on individual rights to accommodate differences in ways of life.[158] But while this is often seen as a suitable solution in societies that are characterized by crosscutting cleavages, it is more problematic where the divides are stable and fairly unidimensional and lead to structural minorities with little hope for sharing power in common institutions. Responses to such situations typically eschew strong integrationist ideals and seek to deal with diversity through accommodation, mainly in the form of consociationalism and/or devolution.[159] It is such a multicultural constitutionalism that

---

[157] For related critiques, see, eg, M J Sandel, 'The Procedural Republic and the Unencumbered Self', *Political Theory* 12 (1984), 81–96; C Taylor, 'The Politics of Recognition' in C Taylor, *Philosophical Arguments*, Cambridge, MA: Harvard University Press, 1995, 225–56.

[158] For a theoretical defence, see B Barry, *Culture and Equality: An Egalitarian Critique of Multiculturalism*, Cambridge, MA: Harvard University Press, 2002.

[159] See the survey of the debate in J McGarry, B O'Leary, & R Simeon, 'Integration or Accommodation? The Enduring Debate in Conflict Regulation' in S Choudhry (ed), *Constitutional Design for Divided Societies: Integration or Accommodation?*, Oxford: Oxford University Press, 2008, 41–88; see also Tierney, *Constitutional Law*.

we might be able to draw on for translation beyond the state. As we shall see, though, even such a vision faces trade-offs and limits in its accommodation of diversity, and these raise doubts as to its suitability in the radically diverse postnational context.

Options

Consociationalism is characterized by an insistence on common decision-making: prominent in a number of smaller European countries especially in the postwar period and later adopted in several other settings, consociation-alism seeks to manage deep disagreement through executive power-shar-ing and the creation of veto positions for minority groups.[160] These force all actors to reach common ground rather than impose their views; none of the constituencies enjoys formal primacy. Societal groups are not only granted autonomy rights for their own cultural and linguistic affairs but also enjoy a particular, protected position in central decision-making structures. Otherwise, consociationalists believe, those groups would be at a perma-nent disadvantage in the struggle over common policies, and ever greater antagonism and conflict would likely ensue.[161]

Federalist responses, on the other hand, focus less on central decision-mak-ing; they emphasize the need to devolve as many state functions as possible to the groups that make up society. This can occur in the form of territorial pluralism in which those functions are exercised by federal units along the lines of inter-group boundaries, potentially in an asymmetrical way.[162] Such an approach can be combined with consociationalist, co-decision arrange-ments at the federal level, but it is feasible only if the relevant groups are ter-ritorially concentrated. Otherwise, devolution has to follow personal rather than territorial lines and is accordingly more limited in its extent; it typically focuses on group rights to govern cultural and educational affairs.

On the postnational level, as most divides follow territorial lines, both consociationalism and territorial federalism, or a combination of both, may provide resources for the accommodation of diversity. This may alleviate

---

[160] See A Lijphart, *Democracy in Plural Societies*, New Haven, CT: Yale University Press, 1978; A Lijphart, *Thinking About Democracy: Power Sharing and Majority Rule in Theory and Practice*, London: Routledge, 2008.

[161] But see also the critiques, eg, D Horowitz, 'Constitutional Design: Proposals Versus Processes' in A Reynolds (ed), *The Architecture of Democracy: Constitutional Design, Conflict Management, and Democracy*, Oxford: Oxford University Press, 2002, 15–36; B Barry, 'Political Accommodation and Consociational Democracy', *British Journal of Political Science* 5 (1975), 477–505.

[162] See, eg, the discussion in McGarry et al, 'Integration or Accommodation?', 63–7.

some of Tully's concerns about uniformity, but it might also dilute the appeal of the constitutionalist project which has originally drawn precisely on the virtues of reason, order, and collective decision-making.

Trade-Offs

Among such trade-offs, the most obvious one concerns the integrative, stabilizing force of constitutionalism. Foundational constitutionalism is typically regarded as a potent tool to integrate society, by creating a common framework as an expression of both common values and collective decision-making processes. The need to find common solutions typically leads to an attenuation of diversity, while accommodationist approaches help entrench the boundaries between different groups and are often seen as widening, rather than closing the gaps in society, thus creating greater instability and potentially leading to secession or break-up.[163] Yet in deeply divided societies, integrationist policies are rarely an option; minority groups are not ready to agree to them for fear of losing out to the majority. And if integration is pursued despite such opposition, it will typically lead to greater friction, resistance, and instability of the overall constitutional structure. Accommodation may not come with the full stabilizing promise of the original, more unitary strain of foundational constitutionalism, but there is little alternative to it when divisions run deep.[164]

The second trade-off concerns the effectiveness of collective decision-making. As I have sketched above, constitutionalism draws much of its appeal from the realization of agency against forces of history and chance. But by many, accommodation is seen precisely as a surrender to such forces. Even if normatively justified,[165] it often appears as a respect for difference based on historically grown, passion-based allegiances quite in contrast with detached, reasoned construction. And accommodationist approaches may dilute the promise of public autonomy on yet another level. Because consociationalism emphasizes the commonality of decision-making and, as a result, veto rights of minority groups, it runs the risk of institutionalizing blockade: it might lead to a 'joint-decision trap'.[166] For the greater the number

---

[163] See, eg, R H Pildes, 'Ethnic Identity and Democratic Institutions: A Dynamic Perspective' in Choudhry, *Constitutional Design*, 173–201.

[164] McGarry et al, 'Integration or Accommodation?', 85–7.

[165] For normative defences of group rights, see W Kymlicka, *Multicultural Citizenship*, Oxford: Clarendon Press, 1995; N Torbisco Casals, *Group Rights as Human Rights: A Liberal Approach to Multiculturalism*, Dordrecht: Springer Verlag, 2006.

[166] F Scharpf, 'Die Politikverflechtungsfalle: Europäische Integration und deutscher Föderalismus im Vergleich', *Politische Vierteljahresschrift* 26 (1985) 323–56 at 346–50.

of groups in society (and in postnational society the number is bound to be high), the greater the risk that collective negotiations collapse.[167] And if unanimity is to be achieved, policies need to be pareto-optimal—they have to benefit each and every group, but this severely reduces the range of possible options and limits prospects of, for example, distributive justice.[168]

A third challenge consociationalism poses to the ideal of public autonomy lies in the extent of individual participation in government.[169] It relies, to a large extent, on the cooperation of *elites*: because genuine consensus will often be elusive, problem-solving requires bargaining, package deals, logrolling among the different groups. This can only be achieved by elites that stand in constant contact with each other and are socialized into cooperation. Stronger participation of a broader public in the various groups renders this cooperation difficult because it is usually focused only on a particular decision, not the whole of the deal struck. Accordingly, as Arend Lijphart stresses, '[i]t is…helpful if [leaders] possess considerable independent power and a secure position of leadership'.[170] Even though this is not incompatible with public participation in general, it considerably limits its scope.[171]

Limits

Yet even with such trade-offs, the accommodation of diversity in foundational constitutionalism has limits. After all, if it wants to retain its central promise—to create a comprehensive framework for all public power in a given polity under the rule of law—constitutionalism has ultimately to resolve the tension between the sovereignty claims of the federal and the group level, if only by defining rules for constitutional amendment and hierarchies between the different levels of law. Visions of a federalism with 'suspended' ultimate authority, influential until the late nineteenth century, are in conflict with this comprehensive ambition and find little reflection in contemporary federal orders.[172] This leaves foundational constitutionalism with two options: either it resolves the sovereignty question in favour of the groups, and their interaction remains a non-constitutionalist affair;

---

[167] Accordingly, also for Lijphart consociational orders ideally operate with no more than four main groups; see Lijphart, *Democracy in Plural Societies*, 56.

[168] On such problems in the EU context see, eg, F Scharpf, 'The Joint-Decision Trap Revisited', *Journal of Common Market Studies* 44 (2006), 845–64 at 851.

[169] See, eg, Dryzek, *Deliberative Global Politics*, 50–1.

[170] Lijphart, *Democracy in Plural Societies*, 50.

[171] For a nuanced account, see McGarry et al, 'Integration or Accommodation?', 82–4.

[172] See text at n 86 above.

it is that of a federation under international law. Or it resolves it in favour of the federal level (for example, by denying group vetos in amendment processes); it can then realize the constitutionalist promise to some extent, but this realization might remain formal as long as some groups actively contest the solution. One may only think of the Canadian constitutional crisis in the 1980s and 1990s, provoked by Québec's insistence on a unilateral right to secede. The federal claim to define the rules for constitutional amendment (including the framework for secession) and thus to regulate the relationship with its constituent units, remained fragile in the face of resistance by a powerful minority—in fact, it antagonized this minority only further.[173] Unless the constitutionalist ambition to create a comprehensive framework meets matching societal conditions, such fragility is bound to continue, and the hope to create a constitutional framework *for* politics keeps being called into question by its dependence *on* politics.[174]

One may seek a way out of this problem by keeping constitutional norms on contested issues relatively open—by interpreting them in minimalist terms, as Cass Sunstein suggests,[175] or along lines proposed by Jeremy Waldron, by entrusting their interpretation to the political process that might reflect dissonance or convergence, as the case may be.[176] The more open the norms and processes, though, the more constitutionalism gives up on one of its key aspirations: to found and structure a polity through a higher law. For such openness, as desirable as it might be, simply moves crucial questions back into everyday political debate.

In divided societies, constitutionalism thus finds itself in a dilemma. It can retain its purity, pursue the integration of society, and seek to level difference, but this is often normatively problematic and practically impossible; it may enflame tensions rather than calm them. The alternative—accommodation—also comes at a high cost: as we have seen, it

---

[173] S Choudhry, 'Does the World need more Canada? The Politics of the Canadian Model in Constitutional Politics and Political Theory' in Choudhry, *Constitutional Design*, 141–72 at 159–71.

[174] On the fragility of constitutions in the face of external factors, see F Schauer, 'Amending the Presuppositions of a Constitution' in S Levinson (ed), *Responding to Imperfection: The Theory and Practice of Constitutional Amendment*, Princeton, NJ: Princeton University Press, 1995, 145–61.

[175] C R Sunstein, *Legal Reasoning and Political Conflict*, Oxford: Oxford University Press, 1996; C R Sunstein, *One Case at a Time: Judicial Minimalism on the Supreme Court*, Cambridge, MA: Harvard University Press, 1999; but see also C R Sunstein, 'Beyond Judicial Minimalism', *Harvard Public Law Working Paper* No 08–40, <http://ssrn.com/abstract=1274200>.

[176] Waldron, *Law and Disagreement*, ch 13.

diminishes the constitutionalist promise as regards the potential for long-term social stability, for public autonomy, and often enough also for the rule of law. After all, in order to remain true to its core, constitutionalism has to maintain the idea of a comprehensive framework that assigns different organs and groups their places. And this requires hierarchies that all too often stand in tension with the (diverging) claims of different parts of society.

This element of hierarchy brings me back to Tully's critique. This critique seems overdrawn in its attack on constitutionalism's 'empire of uniformity'—constitutionalist thought and practice know more ways of accommodating difference than Tully gives credit for. But he is right in pointing to the fact that the supposed commonality of the constitutional project requires members of the 'nation' to recognize it as the *primary* political framework, taking precedence over whatever other structures might exist in sub-groups. It presupposes the acceptance of a priority of the common over the particular (typically within limits of human rights)—an acceptance we might not find among distinct cultural groups within states, and certainly not among states vis-à-vis the 'common' European or global realm. This emphasis on the collective, the common framework, poses not only normative problems from the perspective of minority groups, but it may also aggravate tensions within society and create less rather than more stability. Sovereign authority is simply too precious, and the quest for it typically attracts pernicious contest and drives competing groups further apart.[177] A constitution that needs to settle fundamental questions (to some extent) then risks becoming an imperial instrument. In a radically diverse society, a constitution may then easily come to be seen, not as a reasoned common framework, but as a hegemonic tool for one part of society to lock in its preferred institutional structure.[178]

Such a dynamic may be difficult to avoid in the binary, hierarchical structure of foundational constitutionalism. We may thus want to look for alternatives that allow us to work around societal divides in a more pragmatic fashion. As John Dryzek puts it, in some circumstances '[t]he peace is disturbed only by philosophers who believe a constitutional solution is required'.[179] If this is true in domestic societies with high degrees of diversity, it will be even more so in the postnational context.

---

[177] Dryzek, *Deliberative Global Politics*, ch 3.

[178] See Tully, *Strange Multiplicity*, chs 2 and 3; R Hirschl, *Towards Juristocracy: The Origins and Consequences of the New Constitutionalism*, Cambridge, MA: Harvard University Press, 2004.

[179] Dryzek, *Deliberative Global Politics*, 64.

IV. CONCLUSION: BEYOND
CONSTITUTIONALISM?

Visions of postnational constitutionalism respond to a widespread anxiety, to a lack of certainty about the foundations and structures of the new, strange, still largely unknown space of the postnational. They promise to tame this space, to organize it in a rational way, to hedge it in along lines we have come to know (and value) in domestic politics over centuries. Postnational constitutionalism is an attempt to establish continuity with central political concepts and domestic traditions; it tries to avoid the normative rupture often feared in discussions of globalization and global governance.

As we have seen, this strategy runs into obstacles. Most approaches to postnational constitutionalism are too thin to redeem the full promise of the domestic constitutionalist tradition and therefore cannot provide the continuity they seek. They emphasize processes of legalization and limitation of postnational governance, but thereby hark back to a particular tradition of power-limiting constitutionalism which in the domestic context has been marginalized by the more demanding and comprehensive strand of foundational constitutionalism. Yet realizing the latter vision in the postnational sphere would have radical implications: it would require massive social and institutional change. A postnational constitutionalism of this kind would not only have utopian overtones; it would also sit uneasily with major—and likely persistent—features of European and global societies. Responding to their diversity may force it into trade-offs as regards its integrative, stabilizing capacity as well as its potential to realize agency and public autonomy. And yet, if the constitutionalist project seeks to redeem a minimum of its foundational aspirations it needs to define (some) principled hierarchies, which in a divided society may well exacerbate tensions further.

This may sound gloomy, but perhaps it is not. So far we had assumed that in the postnational realm we did indeed want to connect to the domestic tradition, that the postnational *ought* to be structured in a way that continued on the constitutionalist path, if perhaps somehow adapted to environmental conditions. But this assumption may well be misguided. After all, constitutionalism—especially its dominant domestic strand, foundational constitutionalism—is a historically very particular form through which to realize central political values, individual liberty, and collective self-government. It embodies a peculiarly modern trust in the ability of humankind to rationally govern itself, in the power of reason in the design of political institutions, and in the strength of those institutions in realizing a common good. After all, the modern constitutionalist project has emerged from Enlightenment thought, and it is today often regarded as a continuation of Kantian political theory.[180]

In its particularity, though, constitutionalism may not be the ideal framework for the postnational space. Having emerged as especially apt for a 'people' to govern itself, it might provide some promise in the European context but will be less suited for the radical diversity that marks the global populace. The ideological divisions of the Cold War might have withered away, but outlooks on life, politics, religion, and justice in the world continue to differ enormously. In these circumstances, the idea of settling the central questions of a polity in constitutionalist form may not only seem unachievable but also undesirable—respect for this diversity may require leaving those questions open, rather than closing the debate. The greater the distance between different groups in a population, the easier a constitutional settlement may appear as imposed by one group on the other, as an imperial tool rather than an expression of common self-government—and this risk becomes particularly acute in the highly diverse context of the postnational.[181]

Yet these difficulties of realizing constitutionalism in the postnational sphere may not be merely evidence of a loss, of a deficit of global politics that we should acknowledge with a melancholical longing for the good old times of the constitutional state. It is a loss, too. But just as the nation-state has long been a problematic political form, so has modern, foundational constitutionalism never been simply an unequivocal 'evolutionary achievement';[182] it has come to sit uneasily already with the diversity, social differentiation and increased regulatory expectations in late modern societies.[183] Facing the difficulty of translating it should sharpen our sense for how the move from national to postnational politics exacerbates such problems, and it should liberate us from the intellectual straightjacket that accompanies the quest for continuity with domestic concepts and traditions. This should allow us to explore alternative visions of politics—to risk a break with what we are familiar with and look beyond constitutionalism for guidance and inspiration.

---

[180] See, eg, Habermas, 'Konstitutionalisierung'.

[181] See Koskenniemi, 'Fate of Public International Law', 19; Walker, 'Holistic Constitution', 305.

[182] But see Luhmann, 'Verfassung als evolutionäre Errungenschaft'.

[183] See n 178 above; K-H Ladeur, 'Postmoderne Verfassungstheorie' in U K Preuß (ed), *Zum Begriff der Verfassung: Die Ordnung des Politischen*, Frankfurt am Main: Fischer, 1994, 304–31; D Grimm, 'Die Zukunft der Verfassung' in Grimm, *Zukunft der Verfassung*, 399–439.

3

The Case for Pluralism

Constitutionalism's difficulties signal a broader challenge for the 'transfer' approach to postnational governance, as I have called it in the introductory chapter.[1] The societal diversity and institutional fragmentation that cause constitutionalism's problems also affect other efforts at using domestic models beyond the state. The rule of law's aspiration to tame politics through legal rules will conflict with the deep contestation characteristic of postnational politics—a contestation prone to undermine the sense of settlement or depoliticization typically associated with a shift to law. Likewise, democracy will struggle with the fragmentation of the postnational space—because of the lack of a social basis for meaningful communication across boundaries and the impossibility to connect to clear, centralized decision-making channels.

The postnational space thus seems to demand new, different answers to the question of how to structure governance; its shape suggests that we may have to break with the political forms we have grown accustomed to in domestic settings. Yet what could such different answers be? And are they likely to fare better than constitutionalism in realizing key political values, such as justice or democracy, in the postnational space?

In this book, I explore one structural alternative to the constitutionalist project—a pluralist vision. Pluralism eschews the hope of building one common, overarching legal framework that would integrate postnational governance, distribute powers, and provide for means of solving disputes between the various layers of law and politics. It is based instead on the heterarchical interplay of these layers according to rules ultimately set by each layer for itself. In pluralism, there is no common legal point of reference to appeal to for resolving disagreement; conflicts are solved through convergence, mutual accommodation—or not at all. It is a vision that takes societal fragmentation to the institutional level.

If such an account is often seen as useful for *analysing* the shape of postnational governance, it is less frequently seen as *normatively* attractive—unlike

---

[1] Chapter 1, III.1.

constitutionalism, it seems simply to surrender to social forces.[2] Pluralism, as Martti Koskenniemi puts it, 'ceases to pose demands on the world'.[3]

As I will try to show in this chapter, this picture underestimates pluralism's virtues. In a postnational society characterized by diversity and rapid change, pluralism has significant strengths in providing adaptability, creating space for contestation, and offering a possibility of steering between conflicting supremacy claims of different polity levels. It is not free from difficulties, but as we have seen in the previous chapter, neither is constitutionalism, and pluralism is less afflicted by the problems that come with an attempt to create hierarchies at odds with societal contestation. It resonates better with the divided allegiances and preferences in postnational society.

The chapter develops this argument in three steps. In Section I, I lay the conceptual ground by identifying different understandings of pluralism and their implications. Section II begins to inquire into the normative appeal of pluralism by developing further the three main arguments suggested so far in the literature—greater adaptability, the provision of contestatory space, and the equidistance to conflicting claims to ultimate authority. Despite their merits, though, such substantive benefits alone will be insufficient to ground our structural choices; they have to be integrated into an account that gives greater weight to procedures in the determination of a polity's structural framework. In Section III, I outline such a more procedural, participatory account and how it would frame the contest between constitutionalism and pluralism. In this vision, individuals' public autonomy provides the anchor and indicates the institutional shape of the postnational order—of an order that, because of divided views on the right levels of decision-making, should reflect rather than contain contestation and thus take a pluralist, not a constitutionalist form.

The normative argument in this chapter seeks to provide a framework for thinking about pluralism's virtues, but in and of itself, it cannot provide ultimate conclusions on how pluralism compares with constitutionalism or how it can respond to challenges from angles such as power, stability, democracy, or the rule of law. For this, we need more empirical work and deeper inquiries into the institutional dynamics of pluralist orders in the varied contexts of postnational governance—a challenge the following chapters will take up.

---

[2] For an example, see J Baquero Cruz, 'The Legacy of the Maastricht-Urteil and the Pluralist Movement', *European Law Journal* 14 (2008), 389–422 at 417–18.

[3] M Koskenniemi, 'The Fate of Public International Law: Between Technique and Politics', *Modern Law Review* 70 (2007), 1–30 at 23.

I. THE PLURALISM OF PLURALISMS

'Pluralism' suggests a particular responsiveness to issues of diversity, and it might also sound appealing as a more positive approach to phenomena of fragmentation that, in the international law literature at least, have provoked considerable anxiety.[4] Yet pluralism has many meanings, and it can serve as a description of the shape and diversity of society, of substantive commitments in matters of rights or institutions, or of the structure of a polity's institutions. It is the latter meaning that interests me most, as it operates on the same (structural) level as constitutionalism and may therefore provide a true alternative. Yet even here, the usage of pluralism varies widely.[5] The differences could be seen as a matter of degree—as between 'soft' and 'hard', 'weak' or 'strong', or 'moderate' and 'radical' pluralism. Analytically, though, they are better captured as differences in kind, as between what may be termed 'institutional' and 'systemic' pluralism.

To illustrate this distinction, and to work out more clearly what could be an alternative model to the constitutionalist one, it is worth taking a closer look at Neil MacCormick's work which has inspired much recent pluralist thinking, especially in the European Union context.[6] MacCormick sought to theorize the impact of the conflicting supremacy claims of the national and Union levels in the EU and came to regard the resulting legal structure as one in which both levels, as systemic units, had internally plausible claims to ultimate authority; their conflict was due to the fact that they did not agree on the ultimate point of reference from which they were arguing. For the national level, national constitutions remained the ultimate

---

[4] See the analysis in M Koskenniemi & P Leino, 'Fragmentation of International Law? Postmodern Anxieties', *Leiden Journal of International Law* 15 (2002), 553–79. For attempts to come to terms with the challenge of fragmentation, see P-M Dupuy, 'L'unité de l'ordre juridique international', *Recueil des Cours de l'Académie de Droit International* 297 (2002), 9–489; O Casanovas, *Unity and Pluralism in Public International Law*, Leiden: Martinus Nijhoff, 2001; J Pauwelyn, *Conflict of Norms in Public International Law: How WTO Law Relates to Other Rules of International Law*, Cambridge: Cambridge University Press, 2003; see also International Law Commission, 'Conclusions of the Work of the Study Group on the Fragmentation of International Law: Difficulties Arising from the Diversification and Expansion of International Law', *Report of the International Law Commission on its Fifty-eighth Session*, UN Doc A/61/10, 251.

[5] For an overview, see R Michaels, 'Global Legal Pluralism', *Annual Review of Law and Social Science* 5 (2009), 243–62.

[6] N MacCormick, 'Beyond the Sovereign State', *Modern Law Review* 56 (1993), 1–18; N MacCormick, 'The Maastricht-Urteil: Sovereignty Now', *European Law Journal* 1 (1995), 259–66; N MacCormick, *Questioning Sovereignty: Law, State, and Nation in the European Commonwealth*, Oxford: Oxford University Press, 1999.

source of authority, and all exercises of public power (including by the EU) had to be traced back to them; for the EU, the EU treaty was seen as independent from, and superior to, national law including national constitutions. In MacCormick's view, there was thus no common legal framework that could have decided the conflict—the two views were (on a fundamental level) irreconcilably opposed; the two levels of law ran in parallel without subordination or external coordination. This description borrowed some of its ideas from sociological and anthropological accounts of legal pluralism that had become influential since the 1970s,[7] but took the idea beyond the relationship of official and non-official law (or norms) that those studies were interested in and applied it to the coexistence of different official systems of law, all with their own *Grundnormen* or rules of recognition. In this sense, MacCormick's approach was one of 'systemic' (or in his words, 'radical') pluralism.[8]

Whether consciously or not, this approach had ancestors not only in legal anthropology[9] and medieval thought,[10] but also in the early theory and practice of federalism.[11] Especially the situation in the United States after the constitution of 1787 had created an awareness that the classical categories—unitary state or federal union under international law—did not adequately reflect the character of federal polities. In the US, the constitution was described as 'neither a national nor a federal Constitution, but a composition of both',[12] and it certainly sought to balance the powers of the federal government and those of the states. More importantly perhaps, it left unsettled rival claims to ultimate authority: throughout the first half of the nineteenth century, such authority was claimed for both the federal and the

[7]   See S F Moore, 'Law and Social Change: the Semi-Autonomous Social Field as an Appropriate Subject of Study', *Law & Society Review* 7 (1973), 719–46; J Griffiths, 'What is Legal Pluralism?', *Journal of Legal Pluralism* 24 (1986), 1–55; S E Merry, 'Legal Pluralism', *Law & Society Review* 22 (1988), 869–96.

[8]   See N MacCormick, 'Risking Constitutional Collision in Europe?', *Oxford Journal of Legal Studies* 18 (1998), 517–32 at 528–32. For a discussion of lineages of legal pluralist thought, see E Melissaris, *Ubiquitous Law: Legal Theory and the Space for Legal Pluralism*, Farnham: Ashgate, 2009, chs 2 and 3.

[9]   On the complicated links between anthropological approaches to legal pluralism and theories of the global legal order, see Michaels, 'Global Legal Pluralism'.

[10]   H J Berman, *Law and Revolution: The Formation of the Western Legal Tradition*, Cambridge: MA: Harvard University Press, 1983, 115–19.

[11]   See O Beaud, *Théorie de la Fédération*, Paris: Presses Universitaires de France, 2007.

[12]   A Hamilton, J Madison, & J Jay, *The Federalist Papers* (L Goldman, ed), Oxford: Oxford University Press, 2008, 192 (J Madison, *Federalist* no 39).

state levels, and the contest was eventually settled only (though perhaps not even conclusively) through the civil war.[13] In Europe, parallel conceptions existed (and were influential until the late nineteenth century[14]), and it was Carl Schmitt who later captured them most cogently in his theory of federal union by placing the undecided, 'suspended' character of ultimate authority at its centre.[15] Some contemporary strands of federal theory seek to revive this heritage.[16]

If MacCormick initially envisioned the EU in a similar way, he softened his account considerably in his later work. Mindful of the risk of friction and collision inherent in an unregulated parallelism of different orders, he came to see a greater potential for coordination in the overarching framework of international law. 'Pluralism under international law', as he terms it, is in fact a monist conception, but one that assigns EU law and domestic constitutional law equal positions and does not subordinate one to the other as a matter of principle.[17] This has been criticized for taking the edge out of the approach, and analytically it is indeed categorically distinct from the systemic pluralism MacCormick had initially diagnosed. It accepts pluralism not on the systemic level, but only in the institutional structure—different parts of one order operate on a basis of coordination, in the framework of common rules but without a clearly defined hierarchy, in a form of what I would call 'institutional pluralism'. This is reminiscent of the 'weak' legal pluralism, which for John Griffiths was analytically unremarkable because it operated in the framework of—and was mandated by—central state law.[18]

The tamed nature of institutional pluralism can be glanced when considering other articulations of it, for example Daniel Halberstam's account of

---

[13] See A R Amar, 'Of Sovereignty and Federalism', *Yale Law Journal* 96 (1987), 1425–520 at 1429–66; R Schütze, 'Federalism as Constitutional Pluralism: "Letter from America"' in M Avbelj & J Komárek (eds), *Constitutional Pluralism in the European Union and Beyond*, Oxford: Hart Publishing, 2010, forthcoming.

[14] See, eg, S Oeter, 'Souveränität und Demokratie als Probleme in der "Verfassungsentwicklung" der Europäischen Union', *Zeitschrift für ausländisches öffentliches Recht und Völkerrecht* 55 (1995), 659–707 at 664–70; M Stolleis, *Geschichte des öffentlichen Rechts in Deutschland*, vol 2, Munich: C H Beck, 1992, 365–8.

[15] C Schmitt, *Verfassungslehre*, 9th edn, Berlin: Duncker & Humblot, [1928] 2003, 371–5.

[16] See Beaud, *Fédération*; R Schütze, *From Dual to Cooperative Federalism: The Changing Structure of European Law*, Oxford: Oxford University Press, 2009; see also C Schönberger, *Unionsbürger: Europas föderales Bürgerrecht in vergleichender Sicht*, Tübingen: Mohr Siebeck, 2005, 124–7.

[17] MacCormick, 'Risking Constitutional Collision'.

[18] Griffiths, 'Legal Pluralism', 5–8.

'interpretive pluralism' under the US Constitution. Pluralism, in this view, denotes the fact that the authority to interpret the US Constitution is ultimately undefined, and that in the extreme case three organs compete for it—Congress, the President, and the Supreme Court.[19] This may indeed lead at times to similar political dynamics as in instances of systemic pluralism such as the EU where *Grundnormen* themselves diverge. In particular, as Halberstam points out, the actors in both cases may have recourse to comparable sources of political authority to bolster their claims.[20] But such similarities should not conceal the crucial difference that lies in the fact that interpretive pluralism operates with respect to a common point of reference—constitutional norms that form a background framework and lay the ground for arguments about authority—while in systemic pluralism such a common point of reference *within* the legal or institutional structure is lacking. In Halberstam's example, conflict might not be fully regulated but occurs in a bounded legal and political universe that contains (some) resources for its solution. Practically, the extent of this difference will depend on how thick the common framework is—in this respect, institutional and systemic pluralism may differ only gradually. If foundational constitutionalism and systemic pluralism mark the extremes of a continuum, institutional pluralism may occupy some place in the middle. Analytically, however, the difference between institutional and systemic pluralism is one in kind, defined by the presence *vel* absence of a common frame of reference.

Other pluralist approaches to postnational law follow a similarly institutionalist route. Mattias Kumm's 'cosmopolitan constitutionalism', for example, presents itself as pluralist as it does not seek to construct firm hierarchies between different levels of law.[21] But this pluralism is embedded in a thick set of overarching norms, such as subsidiarity, due process, or democracy, that are meant to direct the solution of conflicts. There may be no one institution to settle disputes, and such disputes may thus, as a matter of fact, remain undecided for a long time. This, however, is typical enough for all kinds of constitutional structures—after all, law or constitutions can never

---

[19] D Halberstam, 'Constitutional Heterarchy: The Centrality of Conflict in the European Union and the United States' in J L Dunoff & J P Trachtman (eds), *Ruling the World? Constitutionalism, International Law and Global Government*, Cambridge: Cambridge University Press, 2009, 326–55.

[20] ibid.

[21] See M Kumm, 'The Cosmopolitan Turn in Constitutionalism: On the Relationship between Constitutionalism in and beyond the State' in Dunoff & Trachtman, *Ruling the World?*, 258–324; see also M Kumm, 'The Legitimacy of International Law: A Constitutionalist Framework of Analysis', *European Journal of International Law* 15 (2004), 907–31.

determine the outcome of conflicts, but only offer certain (institutional, normative) resources for their solution. Kumm's proposal may indeed be institutionally pluralist, but structurally it retains (as its self-description as cosmopolitan *constitutionalism* suggests) a constitutionalist character: in his vision, it is rules of 'hard law'—constitutional rules—that guide and contain conflict resolution. To use another example, Paul Schiff Berman situates his own approach clearly on the pluralist rather than the constitutionalist side[22] and his account of the hybrid and contested nature of the global legal order is close to the systemic pluralism we see in the earlier work of MacCormick. Yet his discussion of the forms that may allow for managing the resulting conflicts recalls the constitutionalist instruments for accommodating diversity I have discussed in Chapter 2: limited autonomy regimes or subsidiarity principles reflect devolutionist ideas, while hybrid-participation regimes are close to models of consociationalism.[23] Even Mireille Delmas-Marty, the most influential French theorist of transnational legal pluralism, tames her initially radical-sounding vision by an eventual attempt to create order through overarching rules, softened by way of margins of appreciation and balancing requirements.[24] Just as the later MacCormick, Delmas-Marty seems to become afraid of the 'messy' picture she describes and clings to some degree of institutionalized harmony.

Harmony is also a prominent aim in another, more ambiguous take on postnational pluralism, that of Miguel Poiares Maduro.[25] Maduro seeks to contain the risk of friction that results from the conflicting claims of national and EU law by introducing, as part of his idea of a 'counterpunctual law', a requirement for both levels to strive for coherence and integrity in the overall order. In the 'internal' pluralism of the EU, this requirement is regarded

---

[22] P S Berman, 'Global Legal Pluralism', *Southern California Law Review* 80 (2007), 1155–237.

[23] ibid, 1196–235.

[24] M Delmas-Marty, *Ordering Pluralism: A Conceptual Framework for Understanding the Transnational Legal World* (N Norberg, trans), Oxford: Hart Publishing, 2009, 149–65. For an earlier proposal, see M Delmas-Marty, *Towards a Truly Common Law: Europe as a Laboratory for Legal Pluralism* (N Norberg, trans), Cambridge: Cambridge University Press, 2002.

[25] M Poiares Maduro, 'Europe and the Constitution: What If This is as Good as it Gets?' in J H H Weiler & M Wind (eds), *European Constitutionalism Beyond the State*, Cambridge: Cambridge University Press, 2003, 74–102; M Poiares Maduro, 'Contrapunctual Law: Europe's Constitutional Pluralism in Action' in N Walker (ed), *Sovereignty in Transition*, Oxford: Hart Publishing, 2003, 501–38; M Poiares Maduro, 'Courts and Pluralism: Essay on a Theory of Adjudication in the Context of Legal and Constitutional Pluralism' in Dunoff & Trachtman, *Ruling the World?*, 356–79.

as a legal one, and the pluralism Maduro describes is therefore integrated in a broader legal framework; it is of an institutional—constitutionalist—kind.[26] Beyond Europe, there is less emphasis on commonality: courts are expected to 'interpret the law, as far as possible, in a manner that minimizes potential jurisdictional conflicts', but this expectation operates on the assumption that 'courts [do not] have an allegiance to competing legal orders'.[27] It should thus be seen as merely a moral requirement for the different actors to show respect to each other across the boundaries of their own laws—a vision resembling a conflict-of-laws approach, much closer to systemic pluralism.

Conflict-of-laws ideas are sometimes used to infuse an ethos of recognition and respect into the rules that define the relationships of different levels of law in the postnational order. Christian Joerges takes this path, but it largely remains within a constitutional mindset, as it defines merely the substantive content of a framework that remains shared.[28] Yet a conflict-of-laws model can also be seen as an architectural inspiration: as an inspiration to manage conflicts between different legal sub-orders not through overarching rules but through reliance on the capacity of those sub-orders to define adequate rules for mutual engagement. As in traditional conflict-of-laws, certain issues could then be subject to more than one set of rules, and the different legal subsystems would seek to define for themselves when to claim authority or cede it to another level. This forms the basis of the approach of Andreas Fischer-Lescano and Gunther Teubner: for them, the global legal order is irredeemably pluralist as the functional differentiation of society is reproduced in a differentiation of legal subsystems, all with their own particular rationalities.[29] Interactions occur in network fashion, through interfaces defined by each subsystem in reaction to its environment, but without the hope for an overarching framework that would structure their relationships; too divergent are their own inner logics. Fischer-Lescano and Teubner's is a systemic pluralism without compromise or melancholical remnants of a constitutional structure, but it is also one in which the inevitability of social forces reigns and emancipatory ideas find little, if any,

---

[26] See Poiares Maduro, 'Courts and Pluralism', 374–5.

[27] ibid, 375.

[28] C Joerges, 'Rethinking the Supremacy of European Law', *EUI Working Paper Law* 2005/12; C Joerges, 'Conflict of Laws as Constitutional Form: Reflections on International Trade Law and the *Biotech* Panel Report', *RECON Online Working Paper* 2007/3.

[29] A Fischer-Lescano & G Teubner, *Regime-Kollisionen: Zur Fragmentierung des globalen Rechts*, Frankfurt am Main: Suhrkamp Verlag, 2006. For an early statement, see G Teubner, 'Global Bukowina: Legal Pluralism in the World Society' in G Teubner (ed), *Global Law Without a State*, Dartmouth: Aldershot, 1997, 3–28.

institutional home. If the critique that pluralism surrenders to the forces that be applies anywhere, then here.

One does not have to be a follower of systems theory, though, to interpret the postnational legal order as systemically pluralist; in fact, many such accounts are driven by sociological observation based on actors and agency. Thus, Francis Snyder's analysis of global legal pluralism is based on the emergence and development of a plurality of 'sites of governance' through the strategic action of economic players across boundaries.[30] And Boaventura de Sousa Santos's approach starts from the uses of law by actors, including social movements, in the interstices between normative orders where different sets of norms conflict and can be played out against each other.[31]

Here is not the place to enter into a discussion of the relative value of these analytical approaches; we will return there in later chapters. The aim of this section is merely to gain greater conceptual clarity about the options at our disposal when thinking about alternatives to constitutionalism. And as we have seen, the 'institutionalist' variant of pluralism represents less an alternative to than a continuation of constitutionalist themes: even though its different expressions in the literature all focus on diversity and contestation, they see this contestation as contained in a common, constitutional framework. In that, they resemble closely the accommodationist variants of constitutionalism discussed in the previous section, and they are likely to share the latter's problems.

In contrast, systemic pluralism has emerged as a distinct alternative that eschews a common framework in favour of a decentred management of diversity. This differs from constitutionalism, but also from the classical dualist approach that has for long dominated debates about the relationship between national and international law. For dualism was built on the idea that those two legal orders were clearly separate—the domestic order applied inside the state whereas the international order regulated states in their mutual interactions. Pluralism instead responds to the increasing enmeshment of different layers of law I have diagnosed in Chapter 1—it acknowledges that a relationship may be governed by competing rules from

---

[30] F Snyder, 'Governing Economic Globalisation: Global Legal Pluralism and European Law', *European Law Journal* 5 (1999), 334–74.

[31] B de Sousa Santos, *Toward a New Legal Common Sense*, London: Butterworths, 2002; B de Sousa Santos, 'Beyond Neoliberal Governance: The World Social Forum as Subaltern Cosmopolitan Politics and Legality' in B de Sousa Santos & C A Rodríguez-Garavito (eds), *Law and Globalization from Below*, Cambridge: Cambridge University Press, 2005, 29–63. See also B Rajagopal, 'Limits of Law in Counter-hegemonic Globalization: The Indian Supreme Court and the Narmada Valley Struggle' in de Sousa Santos & Rodríguez-Garavito, *Law and Globalization from Below*, 183–217.

a number of these layers. In this vision, domestic and international law also do not exhaust the range of competing layers—other regionally, personally, or functionally defined layers may complement them. Thus while dualism focuses on two separate spheres and their relationship, pluralism deals with interactions among multiple, enmeshed orders.

Pluralism may thus be a distinct concept, but whether it is also normatively appealing is another matter. Most accounts of pluralism in postnational law are of an analytical kind, and even those who highlight its normative virtues typically emphasize the risk of friction it entails.[32] And from the perspective of most modern political theory, the irregularity of pluralist structures must appear as diametrically opposed to a reasoned, justifiable structure of government.[33] The risk that pluralism represents no more than a transitional, perhaps (for the time being) inevitable digression from a good order is therefore real. But as I will try to show in the remainder of the chapter, seeing systemic pluralism in these terms would downplay the features that make it attractive in a postnational space that, after all, looks very different from the world of the nation-state constitutionalism has so effectively come to inhabit.

II. PLURALIST VIRTUES

Most of the interest in pluralism in postnational law has, as I have just mentioned, focused on the analytical aspect rather than the normative case, and much of it has been accompanied by that systems-theoretical sense of inevitability that sees pluralism largely as an unavoidable consequence of the dynamics of society.[34] Yet once beyond that sentiment, the literature offers three main strands of normative arguments for pluralism (or intimations thereof). One highlights the capacity for adaptation, the second the space for contestation pluralism provides, the third its usefulness for building checks and balances into the postnational order. All three strands capture important aspects of pluralism's appeal, but as will become clear, they are ultimately insufficient to ground a pluralist order.

1. Adaptation

As any order based on law, constitutionalism is in a constant tension with changing social circumstances. Whatever view one holds on the methods

---

[32] eg, Poiares Maduro, 'Europe and the Constitution'.

[33] P Allott, 'Epilogue: Europe and the Dream of Reason' in Weiler & Wind, *European Constitutionalism*, 202–25.

[34] See Fischer-Lescano & Teubner, *Regime-Kollisionen*, ch 3.

of constitutional interpretation, written text, judicial precedent, or previous constitutional moments will always play an important, sometimes the decisive role.[35] Whether in a stronger or weaker form, a constitution always ties a polity to its past and thus creates tensions in the present.

Pluralism promises to relax such ties, to allow for adaptation to new circumstances in a more rapid and less formalized way: by leaving the relationships between legal sub-orders undetermined, it keeps them open to political redefinition over time. Whether or not this is advisable in domestic politics, it certainly has some appeal in the postnational space. Here, social and political relations are much more in flux, ideas about political justice are constantly shifting, and our imagination of what governance arrangements may be feasible keeps changing. This means, on the one hand, that rules we might formulate today may soon look outdated because of a change of our normative sentiments or an expanded horizon of institutional options. On the other hand, such rules may soon seem anachronistic because of a change in the structure of society. All constitutions are as much expressions of abstract normative values as they are reflections of a particular social structure, and they tend to stabilize and immunize that structure. For example, in the elaboration of a postnational constitution we would currently operate under the constraint that beyond the state social cohesion and communicative structures are such that we have to ground democracy in something other than the classical idea of a relatively unitary postnational 'people' and that we would have to give significant weight to national democratic deliberations in order to legitimize postnational decision-making. This constraint, however, may ease over time, particularly in contexts of strong integration like the European Union,[36] and if this happened it would open up manifold new procedural and institutional possibilities. Exploiting these possibilities would be much easier in an order in which the old structure is not inscribed in institutional settings that defy informal change. Think only of the equality of US states in the Senate: whereas in the late eighteenth century, population differences among states were small enough to make such a solution allowable, they have now grown to proportions that place the institutional structure under significant strain.

---

[35] This is obvious in originalist approaches, but even for a theory that places as much emphasis on moral theory as Ronald Dworkin's, the dimension of 'fit' with history continues to provide a central anchor; see R Dworkin, *Law's Empire*, Cambridge, MA: Harvard University Press, 1986.

[36] For one vision of such a trajectory, see J Habermas, *The Postnational Constellation* (M Pensky, trans), Cambridge, MA: MIT Press, 2001, ch 4.

Because of the high hurdles for adaptation, though, change is most unlikely to happen.[37]

All constitutional settings, including domestic ones, face this challenge of adaptation, but it is particularly pronounced in the postnational context where the speed and magnitude of social and institutional change are today much greater than in most domestic settings. Freezing particular solutions in constitutional form then risks rendering them soon obsolete or even positively harmful; keeping institutional settings flexible in a pluralist structure may be the better option.

Such an argument may gain particular force because of the divided character of postnational society. As we have seen above, most constitutionalist responses to this fact involve institutional structures that accommodate but thereby also stabilize societal divides. This is most pronounced in consociationalist settings where rights that attach to particular groups are likely to reinforce existing group divides and maintain them even if individuals' identities change.[38] As Richard Pildes has recently emphasized, in divided societies adaptability and dynamism are primary virtues of institutional settlements as they allow for a reflection of changing social circumstances—more than particular institutional provisions at the outset, revisability may help reflect and further social integration over time.[39] And though he focuses on the (limited) options for adaptation that exist *within* a constitutional framework, choosing a pluralist setting instead might be a further-reaching step towards that aim.

Another virtue deriving from adaptability may be a greater capacity for learning. Charles Sabel has repeatedly argued that heterarchical networks and revisable rather than rigid norms facilitate processes of experimentation and mutual learning better than hierarchies with rigid norms.[40] Because they rely on the engagement and experiences of all actors, they are able to generate sounder insights than hierarchical organizations, and because of the easier revisability they are better able to respond to changes in both circumstances and knowledge. This holds especially when the regulatory

---

[37] R H Pildes, 'Ethnic Identity and Democratic Institutions: A Dynamic Perspective' in S Choudhry (ed), *Constitutional Design for Divided Societies: Integration or Accommodation?*, Oxford: Oxford University Press, 2008, 173–201 at 174.

[38] For a survey of such claims, see J McGarry, B O'Leary, & R Simeon, 'Integration or Accommodation? The Enduring Debate in Conflict Regulation' in Choudhry, *Constitutional Design*, 41–88 at 71–8.

[39] Pildes, 'Ethnic Identity', 184–201.

[40] See, eg, C F Sabel & J Zeitlin, 'Learning from Difference: The New Architecture of Experimentalist Governance in the EU', *European Law Journal* 14 (2008), 271–327.

landscape is characterized by great diversity and the issues at stake involve significant uncertainty and change at a quick pace. In postnational governance, the former is generally true and the latter in most areas, so pluralist, heterarchical structures may be particularly adequate here—a point I will return to in Chapter 7 when I look more closely at the dynamics of pluralist orders in postnational politics.

However, adaptability, transformative capacity, and openness to learning have a downside: greater flexibility comes with the risk of a surrender to social forces. It may be highly beneficial in benign circumstances, when the relevant actors show the required disposition for responding to argument and exchanging experiences and knowledge. Adaptability in the institutional structure may also be desirable when social change goes in the right direction (whichever that may be): then flexible structures will also change for the better rather than hold progress back. But none of this can be taken for granted; when shifts take an adverse direction and actors show less goodwill, more rigid forms may prove preferable. Pluralism's greater adaptability may thus be a virtue only in certain, potentially quite limited conditions.

2. Contestation

If the argument from adaptation is based on an optimistic view of the social environment and its trajectory, that from contestation starts from a more pessimistic one. It assumes that constitutional frameworks are typically elite products, expressions of power and social hegemony, and that the element of disruption and openness in a pluralist order may provide greater contestatory space for weaker actors.[41]

This argument can take a weak or a strong form. In its weak form, it is based on an appreciation of the *current* political constraints that attempts at postnational constitutionalisation would face. After all, international politics remains dominated by intergovernmental bargaining in which the pursuit of states' self-interest on the basis of material power plays at least a prominent, perhaps the dominant role.[42] As a result, current structures follow an unjust distribution of power to an inordinate extent, and efforts at reconceiving them in a constitutional fashion are bound to stabilize and reinforce the inequalities behind them—the re-reading of the UN Charter

---

[41] Thus the emphasis on subaltern, alternative legalities in de Sousa Santos, *New Legal Common Sense*, chs 3 and 9.

[42] See, eg, R O Keohane, 'Governance in a Partially Globalized World', *American Political Science Review* 95 (2001), 1–13.

as a constitution is a good example here.[43] But the current distribution of power also limits the options we could imagine to form part of a fresh constitutional settlement, and it certainly limits what we could hope to achieve in such a settlement—it may largely end up in an institutionalization of the preferences of the dominant actors of the day, as many large-scale attempts at institutionalization have before.[44] Even in the European Union, where the intergovernmental mode of operation may have been complemented by broader, transnational, and civil society-oriented politics to a greater extent than elsewhere, large-scale institutional change so far appears to have followed an intergovernmental logic, based on self-interest and power.[45] An explicit attempt at constitution-making may trigger a shift here, as it has with the establishment of the convention process leading up to the 2004 draft constitutional treaty. But even this convention seems to have operated largely in the shadow of what dominant players could be expected to agree to and thus may not have seriously challenged the intergovernmental mode.[46] For truly different (and fairer) processes, one might have to wait for a more radical transformation of European and global politics. Assuming that alternative forms of power (ideational, communicative) are likely to play a stronger rather than weaker role in the future, seeking a constitution now would only benefit those holding the greatest material power today: it would allow them to 'lock in' their dominant position.

This argument for pluralism, based on the fluidity of the postnational order and the role of material power in it, is powerful, but it is also transitional. Pluralism appears as an attractive option for times of change when better alternatives cannot be realized. But it continues to lack appeal as a long-term vision of what the global order should look like—it seems constitutionalism

---

[43] B Fassbender, 'The United Nations Charter as Constitution of the International Community', *Columbia Journal of Transnational Law* 36 (1998), 529–619, highlights the critical potential of the constitutional idea, especially as regards the issue of veto powers, but the greater legitimation the unequal structure of the UN would gain from such a move is on balance far weightier.

[44] G J Ikenberry, *After Victory: Institutions, Strategic Restraint, and the Rebuilding of Order After Major Wars*, Princeton, NJ: Princeton University Press, 2001.

[45] A Moravcsik, *The Choice for Europe: Social Purpose and State Power from Messina to Maastricht*, London: UCL Press, 1998.

[46] P Magnette & K Nicolaïdis, 'The European Convention: Bargaining in the Shadow of Rhetoric', *West European Politics* 27 (2004), 381–404; but see also the different emphasis in the appraisals by J E Fossum & A J Menendez, 'The Constitution's Gift? A Deliberative Democratic Analysis of Constitution Making in the European Union', *European Law Journal* 11 (2005), 380–410; C Karlsson, 'Deliberation at the Convention: The Final Verdict', *European Law Journal* 14 (2008), 604–19.

still provides the better alternative once postnational politics has become more settled and 'domesticated'.

The strong version of the argument from contestation, however, is of a less transitional nature. In this variant, the contestatory space pluralism opens up will be crucial to any postnational order, not just the current one. This depends on a much more pessimistic appraisal of the prospects of reform in the official institutional setting: it typically starts from the view that tools for counter-hegemonic action are necessary in any polity, and that a pluralist legal order would facilitate their exercise. In the argument put forward for example by Boaventura de Sousa Santos, alternative legalities can become central tools for the articulation of subaltern politics against the mainstream forms of global governance sustained by dominant economic and military power.[47]

What distinguishes this approach from the weak version of the argument is the lack of hope eventually to institutionalize a just or legitimate order in a constitutionalist form, and in this it connects with some of the critiques of modern constitutionalism I have sketched in Chapter 2. As we have seen, for James Tully constitutions in multicultural societies are typically expressions of dominant cultures, and he therefore seeks to destabilize processes of constitutionalisation in the modern, foundational way.[48] This analysis resonates with broader critiques. Constitutionalism's aspiration to establish an impartial framework is questioned also by those who, like Chantal Mouffe, are sceptical about the chances for attaining a neutral consensus in diverse societies more generally.[49] This does not have to go as far as to deny the possibility of reasoned deliberation and consensus between worldviews altogether, as some postmodernists do. Mouffe's scepticism is grounded in the observation that in practice forms of consensus are typically expressions not of an inclusive process leading to an impartial result, but instead of social mechanisms that favour powerful actors whose dominance is then concealed by the supposed neutrality of broad agreement. And those conditions which political theorists defend to ground impartial consensus favour a particular rationality and abstract so much from the circumstances of the individual (in social relations, language, culture) that they can hardly count as truly inclusive.[50] Mouffe's viewpoint is mirrored, for example, in Ran Hirschl's much more empirically minded, comparative study of the political

---

[47] de Sousa Santos, *New Legal Common Sense*, ch 9; de Sousa Santos, 'Beyond Neoliberal Governance'.

[48] See Chapter 2, III.2 and 3.

[49] C Mouffe, *The Democratic Paradox*, London: Verso, 2000, ch 4.

[50] ibid, 92–6.

origins of recent constitutionalization and the concomitant emergence of judicial review.[51] Hirschl interprets these developments, despite their apparent claim to inclusiveness and impartiality, as attempts by political elites to lock in their privileged position and defend it from challenge; constitutions then come to appear as hegemonic tools. If this is true, one would indeed want to deny them full legitimation and provide space for continuous contestation on a fundamental level—something a pluralist, heterarchical order may indeed be able to do.

The argument from contestation usefully draws attention to the fact that law—including constitutions—is not the product of abstract ideas but of real, and normally problematic, social and political processes. Whether or not one accepts the argument then comes to depend on one's general views about the degree to which such processes can be transformed. Caution is warranted here: also in domestic politics we will hardly ever find the ideal communicative structures that would render a truly fair consensus possible; constitutions, as a result, typically display some of the features of power politics Hirschl's study identifies. If this holds true in the relatively well-integrated, homogeneous contexts of nation-states, we can expect it to be even more pronounced in the far more divided postnational space in which organized material power (through states) is generally seen to play an even more dominant role. Even if constructivists have rightly pointed to the continued (and perhaps increased) impact of ideas and values and the concomitant influence of arguments in international politics, this need not imply a weakening of power in this context; after all, material power is often enough reflected in, and furthered through, ideas and values.[52] There is little hope for transcending the predominance of power in the postnational space—neither in the near future nor in the long term, especially if we take the limited success of such attempts in the more benign domestic context as a guide.

In these circumstances, an attempt at constitution-making can appear as simply another hegemonic move.[53] But it may also give the communicative power of weaker actors a greater role: the powerful may be willing to make concessions in order to gain stronger legitimacy for an order that is overall beneficial to them, and this may help change the political logic

[51] R Hirschl, *Towards Juristocracy: The Origins and Consequences of the New Constitutionalism*, Cambridge, MA: Harvard University Press, 2004.

[52] On links between realist/rationalist and constructivist approaches in world politics, see I Hurd, *After Anarchy: Legitimacy and Power in the United Nations Security Council*, Princeton, NJ: Princeton University Press, 2007; also T Risse, '"Let's Argue!" Communicative Action in World Politics', *International Organization* 54 (2000), 1–39.

[53] See Koskenniemi, 'Fate of Public International Law', 19.

of the postnational space to some extent. It may also provide tools that can be mobilized later for a transformation of the structure quite at odds with that intended at the inception; powerful actors may well be trapped in their own argumentative and legal strategies.[54] This only reflects the janus-faced character of law as both a tool of the powerful as well as an instrument of resistance;[55] which of them gains the upper hand depends on the environment and the success of mobilization on either side. Balakrishnan Rajagopal has recently pursued this ambiguity with a focus on legal pluralism, tracing the ways in which the multiplicity of applicable legal orders granted social activists in India space but also meant that successes in one order did not necessarily translate into the others.[56] Thus a pluralist structure does not, in and of itself, allow for more effective contestation than a constitutionalist one.[57] Whether it does will depend on the context: the greater the power differential behind a potential constitution, and the more that constitution is likely to reflect it, the greater is the likelihood that a pluralist order will provide more effective tools of contestation and delegitimation than the concessions that might be extracted in a constitutional settlement. As I will discuss in greater detail in Chapter 7, in postnational politics this likelihood is relatively high.

3. Checks and Balances

The most common argument for a pluralist order stems from an analogy with checks and balances in domestic constitutions. This analogy is grounded in the difficulty of justifying the supremacy of any level of postnational governance over the others: if no level can claim superiority, a constitutionalist order that implies ultimate authority (if only that of the constitution, the common framework) will appear problematic.[58] In order to respect the competing claims of the different levels, we might instead choose a path that aims not so much at integration but at dissociation: one that keeps an equal distance from the ideals of all of them, that refrains from according full control over decisions—through veto rights or otherwise—to

---

[54] See Risse, 'Let's Argue', 32–3, on such 'self-entrapment'.

[55] In the context of international law, see N Krisch, 'International Law in Times of Hegemony: Unequal Power and the Shaping of the International Legal Order', *European Journal of International Law* 16 (2005), 369–408.

[56] Rajagopal, 'Limits of Law'.

[57] de Sousa Santos, *New Legal Common Sense*, 98, 495.

[58] See Poiares Maduro, 'Europe and the Constitution'; Berman, 'Global Legal Pluralism', 1179–96; Halberstam, 'Constitutional Heterarchy'; A Torres Pérez, *Conflicts of Rights in the European Union: A Theory of Supranational Adjudication*, Oxford: Oxford University Press, 2009, 66–9.

either of the competing collectives. If all constituencies are to have decision-making powers beyond merely being listened to, but shall not be able to dictate or veto a particular decision, then no decision can fully bind them all, and each level has to retain the right to challenge it. The resulting picture of postnational governance would then be one of a constant potential for mutual challenge: of decisions with limited authority that may be contested through diverse channels until some (perhaps provisional) closure might be achieved. It would be a picture of checks and balances that result in a form of systemic pluralism.

The first step in this argument is indeed plausible if we consider the normative grounding of the competing polities. Different collectives—subnational, national, regional, or global—have a strong initial case, based on culture, nationalism, cosmopolitanism etc, but they all come with serious deficits as well. Subnational and national constituencies are limited in that they cannot fully respond to the needs and interests of those outsiders that are affected by their decisions or have a claim to be considered, for example for reasons of transboundary justice.[59] The global polity is not capable of instituting structures of democratic participation nearly as thick and effective as those possible on the national level. It is too far removed from individuals, and intergovernmental negotiations will never come with the deliberative structures necessary for effective public involvement; moreover, as mentioned above, we face serious limits of communication across cultural, linguistic, and political boundaries.[60] Regional levels typically combine the advantages, but also the problems of the lower and higher levels—they are not fully inclusive and their democratic structures are not sufficiently deep.[61]

It might be tempting to see these tensions simply as a reflection of competing approaches in political and democratic theory. For example, a cosmopolitan model would delimit the relevant collectives according to the scope of individuals who are significantly affected by particular issues or decisions; as a result, it would locate the relevant collective on a relatively high level.[62]

---

[59] See, eg, I M Young, *Inclusion and Democracy*, Oxford: Oxford University Press, 2000, 246–51.

[60] See, eg, J Habermas, 'Hat die Konstitutionalisierung des Völkerrechts noch eine Chance?' in J Habermas, *Der gespaltene Westen*, Frankfurt am Main: Suhrkamp Verlag, 2004, 113–93, 137–42.

[61] In a similar vein, Halberstam, 'Constitutional Heterarchy', reconstructs the competing views as deriving from the three values of 'voice, expertise and rights' that create competing authority claims.

[62] eg, D Held, *Democracy and the Global Order*, Cambridge: Polity Press, 1995; D Held, 'Democratic Accountability and Effectiveness from a Cosmopolitan Perspective', *Government & Opposition* 39 (2004), 365–91.

Liberal nationalists, however, would emphasize the importance of social ties for the realization of requirements of justice, and would therefore keep decisions on a lower, largely national level.[63] More republican-minded theories would seek to balance communal ties with concerns about the effectiveness and inclusiveness of self-government regarding issues of broader reach.[64] Those theories that regard some form of historical or cultural *demos* as central to democracy will hardly accept fundamental decisions taken beyond the national level.[65] Others that are primarily concerned about the discursive conditions for democratic decision-making may accept regional but perhaps not global institutions.[66]

This list could easily be extended, but the details of the various approaches matter less than the broader point that the difficulties in the determination of the right level of governance may boil down to a need to choose between theoretical frameworks. Once this choice is made, one could then proceed to assign particular issues to levels of decision-making and would arrive either at a federal-style model with the global level at the (thin) top; at an intergovernmental one that retains the nation-state as the main anchor of the overall edifice; or at some other broadly coherent structure depending on the particular substantive principle at work. The tensions that seemed to suggest a pluralist order would then appear merely as a result of theoretical indecision.

Yet the solution may not be so easy. In the previous chapter, I mentioned Iris Young's point that abstract principles, such as inclusion of all those affected by a decision, are in tension with the actual allegiances of individuals and that any institutional structure has to reflect those countervailing concerns.[67] This can be redescribed as a tension in the liberal project between two directions of autonomy: one insisting on the individual's right to co-determine whatever decision has an effect on her, the other emphasizing the importance for autonomy of the individual's (cultural, social) particularity that should be reflected in the decision-making framework. Here lurks a deeper conflict that in the domestic context long remained inconsequential and only came to the surface once traditional models of politics

---

[63] eg, D Miller, *National Responsibility and Global Justice*, Oxford: Oxford University Press, 2007.

[64] eg, S Benhabib, *The Rights of Others*, Cambridge: Cambridge University Press, 2004, 217–21.

[65] eg, P Kirchhof, 'Der deutsche Staat im Prozeß der europäischen Integration' in J Isensee & P Kirchhof (eds), *Handbuch des Staatsrechts der Bundesrepublik Deutschland*, vol VII, Heidelberg: C F Müller Verlag, 1992, 855–87.

[66] eg, Habermas, 'Konstitutionalisierung'.

[67] Young, *Inclusion*, ch 7.

were called into question. It is, in James Bohman's words, 'the fundamental tension between universality and particularity that is built into the constitutions of modern states'.[68] The modern state was built onto a relative congruence not only between decision-makers and decision-takers, but also on that between a particular social community and the scope of those affected by political decisions. However much this community may have been imagined or (forcibly) constructed,[69] the resulting congruence allowed to construct democratic participation in a coherent, unitary way. Tensions between community allegiances and political structures only became apparent where subnational groups retained or developed a stronger collective consciousness that made them claim self-determination on their own. Federal, sometimes asymmetrical arrangements were the typical, though not always stable institutional response to such claims.[70]

If the tension between the scope of communities and that of affected individuals could be largely contained in the context of the nation-state, in the postnational context the gap is too big for a similar containment to work. The conflicting principles may be formulated differently depending on the theoretical framework one operates in, but however the precise conceptualization, the tension between them is likely to condition the institutional structure to a significant extent. For many issue areas, it will prevent singling out one collective as determinative; instead, several levels will have claims with similar degrees of justification, and the structural framework should grant them equal importance. Doing so in forms of co-decision (as in consociationalism) would risk serious blockade in a context such as the postnational where the number of players is high.[71] The best solution might then be a pluralist one: one that withholds full legitimacy from all of the different levels, does not grant any of them ultimate decision-making capacity and instead establishes equidistance to all of them.

---

[68] J Bohman, *Democracy across Borders*, Cambridge, MA: MIT Press, 2007, 29; see also S Benhabib, 'Reclaiming Universalism: Negotiating Republican Self-Determination and Cosmopolitan Norms', *The Tanner Lectures on Human Values* 25 (2005), 113–66 at 132 ('The tension between universal human rights claims and particularistic cultural and national identities is constitutive of democratic legitimacy').

[69] B Anderson, *Imagined Communities: Reflections on the Origin and Spread of Nationalism*, London: Verso, 1983; W Connor, 'Nation-Building or Nation-Destroying?', *World Politics* 24 (1972), 319–55.

[70] See S Tierney, *Constitutional Law and National Pluralism*, Oxford: Oxford University Press, 2004; and the discussion in Chapter 2, III.3.

[71] See Chapter 2, III.3.

Functionally, such an approach may indeed be close to domestic constitutional checks and balances—in both cases, no single site enjoys ultimate decision-making powers but has to face checks by others that, in some respects, may have equally strong claims to authority.[72] However, as I have pointed out in the conceptual discussion above, domestic checks and balances are typically part of a structured constitutional framework and operate in a common frame of reference—in our context, they would instead operate between such frameworks, not within one of them. In this way, the checks-and-balances idea is radicalized and taken to the systemic level; it has to be if the equal, fundamental deficits of the different polities are to be reflected.

III. PLURALISM AND PUBLIC AUTONOMY

Checks and balances sound immediately attractive, almost uncontroversial on a background of modern constitutional theory, but the above account leaves open a crucial question: who should be entitled to check whom, and why? To some extent, the response may seem too obvious in the context from which the idea originates, the European Union. Here both the national and the European levels have a strong basis both in abstract normative terms and in social practices as they have developed over the last decades. In this case, it might seem clear that checks and balances between those two polity levels are appropriate, and it might also make the proposition attractive that they should grant each other some 'constitutional tolerance'—that they should refrain from demanding obedience from one another but rather operate on a basis of mutual invitations to cooperate.[73] A pluralist order might be much more suited to such a vision than a constitutionalist one that comes with hierarchies and obligations to comply with the other's orders.

However, the situation is less clear-cut once we move beyond the European to the global realm. Here too, as I have sketched above, there are good arguments for different levels of decision-making on issues of transboundary concerns, yet what this implies in practice is far less obvious. A multiplicity of different regimes are vying for authority, and their relationship with one another and with regional or state organs is far from settled. Should the UN, the World Trade Organization (WTO), or the Financial Action Task Force (FATF) be equally entitled to 'tolerance' from states? Are regimes such as those of the Agreement on the Application of Sanitary and Phytosanitary Measures (SPS Agreement) and the Biosafety Protocol—the subject of Chapter 6—on an equal footing and related to one another only as a matter

---

[72] Halberstam, 'Constitutional Heterarchy'.

[73] J H H Weiler, 'In Defence of the Status Quo: Europe's Constitutional *Sonderweg*' in Weiler & Wind, *European Constitutionalism*, 7–23.

of tolerance, or are there hierarchies at play? And can states or regional enti-ties only expect tolerance from global bodies or claim more, perhaps an ulti-mate right to decide? The determination of the relevant collectives and of their link to particular institutions, seemingly easy in the European context, proves to be highly problematic on the global level.

The most obvious solution here would be to go back to the normative arguments discussed in the last section and probe further into how they would apply to those multiple regimes. The conflicting arguments for keep-ing decision-making at lower or higher levels might play out differently for the different regimes, and in some cases mutual tolerance might be called for, in others not. We might think, for example, that if decision-making on the global level is primarily justified by greater inclusion of those affected, a body such as the Financial Action Task Force (FATF), with a very limited membership but far-reaching effects on outsiders, hardly deserves deference or respect.[74] On the other hand, the Kyoto Protocol's climate change regime could be seen to respond to the need for non-exclusive, global solutions for transboundary environmental problems and thus to warrant a high degree of tolerance (and perhaps compliance) from states.

1. Pluralisms of Choice

This approach seems fairly straightforward but it is only superficially so. For the method we have used so far, relying as it does on a substantive evalua-tion of the claims of different regimes or collectives, contrasts starkly with pluralist approaches developed by political theorists for the domestic level, which typically start from some form of choice of the individuals involved. In order to gain a clearer view of the difference, it is worth analysing these domestic theories briefly before we return to the postnational level.

Pluralist theories of the state have typically been grounded in the freedom of association. An early influential strand of this kind was English political pluralism, associated especially with Frederick William Maitland, G D H Cole, John Neville Figgis, and Harold Laski.[75] For them, a political order based on voluntary associations appeared superior to a state-centred one because it promised individuals greater control of their own affairs. Because

---

[74] On the legitimacy problems of the FATF, see R Hülsse, 'Even Clubs can't do Without Legitimacy: Why the Anti-money Laundering Blacklist was Suspended', *Regulation & Governance* (2008), 459–79.

[75] See P Q Hirst (ed), *The Pluralist Theory of the State*, London: Routledge, 1989, 1–47; D Nicholls, *The Pluralist State: The Political Ideas of J N Figgis and his Contemporaries*, 2nd edn, Basingstoke: Macmillan, 1994; also D Runciman, *Pluralism and the Personality of the State*, Cambridge: Cambridge University Press, 1997.

they originated in individual choice, such associations were also independent from the state in their basis of legitimacy and possessed non-derived powers. Laski, in some of his works, took this so far as to assert that the state was in effect just another association, with no *a priori* claim to supremacy and dependent on acceptance by other associations and individuals whenever it sought to act on them.[76] Yet despite their general emphasis on the importance of associations, most English pluralists, including Laski in his most influential writings, accepted a superior role of the state as a guardian of the system: as a guarantor of the freedom of association, as an enforcer of common norms, and as an arbiter between associations.[77]

These theories thus defend forms of institutional, not systemic, pluralism, but here this fact interests me less than their foundation. As we have seen, protagonists of postnational pluralism have typically determined the relevant collectives on an objective basis, starting from substantive theories of where decision-making power should lie. In contrast, the English pluralists used as a foundation individuals' choices of the associations they want to form part of. Even if these choices might not settle the question entirely (as we have seen, a framework of common norms was still seen as necessary), such an approach is nevertheless of a distinctly more participatory, proceduralist character than its postnational analogues. Contemporary theorists of pluralism in the domestic context, such as Paul Hirst and William Galston, follow this participatory path.[78]

The distinctive character of such an approach is demonstrated in Chandran Kukathas's recent work which develops the idea of freedom of association further and radicalizes its institutional implications.[79] In Kukathas's vision, society is an 'archipelago' of (partly overlapping) associations that coexist both next to each other and on different levels, but not in hierarchical relationships: all depend on negotiations and compromises with the others; none can command; and the basic operational principle is toleration. In this order, the state occupies an elevated place but is confined to an even more minimal role than in the approaches mentioned above. It is supposed to

---

[76] See H J Laski, 'Law and the State' in Hirst, *Pluralist Theory*, 197–227 at 214; also P Q Hirst, 'Introduction' in Hirst, *Pluralist Theory*, 1–45 at 28.

[77] See Hirst, *Pluralist Theory*, 28–30; Nicholls, *Pluralist State*, ch 5; H J Laski, 'The Problem of Administrative Areas' in Hirst, *Pluralist Theory*, 131–63 at 155.

[78] See P Q Hirst, *Associative Democracy*, Cambridge: Polity Press, 1994; W A Galston, *Liberal Pluralism*, Cambridge: Cambridge University Press, 2002, ch 9.

[79] C Kukathas, *The Liberal Archipelago*, Oxford: Oxford University Press, 2003. Kukathas bases freedom of association not on autonomy but on freedom of conscience (ibid, 36–7); but this difference is of little importance in the present context.

ensure order as an 'umpire' between associations, but questions of justice are out of its reach since they are contested among different associations and no neutral ground can be found to adjudicate between them. What is just and right must therefore remain undecided; competing views will seek to broaden their support but cannot be enforced against associations that are unwilling to share them.[80]

In Kukathas's vision, thus, toleration operates between the polities founded upon individuals' allegiances, not between collectives delineated in the abstract. What is more, an abstract delineation would be groundless: there are no overarching principles of justice that would transcend those produced within the different islands of the archipelago. Those islands owe each other respect merely because they are forms of individual association, not for any further-reaching qualities. If associational choices diverge, therefore, the structure will necessarily be pluralist; if they do not, it will not. Here the participatory, association-based logic gains its clearest form; and its implications are not limited to the diverse domestic societies that form the primary focus of Kukathas's work but extend well into the international, postnational spheres.[81]

2. Public Autonomy and the Scope of the Polity

One does not have to share all Kukathas's conclusions, or his libertarian outlook, to see the force of this kind of approach. By insisting on the centrality of individuals' allegiances and choices for the determination of the polity, it relates much more closely than an abstract, objective approach with the emphasis on procedure in most contemporary political theory.

This emphasis has always been characteristic of civic republican approaches that have placed popular sovereignty at the centre of their concern; for them, the (political) 'liberties of the ancients' had to trump, or at least parallel the (private) 'liberties of the moderns'. But also for neo-republicans who reject the 'populist' character of such a recourse to the 'ancients',[82] the primary good—non-domination—depends crucially on participatory opportunities for individuals, be they expressed as possibilities for contestation[83] or the capacity for individuals 'as free and equal citizens to form and

---

[80] ibid, ch 6, and especially 252 ('The state should not be concerned about anything except order or peace').

[81] ibid, 27–9.

[82] See P Pettit, *Republicanism: A Theory of Freedom and Government*, Oxford: Oxford University Press, 1997, 7–8.

[83] ibid, 183–205.

change the terms of their common life together'.[84] Perhaps less naturally, most contemporary liberals share in the emphasis on participation. Thus David Held regards as crucial to liberal democracy the ability for individuals 'to choose freely the conditions of their own association',[85] and Jeremy Waldron sees participation as 'the right of rights' that allows for the creation of political structures in the face of substantive disagreement—for Waldron, it is indeed participation all the way down.[86] And John Rawls, responding to Habermas's charge that his views emphasized abstract rights over the exercise of popular sovereignty, insists that the people's constituent power has long been a cornerstone of liberal constitutional and political (as opposed to merely moral) theories.[87]

If participation and the public autonomy of citizens are so central, their reach has to extend to all elements of the framework of a polity. In constitutional settings, this is realized through the idea of a 'dualist' democracy: a comprehensive role for popular sovereignty in the making of a constitution, where it defines all terms of the constitutional settlement, and a more attenuated role in the operation of daily politics within the constitutional frame.[88] However, if participation is thought to extend to all questions of a constitutional character, it also has to apply to the scope of the polity—the reach of the constitutional frame—itself. If individuals are 'to choose freely the conditions of their own association',[89] they have to be able to determine with whom to associate. As James Bohman puts it, 'to the extent that borders and jurisdictions set the terms of democratic arrangements, they must be open to democratic deliberation'[90]—and, we can add, revision.

Yet applying democracy to itself seems to lead into an infinite regress—in order to determine the scope of the polity, we must already know that scope for otherwise a democratic determination could not take place. This

---

[84] Bohman, *Democracy across Borders*, 45.

[85] Held, *Democracy and the Global Order*, 145

[86] J Waldron, *Law and Disagreement*, Oxford: Oxford University Press, 1996, chs 11 and 13.

[87] J Rawls, 'Reply to Habermas' in J Rawls, *Political Liberalism*, New York: Columbia University Press, 1996, 372–434 at 415.

[88] See B Ackerman, *We the People*, vol 1, Cambridge, MA: Harvard University Press, 1991, ch 1; see also J Rawls, *Political Liberalism*, New York: Columbia University Press, 1996, 233.

[89] Held, *Democracy and the Global Order*, 145.

[90] Bohman, *Democracy across Borders*, 17.

chicken-and-egg problem[91] did not pose grave difficulties during the era of the nation-state: the determination of the polity seemed self-evident and fixed—democratic politics took place in the national realm, providing the ground for views such as Robert Dahl's that '[t]he criteria of the democratic process presupposes [sic] the rightfulness of the unit itself'.[92] The scope of the polity seemed only conceivable as exogenous to the democratic process, as settled prior to its operation, usually through historical events, sometimes a constitution.

This corresponds with the observation that the collective behind democratic self-determination is only ever reflectively constituted, that is, through the attribution of a later act as a representation of the supposed entity.[93] Normatively, though, this remains unsatisfactory as it excludes public autonomy from one of the most consequential areas of our political framework, and it can also hardly be presented as necessary to cope with an *exceptional* problem. For democracy's beginnings are *typically* marred with similar paradoxes: if we want the rules of democracy to be subject to democratic determination, we end up in an infinite regress.[94] Yet there are ways out of this problem. Take only the most prominent challenge, that of democracy's relationship with rights, such as free speech or equality of the vote. Like the scope of the polity, these are both a precondition for, and in need of definition by, the democratic process. If popular sovereignty is no longer conceived as the mere exercise of will by a given collective and therefore depends on qualitative attributes such as rights to count as such, and if rights are no longer just given but require procedural elaboration through democratic action, the two are mutually dependent, but in a circular way. None can be thought independent of the other, both require the other to even come into existence.[95] This relationship is captured in Habermas's diagnosis of a 'co-originality' of private and public autonomy where neither

---

[91] See I Shapiro & C Hacker-Cordón, 'Outer Edges and Inner Edges' in I Shapiro & C Hacker-Cordón (eds), *Democracy's Edges*, Cambridge: Cambridge University Press, 1999, 1–16 at 1.

[92] R A Dahl, 'Federalism and the Democratic Process' in J R Pennock & J W Chapman (eds), *NOMOS XXV: Liberal Democracy*, New York: New York University Press, 1983, 95–108 at 103 (emphasis omitted).

[93] See H Lindahl, 'Constituent Power and Reflexive Identity: Towards an Ontology of Collective Selfhood' in M Loughlin & N Walker (eds), *The Paradox of Constitutionalism: Constituent Power and Constitutional Form*, Oxford: Oxford University Press, 2008, 9–24.

[94] H S Richardson, *Democratic Autonomy*, Oxford: Oxford University Press, 2002, 67.

[95] See Chapter 2, II.3.

can be thought as prior to the other. But this holds only insofar as we are concerned with their *positive* dimension—in order to become positive law, to become institutionalized, the two have to complement each other. In the *moral* dimension, however, we can theorize the rights individuals have to grant each other and introduce them as presuppositions of an institutionalization through public autonomy—aware of their imperfection, their need to be reinterpreted in the very processes by which such public autonomy constitutes itself.[96]

Democracy's relationship with its preconditions is thus complex, even circular, and this complexity is not limited to the question of the scope of the polity but reaches much further. There is thus no reason to abandon normative theorizing about these preconditions—otherwise, democratic theory would surrender precisely at the point where it is confronted with its most serious challenges. In fact, important strands of contemporary political theory have sought to tackle precisely the question of the relevant polity, albeit under a different heading and in the domestic, not the postnational framework. The recent interest in the rights of minority groups is, at least in part, about the multiplication and contestation of polities within the state setting. We have already seen some of the implications in Chandran Kukathas's work, but also those theories operating on more classical liberal ground are ultimately concerned with the scope of the polity. Will Kymlicka's influential vision of group rights, for example, not only focuses on the classical individual or collective rights to protect cultural spaces from state intervention, but also takes into view the political rights necessary for the realization of individual autonomy.[97] Self-government rights—through distinct group institutions as well as through participation in central decision-making structures of the state—are crucial to this approach. But this is only another way to express the idea that within the state different polities compete. And this idea is taken further by those who call for the recognition of difference beyond the realm of classical minorities—difference on the basis of culture, gender, belief etc. What had classically merely engendered calls for negative individual rights, has now often turned into arguments for political rights—for the acceptance of a multiplicity of publics that need to be related to formal institutions in novel, often still uncharted ways.[98]

---

[96] J Habermas, *Between Facts and Norms* (W Rehg, trans), Cambridge, MA: MIT Press, 1996, ch 3, especially p 128; in a similar vein, Rawls, 'Reply to Habermas', 409–21.

[97] W Kymlicka, *Multicultural Citizenship*, Oxford: Clarendon Press, 1995.

[98] See, eg, Young, *Inclusion*, chs 3 and 5.

3. From Public Autonomy to Pluralism in Postnational Law

We have now established a basis for thinking about the structure of the post-national order, one in which the public autonomy of citizens, not abstract moral considerations, carries the central burden. This emphasis may, as Waldron has noted in a similar context, lead to 'a dissonance between what one takes to be the right choice and what one takes to be the authoritative choice in political decision-making',[99] but as he points out, this is an unavoidable dissonance in any theory of political authority operating in circumstances of disagreement.[100] Thus we might think that a state-based, a global constitutionalist, or indeed a pluralist order would be most justified in the light of abstract precepts of morality and political theory, but it is only by observing the practices of public autonomy that we can determine which type of order would deserve acceptance. As we will see below, a pluralist order does indeed seem to resonate well with such practices at the present time.

Social Practices

Identifying practices of public autonomy in the postnational context is not an easy task. In the absence of structured public discourses on what the postnational order should look like (instances one might liken to those of 'constitution-making'), indications of how citizens relate to diverging visions of that order remain vague. And what we know about them is likely to engender some pessimism about the possibility of transnational polities. Even in the (politically closely integrated and socially relatively homogeneous) EU context, people still identify to a much greater extent with their national polity than with a European one.[101] One might thus share Alexander Wendt's scepticism as to the possibility of transcending national allegiances—and thus socially grounding deeper postnational integration, perhaps a 'world state'—in the foreseeable future.[102] This certainly casts doubts on visions of cosmopolitanism and global constitutionalism that situate ultimate authority in a (however much imagined) global constitution—for this would imply a primacy of the polity framework determined in a global polity which does not correspond, even remotely, with the preferences expressed by citizens.

---

[99]   Waldron, *Law and Disagreement*, 246.

[100]   ibid.

[101]   Eurobarometer of Autumn 2003, 27–8, available at: <http://ec.europa.eu/public_opinion/archives/eb/eb60/eb60_en.htm>: only 3 per cent of respondents regarded themselves as Europeans only; another 7 per cent as Europeans first and then citizens of their own country.

[102]   A Wendt, 'A Comment on Held's Cosmopolitanism' in Shapiro & Hacker-Cordón, *Democracy's Edges*, 127–33.

Yet does this imply a return to the primacy of national polities? It probably would if we were faced with a binary choice: if individuals had to choose between being part of a transnational (global or European) and a national polity, we could safely assume that they would opt for the latter. As we have already seen in Chapter 2, in the European context, when asked to rank their different identifications, citizens rank that with their member state consistently, and by a large margin, higher than that with Europe. However, more than half see themselves not solely as 'nationals' but also as 'Europeans'.[103] This suggests a multiplication of feelings of belonging among relatively large parts of the population, certainly beyond the elites that are typically thought to be more cosmopolitan-minded.[104] How deep this runs, and to what degree it might extend beyond Europe, is unclear; comprehensive data on such questions on a worldwide scale is simply lacking. However, anecdotal evidence shows that citizens might be more ready to grant global institutions extensive powers than is often assumed. For example, in the US, a 2009 poll found that more than a quarter of respondents supported 'a leading role [for the United Nations] where all countries are required to follow U.N. policies'.[105] In a 2004 poll, 68 per cent of respondents supported majority decision-making in international economic organizations while only 29 per cent insisted on a veto power for the US;[106] other polls suggest that at least one-third, and possibly as many as two-thirds, of Americans want the US to comply with WTO dispute-settlement decisions even when they conflict with domestic policies.[107] And a 1999 poll found that 73 per cent of respondents regarded themselves as 'citizens of the world' as well as citizens of the United States.[108] Relatively broad acceptance of global decision-making can also be

---

[103] See N Fligstein, *Euroclash: The EU, European Identity, and the Future of Europe*, Oxford: Oxford University Press, 2008, ch 5; J A Caporaso & M Kim, 'The Dual Nature of European Identity: Subjective Awareness and Coherence', *Journal of European Public Policy* 16 (2009), 19–42 at 23–30.

[104] For such a focus on elites, see Wendt, 'Held's Cosmopolitanism', 128–9.

[105] Gallup, 'Americans Remain Critical of the United Nations', 13 March 2009, <http://www.gallup.com/poll/116812/Americans-Remain-Critical-United-Nations.aspx>.

[106] Chicago Council on Foreign Relations, 'Global Views 2004: American Public Opinion and Foreign Policy', 42, <http://www.ccfr.org/UserFiles/File/POS_Topline%20Reports/POS%202004/US%20Public%20Opinion%20Global_Views_2004_US.pdf>.

[107] See the conflicting evidence in Chicago Council, ibid, and that reported in Americans and the World, 'International Trade', <http://www.americans-world.org/digest/global_issues/intertrade/wto.cfm>.

[108] See the report, Americans and the World, 'Globalization', <http://www.americans-world.org/digest/global_issues/globalization/values.cfm>.

found in worldwide polls. In 2007, between 26 and 78 per cent of respondents in sixteen countries (and pluralities or majorities in ten of them) agreed that their country 'should be more willing to make decisions within the United Nations even if this means that [their country] will sometimes have to go along with a policy that is not its first choice'.[109]

We should not read too much into these data,[110] but they do suggest that the nation-state is no longer the sole focus of political loyalties. Instead, they reflect a multiplicity of overlapping, sometimes conflicting identities and loyalties, of varying acceptances of different political structures depending on the issue and the situation at hand.[111] This is closely linked to the diagnosis of a multiplication of 'publics', of structures of communication and identification, both in domestic and transnational relations.[112] In this picture, loyalties to subnational groups meet (and conflict) with national allegiances, just as cosmopolitan leanings interact (sometimes clash) with loyalties for regional, national, subnational collectives.[113]

If we think that such facts matter as part of the practices by which individuals determine the shape and size of their polities, we might indeed regard as most adequate a framework in which ultimate authority is diffused. As Michael Sandel suggests,

> [o]nly a regime that disperses sovereignty both upward and downward can combine the power required to rival global market forces with the differentiation required of a public life that hopes to inspire the reflective allegiance of citizens.[114]

In this vein, a pluralist postnational order may well be the best reflection of contemporary social practices—or at least a better reflection of them than either nationalist or global constitutionalist visions.

---

[109] WorldPublicOpinion.org, 'World Publics Favor New Powers for the UN', 9 May 2007, <http://www.worldpublicopinion.org/pipa/articles/btunitednationsra/355.php?lb=btun&pnt=355&nid=&id=>.

[110] On problems with the European data, based on Eurobarometer polls, see Caporaso & Kim, 'European Identity', 23.

[111] For a similar description, see, eg, M J Sandel, *Democracy's Discontent*, Cambridge, MA: Harvard University Press, 1996, 350.

[112] J Dryzek, *Deliberative Global Politics: Discourse and Democracy in a Divided World*, Cambridge: Polity Press, 2006; Bohman, *Democracy across Borders*.

[113] On the two directions of shifts of loyalties, see also Torbisco Casals, 'Beyond Unity and Coherence: The Challenge of Legal Pluralism in a Post-National World', *Revista Jurídica de la Universidad de Puerto Rico* 77 (2008), 531–51.

[114] Sandel, *Democracy's Discontent*, 345.

Public Autonomy

Social practices alone, however, will be insufficient to ground a normatively satisfactory conception of the postnational order. Throughout the previous sections, and in contrast to the more abstract moral approaches that have so far dominated the debate, I have emphasized participation and public autonomy as crucial elements of such a conception. But 'public autonomy' is not exhausted by a mere expression of attitudes or will by citizens. If we think of public autonomy as an expression of a right to 'self-legislation', the element of will has to be complemented by a specification of the conditions under which it can coincide with everybody else's self-legislation: for it is only conceivable as a consequence of the equal autonomy of all. In a Habermasian interpretation, social practices deserve the attribute 'public autonomy' when they concretize the discursive requirements that allow all to be the authors of the rules to which they are subject. As we have seen above in the example of rights, this leads to a circular relationship between social practices and the conditions under which they acquire normative, democratic significance: for the practices have to both satisfy and specify such conditions. Popular sovereignty in this reading

> is no longer embodied in a visibly identifiable gathering of autonomous citizens. It pulls back into the, as it were, 'subjectless' forms of communication circulating through forums and legislative bodies.[115] In the constitution-making acts of a legally binding interpretation of the system of rights, citizens make an originary use of a civic autonomy that thereby constitutes itself in a self-referential manner.[116]

Social practices therefore constitute exercises of public autonomy when they can be understood as a specification of the idea of 'self-legislation'. For Habermas, public autonomy is typically exercised within an existing polity frame; in fact, the discursive conditions of democracy 'explain the performative meaning of the practice of self-determination on the part of legal consociates who recognize one another as free and equal members of an association they have joined voluntarily'.[117] Yet constructively, there is no need to limit this approach to the discourse *within* a pre-established association—if, as I have argued above, democracy must apply to the determination of the polity itself, the reach of public autonomy has to extend to the processes by which an association, or multiple associations, are formed.[118]

---

[115] Habermas, *Between Facts and Norms*, 136.

[116] ibid, 128.

[117] ibid, 110.

[118] If one sees discursive requirements, as Habermas does, as the necessary *implications* of communicative practices, a restriction to the national polity seems

Processes pertaining to the scope of a polity would then count as an exercise of public autonomy when they represent a plausible interpretation of what it means, for self-legislating individuals, to order the global political space.

It is at this point that more substantive considerations about the right scope of the polity re-enter the debate. As we have seen in the discussion in Section II, various theoretical frameworks compete here—cosmopolitan, republican, nationalist, etc. Yet one defining trait of the debate, certainly from a broadly liberal perspective, is the tension between universality and particularity: the tension between an emphasis on inclusiveness of all those affected, on the one hand, and an insistence on self-determination by groups with particular commonalities and common goals, on the other. There is little ground for prioritizing one of these aspects over the other, and as I have shown above, this difficulty, and the more general problem of countervailing principles, has led commentators to argue for a pluralist order as a means to accommodate the different claims.[119]

As we now return to the issue from a more procedural vantage point, this competition of plausible approaches suggests that individuals have multiple options when it comes to defining what it would mean, for self-legislating individuals, to order the global political space. Yet any determination of the relevant polity through the social practices of some will always have to give an account of how it takes seriously, on the one hand, the claims of outsiders to be included and, on the other, the claims of groups of insiders to pursue their particular goals through their own structures. If it cannot give an account of how to strike that balance, it will hardly count as an exercise of public autonomy.

Plural Polities and Institutions

What kind of order does this suggest after all? As we have seen, social practices pertaining to the structure of the postnational order, reflecting as they do a multiplicity of identities and loyalties, would certainly allow for, and probably favour, an order that disperses ultimate authority, that leaves contests for ultimate authority open—a pluralist order. Such an order would not stand in tension with the idea of self-legislation whose implications for public autonomy I have just sketched. It might indeed be a way to avoid singling out one level of decision-making over others: it might steer clear from the absolute (and problematic) claims of all polities and bring them into a relationship

---

hardly warranted: even within the nation-state, communication with most others only takes place in a mediated way, so the difference with the postnational realm is largely a gradual one.

[119] See Section II.3 above.

of checks and balances.[120] For alternative accounts, a justification in terms of public autonomy is more difficult. This is clearest for global constitutionalist models which, as I have already mentioned, do not resonate well with current social practices. And nationalist models, which are closer to such practices, have problems showing a sufficient orientation towards inclusiveness. They may rightly claim that decision-making in a national framework allows for denser democratic deliberation and thicker forms of solidarity,[121] but this is an argument based on benefits to insiders, and it does not seem to give much weight to the right of outsiders to be self-legislating. This problem should at least caution us not to interpret social practices too easily in purely nationalist terms.

This framework should also be able to guide us when it comes to the more concrete shape of such a pluralist order. As I mentioned above, conceptualizations of pluralism in the European Union typically do not (and need not) problematize the question of which polities (and what institutions) deserve respect—too obviously are these the national and European polities and their respective institutions. Beyond the EU, though, the candidates are many and their credentials often unclear; moreover, the link between polities and institutions will often be tenuous.

Which polities deserve respect and tolerance will then depend, again, on the degree to which they are based on practices of public autonomy: on social practices that concretize the idea of self-legislation. The weight of a collective's claim will follow from the strength of its social grounding, of the participatory practices that support it as well as the plausibility of its attempt to balance inclusiveness and particularity. And whether an *institution* deserves respect will result from the links it has with a given polity. An international institution may, for example, derive its powers from national polities and thus benefit from their standing if it is sufficiently controlled by them. Or it may claim to represent a broader, transnational (and necessarily less graspable) polity; if this claim succeeds, it will then depend on whether there is actual social support for such a polity and its institutional expression.

In all cases, such support will have to be scrutinized as to its public autonomy credentials: as to its deliberative pedigree as well as its inclusiveness or the strength of its argument for furthering particular goals. Thus, polities and institutions will not deserve respect if they are based on exclusion, leaving out substantial parts of those affected by its decisions, without providing a compelling justification. Cases such as the Organisation for Economic Co-Operation and Development (OECD) negotiating foreign investment rules mainly targeted at outsiders, the Basel Committee drawing up financial

---

[120] ibid.

[121] See Miller, *National Responsibility and Global Justice*.

regulation for the rest of the world, or the FATF enforcing money-laundering standards against recalcitrant third parties would be the most obvious examples.[122] Likewise, private regulation may easily fail to satisfy public autonomy demands—it typically represents rule-making efforts by corporate actors without broader civil society input or a link to domestic political processes. For example, the *lex mercatoria*—so celebrated by Teubner[123]—will have to be scrutinized for its links to public processes beyond the reciprocal commitments of global traders. Some forms of private regulation may be able to make more plausible claims: the Forest Stewardship Council, for example, has established a complex institutional structure by which it integrates civil society and business groups as well as state representatives in its decision-making.[124]

More broadly, where a polity shows a strong mobilization of deliberative resources or puts forward an effective claim to respect for particular values, it might gain standing vis-à-vis others, and it might endow institutions that represent it with a strong position in the global institutional interplay. As we will see in Chapter 6, in the dispute over trade with genetically modified organisms (GMO) products, WTO law can base its claim to regulatory power on delegation from and broader inclusiveness than national or regional settings, but the latter point suffers from its refusal to take account of the widely supported Biosafety Protocol. On the other hand, the European, national and local insistence on ultimate decision-making power puts forward a claim deeply rooted in popular sentiment and democratic practices, thus counterbalancing its lack of inclusiveness to a certain extent. None of these sites of governance can assert a full realization of public autonomy, which is in any event elusive in postnational governance. But the picture is one of gradual differences—some sites' claims have a stronger justification than others.

In practice, a claim's effectiveness will hinge on its persuasiveness to other collectives and institutions. For if we take seriously the multiplication of polities and their pluralist, heterarchical character, we will not conceive of any overarching, unifying polity, institution, or framework of rules. We will instead lean towards the conflict-of-laws model I have sketched earlier

---

[122] On those processes, see, eg, J Salzman, 'Labor Rights, Globalization and Institutions: The Role and Influence of the Organization for Economic Cooperation and Development', *Michigan Journal of International Law* 21 (2000), 769–848 at 805–31; M S Barr & G P Miller, 'Global Administrative Law: The View from Basel', *European Journal of International Law* 17 (2006), 15–46; Hülsse, 'Clubs'.

[123] See, eg, Teubner, 'Global Bukowina'.

[124] See E Meidinger, 'The Administrative Law of Global Public-Private Regulation: The Case of Forestry', *European Journal of International Law* 17 (2006), 47–87.

as an example of systemic pluralism: a model that requires each polity, in an exercise of public autonomy through its institutions, to define the terms on which it interacts with others. Different polities may then come to conflicting terms: as the idea of public autonomy leaves concretization to social practice, such conflicts are only to be expected. Yet this does not imply an all-out laissez-faire; as we have seen, to deserve the attribute of 'public autonomy', social practices have to meet substantial conditions—if not in legal, then in moral terms.

The resulting structure of the postnational order is likely to be complex and fluid, constantly subject to readjustment and challenge. Different polities compete for recognition, and different institutions seek to link with them (though not necessarily in exclusive ways) to ground their standing. This pluralist structure might resemble an 'archipelago'[125] and will be hard to navigate, but this difficulty is only a reflection of the undecided, diverse character of postnational society in which a recognition of the need to cooperate coincides with the insistence on local, particular allegiances and values. We have to respect this if we are to take seriously the idea of individuals as self-legislating equals in the definition of the political framework. Pursuing unity and coherence through clear-cut hierarchies or constitutionalization would be an imposition on them, however well-meaning or advisable in the abstract.

IV. CONCLUSION

In the search for paradigms for the emerging postnational order, pluralism has long been seen as, at best, a fitting description. Normatively, it has been regarded as inferior to constitutionalist models that promise a principled, reasoned framework for a structure of global governance which today appears as accidental, haphazard, and driven by material power rather than good argument. In this chapter, I have tried to show that this view seriously underestimates pluralism's normative appeal. For not only does a pluralist order have considerable strengths in terms of its adaptability, of the space for contestation it opens up, and of the checks and balances between different polities that it creates by leaving the relationships between legal systems undefined. Pluralism is also closer to foundational ideals of political order— namely public autonomy—than rival approaches: the plural, divided identities, loyalties, and allegiances that characterize postnational society are better reflected in a multiplicity of orders than in an overarching framework that implies ultimate authority.

[125] Kukathas, *Liberal Archipelago*.

Connected to the ideal of public autonomy, pluralism is also not the laissez-faire approach it is sometimes thought to be. Instead, polities and institutions gain respect from others only if they reflect a vision of how self-legislating equals might order the postnational political space—if they are grounded in social practices with deliberative pedigree and can make a claim to bring inclusiveness and attention to particularity into a plausible balance. This kind of pluralism does indeed 'pose demands on reality',[126] yet the demands are not institutionalized in an overarching legal framework, and such an institutional openness naturally creates anxiety regarding stability, the rule of law, and the influence of power. But pluralism does not necessarily fare worse in these respects than a constitutionalism realistically constructed. For in the non-ideal circumstances of postnational society, we could not expect to attain constitutionalism in its ideal fom: as in divided domestic societies, the necessary accommodation of diversity is likely to weaken its promise of a reasoned, principled order to a significant extent. After all, constitutionalism, just as pluralism, is heavily conditioned by the society it operates in.

This suggests that in the conceptualization and construction of the postnational order we should proceed with significant caution. Caution, first, as regards the deficits of the competing visions: for in the non-ideal circumstances of postnational society, all attempts at constructing order will have serious weaknesses, and it is of little use to compare them to ideal models or to domestic political orders which often operate in far more benign conditions. Caution, secondly, as regards the transferability of domestic models: for we cannot expect those models to achieve the same goals and further the same values in the postnational as in the domestic context. As we have seen in Chapter 2, constitutionalism in its weaker, accommodatory form responds to diversity, but it fails to realize democracy and the rule of law to the same extent as the ideal form promises. And caution, thirdly, as regards the prospects of institutionalization: most modern political theory is closely linked to the idea that institutions and law, if rightly designed, are crucial to furthering political justice. In the postnational realm, though, this is less certain: here, as in other highly unequal settings, institutions may instead largely serve to reflect and entrench the interests and values of particular actors, of particular parts of society.

Such caution should prevent us from jumping to conclusions in favour of legalization and constitutionalization, but also from leaping into the opposite direction. In this chapter, I have presented a normative argument for pluralism, but one of a relatively abstract kind. Many important normative concerns have only been touched upon, if at all—we may still wonder

---

[126] *Pace* Koskenniemi, 'Fate of Public International Law', 23.

whether a stable and fair political order is indeed possible in a pluralist setting or whether pluralism allows us to realize ideals of democracy and the rule of law. Many commentators have voiced such concerns, and I will address them more directly in Chapters 7 and 8.

However, before we are able to form a clearer view on them—and on the prevalence and functioning of pluralism in postnational law more generally—we should leave the current level of abstraction and look in greater detail at central areas of postnational governance in which constitutionalist and pluralist analyses are in particular tension. In Chapters 4 to 6, I will thus analyse the European human rights regime, UN sanctions and their implementation, and global risk regulation in the example of the dispute over trade in GMO products. European human rights are often seen as a particularly good example of postnational constitutionalization; global security poses a particular challenge for stability; and the GMO dispute has been termed an exemplary case of 'when cooperation fails'[127] because of rival regulatory approaches. These instances thus present hard cases for the pluralist vision, and though three case studies are certainly too narrow to ground ultimate conclusions, they should allow us better to gauge the virtues and vices of constitutionalism and pluralism in the postnational order. The final chapters will then draw the insights from the case studies together and place them into perspective. It is only then that we will see whether the broad normative argument advanced in the present chapter holds up to scrutiny.

---

[127] M A Pollack & G C Shaffer, *When Cooperation Fails: The International Law and Politics of Genetically Modified Foods*, Oxford: Oxford University Press, 2009.

PART II

PLURALISM IN POSTNATIONAL PRACTICE

4

The Open Architecture of European Human Rights Law

European human rights law is often regarded as a poster child of postnational constitutionalization. Its development does indeed seem to follow a clear progress narrative: the European Court of Human Rights (ECtHR), initially simply an international tribunal, has shed its modest origins and begun to resemble a supranational constitutional court, with broad decision-making powers, an ever stronger anchoring in the domestic legal orders of member states, and general acceptance of its authority as the ultimate arbiter of human rights disputes in Europe. In this vein, the story of the Strasbourg Court appears as part of the successful implementation of a constitutional model of politics, in which the law lays down the ground rules of political life and enforces them through effective judicial bodies.[1] The European Convention of Human Rights (ECHR), so it seems, had become a constitutional instrument, and the ECtHR has been happy to reinforce that vision in its jurisprudence.[2]

---

[1] See, eg, C Walter, 'Die Europäische Menschenrechtskonvention als Konstitutionalisierungsprozeß', *Zeitschrift für ausländisches öffentliches Recht und Völkerrecht* 59 (1999), 961–83; F Hoffmeister, 'Die Europäische Menschenrechtskonvention als Grundrechtsverfassung und ihre Bedeutung in Deutschland', *Der Staat* 40 (2001), 349–81; E de Wet, 'The Emergence of International and Regional Value Systems as a Manifestation of the Emerging International Constitutional Order', *Leiden Journal of International Law* 19 (2006), 611–32; see also the discussion in J-F Flauss, 'La Cour européenne des droits de l'homme est-elle une Cour constitutionnelle?', *Revue française de droit constitutionnel* 36 (1998), 711–28. Related ideas are voiced, for example, by J A Frowein, 'The European Convention on Human Rights as the Public Order of Europe', *Collected Courses of the Academy of European Law*, vol 1:2 (1992), 267–358; S Greer, *The European Convention on Human Rights: Achievements, Problems and Prospects*, Cambridge: Cambridge University Press, 2006, 165–89 (the ECtHR as a court with a 'constitutional mission').

[2] ECtHR, Judgment of 23 March 1995, *Loizidou v Turkey (preliminary objections)*, para 75; ECtHR, Judgment of 30 June 2005, *Bosphorus Hava Yolları Turizm v Ireland*,

At times, though, this narrative has to face a less harmonious reality, and when this happens, particular indignation ensues. Thus, when in its October 2004 *Görgülü* judgment the German Constitutional Court signalled limits to its loyalty to the ECtHR,[3] it provoked an outcry not only among scholarly commentators but also in the press and led Strasbourg judges to drop their typical reserve and voice frustration in public. The president of the ECtHR and the German judge on the Court expressed serious concerns about the ramifications of the German judgment, prompting a vigorous reply by the Constitutional Court's president, all in prominent places in the German press.[4] What the Constitutional Court had done was to hold that domestic courts could (and should) disregard Strasbourg judgments when they are incompatible with central elements of the domestic legal order, legislative intent, or constitutional provisions.[5] This would have been unsurprising if it had concerned the place of other international agreements in German law. In the case of the ECHR, it ran counter to an entrenched constitutionalist vision and thus sparked massive reactions.

Görgülü was widely interpreted as a warning shot in response to an ECtHR judgment a few months earlier, which had censured the German court's approach to the right of celebrities from media intrusion.[6] Other courts, too, have fired such shots: in late 2009, for example, the Italian Constitutional Court emphasized that national courts did not have to follow Strasbourg jurisprudence when this would produce a conflict with constitutional

---

para 156 (the Convention as a 'constitutional instrument of European public order').

[3] Bundesverfassungsgericht, Judgment of 14 October 2004, *Görgülü*, 2 BvR 1481/04, BVerfGE 111, 307. An English translation is available at: <http://www.bverfg.de/entscheidungen/rs20041014_2bvr148104en.html>.

[4] See 'Im Ausland mißverständlich', Frankfurter Allgemeine Zeitung, 23 October 2004, 5; 'Welches Gericht hat das letzte Wort?', Frankfurter Allgemeine Zeitung, 10 December 2004, 4; and the interviews with the then president of the ECtHR, Luzius Wildhaber, 'Das tut mir weh', Der Spiegel 47/2004, 15 November 2004, 50; and with the president of the German Constitutional Court, Hans-Jürgen Papier, 'Straßburg ist kein oberstes Rechtsmittelgericht', Frankfurter Allgemeine Zeitung, 9 December 2004, 5. The strong resonance in the German press is reflected in editorials by Reinhard Müller, 'Das letzte Wort', Frankfurter Allgemeine Zeitung, 23 October 2004, 1; and Heribert Prantl, 'Juristisches Röhren', Süddeutsche Zeitung, 20 October 2004, 4.

[5] For a short summary and comment on the decision, see F Hoffmeister, 'Germany: Status of European Convention on Human Rights in Domestic Law', *International Journal of Constitutional Law* 4 (2006), 722–31.

[6] ECtHR, Judgment of 24 June 2004, *Von Hannover v Germany*.

norms.[7] It did so explicitly, in an aside irrelevant for the case at hand, with a tone quite different from a landmark ruling two years earlier[8]—and just two weeks after the ECtHR had found the presence of crucifixes in Italian classrooms to be in violation of the Convention,[9] much to the dismay of the Italian public.[10]

Such elements of resistance, or attempts at distancing, cast doubt on the constitutionalization narrative. There is no question that the ECtHR has, over the almost fifty years of its existence, gained remarkable authority; that its judgments enjoy high rates of compliance; and that they are now regularly cited by national courts in many, perhaps most member states.[11] Yet this ever closer linkage between the national and European levels of human rights protection has been accompanied by reservations in many national legal systems, and in remarkably similar terms. As a result, it is no longer useful to see domestic and European human rights law, in the classical domestic/international dichotomy, as different legal orders—the European human rights regime is, in the vocabulary introduced in Chapter 1, an example of 'postnational law'.[12] But it also does not form an integrated whole, neatly organized according to rules of hierarchy and a clear distribution of tasks as the constitutionalist vision would have it.

This chapter argues that the order we see emerging instead is a 'pluralist' one—pluralist in the sense I have outlined in the previous chapter. It is an order in which the relationships of the constituent parts are governed not by an overarching legal framework but primarily by politics, often judicial politics; where we find heterarchy, not hierarchy.[13] I seek to substantiate

---

[7] Corte Costituzionale, Judgment of 16 November 2009, Sentenza 311/2009.

[8] Corte Costituzionale, Judgments of 22 October 2007, Sentenze 348 & 349/2007.

[9] ECtHR, Judgment of 3 November 2009, *Lautsi v Italy*.

[10] See, eg, J Hooper, 'Human Rights Ruling Against Classroom Crucifixes Angers Italy', 3 November 2009, <http://www.guardian.co.uk/world/2009/nov/03/italy-classroom-crucifixes-human-rights>.

[11] For comparative studies, see R Blackburn & J Polakiewicz (eds), *Fundamental Rights in Europe: The European Convention on Human Rights and its Member States, 1950–2000*, Oxford: Oxford University Press, 2001; H Keller & A Stone Sweet (eds), *A Europe of Rights: The Impact of the ECHR on National Legal Systems*, Oxford: Oxford University Press, 2008.

[12] See also H Keller & A Stone Sweet, 'Assessing the Impact of the ECHR on National Legal Systems' in Keller & Stone Sweet, *Europe of Rights*, 677–712 at 710.

[13] For related accounts in the ECHR context, see M Delmas-Marty, *Towards a Truly Common Law: Europe as a Laboratory for Legal Pluralism* (N Norberg, trans), Cambridge: Cambridge University Press, 2002; E Lambert, *Les effets des arrêts de*

this claim in Section I of this chapter by showing that the friction apparent in *Görgülü* and in the Italian case is the norm rather than the exception in European human rights law. I do this through case studies of Spain and France, which are generally regarded as fitting the constitutionalist narrative of European human rights law well; in both, however, surface appearance and actual practice diverge considerably.

In Section II, I take up one of the concerns about pluralism sketched at the end of Chapter 3—the claim that it is bound to produce instability rather than order. To address this issue I try to show how the European human rights regime, despite its pluralism and contestation about fundamentals, has come to work—how mutual accommodation rather than friction has come to characterize its everyday operation. Here, I have chosen two orders—the European Union and the United Kingdom—which exhibit a strong pluralism on a formal level but a remarkable degree of harmony and convergence in practice, and I am interested in how this harmony has come about and why. In Section III, I draw on this material to reflect more generally on the respective virtues of pluralism and constitutionalism in the construction of a postnational legal order, and on some of the conditions for the stability and success of such a pluralist structure.

I. THE OPENNESS OF EUROPEAN HUMAN RIGHTS LAW

Even though the German judgment in *Görgülü* caused such concern, Germany had never been a model case for the constitutionalist story. The ECHR is incorporated into German law, but only with the rank of a statute. Its position is strengthened by a presumption that other statutes are not intended to violate it, and by the Constitutional Court's view, expressed since the 1980s, that it can have recourse to the Convention when interpreting fundamental rights in the *Grundgesetz*. Yet in practice, though actual friction has been rare, the ECHR has played a limited role in German jurisprudence, due in large part to the strength of domestic rights and the Constitutional Court's case law on them.[14]

---

la *Cour européenne des droits de l'homme: Contribution à une approche pluraliste du droit européen des droits de l'homme*, Brussels: Emile Bruylant, 1999.

[14] See A Zimmermann, 'Germany' in Blackburn & Polakiewicz, *Fundamental Rights in Europe*, 335–54; J A Frowein, 'Der europäische Grundrechtsschutz und die deutsche Rechtsprechung', *Neue Zeitschrift für Verwaltungsrecht* 21 (2002), 29–33; C Gusy, 'Die Rezeption der EMRK in Deutschland' in C Grewe & C Gusy (eds), *Menschenrechte in der Bewährung: Die Rezeption der Europäischen Menschenrechtskonvention in Frankreich und Deutschland im Vergleich*, Baden-Baden:

The constitutionalist story thus finds stronger support in other parts of Europe, with countries such as Belgium, the Netherlands, or Switzerland at the forefront; here, the ECHR can be seen as a 'shadow constitution' replacing a national bill of rights.[15] This trend has more recently been reinforced by the high status the Convention enjoys in many of the new member states in Central and Eastern Europe, even if it may still be too early to draw conclusions on its practical impact.[16] But high status does not necessarily translate into general compliance, as is reflected, for example, in the case of Austria. In Austria the Convention enjoys constitutional rank and Austrian courts, especially the Austrian Constitutional Court, cite Convention articles as well as Strasbourg jurisprudence regularly and extensively.[17] Yet in its 1987 *Miltner* judgment (which is remarkably similar to *Görgülü*), the Constitutional Court had already made it clear that there were limits to its loyalty to Strasbourg, and if the ECtHR stretched its law-making functions too far, it would not be able to follow it.[18] The particular problem that provoked this holding was solved by legislation and open friction has been rare since, but the *Miltner* judgment has not been overturned and instances of Viennese resistance to Strasbourg remain.[19]

In what follows, as indicated above, I will concentrate on two other cases that are generally seen to reflect the constitutionalist trajectory. This is particularly so for Spain where the ECHR enjoys supra-legislative status and is also a constitutionally mandated tool for the interpretation of the Spanish

Nomos, 2005, 129–58; E Lambert Abdelgawad & A Weber, 'The Reception Process in France and Germany' in Keller & Stone Sweet, *Europe of Rights*, 107–59.

[15] See Keller & Stone Sweet, 'Assessing the Impact', 686; K Chryssogonos, 'Zur Inkorporation der Europäischen Menschenrechtskonvention in den nationalen Rechtsordnungen der Mitgliedstaaten', *Europarecht* 36 (2001), 49–61.

[16] For initial assessments, see H Keller, 'Reception of the European Convention for the Protection of Human Rights and Fundamental Freedoms (ECHR) in Poland and Switzerland', *Zeitschrift für ausländisches öffentliches Recht und Völkerrecht* 65 (2005), 283–349; M Krzyz.anowska-Mierzewska, 'The Reception Process in Poland and Slovakia' in Keller & Stone Sweet, *Europe of Rights*, 531–602; A Nußberger, 'The Reception Process in Russia and Ukraine', ibid, 603–74.

[17] See H Tretter, 'Austria' in Blackburn & Polakiewicz, *Fundamental Rights in Europe*, 103–65; D Thurnherr, 'The Reception Process in Austria and Switzerland' in Keller & Stone Sweet, *Europe of Rights*, 311–91.

[18] Verfassungsgerichtshof, Judgment of 14 October 1987, *Miltner*, VfSlg 11500/1987, available at: <http://www.ris.bka.gv.at/vfgh/>.

[19] On a recent problematic case, see W Karl & E C Schöpfer, 'Österreichische Rechtsprechung zur Europäischen Menschenrechtskonvention im Jahr 2004', *Zeitschrift für öffentliches Recht* 61 (2006), 151–200 at 158–9, 198–200.

Constitution; as a result, the Spanish Constitutional Court is one of the most active in the reception of Strasbourg jurisprudence. In France, the reception process has been slower and less enthusiastic, but here, too, the constitution grants the Convention a rank above statutes, and French courts are generally regarded as having reflected this status with increasing faithfulness to Strasbourg.[20] Yet in both cases, the stories are not as clear-cut as the narrative of gradual progress suggests.

1. The Spanish Embrace and its Limits

At first sight, the situation in Spain seems straightforward. Spain is generally regarded as a particularly faithful follower of Strasbourg, and the Spanish Constitutional Court usually ranks among the national courts that cite the ECHR and Strasbourg jurisprudence the most.[21] This is not surprising, given the importance of the Convention in the transition from Franco's dictatorship: as much as it was important for Spain on the international level to demonstrate membership in the club of Western democratic countries, its authority was of great use in stabilizing its new democratic institutions—and particularly the new *Tribunal Constitucional*—internally.[22]

As a result, the ECHR occupies an important position in the Spanish legal order. It ranks, like other treaties, above ordinary legislation,[23] but it is also central to the interpretation and development of the individual rights

---

[20] On the comparative assessment of these cases, see Keller & Stone Sweet, 'Assessing the Impact', 705.

[21] See M-A Eissen, 'L'interaction des jurisprudences constitutionnelles nationales et de la jurisprudence de la Cour européenne des Droits de l'homme' in D Rousseau & F Sudre (eds), *Conseil constitutionnel et Cour européenne des droits de l'homme: Droits et libertés en Europe*, Paris: Editions STH, 1990, 137–215 at 146–7; M C Soriano, 'The Reception Process in Spain and Italy' in Keller & Stone Sweet, *Europe of Rights*, 393–450.

[22] On the constitutional history, see L Martín-Retortillo Baquer, 'La recepción por el Tribunal Constitucional de la jurisprudencia del Tribunal Europeo de Derechos Humanos', *Revista de Administración Publica* 137 (1995), 7–29 at 8, 12. On the concrete points of dispute over the insertion of a reference to international human rights instruments, see L Martín-Retortillo Baquer, 'Notas para la historia del apartado segundo del artículo 10 de la Constitución' in L Martín-Retortillo Baquer, *La Europa de los derechos humanos*, Madrid: Centro de estudios políticos y constitucionales, 1998, 177–92; A Sáiz Arnaiz, *La apertura constitucional al derecho internacional y europeo de los derechos humanos: El artículo 10.2 de la Constitucion Española*, Madrid: Consejo General del Poder Judicial, 1999, ch 1.

[23] Art 96(1) of the Spanish Constitution. The superior rank has been widely accepted, though only after some disputes in the literature; see G Escobar Roca,

enshrined in the constitution. According to Article 10(2) of the constitution, the 'basic rights and liberties . . . shall be interpreted in conformity with the Universal Declaration of Human Rights and the international treaties and agreements on those matters ratified by Spain', and this has in practice meant primarily the ECHR.[24] In recent years, the *Tribunal Constitucional* (TC) has cited the Convention in one out of five decisions, and in three out of five of its most important—plenary—decisions in individual rights cases,[25] and in a significant number of cases, it has referred to the Convention as the basis for substantial shifts in its case law.[26]

Yet if Article 10(2) seems to demand the strict observance of the ECHR (and of ECtHR jurisprudence[27]) in the interpretation of individual rights, the clause 'in conformity' (*de conformidad*) has often been understood in a flexible way.[28] Sometimes the TC suggests a tight link between the Convention and the content of constitutional rights, understanding Article 10(2) as

'Spain' in Blackburn & Polakiewicz, *Fundamental Rights in Europe*, 809–31 at 812–13.

[24] On the special role of the ECHR, see STC 245/1991, FJ 3; STC 91/2000, FJ 7 (judgments of the *Tribunal Constitucional* are available at: <http://www.tribunal-constitucional.es/en/jurisprudencia/Pages/Buscador.aspx>). A Queralt Jiménez, *La interpretación de los derechos: del Tribunal de Estrasburgo al Tribunal Constitucional*, Madrid: Centro de Estudios Políticos y Constitucionales, 2008, 375–99, demonstrates the TC's preference for the ECHR over the International Covenant on Civil and Political Rights.

[25] Queralt Jiménez, *Interpretación*, 207–10.

[26] ibid, chs 4–6. See also the cases in Sáiz Arnaiz, *Apertura constitucional*, 245–66; Escobar Roca, 'Spain', 815–21. For an important instance of a shift, see, eg, STC 167/2002 of 18 September 2002.

[27] The TC does not make a difference between Convention and jurisprudence, recognizing that it is for the ECtHR 'to concretize the content of the rights recognized in the Convention'; STC 91/2000 of 30 March 2000, FJ 7. Likewise, most of the literature accepts that the status of ECtHR case law is on a par with the Convention as such; see only E García de Enterría, 'Valeur de la jurisprudence de la Cour européenne des Droits de l'Homme en droit espagnol' in F Matscher & H Petzold (eds), *Protecting Human Rights: The European Dimension: Studies in honour of G J Wiarda*, Cologne: Heymanns, 1988, 221–30 at 224; J Delgado Barrio, 'Proyección de las decisiones del Tribunal Europeo de Derechos Humanos en la jurisprudencia española', *Revista de Administración Publica* 119 (1989), 233–52 at 242–5. But see also Sáiz Arnaiz, *Apertura constitucional*, 167–8, who observes a lack of theoretical grounding in the TC's references to ECtHR decisions.

[28] See also Sáiz Arnaiz, *Apertura constitucional*, 207–8, 234–5.

'imposing' a certain reading;[29] but often enough, it uses more ambiguous formulae, describing the ECHR as an 'interpretative criterion' that has to be 'taken into account' in or should 'orient' constitutional interpretation.[30] The actual status of the Convention in the interpretation of fundamental rights thus remains unclear; the TC keeps shifting ground, but ultimately retains flexibility as to the weight it accords Strasbourg judgments, and the ECHR in general.

The affirmation of this flexibility has been most noticeable in two distinct clusters of cases. The first of them concerns the execution of judgments of the ECtHR in Spain. In Spain, as has long been the case in most of Europe, reopening proceedings after they have been closed by a final judgment faces high hurdles, and the ECtHR finding a Convention violation in a given case generally does not suffice. As a result, Spanish courts have traditionally not reacted to such findings, but in 1991, the TC initiated a shift and set aside a domestic judgment found to have violated the right to a fair trial. In the *Bultó* case, it held that because of Article 10(2) a violation of the ECHR constituted in itself also a violation of a constitutional right, and that as a consequence, the TC was under a duty to remedy this violation if no other means were available.[31] This reasoning was a radical enough departure from traditional doctrine to provoke not only a very strong dissenting opinion but also an outcry in the scholarly literature; for the critics, the TC had tied the rights under the Spanish constitution too closely to the jurisprudence of the ECtHR.[32] And indeed, the *Tribunal Constitucional* did not maintain this approach for long.

---

[29] STC 147/2000 of 29 May 2000, FJ 4a. For similar formulae, see STC 167/2002 of 18 September 2002, FJ 9; STC 206/1998 of 26 October 1998, FJ 4; STC 36/1991 of 14 February 1991, FJ 5.

[30] STC 119/2001 of 24 May 2001, FJ 6. Similar formulae can be found in STC 113/1987 of 3 July 1987, FJ 2; STC 24/1981 of 14 July 1981, FJ 4; STC 36/1984 of 14 March 1984, FJ 3. On other international instruments, see STC 38/1981 of 23 November 1981, FJ 4; STC 292/2000 of 30 November 2000, FJ 3; STC 70/2002 of 3 April 2002, FJ 7a.

[31] STC 245/1991 of 16 December 1991; the ECtHR judgment was *Barberà, Messegué and Jabardo v Spain* of 6 December 1988. For a similarly strong linkage between constitutional right and ECHR, see STC 36/1991 of 14 February 1991, FJ 5.

[32] See only C Ruiz Miguel, *La ejecución de las sentencias del Tribunal Europeo de Derechos Humanos*, Madrid: tecnos, 1997, at 138–51; also J A Carrillo Salcedo, 'España y la protección de los derechos humanos: el papel del Tribunal Europeo de Derechos Humanos y del Tribunal constitucional español', *Archiv des Völkerrechts* 32 (1994), 187–201 at 199. But see also the more positive assessment in J L Requejo Pagés, 'La articulación de las jurisdicciones internacional, constitucional y ordinaria en la defensa de los derechos fundamentales', *Revista Española de Derecho Constitucional* 12 (1992) 35 at 179–99.

Two years after *Bultó*, it departed from it rather silently in an unpublished decision in which it emphasized that the TC and the ECtHR operated 'in distinct legal orders'; that the TC, subject only to the Spanish Constitution, enjoyed 'independence in its task of interpretation under Article 10(2)'; and that it was in no way hierarchically subordinate to the Strasbourg court.[33] This new position was a response to a Strasbourg decision in a case (*Ruiz Mateos*) that for more than ten years had attracted much public attention in Spain; and it might have been provoked by the fact that the ECtHR judgment presented a direct challenge to earlier decisions of the TC itself.[34] However, the *Tribunal* has affirmed this more restrictive stance in a number of cases since,[35] and while the result might not differ much from the situation in other countries, the sequence of cases is remarkable as an attempt to reclaim supremacy (and flexibility) after experimenting with a closer link between national and European systems of human rights protection.

A similar dynamic emerges in the second set of cases, which also reflects a broader cultural gap between Spanish and European conceptions of rights.[36] It concerns the effects of environmental pollution on the health and well-being of individuals; an issue that the ECtHR began to tackle from the angle of the right to a private life in the early 1990s.[37] In 1994, it applied its approach in a Spanish case, *López Ostra*, and found that the government had failed to protect the applicant sufficiently from the smells, noise, and polluting fumes emanating from a waste treatment plant nearby.[38] The judgment met with much criticism in Spanish doctrine,[39] and initially with an evasive

[33] TC, Admissibility decision of 31 January 1994, Amparo no 2292/93, in Ruiz Miguel, *Ejecución de las sentencias*, 181–3. The TC's attempts at distinguishing the case from the earlier one were rather weak; see ibid, 151–6.

[34] ECtHR, Judgment of 23 June 1993, *Ruiz-Mateos v Spain*.

[35] See ATC 96/2001 of 24 April 2001 (citing the admissibility decision of 11 March 1999) in the *Castillo Algar* case; STC 313/2005 of 12 December 2005, FJ 3, in the *Perote Pellón* case; and STC 197/2006 of 3 July 2006, in the *Fuentes Bobo* case; see also M Revenga Sánchez, 'En torno a la eficacia de las Sentencias del TEDH: Amparo de ejecución o afianzamiento de doctrina? Una propuesta de reforma', *Revista española de Derecho Europeo* 2004, 521–38 at 527–59. But see also, for a slight shift regarding criminal cases, STC 240/2005 of 10 October 2005, FJ 6.

[36] On these cases, see also Queralt Jiménez, *Interpretación*, 341–51.

[37] See especially ECtHR, Judgment of 21 February 1990, *Powell and Rayner v United Kingdom*.

[38] ECtHR, Judgment of 9 December 1994, *López Ostra v Spain*.

[39] Cf Escobar Roca, 'Spain', 825.

reaction by the TC.[40] It was only seven years later that the *Tribunal* considered the possibility—clearly suggested by the Strasbourg jurisprudence—of an extensive interpretation of the right to privacy (*intimidad*) and to a home in the Spanish constitution. In the 2001 *Moreno Gómez* case, the TC indeed affirmed that this right, as well as the right to physical integrity, might be affected by environmental factors, and in the particular case by an elevated level of outside noise.[41] Yet it stopped short of subscribing fully to the ECtHR's approach, noting—in contrast to its previous jurisprudence—that Article 10(2) did not require a 'literal translation' (*traslación mimética*) of ECtHR decisions, and pointing to the 'normative differences' between the Convention and the constitution.[42] Consequently, it set a high threshold for finding an interference with fundamental rights,[43] and in the present instance did not find that this threshold had been reached. This result, and the more restrictive approach in general,[44] are not surprising in a rather noisy country where tolerance levels are high; the difference in approach from much of the rest of Europe became evident when, three years later, the ECtHR unanimously found a violation of the right to a private life in the same case.[45] What is interesting, however, is the fact that this difference has found reflection in the principles guiding the TC's reception of Strasbourg jurisprudence and has led to a result quite far removed from the 'conformity' with the ECHR that Article 10(2) requires and that, thus far, had not been interpreted so liberally.[46]

   The link between the Spanish Constitution and the ECHR, very close in *Bultó*, later somewhat loosened but still tight, has thus become weaker, offering significant discretion to the *Tribunal Constitucional* in deciding when to follow Strasbourg and how. This should not make us overlook the fact that, as mentioned above, the TC refers to the ECHR and to ECtHR decisions frequently and, in fact, as a matter of normalcy. But this practice appears less as a result of a principled linkage than as a favourable exercise of discretion by

---

[40] STC 199/1996 of 3 December 1996, FJ 2–3, 6. Because the applicant sought the criminal prosecution of those responsible for pollution, the TC could also distinguish the case from that decided by the ECtHR in *López Ostra*; see FJ 4.

[41] STC 119/2001 of 24 May 2005, FJ 5.

[42] ibid, FJ 6.

[43] On the difference from the ECtHR's approach, see the analysis in Queralt Jiménez, *Interpretación*, 345–9.

[44] Later confirmed in STC 16/2004 of 23 February 2004.

[45] ECtHR, Judgment of 16 November 2004, *Moreno Gómez v Spain*.

[46] For a similar approach with regard to the UN Human Rights Committee, see STC 70/2002 of 3 April 2002, FJ 7; Queralt Jiménez, *Interpretación*, 375–99.

the TC in the great number of cases in which the stakes are not too high.[47] For a *Tribunal* that is now in a much less precarious position than in the early years, preserving autonomy seems to have taken precedence over fostering close ties with Strasbourg.

2. *The French* dialogue des juges

The French trajectory is quite different, though perhaps more typical of the general constitutionalist story. Initially convinced that the Convention was a way not to learn but to teach others, France long remained sceptical, ratified it only in 1974 and waited until 1981 to accept individual complaints. Over time, however, the French political and judicial systems have grown increasingly open, reaching a stage where smooth reception is the rule and the constitutionally mandated superiority of the ECHR over domestic legislation is now widely accepted.[48]

In this picture, France is a story of gradual, if slow, progress. The *Conseil constitutionnel*, the equivalent to a constitutional court, rejects the use of the Convention as a standard against which it can measure statutes, but has over time become more receptive to the ECHR, adapting its jurisprudence on domestic liberties to Strasbourg case law without mentioning it.[49] The *Cour de cassation* began to recognize the ECHR's direct effect in the the mid-1970s, made use of it with growing readiness from the 1980s on, and it also

---

[47] For a similar account, see Sáiz Arnaiz, *Apertura constitucional*, 160–1; for a normative defence of such a practice, see V Ferreres Comella, 'El juez nacional ante los derechos fundamentales europeos. Algunas reflexiones en torno a la idea de diálogo', in *Integración europea y poder judicial*, Bilbao: Instituto Vasco de Administración Publica, 2006, 227–65 at 228–37, 244–9.

[48] See generally E Steiner, 'France' in C A Gearty (ed), *European Civil Liberties and the European Convention on Human Rights*, The Hague: Kluwer Law International, 1997; C Dupré, 'France' in Blackburn & Polakiewicz, *Fundamental Rights in Europe*, 313–33; L Heuschling, 'Comparative Law and the European Convention on Human Rights in French Human Rights Cases' in E Örücü (ed), *Judicial Comparativism in Human Rights Cases*, London: UKNCCL and BIICL, 2003, 23–47; M Fromont, 'Le juge français et la Cour européenne des droits de l'homme' in J Bröhmer et al (eds), *Internationale Gemeinschaft und Menschenrechte: Festschrift für Georg Ress*, Cologne: Heymanns, 2005, 965–77; Lambert Abdelgawad & Weber, 'France and Germany'.

[49] See, eg, O Dutheillet de Lamothe, 'European Law and the French Constitutional Council' in G Canivet, M Andenas, & D Fairgrieve (eds), *Comparative Law Before the Courts*, London: BIICL, 2004, 91–8; B Mathieu, 'De quelques exemples récents de l'influence des droits européens sur le juge constitutionnel français', *Dalloz* 2002, no 18, 1439–41.

reacted to Strasbourg judgments often with great speed.[50] Today, commentators observe a normalization, even 'banalization', of the *Cour de cassation*'s use of the ECHR as a check on domestic legislation.[51] The *Conseil d'Etat*, the highest administrative court, has shown greater reluctance and began to recognize the superior rank of the ECHR only in 1990. Since then, however, Strasbourg jurisprudence is reflected much more broadly—the *Conseil d'Etat* now mentions the Convention in more than half its decisions and has, in a remarkable shift, even begun to cite ECtHR case law.[52]

Yet if this general picture reflects a strong domestic anchoring of the Convention and its case law, it also conceals significant friction. Despite the primacy of the ECHR provided for in the constitution, French scholars and judges prefer to see the relationship between the legal orders as one of coordination and that of French and European judges as a 'dialogue'.[53] In this vein, they often regard the authority of ECtHR judgments as limited, especially in cases to which France has not been a party.[54] And even though the image of dialogue suggests harmony, it conceals, as one French scholar puts it, 'the discrete but real play of power between jurisdictions and the capacity of resistance as well as adaptation'.[55]

---

[50] See R de Gouttes, 'Le juge judiciaire français et la Convention européenne des droits de l'homme: avancées et reticences' in P Tavernier (ed), *Quelle Europe pour les droits de l'homme?*, Brussels: Emile Bruylant, 1996, 217–34; R de Gouttes, 'La Convention Européenne des Droits de l'Homme et le juge français', *Revue Internationale de Droit Comparé* 51 (1999), 7–20; Steiner, 'France', 294–8.

[51] P Wachsmann, quoted in F Sudre, 'Vers la normalisation des relations entre le Conseil d'Etat et la Cour européenne des droits de l'homme', *Revue française de droit administratif* 2006, 286–98 at 287.

[52] See Lambert Abdelgawad & Weber, 'France and Germany', 128; R Abraham, 'Le juge administratif français et la cour de Strasbourg' in Tavernier, *Quelle Europe*, 235–47; Sudre, 'Vers la normalisation', especially 287–8; Conseil d'Etat, Decision of 20 December 2005, no 288253.

[53] See Abraham, 'Le juge administratif français', 245–7; Sudre, 'Vers la normalisation'; J Andriantsimbazovina, *L'autorité des décisions de justice constitutionnelles et européennes sur le juge administratif français*, Paris: LGDJ, 1998, 441–515; Heuschling, 'Comparative Law and the ECHR', 35; also de Gouttes, 'Le juge judiciaire', 234; and the similar approaches in L Potvin-Solis, *L'effet des jurisprudences européennes sur la jurisprudence du Conseil d'Etat français*, Paris: LGDJ, 1999; Lambert, *Effet des arrêts de la CourEDH*.

[54] On the scholarly dispute over whether Strasbourg jurisprudence enjoys interpretative authority at all, or whether French courts remain free to interpret the Convention themselves, see Heuschling, 'Comparative Law and the ECHR', 30–2.

[55] Mathieu, 'Quelques examples récents', 1439–41.

This capacity of resistance has indeed become apparent in a number of cases. It has been verbalized most strongly in the *Conseil d'Etat*, and in particular by its *Commissaires du Gouvernement* (CdG), the official amici of the *Conseil*. Already in 1978, one of them had insisted that the *Conseil d'Etat* had 'an autonomous and sovereign power of interpretation entirely comparable to the power to interpret domestic rules'; conflicts with the ECtHR were thus not solved legally, as a matter of principle, but should be avoided for reasons of 'convenience and political realism'.[56] And still in 1997, another CdG stated that 'when you apply the provisions of the Convention, you attach a lot of importance to the latest interpretation given by the European Court, but you cannot consider yourself as being legally bound by this interpretation'.[57]

The limits of the ECtHR's authority over French courts became clearer in the dispute over the *Poitrimol* case—an example of resistance or, in the words of an advocate-general at the *Cour de cassation*, 'rebellion' of French courts against Strasbourg.[58] In its 1993 *Poitrimol* decision, the ECtHR regarded a classical element of French criminal procedure—the loss of the right of appeal for an accused who fails to appear in person—as a violation of the right to a fair trial.[59] Over the next six years, despite further condemnations of France in Strasbourg,[60] French courts refused to set aside their procedural rules. At first, they ignored the ECtHR's judgment; later, they openly defied it by insisting on their own interpretation of Article 6 ECHR; and only in 1999 did the *Cour de cassation* shift its approach to some extent, thereby anticipating a legislative amendment adopted in 2000.[61] In 2001, it finally accepted the authority of the ECtHR on a parallel issue, with the reporting judge noting

---

[56] Conclusions of D Labetoulle, cited in Heuschling, 'Comparative Law and the ECHR', 32.

[57] Conclusions of G Bachelier, cited ibid.

[58] de Gouttes, 'Le juge judiciaire', 232–3.

[59] ECtHR, Judgment of 23 November 1993, *Poitrimol v France*.

[60] ECtHR, Judgments of 29 July 1998, *Omar v France*, *Guérin v France*; Judgment of 14 December 1999, *Khalfaoui v France*.

[61] Cour de cassation, Judgment of 19 January 1994, no 93-80163, *Bulletin criminel* 1994, no 27, 50; Judgment of 7 February 1994, no 93-81533; Judgment of 9 January 1995, no 94-81696, *Bulletin criminel* 1995, no 7, 18; Judgment of 30 June 1999, *Rebboah*, no 98-80923, *Bulletin criminel* 1999, no 167, 478; also Judgment of 24 November 1999, *Zutter*, no 97-85694, *Bulletin criminel* 1999, no 273, 858. On the legislation, see Law no 2000-516 of 15 June 2000, *Journal Officiel*, no 138, 16 June 2000, 9038. See also M Fromont, 'Die Bedeutung der Europäischen Menschenrechtskonvention in der französischen Rechtsordnung', *Die Öffentliche Verwaltung* 58 (2005), 1–10 at 7.

'the superior principle of the European Convention, which takes precedence over our contrary domestic rules'.[62]

The theoretical underpinnings of these years of resistance become a little more concrete in statements of one of the advocates-general at the *Cour*, Regis de Gouttes. In his view, the decisions in the wake of *Poitrimol* draw a limit of Strasbourg's authority in the 'fundamental principles of French law' or in constitutional norms such as the effectiveness of the judiciary.[63] If this interpretation is correct (and advocates-general's views are usually accorded much weight in the French legal system[64]), the situation in France does not differ much from that in Austria or Germany: French courts then do not merely disagree with Strasbourg on the interpretation of the ECHR but they set autonomous limits and protect a constitutional core from European interference.[65] However, framing it in such principled terms should not hide the political context of French resistance in the *Poitrimol* case. *Poitrimol* was decided by a 5—4 majority in the ECtHR, with strong dissenting opinions, and there was thus reason for hope that the court might later change course. This hope crumbled when, in 1998, the ECtHR confirmed *Poitrimol* in two Grand Chamber judgments with majorities of 18—3 and 20—1, respectively.[66] The ensuing shift of the *Cour de cassation* (and French legislation) was then likely due not so much to a shift in principle but to the 'political realism' emphasized already in the above-mentioned CdG statement of 1978.

The situation was somewhat different in the second, and even more prominent, example of French judicial 'rebellion', concerning the role of the judicial amici in French courts and especially the advocates-general at the *Cour de cassation* and the CdG at the *Conseil d'Etat*.[67] In its 1991 *Borgers* decision, to the surprise of many observers, the Strasbourg Court abandoned its earlier approach and found the privileged position of the advocate-general in

---

[62] Cour de Cassation, Judgment of 2 March 2001, *Dentico*, no 00-81388, *Bulletin d'Information de la Cour de Cassation* no 533, 15 April 2001, also with the report of the reporting judge and the conclusions of the advocate-general.

[63] de Gouttes, 'Le juge judiciaire' and 'CEDH et juge français'.

[64] On their traditionally central role in French judicial decision-making, see M Lasser, 'The European Pasteurization of French Law', *Cornell Law Review* 90 (2005), 995–1083 at 1005–8.

[65] I am grateful to Wibren van der Burg for insisting that I clarify this point.

[66] ECtHR, Judgments of 29 July 1998, *Omar v France* and *Guérin v France*. In *Omar*, the French judge Pettiti was the only one to dissent. On the importance of these judgments for the *Cour de cassation*'s change of approach, see the conclusions of the advocate-general de Gouttes, in Cour de Cassation, *Dentico*.

[67] See also the detailed assessment in Lasser, 'European Pasteurization'.

the Belgian Court of Cassation to violate the right to a fair trial.[68] This presented a challenge not only for Belgium, but also for similar courts in other countries[69] and especially in France. Thus, the French *Cour de cassation* soon undertook a vigorous defence of its advocates-general: it made some procedural amendments and in a much-noted judgment, emphasized their impartiality and maintained the conformity of the institution with the idea of a fair trial.[70] However, the ECtHR was not impressed and in its 1998 *Reinhardt and Slimane-Kaïd* decision,[71] it found against France (though in a softer tone than in previous judgments and with less radical demands[72]), thereby initiating a process that eventually brought about significant changes in the *Cour de cassation*'s organization and procedure.[73]

If this attempt at resistance was thus largely unsuccessful, that of the *Conseil d'Etat* fared significantly better. Given the latter's similar structure, it was only a matter of time before it came under ECtHR scrutiny as well; thus, shortly after the *Reinhardt and Slimane-Kaïd* judgment, the *Conseil d'Etat* decided to anticipate future cases and advance an own, alternative interpretation of the requirements of a fair trial, with an emphasis on the *judicial* role of the CdG: she being part of the judicial body and thus not subject to the adversarial procedure requirements in Article 6(1) of the Convention.[74] This stance soon found support from the European Court of Justice (ECJ). Seeking to protect the role of its own advocates-general, the ECJ stressed that they acted as 'Member[s] of the Court of Justice itself' and took part in the judicial function in full independence from outside authorities.[75]

---

[68] ECtHR, Judgment of 30 October 1991, *Borgers v Belgium*; explicitly departing from Judgment of 17 January 1970, *Delcourt v Belgium*.

[69] ECtHR, Judgments of 20 February 1996, *Vermeulen v Belgium* and *Lobo Machado v Portugal*.

[70] See Lasser, 'European Pasteurization', 1020; Cour de cassation, Judgment of 18 December 1996, *Fontaine*, no 96-82746.

[71] ECtHR, Judgment of 31 March 1998, *Reinhardt and Slimane-Kaïd v France*; affirmed in ECtHR, Judgment of 8 February 2000, *Voisine v France*; 26 July 2002, *Meftah and others*; 27 November 2003, *Slimane-Kaïd (no 2)*; 5 February 2004, *Weil*.

[72] See especially the observations in the dissenting opinion of Judge de Meyer, *Reinhardt and Slimane-Kaïd v France*.

[73] See Lasser, 'European Pasteurization', 1049–51, 1060–2; and the speech by procureur général Burgelin of 11 January 2002, available at: <http://www.courdecassation.fr/publications_cour_26/rapport_annuel_36/rapport_2001_117/>.

[74] Conseil d'Etat, Judgment of 29 July 1998, *Esclatine, Recueil Dalloz* 1999, Jurisprudence, 89. See also the Conclusions of CdG Chauvaux, ibid, 85–9.

[75] ECJ, Order of 4 February 2000, *Emesa Sugar*, C-17/98, paras 11–16.

With this move, both courts sought to distinguish themselves from institutions the ECtHR had already found wanting, including the French *Cour de cassation*—rather disingenuously so, given the largely parallel position of the judicial amici in all of them.[76] Nevertheless, this strategic stance, coupled with the strength of the concerted resistance, proved relatively successful. In its 2001 *Kress* judgment, the ECtHR recognized the special, *'sui generis'* nature of the CdG and, though pointing out that his independence and impartiality were not sufficient to remove all doubts regarding his role in the proceedings, the court proved far more lenient than in its earlier cases.[77] It found the participation of the CdG in the deliberations of the bench to be in violation of the right to a fair trial, but gave carte blanche to its role in the proceedings before the *Conseil d'Etat*. Most significantly, and contrary to its stance in *Reinhardt and Slimane-Kaïd*, it did not question the privileged access of the CdG to the reporting judge's draft judgment prior to the hearings.[78] Thus, the central procedural role of the CdG remained largely intact, and even though the *Kress* judgment has come under serious fire in the French literature,[79] it has also been described, more accurately, as 'Solomonic'.[80] This has not, however, led the *Conseil d'Etat* to implement it in any meaningful way. In another round of resistance, encouraged by scholarly calls for only

[76] On the independence and judicial function of the advocates-general at the *Cour de cassation*, see J Thierry, Case note, *Recueil Dalloz* 2000, Commentaires, 653–4; and the description in the ECtHR, *Reinhardt and Slimane-Kaïd v France*, paras 74–5.

[77] ECtHR, Judgment of 7 June 2001, *Kress v France*.

[78] On this practice, see the description ibid, para 43; the issue was not taken up in the assessment of the violation of the Convention; see also R de Gouttes 'L'intervention du Ministère public au cours de la phase d'instruction: La situation à la Cour de cassation' in I Pingel & F Sudre (eds), *Le ministère public et les exigences du procès équitable*, Brussels: Bruylant, 2003, 63–80 at 72–4; B Genevois, 'L'intervention du Ministère public au cours de la phase d'instruction: La situation au Conseil d'Etat', ibid, 81–93, 91. On a point left vague in *Kress*, the precise form in which the parties are informed about the tenor of the CdG's conclusions and can respond to them, the ECtHR and the *Conseil d'Etat* engaged in another exchange; see Sudre, 'Vers la normalisation', 292.

[79] See only J Andriantsimbazovina, '"Savoir n'est rien, imaginer est tout": libre conversation autour de l'arrêt Kress de la Cour européenne des droit de l'homme', *Recueil Dalloz* 2001, 2611–18; V Haïm, 'Faut-il supprimer la Cour européenne des droits de l'homme', *Recueil Dalloz* 2001, 2988–94.

[80] R Drago, Case note, *Recueil Dalloz* 2001, 2624–7 at 2626; see also Andriantsimbazovina, 'Savoir n'est rien', 2617.

'modest, symbolic reforms',[81] it has interpreted the judgment very narrowly, reading the condemnation of the CdG's 'participation' in the deliberations of the bench as implying the possibility for him to 'attend' these deliberations silently.[82] This strategy, like that of the *Cour de cassation* in the *Poitrimol* episode, sought to exploit a division in the ECtHR: *Kress* was decided by a narrow majority of 10—7 in the Grand Chamber, with a vigorous joint dissent, thus indicating that there might be hope for a future shift.[83] Yet Strasbourg did not flinch: in its 2006 *Martinie* decision, the Grand Chamber flatly—and with a clear 14—3 majority—rejected the challenge and upheld *Kress*, insisting that it could only be interpreted as ruling out not only active participation but also mere attendance of the CdG.[84] In response, the French government brought the procedure into line with ECtHR demands and renamed the CdG into *rapporteur public*.[85]

The two episodes I have sketched here, around *Poitrimol* and *Borgers*, now allow us a slightly clearer picture of what the French vision of a 'dialogue des juges' might imply. As we have seen, French practice now routinely follows ECtHR jurisprudence, but it ultimately reflects a 'oui, mais …' vis-à-vis Strasbourg,[86] given the rejection of its interpretation in a few cases with high stakes. The conditions for this rejection are not clearly defined; we can discern a limit to Strasbourg's interpretative authority only in a notion as vague as 'fundamental principles of French law'.[87] Yet this vagueness may, again, be useful: it allows the courts great flexibility; they can stage

---

[81] Drago, Case note, 2626.

[82] See B Genevois, 'L'intervention du Ministère public au cours du délibéré: La situation au Conseil d'Etat' in Pingel & Sudre, *Le ministère public*, 189–97 at 196–7; Sudre, 'Vers la normalisation', 291–7. The French response took the form of two directions of the president of the judicial division of the *Conseil d'Etat* of 2001 and 2002 and a governmental decree of 2005; see ECtHR, Judgment of 12 April 2006, *Martinie v France*, para 52, and the Decree no 2005-1586 of 19 December 2005, in *Revue française de droit administratif* 2006, 298–9.

[83] On this hope see, eg, Sudre, 'Vers la normalisation', 293.

[84] ECtHR, *Martinie v France*. See also, in the same vein, the Chamber Judgment of 5 July 2005 in *Marie-Louise Loyen and other v France*, para 63.

[85] Décrée 2006-964, 1 August 2006, gives the parties the right to object to the CdG's presence in the deliberations of the *Conseil d'Etat* and removes him from deliberations in other administrative courts. Décrée 2009-14, 7 January 2009, allows the parties to present an oral response to the conclusions of the *rapporteur public*.

[86] de Gouttes, 'Le juge judiciaire', 219.

[87] Criteria are similarly vague in the approaches of Andriantsimbazovina, *Autorité des décisions*; Potvin-Solis, *Effet des jurisprudences européennes*.

resistance against the ECtHR whenever they think its interference in French law and institutions has gone too far; and they can also take into account the political context, most notably the chances of changing Strasbourg juris- prudence, as we have seen in the *Cour de cassation*'s attack on *Poitrimol* and the *Conseil d'Etat*'s challenge of *Kress*. Thus, if the idea of 'dialogue' favours transnational judicial conversations about principled questions of interpre- tation, it also opens space for discretion and realism: in short, for judicial politics.[88] The joint between the French legal order and the ECHR is thus buffered by a political element—an element that is not fully determined by law but leaves the relationship, to an important extent, open.

II. MUTUAL ACCOMMODATION IN A PLURALIST ORDER

As the Spanish and French cases show, even in countries generally regarded as examples of the constitutionalist story, progress in the direction of a uni- fied, well-ordered European human rights law with the ECHR at its top is not unequivocal. The challenges to the constitutionalist narrative are not only factual, in that domestic courts sometimes do not follow Strasbourg judgments, evade them, or misinterpret them. They are instead of a prin- cipled nature: domestic courts assert a power to decide on the limits of the authority of the ECtHR, and because of the very vague indications as to when this power can be exercised, it appears as essentially discretionary. In this, the French and Spanish cases are very similar to the German and Austrian ones mentioned at the beginning. The Austrian Constitutional Court saw the limits to Strasbourg authority in the 'constitutional principles of state organisation',[89] and according to the German Constitutional Court, ECtHR judgments have to be 'taken into account' by German courts but may have to be 'integrated', that is, adapted to fit into the domestic legal sys- tem; they have to be disregarded when they run counter to legislative inten- tion or are 'contrary to German constitutional provisions'.[90] The German threshold for disregarding Strasbourg decisions thus appears lower than in the other cases considered, but the standards are similarly vague and allow the Constitutional Court to decide with wide discretion when it wants a decision to be followed and when not.[91]

---

[88] See also the observation in Potvin-Solis, ibid, 728.

[89] See Verfassungsgerichtshof, *Miltner.*

[90] See Bundesverfassungsgericht, *Görgülü*, paras 58, 62.

[91] The German Constitutional Court has explicitly reserved its right to supervise the interpretation of these guidelines by lower courts, see ibid, para 63.

In all those cases, from the perspective of the domestic courts national constitutional norms emerge as ultimately superior to European human rights norms and national courts as the final authorities in determining their relationship. This seems to hold more broadly: asked about their relationship to Strasbourg, 21 out of 32 responding European constitutional courts declared themselves not bound by ECtHR rulings.[92] Their position here is similar to the one now adopted by many courts when 'borrowing' human rights interpretations from other courts: it stipulates a horizontal relationship in which the borrowing court enjoys discretion and control over the reception process.[93] This contrasts with the constitutionalist narrative, but it much resembles the situation in European Union law, where—in the influential interpretation of Neil MacCormick—two different systemic perspectives conflict and both the European and the national legal orders, through their respective courts, claim to wield ultimate authority.[94] The relationship between the two levels is then determined not by one overarching rule, but by an oversupply of competing rules, among which solutions can only be found through political negotiations, often in the form of judicial politics.

If this sounds highly conflictual, reality has proven to be rather harmonious. We have already seen in the cases of Spain and France how, despite national courts' insistence on their final authority, the normal, day-to-day operation of the relationship with the Strasbourg Court has lately been highly cooperative, and friction has been rare. This picture seems, apart from a few exceptions, generalizable: compliance rates with ECtHR judgments are regarded as high,[95] and national courts in many jurisdictions refer

---

[92] M Melchior & C Courtoy, 'The Relations between the Constitutional Courts and the Other National Courts, Including the Interference in this Area of the Action of European Courts: Part III', *Human Rights Law Journal* 23 (2002), 327–30 at 327.

[93] See, eg, A-M Slaughter, 'A Typology of Transjudicial Communication', *University of Richmond Law Review* 29 (1994), 99–137 at 124–5; C McCrudden, 'A Common Law of Human Rights? Transnational Judicial Conversations on Constitutional Rights', *Oxford Journal of Legal Studies* 20 (2000), 499–532 at 503–10.

[94] N MacCormick, 'Beyond the Sovereign State', *Modern Law Review* 56 (1993), 1–18; see also C Richmond, 'Preserving the Identity Crisis: Autonomy, System and Sovereignty in European Law', *Law and Philosophy* 16 (1997), 377–420. See also Chapter 3, I and Chapter 5, II.3.

[95] See Greer, *European Convention*, 60–135. There are, however, no systematic studies on the issue. On problems with execution, see M Marmo, 'The Execution of Judgments of the European Court of Human Rights—A Political Battle', *Maastricht Journal of European and Comparative Law* 15 (2008), 235–58 at 238–42.

to Strasbourg jurisprudence as a matter of normalcy.[96] The ECHR has thus been termed 'the most effective human rights regime in the world'.[97] Also in Germany, despite the reservations of the Constitutional Court and a certain reluctance of courts to cite ECtHR cases, Strasbourg judgments are generally followed, sometimes without openly acknowledging that they are at the origin of a jurisprudential shift.[98] Even—or especially—after *Görgülü*, the Bundesverfassungsgericht has come to analyse Strasbourg case law in quite some detail.[99] and its president has emphasized the cooperative nature of the relationship between the courts.[100]

If we want to understand how this harmony in the face of a pluralist order has come about, we have to take a closer look at the judicial strategies and the interplay between the different courts. For this purpose, I have chosen to look at two cases in which the formal framework is obviously pluralist, thus clearly leaving domestic courts room for distancing themselves from Strasbourg if they so wish. The United Kingdom is one such case, as the 1998 Human Rights Act explicitly leaves the status of ECtHR judgments open; the other is the European Union, which is not even a party to the ECHR, with the result that any effect of Convention rights on the EU legal order and ECJ jurisprudence can always only be indirect. The aim of this inquiry is not to provide a comprehensive account of the gradual construction of the ECtHR's authority; this would be beyond the scope of this book.[101] My aim is more modest: to gain insights into why the different courts have not used their discretionary space in a

---

[96] Cf the surveys in Blackburn & Polakiewicz, *Fundamental Rights in Europe*; Keller & Stone Sweet, *Europe of Rights*.

[97] H Keller & A Stone Sweet, 'The Reception of the ECHR in National Legal Orders' in Keller & Stone Sweet, *Europe of Rights*, 3–28 at 3.

[98] See the references in n 14 above.

[99] See, eg, Bundesverfassungsgericht, Judgment of 13 December 2006, 1 BvR 2084/05, *Neue Zeitschrift für Verwaltungsrecht* (2007), 808 (on membership of a hunting association).

[100] H-J Papier, 'Koordination des Grundrechtsschutzes in Europa—die Sicht des Bundesverfassungsgerichts', *Zeitschrift für Schweizerisches Recht* 124 (2005) II, 113–27 at 127; 'Straßburg ist kein oberstes Rechtsmittelgericht'.

[101] We still lack general studies on the construction of the ECtHR's authority; for an initial attempt, see L R Helfer & A-M Slaughter, 'Toward A Theory of Effective Supranational Adjudication', *Yale Law Journal* 107 (1997), 273–391. Much more work has been done on the European Union; see only A-M Slaughter, A Stone Sweet, & J H H Weiler (eds), *The European Courts and National Courts*, Oxford: Hart Publishing, 1997; K J Alter, *Establishing the Supremacy of European Law: The Making of an International Rule of Law in Europe*, Oxford: Oxford University Press, 2001; A

more conflictual way, and thereby to begin to understand how the plural-ist structure has favoured (or hampered) the creation of a stable legal and political order in the context of the ECHR.

1. Judicial Conversations between European Courts

Rather surprisingly, the relationship between the ECtHR and the ECJ is not so dissimilar to the French and Spanish pictures, even though it rests on a fundamentally different basis. On a purely formal level, the ECHR and the law of the European Communities (EC) have long been unconnected: since the EC is not a party to the ECHR, Community acts remain outside the jurisdiction of the Strasbourg organs, and neither the Convention nor judgments of the Strasbourg Court create direct obligations for the EC. Yet despite this clear separation—a strong formal pluralism—the Strasbourg and Luxembourg courts have initiated a dialogue that, over time, has led to a remarkable convergence between their legal orders.[102]

Their relationship has evolved in broadly three phases, but though the trajectory might look like steady progress overall, it was not without fric-tions and setbacks. Initially, engagement between the judicial systems was limited. In its early years, the ECJ refused to deal with human rights issues altogether; only faced with growing concerns among member states and their constitutional courts did it begin to regard fundamental rights as gen-eral principles of Community law, and from the mid-1970s on it mentioned the ECHR explicitly.[103] Throughout this time, and until the late 1980s, the European Commission of Human Rights (EComHR) declared inadmissible all applications directed against Community acts solely on the ground that the EC was not a party to the Convention.[104] This changed with the increase in the EC's human rights-sensitive functions, and in 1990, the EComHR held that member states had to ensure a level of protection 'equivalent' to that of

Stone Sweet, *The Judicial Construction of Europe*, Oxford: Oxford University Press, 2004.

[102] In this discussion, I am much indebted to L Scheeck, 'The Relationship between the European Courts and Integration through Human Rights', *Zeitschrift für ausländisches öffentliches Recht und Völkerrecht* 65 (2005), 837–85.

[103] On the general development, see B de Witte, 'Community Law and National Constitutional Values', *Legal Issues of European Integration* 1991:2, 1–22; A Stone Sweet, 'Constitutional Dialogues in the European Community' in Slaughter, Stone Sweet, & Weiler, *European Courts and National Courts*, 305–30 at 317–19.

[104] EComHR, Decision of 10 July 1978, *Confédération Française Démocratique du Travail v EC*, alternatively: *Their Member States*, Decisions and Reports 13, 231.

the ECHR when they transferred powers to the EC—a requirement it found to be met at that point.[105]

In the early 1990s, the relationship thus seemed to be one of harmony at a relatively safe distance; and it improved further with political efforts to make the EC accede to the ECHR. These efforts were, however, brought to a halt in 1996 when the ECJ, in its famous Opinion 2/94, found the EC lacked the powers to accede: integrating it into the institutional framework of the Convention (ie, subjecting its organs, including the ECJ, to the ECtHR) was of constitutional importance and thus required a formal amendment of the treaties.[106] The ECtHR countered with what is widely regarded as a 'warning shot' for Luxembourg.[107] In its *Cantoni* judgment, it left the deferential path staked out earlier and subjected to full scrutiny a French provision identical to an EC directive, thus effectively denying Community acts the privileged treatment the 'equivalent protection' doctrine implied.[108] In the following years, the ECJ improved its record, citing ECtHR judgments more frequently and in greater detail[109] and even using them in 1998 to hold, for the first time, that a Community act violated fundamental rights.[110] The ECtHR, though, continued to assert itself: in its 1999 *Matthews* judgment, it applied normal Convention standards to the exclusion of Gibraltar from elections to the European Parliament, finding the United Kingdom in violation of the right to free and fair elections.[111]

Matthews was widely seen as signalling a willingness on the part of Strasbourg to extend its control into the area of EC law with greater self-confidence.[112] Yet it was followed by a much calmer period. Over the next six years, the ECtHR found all challenges, direct or indirect, of EU measures

---

[105] EComHR, Decision of 9 February 1990, *M & Co v Germany*, Decisions and Reports 64, 138.

[106] Opinion 2/94 of 28 March 1996, ECR 1996, I-1759, paras 34–6.

[107] See D Spielmann, 'Human Rights Case Law in the Strasbourg and Luxembourg Courts: Conflicts, Inconsistencies, and Complementarities' in P Alston (ed), *The EU and Human Rights*, Oxford/New York: Oxford University Press, 1999, 757–80 at 773; also Scheeck, 'Relationship between the European Courts', 865–6.

[108] ECtHR, Judgment of 22 October 1996, *Cantoni v France*.

[109] See, eg, ECJ, Judgment of 26 June 1997, C-368/95, *Familiapress*, ECR 1997, I-3689, paras 24–6.

[110] ECJ, Judgment of 17 December 1998, C-185/95, *Baustahlgewebe*, ECR 1998, I-8417.

[111] ECtHR, Judgment of 18 February 1999, *Matthews v United Kingdom*, paras 31–5.

[112] See I Canor, 'Primus Inter Pares: Who is the Ultimate Guardian of Fundamental Rights in Europe?', *European Law Review* 25 (2000), 3–21; Scheeck, 'Relationship between the European Courts', 866.

to be inadmissible on grounds unrelated to the character and legal status of the EU, thus leaving the door open for scrutiny in principle but avoiding friction in the particular case.[113] This deferential stance was sometimes surprising, for example in the *Emesa Sugar* case in which the ECJ had challenged Strasbourg's jurisprudence on the role of the advocate-general.[114] In another high-profile case, *Senator Lines*, evasion became possible when the EU's Court of First Instance (CFI) quashed the respective fine shortly before the Strasbourg judgment was to be rendered, prompting suspicions that the CFI's decision might have been driven by strategic concerns.[115] Overall, the ECJ's approach during this time certainly facilitated the ECtHR's cautious attitude: references to Strasbourg jurisprudence had become normal, several judgments reflected a greater emphasis on human rights as opposed to economic freedoms,[116] and in some much-noted instances the ECJ rectified inconsistencies between its jurisprudence and ECtHR judgments.[117] This friendly interplay between the courts mirrored political developments—the ECHR was granted a prominent place in the EU Charter of Fundamental Rights in 2000;[118] and the draft constitutional treaty of 2004 contained an obligation for the EU to accede to the Convention.[119] When ratification of the treaty failed, however, the ECtHR stepped back to the fore and used its *Bosphorus* judgment to set out with greater clarity its vision of the relation-

---

[113] See ECtHR, Decision of 23 May 2002, *Segi and Gestoras Pro-Amnistia v Germany and others*; Decision of 10 March 2004, *Senator Lines v the 15 Member States of the European Union*; Decision of 13 January 2005, *Emesa Sugar BV v Netherlands*; see also C Costello, 'The Bosphorus Ruling of the European Court of Human Rights: Fundamental Rights and Blurred Boundaries in Europe', *Human Rights Law Review* 6 (2006), 87–130 at 94–6.

[114] See ECJ, *Emesa Sugar*; on the French side of the same story, see text at nn 67–84 above.

[115] See CFI, Judgment of 30 September 2003, T-191/98 et al, *Atlantic Container Line and others*, ECR 2003, II-3275; see Scheeck, 'Relationship between the European Courts', 866–8.

[116] ECJ, Judgment of 12 June 2003, C-112/00, *Schmidberger*, ECR 2003, I-5659; Judgment of 14 October 2004, C-36/02, *Omega Spielhallen*, ECR 2004, I-9609.

[117] See especially ECJ, Judgment of 22 October 2002, C-94/00, *Roquette Frères*, ECR 2002, I-9011, explicitly departing from the decision in ECJ, Judgment of 21 September 1989, C-227/88, *Hoechst*, ECR 1989, 2859.

[118] Charter of Fundamental Rights of the European Union, *Official Journal EU*, 2000, C 364/1, Preamble and Arts 52(3) and 53; see below for more detail.

[119] Treaty establishing a Constitution for Europe, *Official Journal EU*, 2004, C310, Art I-9 and Part II. The ECHR sought to allow for this in Additional Protocol no 14.

ship with EU law.[120] Accepting that 'equivalent protection' was generally assured in the EU, it established that it would only scrutinize individual cases for 'manifest deficiencies' in rights protection. In the case before it, it did not find such deficiencies, and it has acted cautiously also in the first cases after *Bosphorus*.[121] But the approach leaves the Court significant flexibility to react to changes in the EU's fundamental rights regime and also points to areas of EU law that might come under more intense scrutiny in the future.[122]

The product of these more than thirty years of interaction is significant convergence and harmony, and this is generally acknowledged by commentators, including the president of the ECtHR.[123] The ECJ has come to refer to the ECHR and Strasbourg case law as a matter of normalcy and usually follows it diligently; likewise, the ECtHR has acknowledged the generally satisfactory level of rights protection in the EU and has, with its 'manifest deficiency' standard, raised the bar for individual challenges.[124] Yet this mutual accommodation remains a matter of choice: the ECtHR retains flexibility in applying its standard; and the ECJ has never acknowledged being tied to Strasbourg's interpretation of the ECHR and has instead used vague notions such as 'source of inspiration' to describe its status, leaving open the possibility of divergence when the ECJ regards it as necessary.[125] To some extent, that stance has also been politically ratified: in the convention drafting the

---

[120] ECtHR, *Bosphorus Hava Yolları Turizm v Ireland*, especially paras 152–8.

[121] See J Callewaert, 'The European Convention on Human Rights and European Union Law: A Long Way to Harmony', *European Human Rights Law Review* (2009), 768–83 at 772–3.

[122] See Costello, 'Bosphorus', 115–18.

[123] See O de Schutter, 'L'influence de la Cour européenne des droits de l'homme sur la Cour de justice des Communautés européennes', *CRIDHO Working Paper* 2005/07, 3; Costello, 'Bosphorus', 114; Wildhaber, quoted ibid.

[124] For other ways of interaction between the courts, see Scheeck, 'Relationship between the European Courts', 868–77; S Douglas-Scott, 'A Tale of Two Courts: Luxembourg, Strasbourg and the Growing European Human Rights *Acquis*', *Common Market Law Review* 43 (2006), 629–65 at 640–4.

[125] See, eg, ECJ, *Omega Spielhallen*, para 33. D Simon, 'Des influences réciproques entre CJCE et CEDH: "Je t'aime, moi non plus?"', *Pouvoirs* 2001, no 96, 31–49 at 37, points out that the acceptance of the ECHR by the ECJ only operates 'within the framework of the structure and objectives of the EC'. On instances of problematic application of the Convention by the ECJ, see Spielmann, 'Human Rights Case Law', 766–70; de Schutter, 'L'influence de la CourEDH', 15–20, 25–6; Douglas-Scott, 'Tale of Two Courts', 656–7; C Costello & E Browne, 'ECHR and the European Union' in U Kilkelly (ed), *ECHR and Irish Law*, Bristol: Jordan Publishing, 2004, 35–80 at 41–6.

Charter of Fundamental Rights, some members wanted to see a reference to the ECtHR's case law as a guide to interpretation, but this was successfully opposed by other members eager not to curtail the ECJ's autonomy by subjecting it directly to another body.[126] In the end, the reference to Strasbourg jurisprudence was included only in the presidium's explanations.[127] The Lisbon Treaty, by providing for the accession of the EU to the Convention, now opens the way to direct review of EU acts by the ECtHR. But it does not strengthen the position of the ECHR (or ECtHR judgments) in EU law—it only codifies the status quo in this respect by referring to the Convention as one of the sources of 'general principles' of the law of the Union.[128]

The overall result is far from hierarchical and well ordered: it might not quite be of 'Kafkian complexity',[129] but it is certainly highly pluralist. How then has it come to be so harmonious in practice? The most obvious explanation would start from the particular situation in which the courts found (and still find) themselves: for most of their existence, both have been highly vulnerable and their authority has been shaky.[130] In that context, the ECtHR may have wanted to subject the EC and later the EU to fuller control, given the gap in human rights protection that widened with the increase in supranational competences. But doing so too aggressively would have risked a backlash from the ECJ that could have been harmful to the ECtHR's position. Moving cautiously, recalibrating its approach according to the ECJ's reaction and the broader legitimacy context it was operating in, was thus the more sensible option.[131] Likewise, for the ECJ, avoiding conflict with the ECtHR was of central importance. Its authority had been

---

[126] See J B Liisberg, 'Does the EU Charter of Fundamental Rights Threaten the Supremacy of Community Law?', *Jean Monnet Working Paper* 4/01, 7–18; also P Lemmens, 'The Relation between the Charter of Fundamental Rights of the European Union and the European Convention on Human Rights–Substantive Aspects', *Maastricht Journal of European and Comparative Law* 8 (2001), 49–67 at 50–5. In the end, the reference to Strasbourg jurisprudence was included only in the presidium's explanations; see Doc Charte 4473/00 Convent 49, Explanation on Art 52.

[127] See Doc Charte 4473/00 Convent 49, Explanation on Art 52.

[128] Arts 6(2) and 6(3) Treaty on European Union.

[129] Douglas-Scott, 'Tale of Two Courts', 639.

[130] See Scheeck, 'Relationship between the European Courts', 870–3, 880–3; Costello, 'Bosphorus', 88–9.

[131] Bringing the ECJ on its side was also useful as a way of strengthening the enforcement of the ECHR within member states, at least as far as their action fell into the ambit of Community law and thus of ECJ supervision; on the latter, see J H H Weiler & N S Lockhart, '"Taking Rights Seriously" Seriously: The European

called into question in the 1960s and 1970s on human rights grounds, and using the ECHR was the most obvious way to allay concerns of national courts, governments, and the public. Following the ECtHR was therefore only prudent: in order to maintain its authority, the ECJ had to accept constraints on its autonomy, even if it managed to keep these constraints limited, first by blocking the EC's accession to the ECHR and then by using vague formulae to describe the Convention's status in Community law.

2. The British Turn toward Strasbourg

If the ECJ reached out to Strasbourg to bolster its authority, it seems the British House of Lords hardly needed such support: resting on centuries of tradition, it could easily forego the additional authority (if any) that a 'European', or 'foreign', court had to offer. So we might expect that the Lords, if given the choice, would insist on their autonomy and keep the ECtHR at a comfortable distance.

Yet this is not quite what happened. Certainly, before the 1998 Human Rights Act (HRA), the Convention was not part of British law and domestic courts only used the ECHR in a limited way, mostly to clarify ambiguities in statutes and the common law, but largely avoiding questions of judicial review of administrative action.[132] However, the situation changed radically—surprisingly radically—with the HRA: in the years since it has come into effect, British courts have come to refer to the Convention and to ECtHR judgments with a frequency and diligence hardly matched anywhere else in Europe.[133] This is all the more surprising as the HRA only requires national courts to 'take into account' Strasbourg jurisprudence in the interpretation of these rights. This vague formula deliberately creates opportunities for divergence; the

Court and its Fundamental Rights Jurisprudence', *Common Market Law Review* 32 (1995), 51–94, 579–627.

[132]   See M Hunt, *Using Human Rights Law in English Courts*, Oxford: Hart Publishing, 1997, chs 4– 6, for a detailed survey; also K Starmer & F Klug, 'Incorporation through the Back Door?', *Public Law* (1997), 223–33; R Blackburn, 'The United Kingdom' in Blackburn & Polakiewicz, *Fundamental Rights in Europe*, 935–1008 at 950–6, 971–91, 999–1003.

[133]   See only K Starmer & F Klug, 'Incorporation through the "Front Door": The First Year of the Human Rights Act', *Public Law* (2001), 654–5; C O'Brien & F Klug, 'The First Two Years of the Human Rights Act', *Public Law* (2002), 649–62. See also the more cautious assessment in N Bamforth, 'Understanding the Impact and Status of the Human Rights Act 1998 within English Law', *NYU Global Law Working Paper* 10/2004; E Wicks, 'Taking Account of Strasbourg? The British Judiciary's Approach to Interpreting Convention Rights', *European Public Law* 11 (2005), 405–28 at 410–25.

government intended it to give domestic courts space to go beyond Strasbourg interpretations but also, for example, to disregard outdated judgments.[134] But the House of Lords refused to make use of this space: the dominant position among the judges is instead one of close attention and loyalty to Strasbourg judgments. This line is reflected in an opinion of Lord Bingham in 2004:

> While such case law [of the ECtHR] is not strictly binding, it has been held that courts should, in the absence of some special circumstances, follow any clear and constant jurisprudence of the Strasbourg court... This reflects the fact that the Convention is an international instrument, the correct interpretation of which can be authoritatively expounded only by the Strasbourg court. From this it follows that a national court subject to a duty such as that imposed by section 2 should not without strong reason dilute or weaken the effect of the Strasbourg case law.... The duty of national courts is to keep pace with the Strasbourg jurisprudence as it evolves over time: no more, but certainly no less.[135]

Formulae such as 'special circumstances' or 'without strong reason' still leave the courts significant flexibility and have led to 'creative dialogues' with the ECtHR as well as open departures from its interpretations.[136] Yet the House of Lords followed Strasbourg case law in most cases, and this included politically sensitive judgments such as *A v Home Secretary* where the Lords found statutory powers to detain terrorist suspects incompatible with the Convention.[137] Even where they had an opinion that was difficult

---

[134] Cf Wicks, 'Taking Account', 406–9; R Masterman, 'Taking the Strasbourg Jurisprudence into Account: Developing a "Municipal Law of Human Rights" under the Human Rights Act', *The International and Comparative Law Quarterly* 54 (2005), 907–32 at 912–13.

[135] House of Lords, Judgment of 17 June 2004, *R v Special Adjudicator, ex parte Ullah* [2004] UKHL 26, para 20. For the initial statements, see Lord Slynn's speeches in House of Lords, Judgment of 9 May 2001, *Alconbury* [2001] UKHL 23, para 26; Judgment of 16 October 2003, *R v Home Secretary, ex parte Amin* [2003] UKHL 51, para 44.

[136] On the dialogue around the ECtHR's *Osman* judgment, see Lord Steyn, '2000–2005: Laying the Foundations of Human Rights Law in the United Kingdom', *European Human Rights Law Review* (2005), 349–62 at 361. On departures, see Lord Rodger, in House of Lords, Judgment of 18 July 2002, *Boyd, Hastie and Spear Saunby and Others* [2002] UKHL 31, para 92 (the ECtHR judgment in question was seen to rely on incomplete information about the domestic situation). For the generally loyal attitude of Lord Rodger, see House of Lords, Judgment of 11 December 2003, *Attorney General's Reference No 2 of 2001* [2003] UKHL 68, para 162.

[137] See only House of Lords, Judgment of 16 December 2004, *A v Home Secretary (Belmarsh)* [2004] UKHL 56; Judgment of 10 April 2003, *Bellinger v Bellinger* [2003] UKHL 21; Judgment of 8 March 2006, *Lambeth and Leeds* [2006] UKHL 10.

to reconcile with ECtHR judgments, they usually went to great lengths to achieve reconciliation through detailed exegesis and thus maintain the authority of the Strasbourg Court.[138] And when a Strasbourg verdict was in open conflict with their own previous jurisprudence, they saw themselves as 'required' to overturn the precedent.[139]

This strong loyalty to Strasbourg is unexpected also because of the wide-spread Eurosceptic sentiment in Britain—a sentiment that could have led the Lords to read the open 'take into account' language in the HRA as an invitation to start building an own, British human rights jurisprudence.[140] This alternative was readily available: it could build on efforts to develop a rights-based 'common law constitutionalism' already undertaken by courts and commentators since the late 1980s.[141] And it is precisely this path that the Court of Appeal has taken in the wake of the HRA. In several judgments, it has declared that the 1998 Act charges the courts with 'develop[ing] a municipal law of human rights by the incremental method of the common law, case by case, taking account of the Strasbourg jurisprudence'; that it did not need to 'stick[] like glue to the Strasbourg texts'; or that its task was only to 'draw out the broad principles which animate the Convention'.[142] In some cases, this has allowed the Court of Appeal to go beyond early Strasbourg

---

[138] See, eg, Lord Hope in House of Lords, *Lambeth and Leeds*. But see also the more ambiguous stance in House of Lords, Judgment of 28 March 2007, *R (Hurst) v Commissioner of the Police* [2007] UKHL 13, and in cases involving privacy and freedom of expression, for example House of Lords, Judgment of 6 May 2004, *Campbell v MGN* [2004] UKHL 22; cf G Phillipson, 'Transforming Breach of Confidence? Towards a Common Law Right of Privacy under the Human Rights Act', *Modern Law Review* 66 (2003), 726–58; R Mulheron, 'A Potential Framework for Privacy? A Reply to *Hello!*', *Modern Law Review* 69 (2006), 679–713. I am grateful to Carol Harlow for drawing my attention to this latter point.

[139] See, eg, Lord Brown in House of Lords, *Lambeth and Leeds*, para 198.

[140] For a suggestion in this direction, see Masterman, 'Taking the Strasbourg Jurisprudence into Account'.

[141] See M Loughlin, 'Rights Discourse and Public Law Thought in the United Kingdom' in G W Anderson (ed), *Rights and Democracy: Essays in UK-Canadian Constitutionalism*, London: Blackstone Press, 1999, 193–213; T Poole, 'Back to the Future? Unearthing the Theory of Common Law Constitutionalism', *Oxford Journal of Legal Studies* 23 (2003), 435–54; also Hunt, *Using Human Rights Law*.

[142] See England and Wales Court of Appeal, Judgment of 6 March 2002, *Tower Hamlets v Runa Begum* [2002] EWCA Civ 239, para 17; England and Wales Court of Appeal, Judgment of 27 March 2002, *R (Amin) v Home Secretary* [2002] EWCA Civ 390, paras 61–2; England and Wales Court of Appeal, Judgment of 17 May 2001, *Aston Cantlow* [2001] EWCA Civ 713, para 43.

jurisprudence and establish more demanding standards,[143] but in others it has been criticized for neglecting the ECtHR's case law[144] and falling short of what it required.[145] In the House of Lords, a similar approach was taken by Lord Hoffmann who insists that Convention rights under the HRA had become domestic, not international rights, and that, when faced with ECtHR judgments that were based on a misunderstanding of British law or were 'fundamentally at odds with the distribution of powers under the British constitution', courts might not have to follow them.[146]

If such a reserved stance had been expected, it is all the more surprising that Lord Hoffmann was quite alone with it in the House of Lords.[147] How can we explain the strong loyalty of the Lords to Strasbourg? The most straightforward answer would see dynamics of judicial empowerment at work: by relying on Strasbourg authority, the House of Lords was able to extend the reach of its judicial review powers beyond what was possible under the common law—in this reading, the HRA 'unleashed' the Lords from the shackles previously imposed by parliamentary supremacy and the separation of powers. Such an explanation is plausible if we think that, already before the HRA, the courts were intent on strengthening their review powers; and the above-mentioned efforts at developing a jurisprudence of common law rights certainly support this view.[148] Yet this explanation also raises

---

[143] See England and Wales Court of Appeal, Judgment of 5 November 2002, *Ghaidan v Godin-Mendoza* [2002] EWCA Civ 1533.

[144] See only Lord Hope in House of Lords, Judgment of 26 June 2003, *Aston Cantlow* [2003] UKHL 37, paras 44–52; I Loveland, 'Does Homelessness Decision-Making Engage Article 6(1) of the European Convention on Human Rights?', *European Human Rights Law Review* (2003), 176–204 at 191–2.

[145] See Lords Bingham, Slynn, and Steyn, in House of Lords, *R v Home Secretary, ex parte Amin*, paras 32, 45, 50–1; and Lord Bingham in House of Lords, Judgment of 8 December 2005, *A v Home Secretary (Torture Evidence)* [2005] UKHL 71, para 51.

[146] See his speeches in House of Lords, Judgment of 11 March 2004, *McKerr* [2004] UKHL 12, paras 64–5; House of Lords, Judgment of 14 November 2002, *R v Lyons* [2002] UKHL 44, para 46; House of Lords, *Alconbury*, para 76. Instead of drawing on Strasbourg case law, he often chooses to look to the tradition of rights under the common law; see only his speech in House of Lords, *A v Home Secretary (Belmarsh)*; for a careful analysis of his position there, see T Poole, 'Harnessing the Power of the Past? Lord Hoffmann and the *Belmarsh Detainees* Case', *Journal of Law and Society* 32 (2005), 534–61.

[147] For a similar position, see Lord Hobhouse in House of Lords, *Attorney General's Reference No 2 of 2001*.

[148] I am indebted to Martin Loughlin for drawing my attention to this point. See Hunt, *Using Human Rights Law*, chs 5 and 6; Loughlin, 'Rights Discourse', for the

problems. First, it is not entirely clear that British courts were indeed so keen on extending their powers of judicial review; otherwise, they might not have closed the door to ECHR arguments as tightly as they did in their 1991 *Brind* judgment.[149] Secondly, and more importantly in our context, a desire for empowerment would not necessarily explain why the Lords should have tied themselves so firmly to Strasbourg jurisprudence—after all, they could also have extended their review powers by building on the common law like the Court of Appeal, and this would have preserved them a greater degree of autonomy, too.

Yet perhaps the degree of loyalty to Strasbourg shown by the House of Lords can be explained in a similar way as that of the ECJ: as an attempt to defend its authority against challenge. This might be counterintuitive given that, as mentioned above, the Lords' authority, unlike that of the ECJ, had been established over centuries before even the ECtHR was created. Yet their role post-HRA was largely new: they had been turned into a quasi-constitutional court with broad review powers over executive and legislative action, and this was in strong tension with previous assumptions about the role of courts under the British constitution.[150] In this new role, the House of Lords enjoyed limited authority, and developing a municipal law of human rights might have appeared as too openly "creative": as a legislative rather than judicial function and therefore subject to greater challenge. Instead, relying closely on Strasbourg jurisprudence may have helped to maintain a more clearly judicial role, one of 'applying' the law, and may have also appeared as merely executing a parliamentary mandate.[151] This would correspond well with the observed general desire of courts to be perceived as non-political actors, servants of the law but not autonomous

developments, also on attempts at sharpening the scrutiny of administrative action to resemble more closely a proportionality test as required under the ECHR. See also J A G Griffith, 'The Brave New World of Sir John Laws', *Modern Law Review* 63 (2000), 159–76, and his 'The Common Law and the Political Constitution', *Law Quarterly Review* 117 (2001), 42–67.

[149] See House of Lords, Judgment of 7 February 1991, *Brind v Home Secretary* [1991] 1 AC 696; and the detailed analysis in Hunt, *Using Human Rights Law*, ch 6.

[150] See, eg, A Tomkins, *Public Law*, Oxford: Oxford University Press, 2003, 102–25, also on earlier inroads into the principle of parliamentary supremacy in the EC context.

[151] See also R Masterman, 'Aspiration or Foundation? The Status of the Strasbourg Jurisprudence and the "Convention Rights" in Domestic Law' in H Fenwick, R Masterman, & G Phillipson (eds), *Judicial Reasoning under the UK Human Rights Act*, Cambridge: Cambridge University Press, 2007, 57–86 at 78, 85.

creators.[152] Thus, even though on a substantive level it meant embracing an innovative internationalist conception of human rights, tying its hand and limiting (or denying) its discretion by reference to Strasbourg might have seemed to the House of Lords the safest option in the new—tempting but slightly uncomfortable—position in which the HRA placed it.[153] It remains to be seen whether in the new UK Supreme Court the judges will feel on more stable ground, and what consequences this might entail.

3. Strasbourg's Accommodation Strategies

The story of convergence between domestic courts and the ECtHR has so far been told from the perspective of the former and has highlighted factors that made domestic courts benefit from forging close links with Strasbourg. However, the gains from a cooperative relationship have usually been greater on the part of the ECtHR. From its inception, the Strasbourg organs were dependent on a positive stance by national authorities; with no enforcement tools at their disposal, compliance had to be essentially voluntary. If the Court and Commission wanted to become influential, they needed to establish, on the one hand, their authority as impartial and trustworthy interpreters of the Convention; on the other, they had to take care not to upset national authorities so much as to provoke a backlash.[154] This posed a dilemma, as the image of impartiality could easily be undermined by sensitivity for the concerns of particular member states, but Strasbourg managed to navigate between the two poles with great talent.[155] In the early years, this involved strong elements of diplomacy: the EComHR often assumed a mediatory rather than adjudicatory role, much to the dismay of many legal scholars, but with the result of allaying member states' fears

---

[152] See A-M Burley & W Mattli, 'Europe before the Court: A Political Theory of Legal Integration', *International Organization* 47 (1993), 41–76 at 72–3; W Mattli & A-M Slaughter, 'Revisiting the European Court of Justice', *International Organization* 52 (1998), 177–210 at 196–8; Alter, *Establishing the Supremacy*, 46.

[153] The different approach of the Court of Appeal and Lord Hoffmann might then be due to a different assessment of how best to shield themselves from attack—for them, referring to national traditions and the common law might seem to carry more weight with sceptics than foreign judgments. Poole, 'Harnessing the Power of the Past', 554–5, 561, sees this concern at the basis of Lord Hoffmann's position. This stance might well be justified given the political dispute over the HRA; on the dispute, see H Fenwick, R Masterman, & G Phillipson, 'The Human Rights Act in contemporary context' in Fenwick, Masterman, & Phillipson, *Judicial Reasoning*, 1–21 at 3–5.

[154] See also Helfer & Slaughter, 'Effective Supranational Adjudication', 307–28.

[155] See ibid, 313–14.

of an overly aggressive enforcement of human rights.[156] Later, as the judicial function became increasingly settled, Strasbourg developed doctrinal tools to navigate thorny issues: the evolutive approach and the margin of appreciation.

Both of these tools are well known; together, they allowed for an incremental expansion of the reach of the Convention, responsive to the pace of progress in member states, but in a doctrinal, not openly political framework.[157] We have already seen a striking example for the evolutive approach in the stance of the ECtHR towards advocates-general; the shift from the 1970 *Delcourt* case to the 1991 *Borgers* case was justified precisely by the need to reflect the 'evolution' of the requirements of a fair trial.[158] This dynamism in interpreting the Convention has often been criticized,[159] and understandably so, as there are hardly any methodological guidelines for how it is to be applied[160]—after all, it is a tool of judicial politics that grants the Court flexibility in responding to circumstances and opportunities. The critique has been even greater with respect to the second tool, the margin-of-appreciation doctrine that limits the stringency of the proportionality test by deferring to the judgment of member states. The extent of this margin depends on a number of criteria; the Court usually emphasizes the degree of consensus among member states, and on particularly contentious issues it has indeed stepped back to await the crystallization of a common European approach and has sought to respond to political movement within the member states concerned.[161] However, the application of

[156] See F-J Hutter, 'Die Erfolgsgeschichte der EMRK—Vom Nachkrieg zur europäischen Friedensordnung' in Grewe & Gusy, *Menschenrechte in der Bewährung*, 36–54 at 46–8.

[157] See P van Dijk & G J H van Hoof, *Theory and Practice of the European Convention on Human Rights*, 3rd edn, The Hague: Kluwer Law International, 1998, 82–95; A Mowbray, 'The Creativity of the European Court of Human Rights', *Human Rights Law Review* 5 (2005), 57–79.

[158] ECtHR, *Borgers v Belgium*, para 24.

[159] See, eg, F Matscher, 'Methods of Interpretation of the Convention' in R S J Macdonald, F Matscher, & H Petzold (eds), *The European System for the Protection of Human Rights*, Dordrecht: Martinus Nijhoff, 1993, 63–81 at 69–70.

[160] This is conceded even by supporters of the approach; see, eg, Mowbray, 'Creativity of the ECtHR', 71.

[161] See H C Yourow, *The Margin of Appreciation Doctrine in the Dynamics of European Human Rights Jurisprudence*, The Hague: Kluwer Law International, 1996, 193–6; Y Arai-Takahashi, *The Margin of Appreciation Doctrine and the Principle of Proportionality in the Jurisprudence of the ECHR*, Antwerp: Intersentia, 2002, 203–4; van Dijk & van Hoof, *Theory and Practice*, 87–91, also on various other factors

this doctrine has been open to the charge of great casuistry, reinforcing the already significant context-specificity of the proportionality test and often preventing generalizable inferences for future cases.[162] Yet this effect is deliberate: even today, there is a lively debate among judges about the degree to which they should formulate general principles or decide primarily on the basis of the facts of a specific case.[163]

The critique of these tools by scholars who regard coherence and legal certainty as central elements of the rule of law[164] is thus understandable, but the value of the resulting flexibility for a court that is in the process of establishing its authority can hardly be overestimated.[165] It helps to avoid clashes with member states and their courts while keeping alive the promise of a more effective human rights protection in the future, thereby also alerting national authorities to the risk that particular policies might one day be regarded as violations. The story of the treatment of transsexuals in Britain is a good illustration of this point: Strasbourg was lenient in 1986, emphasizing the lack of consensus in Europe and the resulting broad margin of appreciation,[166] but tightened its jurisprudence considerably over the next decade, warning Britain that it had to keep the situation under review.[167] When the political response was muted and even provoked explicit criticism by the Court of Appeal, the ECtHR eventually came to find a violation of the

influencing the extent of the margin. See also the example of transsexualism discussed below.

[162] See J A Brauch, 'The Margin of Appreciation and the Jurisprudence of the European Court of Human Rights', *Columbia Journal of European Law* 11 (2004), 113–50, 125; Greer, *European Convention*, 223, 323; also van Dijk & van Hoof, *Theory and Practice*, 91–5.

[163] See L Wildhaber, 'Ein Überdenken des Zustands und der Zukunft des Europäischen Gerichtshofs für Menschenrechte', *Europäische Grundrechte-Zeitschrift* 36 (2009), 549–53 at 547–8.

[164] See, eg, M R Hutchinson, 'The Margin of Appreciation Doctrine in the European Court of Human Rights', *ICLQ* 48 (1999), 638–50; Brauch, 'Margin of Appreciation'.

[165] See R S J Macdonald, 'The Margin of Appreciation' in Macdonald, Matscher, & Petzold, *European System*, 83–124 at 122–4; van Dijk & van Hoof, *Theory and Practice*, 95; Helfer & Slaughter, 'Effective Supranational Adjudication', 316–17; R Goodman & D Jinks, 'How to Influence States: Socialization and International Human Rights Law', *Duke Law Journal* 54 (2004), 621–703 at 702.

[166] ECtHR, Judgment of 17 October 1986, *Rees v United Kingdom*, especially para 37.

[167] ECtHR, Judgment of 27 September 1990, *Cossey v United Kingdom*, para 42; Judgment of 30 July 1998, *Sheffield and Horsham v United Kingdom*, para 60. See also Arai-Takahashi, *Margin of Appreciation*, 72–4.

Convention on the basis of a much-reduced margin of appreciation.[168] Here, the ECtHR, rather than merely stating the law, was administering change in a dialogue with national institutions that benefited much from the flexibility of its doctrinal tools.

However, these tools have not always led to an extension of human rights protection; sometimes they have also allowed for retreat in reaction to national concerns. We have already seen above how Strasbourg modified and limited its jurisprudence on the role of advocates-general when faced with the opposition of the *Conseil d'Etat*.[169] Another example is the shift in the ECtHR's stance towards the implementation of the Convention in domestic law. The Convention is not explicit about a need for incorporation, but in the 1970s, the Court described such incorporation as a 'particularly faithful reflection of the drafters' intention'.[170] However, faced with the continuing resistance of a number of states—especially the UK and the Scandinavian countries—it began to limit itself to stating that there was no preferred way of achieving compliance with the Convention and that incorporation was not legally required.[171] It became again slightly more demanding in its 1991 *Vermeire* judgment when it censured Belgium for its failure to amend legislation on illegitimate children following the *Marckx* judgment twelve years earlier.[172] Yet its general approach remained cautious until the early 2000s when the negotiations on Additional Protocol No 14 gave questions of execution greater political weight.[173] Thus, in 2004, the Court returned to a more determined language, holding that states were obliged to modify their domestic law if this was necessary to end violations of the Convention and fully comply with ECtHR judgments.[174]

---

[168] ECtHR, Judgment of 11 July 2002, *Christine Goodwin v United Kingdom*. The UK was again censured in ECtHR, Judgment of 23 May 2006, *Grant v United Kingdom*.

[169] See text at nn 74–85 above.

[170] ECtHR, Judgment of 18 January 1978, *Ireland v United Kingdom*, para 239.

[171] See, eg, ECtHR, Judgment of 21 February 1986, *James and others v United Kingdom*, para 84.

[172] ECtHR, Judgment of 29 November 1991, *Vermeire v Belgium*, paras 23–8.

[173] See Greer, *European Convention*, 159–65; V Colandrea, 'On the Power of the European Court of Human Rights to Order Specific Non-monetary Measures: Some Remarks in Light of the Assanidze, Broniowski and Sejdovic Cases', *Human Rights Law Review* 7 (2007), 396–411. On measures to strengthen the execution of judgments in general, see Marmo, 'Execution of Judgments'.

[174] ECtHR, Judgment of 17 February 2004, *Maestri v Italy*, para 47; Judgment of 8 April 2004, *Assanidze v Georgia*, para 198; see also the Recommendation Rec(2004)6

And following an invitation by the Council of Europe's Committee of Ministers, it also began to identify systemic problems in member states that required a broader legislative response.[175] This still falls short of its initial approach and certainly does not reflect a general duty to incorporate the Convention, but it shows the Court's particular sensitivity to the political process and its readiness to react to resistance as well as encouragement. After all, the process of accommodation in the ECHR framework is not a one-way street leading to ever greater authority of Strasbourg;[176] instead, it is a mutual process in which signals from political actors, including courts, feed back into ECtHR jurisprudence.

III. PLURALISM'S APPEAL

As we have seen, in the day-to-day operation of the European human rights regime, the pluralist structure of European human rights law has mostly produced not conflict and friction but harmony and convergence. The different courts involved have not made aggressive use of their discretionary space; instead, they have sought to accommodate each other in a cooperative relationship. Yet has this happened despite, or perhaps because of, the pluralist structure?

1. The Success of the European Human Rights Regime

On one level, this success has little to do with the institutionalist structure of the regime, but is the result of favourable political circumstances. The ECHR benefited much from the geopolitical environment, as it allowed Western European states to demonstrate their commitment to human rights in the face of the Soviet challenge.[177] Within Europe, the absence of concentrated power facilitated the operation of the Convention mechanism: none of the most powerful member states could expect to see its preferences fully

---

of the Committee of Ministers to member states on the improvement of domestic remedies, of 12 May 2004.

[175] ECtHR, Judgment of 22 June 2004, *Broniowski v Poland*, paras 189–94; Resolution Res(2004)3 of the Committee of Ministers on judgments revealing an underlying systemic problem, of 12 May 2004.

[176] On controversies within the Court about a potential 'one-way street' model of rights interpretation, see Wildhaber, 'überdenken'.

[177] See A W B Simpson, 'Britain and the European Convention', *Cornell International Law Journal* 34 (2001), 523–54 at 542–54; D Nicol, 'Original Intent and the European Convention on Human Rights', *Public Law* (2005), 152–72; also A Moravcsik, 'The Origins of Human Rights Regimes: Democratic Delegation in Postwar Europe', *International Organization* 54 (2000), 217–52 at 242.

reflected in the Convention; the UK, France, and Germany all had to accept that ECtHR jurisprudence drew on a range of traditions.[178] And for most of the life of the Convention, its members (then mainly Western European) shared relatively homogeneous political systems and cultural values;[179] increasing international convergence on the content of human rights—signalled for example by the growing practice of transnational judicial borrowing—was of additional help.[180] In this situation, divergence among member states was limited, violations were usually not terribly grave, and the findings of violations were not particularly concentrated. Though some countries lost more often than others in Strasbourg, none of them was a clear outlier that could have challenged the system or would have made resistance a routine position.[181] Beyond that, member states had a sufficient stake in a working system to accept occasional defeat. Their interests in it were quite varied, ranging from bolstering the human rights credentials of the West to spreading one's own values, protecting human rights achievements from potential domestic challenge, and signalling a commitment to liberal democracy so as to enter (or maintain membership in) the Western club.[182] For most countries, and most of the time, these benefits of membership outweighed the costs, and gradually reputational concerns also came to solidify the regime.

The formal structure of the regime had little impact on all this, except of course the costs for member states—the scope of the obligations under the Convention and the likelihood of being found in violation. The initial design of the ECHR kept these costs low: the Convention reflected a minimal

---

[178]   On the problems of superpower status for participation in international human rights regimes, see A Moravcsik, 'Why Is US Human Rights Policy So Unilateralist?' in S Patrick & S Forman (eds), *Multilateralism and US Foreign Policy*, Boulder, CO: Lynne Rienner, 2002, 345–76 at 348–50.

[179]   On the importance of this point, see R Bernhardt, 'Commentary: The European System', *Connecticut Journal of International Law* 2 (1987), 299–301 at 299–300; E A Posner & J C Yoo, 'Judicial Independence in International Tribunals', *California Law Review* 93 (2005), 1–74 at 55; but see also the more cautious assessment in Helfer & Slaughter, 'Effective Supranational Adjudication', 335–6.

[180]   On judicial borrowing, see n 93 above.

[181]   When this might have happened to Greece, Greece left the Convention system; see Greer, *European Convention*, 26. Turkey, the other systematic outlier, had a particular interest in showing a commitment to human rights. Russia's position today is likely to pose more serious problems.

[182]   See Simpson, 'Britain and the ECHR'; Moravcsik, 'Origins of Human Rights Regimes'; Gusy, 'Rezeption der EMRK'; also E Voeten, 'The Politics of International Judicial Appointments: Evidence from the European Court of Human Rights', *International Organization* 61 (2007), 669–701.

consensus, and many member states believed it did not require changes to their laws and institutions.[183] As we have seen, the Strasbourg organs have been careful not to raise these costs too suddenly: while giving Convention rights increasing bite over time, they did so in an incremental fashion that never departed too much from the level of rights protection already consolidated in member states. The evolutionary approach to interpretation and the related margin-of-appreciation doctrine—central political tools in a pluralist order[184]—thus quite likely helped stabilize the European human rights regime to a significant extent.[185] Most observers recognize that, even if they have constitutionalist sympathies and are sceptical of the political nature of these tools.[186]

However, we might find a broader effect of pluralism when we return to the focus of previous sections: the interaction of courts. The courts have played a crucial role in the development of the overall regime, both on the European level where the Strasbourg Court has stimulated large-scale change, and on the domestic level where courts have anchored the Convention in domestic societies. Studies of the influence of international human rights norms generally attach much weight to 'institutionalisation and habitualisation' on the domestic level;[187] and courts are widely regarded as central to the micro-processes of implementation and compliance in transnational dispute resolution.[188] Because of the strength of the rule of law in most member states of the Convention, non-compliance with domestic court decisions comes at a high cost for political actors; if a domestic court thus gives effect to ECtHR judgments, this often guarantees compliance more broadly.[189]

---

[183] Hutter, 'Erfolgsgeschichte', 42–5.

[184] See Delmas-Marty, *Towards a Truly Common Law*, 71–4; and text at nn 157–68 above.

[185] See Helfer & Slaughter, 'Effective Supranational Adjudication', 314–17; Goodman & Jinks, 'How to Influence States', 702. See also Hutter, 'Erfolgsgeschichte', 46–8, on the early work of the Commission.

[186] See Greer, *European Convention*, 214; van Dijk & van Hoof, *Theory and Practice*, 95.

[187] T Risse & S C Ropp, 'International Human Rights Norms and Domestic Change: Conclusions' in T Risse, S C Ropp, & K Sikkink (eds), *The Power of Human Rights: International Norms and Domestic Change*, Cambridge: Cambridge University Press, 1999, 234–78 at 249–50, 277.

[188] R O Keohane, A Moravcsik, & A-M Slaughter, 'Legalized Dispute Resolution: Interstate and Transnational', *International Organization* 54 (2000), 457–88 at 478.

[189] Greer, *European Convention*, 279.

2. The Decision-Making of Courts

How has the pluralist structure of the European human rights regime then influenced the likelihood of cooperation among the courts? If court action were determined primarily by formal rules, we would expect domestic courts to follow Strasbourg decisions more readily in a constitutionalist order in which European norms enjoy primacy over domestic ones. But already our limited survey of judicial dialogues has shown that the formal setting has only played a limited role. In France, despite the ECHR's supremacy over domestic statutes, courts have been reluctant to exercise review powers; on the other hand, the ECJ has given effect to ECtHR jurisprudence despite the absence of a formal basis. This corresponds with the observation that the incorporation of the Convention is not a dominant factor for compliance.[190] Of course, this does not imply that form is entirely inconsequential: the example of the UK shows well that the absence of a formal mandate to apply the ECHR made the courts reluctant to use it; only after the HRA did they feel authorized to so. Yet, while form certainly played a role in setting the boundaries of court action, it was hardly determinative of it[191]—a finding that is consistent with studies of other higher courts.[192]

Which other factors are then likely to have had an impact on court action vis-à-vis Strasbourg? Studies of courts suggest that decision-making is typically influenced by three groups of factors: attitudinal, normative, and strategic ones.[193] All of these also appear to be relevant in our context, though

---

[190] See Keller & Stone Sweet, 'Assessing the Impact', 683–6; also Lambert, *Effets des arrêts de la CourEDH*, 209, 378–9; Queralt Jiménez, *Interpretación*, 152–4; Greer, *European Convention*, 83–5 (though with methodological problems); and the account in Helfer & Slaughter, 'Effective Supranational Adjudication', 306–7.

[191] See also J Polakiewicz, *Die Verpflichtungen der Staaten aus den Urteilen des Europäischen Gerichtshofs für Menschenrechte*, Berlin/Heidelberg: Springer Verlag, 1993, 331.

[192] See J L Gibson, 'Judicial Institutions' in R A W Rhodes, S A Binder, & B A Rockman (eds), *The Oxford Handbook of Political Institutions*, Oxford: Oxford University Press, 2006, 515–34 at 518; in the EC law context, Mattli & Slaughter, 'Revisiting the ECJ', at 203. This is true even for scholars who emphasize the legal aspect; see M A Bailey & F Maltzman, 'Does Legal Doctrine Matter? Unpacking Law and Policy Preferences on the US Supreme Court', *American Political Science Review* 102 (2008), 369–84.

[193] Gibson, 'Judicial Institutions'; see also M Shapiro, 'Political Jurisprudence' in M Shapiro & A Stone Sweet, *On Law, Politics, and Judicialization*, Oxford: Oxford University Press, 2002, 19–54; J A Segal, 'Judicial Behavior' in K E Whittington, R D Kelemen, & G A Caldeira (eds), *The Oxford Handbook of Law and Politics*, Oxford: Oxford University Press, 2008, 19–33.

their relative weight is difficult to determine in the absence of broader, integrated studies of decision-making in the courts we are concerned with here.[194] These three categories should provide a useful prism for further exploration, even if, as Helen Keller and Alec Stone Sweet note, 'no single factor, or simple combination of factors, can explain the choices judges have made'.[195]

Attitudes. American studies of courts, particularly the US Supreme Court, often find judicial decision-making to be centrally influenced by the ideological and political attitudes of the judges.[196] This is likely to find reflection in European courts, but probably, for institutional and cultural reasons, in a weaker form.[197] Moreover, the main divisions on the ECtHR itself reflect less a left–right than an activism–restraint spectrum and so are more difficult to map onto dominant political cleavages. To some extent, however, the two dimensions appear as linked, and we can expect left-leaning judges to be somewhat more positively inclined towards Strasbourg judgments that extend rights protection and overcome national limitations.[198] It is also likely that, on average, conservative judges have stronger nationalist attitudes that make them more sceptical of ECtHR oversight as a matter of principle. And one might suspect that domestic judges—regardless of their political background—will often be inclined to see a solution enshrined in their own law as superior to one coming from a foreign source, in part simply because they are used to applying the national law and have internalized its supposed value. This might result in some bipartisan bias against Strasbourg attempts at change.

---

[194] Some attempts at this exist; see, eg, G Vanberg, *The Politics of Constitutional Review in Germany*, Cambridge: Cambridge University Press, 2005; P C Magalhães, *The Limits to Judicialization: Legislative Politics and Constitutional Review in the Iberian Democracies*, PhD Diss, University of Ohio, 2003, <http://www.ohiolink.edu/etd/send-pdf.cgi?osu1046117531>, especially ch 7; Alter, *Establishing the Supremacy*. See also, for related inquiries, C Landfried, *Bundesverfassungsgericht und Gesetzgeber*, Baden-Baden: Nomos, 1984; C Landfried (ed), *Constitutional Review and Legislation: An International Comparison*, Baden-Baden: Nomos, 1988; A Stone Sweet, *The Birth of Judicial Politics in France: The Constitutional Court in Comparative Perspective*, Oxford: Oxford University Press, 1992; A Stone Sweet, *Governing with Judges: Constitutional Politics in Europe*, Oxford: Oxford University Press, 2000.

[195] Keller & Stone Sweet, 'Assessing the Impact', 705.

[196] eg, J A Segal & H J Spaeth, *The Supreme Court and the Attitudinal Model*, New York: Cambridge University Press, 1992.

[197] Voeten, 'Politics of International Judicial Appointments', 680; but see also the findings for Portugal and Spain in Magalhães, *Limits to Judicialization*, 293–315.

[198] See Voeten, 'Politics of International Judicial Appointments', 677–8.

Normative commitments. Most studies of courts also show that judges' pursuit of their political preferences on the bench is strongly conditioned by the beliefs they hold about the right role of the courts.[199] As regards the stance of domestic courts towards the ECtHR, this will play out in a number of ways. First, the more judges value judicial restraint vis-à-vis the political branches, the less they will approve of attempts by any court—including Strasbourg—at checking politics. We can see this reflected, for instance, in the reluctance of British courts and the French *Conseil d'Etat* to use the ECHR to extend their review powers even though they had formal opportunities to do so; ideas about parliamentary supremacy are likely to have played an influential role here.[200] Even more importantly in our context, domestic judges, socialized in a national constitutional setting, will usually have internalized a vision of the domestic constitution as the final point of reference, and of domestic decision-makers and judges as having the final word. Their institutional commitments will thus reflect some scepticism as regards supranational supremacy claims.[201] Thirdly, normative commitments will also derive from judges' conceptions of the proper forms of argument and persuasion; after all, it is the particular form of reasoning that distinguishes judicial from political decision-making.[202] Much of the success of the ECJ has been attributed to its demonstrative autonomy from politics as well as its formalist style of reasoning,[203] and in the generally formalist legal culture of Europe, this factor is likely to have been influential for the reception of the ECtHR as well.[204]

Strategic considerations. The third group of factors usually seen as relevant to judicial decision-making is of a strategic nature. Among these factors are the pursuit of personal goals of judges, such as securing reelection, but also, and perhaps primarily, the strengthening of the position, authority, and legit-

---

[199] eg, Gibson, 'Judicial Institutions', 518–21; T M Keck, 'Party, Policy, or Duty: Why Does the Supreme Court Invalidate Federal Statutes', *American Political Science Review* 101 (2007), 321–38; Bailey & Maltzman, 'Does Legal Doctrine Matter?'. See also Shapiro & Stone Sweet, *On Law, Politics, and Judicialization*, Part 2, on path-dependence and precedent in judicial decision-making.

[200] See text at nn 49–52, 132, and 149 above.

[201] See N MacCormick, 'The Maastricht-Urteil: Sovereignty Now', *European Law Journal* 1 (1995), 259–66 at 264–5.

[202] See M Shapiro, 'The Success of Judicial Review and Democracy' in Shapiro & Stone Sweet, *On Law, Politics, and Judicialization*, 149–83 at 165–76.

[203] J H H Weiler, 'A Quiet Revolution: The European Court of Justice and its Interlocutors', *Comparative Political Studies* 26 (1994), 510–34 at 520–1.

[204] See Helfer & Slaughter, 'Effective Supranational Adjudication', 312–14, 318–23, 326–8.

imacy of the court as an institution.[205] The importance of such strategic factors in a supranational context has been demonstrated with respect to the EU, where European law mobilized lower national courts by giving them opportunities for greater institutional influence; in contrast, the highest national courts often rejected stronger review powers over the political branches because using European law for this purpose would have implied a loss of their position at the top of the judicial hierarchy and thus of their autonomy in favour of the ECJ.[206] A desire to preserve autonomy also seems at play in our context, particularly clearly in courts' efforts formally to retain the last word on whether to follow Strasbourg decisions or not—a point all the courts studied here have insisted upon. Likewise, in all the cases discussed, enhancing the courts' authority seems to have been important, most obviously for the Spanish *Tribunal Constitucional* in the transition from dictatorship, and for the ECJ in coping with challenges by domestic courts. But as the British and French cases show—and a similar finding applies to French courts in the EU context[207]—this does not always translate into strategies of institutional expansion. Courts are not always keen to extend their powers, even if the formal setting allows for it; convictions about their rightful place, considerations of legitimacy, or fear of a backlash[208] might prevent them from doing so.

3. The Impact of Pluralism

How then has the pluralist structure affected those different factors in the context of the ECHR? As mentioned above, compared to constitutionalism, pluralism appears as the weaker option with respect to *form*, but then form seems to have played only a limited role. As regards the other factors, the picture is not unambiguous, but it reveals a number of significant advantages of a pluralist structure.

This is already visible when we consider judges' *attitudes*. As mentioned above, ECtHR jurisprudence is not easily classifiable as left or right, but

---

[205] eg, L Epstein & J Knight, 'Toward a Strategic Revolution in Judicial Politics', *Political Research Quarterly* 53 (2000), 625–61; Alter, *Establishing the Supremacy*, 45–7; see also Mattli & Slaughter, 'Revisiting the ECJ', 190–4; and Gibson, 'Judicial Institutions', 521–30.

[206] See J H H Weiler, 'The Transformation of Europe', *Yale Law Journal* 100 (1991), 2403–83 at 2426; Burley & Mattli, 'Europe before the Court', at 63–4; in the same vein, but with more nuanced assessments, see Mattli & Slaughter, 'Revisiting the ECJ', 190; Alter, *Establishing the Supremacy*, 45–52.

[207] See Alter, *Establishing the Supremacy*, 141–2.

[208] On the risk of a backlash against judicial incorporation of the ECHR in the UK before the HRA, see Starmer & Klug, 'Incorporation through the Back Door', 233.

in many cases, Strasbourg activism will be greeted more readily by the domestic left. Insofar as political attitudes play a role in the courts, national resistance to the ECtHR is likely to be more pronounced among conservative judges; and this resistance should be attenuated by the incrementalism characteristic of a pluralist order. After all, incrementalism serves to limit demands for change; it reduces the degree of challenge and allows for a process of slow socialization into the Strasbourg conception of rights. Likewise, insofar as we can assume that domestic judges have a preference for solutions enshrined in their own laws over those emanating from a foreign source, incrementalism softens the blow; it only demands limited changes at any given moment and also reacts to the evolution of domestic law.

Advantages of a pluralist order also emerge with respect to judges' *normative commitments*. Again, incrementalism limits the challenge for judges who favour judicial restraint vis-à-vis politics and for those who have a principled commitment to the national constitution as the final point of reference. And pluralism's other distinctive characteristic, its readiness to leave questions of principle open, further reduces problems for the latter group; their insistence on ultimate national supremacy is not challenged categorically, as it would be in a constitutionalist order; pluralism instead seeks to work around it. However, from a perspective of argument and persuasion, pluralism's appeal appears more ambivalent. The incrementalist element certainly helps tune supranational demands to what domestic courts seem ready to embrace, and it may lead to forms of dialogue that bring the different levels closer together over time.[209] But the stronger political component of pluralism might also make persuasion more difficult: it can make an international court appear as a political body and thereby taint its legal arguments. Escaping such appearances while remaining politically sensitive means walking a precariously fine line.

Somewhat ambiguous is pluralism's role also when it comes to *strategic factors*. By making plain the element of discretion and choice, it prevents domestic courts from hiding entirely behind a Strasbourg decision in order to justify an own expansion of review powers; any such expansion requires a defence on additional grounds. But if a domestic court has a stronger standing than the international body, it might actually benefit from the dissociation that comes with pluralism.[210] On the other hand, clearer advantages are discernible with

---

[209] On the benefits of judicial dialogue for creating authority and legitimacy in the EU context, see A Torres Pérez, *Conflicts of Rights in the European Union: A Theory of Supranational Adjudication*, Oxford: Oxford University Press, 2009, ch 5.

[210] This may have influenced the approach of the Court of Appeal in the UK; see n 153 above.

respect to courts' desire to defend their autonomy: the pluralist order, unlike a constitutionalist one, allows domestic courts to insist on their final authority, and they have done so in all cases studied here. Without the possibility of such insistence, pragmatic accommodation from all sides would have been considerably less likely. At the same time, the vulnerability that comes with the contested supremacy claims in a pluralist structure may well have attuned courts towards cooperation rather than the imposition of a final say.[211]

In sum, then, pluralism's contribution to the stability of the European human rights regime seems significant. We might not be able to quantify the role of the different factors presented here or even determine their relative weight for the different courts involved; this would require an extensive, comparative study of decision-making in those courts. But the discussion has shown that on a number of issues we can expect domestic courts to care about, the incrementalism and openness of pluralism might well have worked to the benefit of the overall regime. It might not always have appeared as overly attractive or convincing to rights activists or staunch cosmopolitans; but it will also have seemed less threatening to the conservatives and committed nationalists who might otherwise have sought to derail the process. Leaving fundamental questions open, pluralism may have allowed for a gentler, and ultimately more successful, way of engaging a variety of actors in the creation of a postnational order—at least in conditions that, as in the European human rights regime, have been favourable enough to allow courts and their dialogues a central role in that process.

IV. CONCLUSION

The constitutionalist narrative of the evolution of the European human rights regime, so powerfully manifested in the reactions to the *Görgülü* judgment, has come to appear more as a story of hope than a reflection of reality. While domestic and European human rights law have indeed become increasingly linked and Strasbourg decisions are regularly followed by national courts, this does not indicate the emergence of a unified, hierarchically ordered system along constitutionalist lines. Instead, as we have seen throughout our case studies, domestic courts insist on the ultimate supremacy of their own legal order over European human rights law, and they have thus created a zone of discretion in deciding whether or not to respect a judgment of the ECtHR, allowing them to negotiate with Strasbourg on issues

---

[211] See also S Oeter, 'Rechtsprechungskonkurrenz zwischen nationalen Verfassungsgerichten, Europäischem Gerichtshof und Europäischem Gerichtshof für Menschenrechte' in *Veröffentlichungen der Vereinigung deutscher Staatsrechtslehrer* 66 (2007), 361–91 at 388.

they feel particularly strongly about. Yet in spite of this divergence on fundamentals, the interplay between the different levels of law has been remarkably harmonious and stable. There have hardly been open clashes; instead, mutual accommodation and convergence have been the norm, facilitated by the flexible and responsive strategies of the courts involved, and especially of the ECtHR itself.

This is initially surprising as pluralism, unlike constitutionalism, is often associated with disorder and the risk of friction. Yet as we have seen, the pluralist structure of the European human rights regime seems to have created favourable circumstances for the generally harmonious dialogue between domestic and European courts. In particular, the strong incrementalism it allows for has limited the extent of the demand for adaptation on the part of national courts and is thus likely to have prevented overreach by Strasbourg and consequently the risk of a backlash. Likewise, pluralism has catered to national courts' desire for maintaining their autonomy; it has allowed them to insist on their superior status in principle and in the shadow of this status to make gradual, pragmatic concessions. In this way, by leaving issues of principle open, the pluralist structure has limited the antagonism between the different institutions involved and has helped them move to a stage where they could mutually benefit from a cooperative relationship.

In those respects, then, the experience of the European human rights regime points to the appeal of pluralist forms of postnational order more generally. In situations where contestation is strong and authorities are not firmly settled, a pluralist order can contribute to the transformation of a regime over time and allow for responsiveness to different actors according to their changing political weight and public legitimacy. By leaving questions of fundamental norms and ultimate authority undecided, pluralism might give postnational law the flexibility it needs in order to deal with principled contestation—contestation might be easier to circumnavigate than in a constitutional order built on the ideal that these questions are settled in one way or another.

This does not suggest easy solutions for other areas of postnational governance. The political environment in which the European human rights regime operates is particularly favourable, and its experiences are therefore not easily transferable. Pluralism may turn out to be less stable and desirable in a less friendly setting. Yet constitutionalism's aspiration to tame unruly politics through establishing a comprehensive rule of law may also run into greater obstacles in broader, more contested spaces. In the next two chapters, I thus turn to the global sphere to examine in more detail what models of order are emerging there and how pluralism and constitutionalism fare in this different—and even more challenging—context.

⁓ 5 ⁓

Sanctions and Rights between Hierarchy and Heterarchy

In the previous chapter, I have analysed a relatively benign case. Human rights, though often enough controversial, generally have such a positive connotation that a multiplicity of human rights regimes may appear simply to multiply the good: to add further layers of protection for the individual, something that in liberal times seems desirable anyway. And the cases in which European and national conceptions of rights have led to clashes between those layers were mostly of limited political salience; their ultimate lack of resolution in a pluralist order could then appear as of little consequence. Moreover, those conflicts all occurred on the background of remarkable homogeneity: with some exceptions, the European human rights regime evolved among countries with similar political systems and social values. And even though the accession wave of the 1990s has led to greater diversity, the core of the regime has remained in place. This fact may have paved the way for a relatively stable pluralist order—in line with Carl Schmitt's dictum that in federal systems the site of ultimate authority can be left undecided only if society and politics are sufficiently homogeneous.[1]

If this were true, pluralism would hardly present a suitable model for the postnational order beyond a few relatively cohesive regions. Yet I have argued in Chapter 3 that it is precisely the pronounced diversity of the global order that makes pluralism attractive there, and it is in the following two chapters that I seek to inquire in greater depth into the promise and problems of pluralist structures in the global context. This chapter will begin by examining the UN sanctions regime in its context of international, regional, and national law. The next chapter will then turn to the example of global risk regulation and analyse the interplay of different layers of law around the dispute over trade and genetically modified organisms, focusing on horizontal exchanges between World Trade Organization (WTO) law and the Biosafety Protocol as well as their interaction with European and national law.

---

[1] C Schmitt, *Verfassungslehre*, 9th edn, Berlin: Duncker & Humblot, [1928] 2003, 375–9.

If the European human rights regime was an 'easy' case, global security governance is quite the opposite. The issues UN sanctions deal with are highly politicized, go to the core of essential state functions, and are often of significant salience in domestic as well as international discourse. If there is an area where one would expect a pluralist order to run into serious obstacles, it is probably this one. Yet as we will see, not only has the regulatory intensity of the field led to a serious enmeshment of different layers of law and thus challenged classical dualist conceptions to a particular extent; it has also produced a pluralist order that has helped reflect and accommodate the serious tensions between actors and policies that are characteristic, and natural, in an area of such salience.

The chapter proceeds in three steps. It first sets the scene by outlining the shape of the UN sanctions regime and its transformation over the last fifteen years. In the second step, it goes on to explore the interaction of legal orders and governance regimes around the issue of sanctions, showing the degree to which layers of law are enmeshed yet not integrated into a coherent whole. Courts have approached this enmeshment with very different strategies, and I use examples from courts in the United Kingdom and the European Union to illustrate how they seek to shape, and cope with, the pluralist legal environment they inhabit (and help create). This is contrasted with the ways by which the EU's internal pluralism has been created and formed, reflecting similarities and differences in structures and judicial visions. The third step uses the case of the sanctions regime to continue the inquiry, begun in the previous chapter, into the stabilizing *vel* destabilizing force of pluralism. As we will see, pluralism appears here less as the cause of the relative instability of the overall sanctions regime than as an expression of underlying, political rather than institutional, obstacles to cooperation.

I. THE TRANSFORMATION OF UN SANCTIONS ADMINISTRATION

In the course of the last two decades, the character of UN sanctions has changed radically, and so have the administrative structure and legal framework in which they operate.[2] This is due in part to the increasing normalization of

---

[2] For an overview of the evolution of the UN sanctions regime, see D Cortright & G A Lopez, *The Sanctions Decade: Assessing UN Strategies in the 1990s*, Boulder, CO: Lynne Rienner, 2000; D Cortright, G A Lopez, & L Gerber-Stellingwerf, 'The Sanctions Era: Themes and Trends in UN Security Council Sanctions since 1990' in V Lowe et al (eds), *The United Nations Security Council and War*, Oxford: Oxford University Press, 2008, 205–25. On the legal issues involved, see J A Frowein & N Krisch, 'Article 41' in B Simma et al (eds), *The United Nations Charter: A*

economic enforcement measures.[3] During the Cold War, the UN Security Council adopted sanctions infrequently (only against Southern Rhodesia and South Africa), and their implementation was largely left to ad hoc, exceptional arrangements. Since 1990, in contrast, they have become a common tool of UN action—the Security Council has used them in more than twenty cases, and in 2010, eleven sanctions regimes were in place simultaneously, many of them involving a variety of particular measures, such as travel bans, asset freezes etc.[4] This has raised the challenge of implementation significantly, but it has also provided an impetus for the normalization and consolidation of structures, both within the UN and in member states.

Yet sanctions have not only increased in scope and extent, they have also undergone a transformation in substance. The sanctions regimes of the early 1990s were aimed at economically isolating the target countries and thereby exerting maximum pressure for behavioural change. Thus, in cases such as Yugoslavia, Haiti, and—most prominently—Iraq, the Security Council adopted 'comprehensive' economic measures, requiring member states to cut all economic relations with the countries concerned.[5] This had only limited success and disastrous humanitarian consequences, discrediting the sanctions for years and leading even then UN Secretary-General Boutros Ghali to call them a 'blunt instrument'.[6] The Council responded with a phase of low activity, before it turned in the late 1990s from 'comprehensive' to 'targeted' (or, rather euphemistically, 'smart') sanctions. Rather than affecting the economy and population as a whole, these were designed to hit particular individuals by freezing their financial assets and banning them from travelling abroad.[7]

While alleviating humanitarian concerns, targeted sanctions raised doubts about their effectiveness, and round after round of expert consultations was

Commentary, 2nd edn, Oxford: Oxford University Press, 2002, 735–49; J M Farrall, *United Nations Sanctions and the Rule of Law*, Cambridge: Cambridge University Press, 2007.

[3] 'Sanctions' and 'enforcement measures' are used here interchangeably, though the latter term is a better characterization in the UN context; see H Kelsen, *The Law of the United Nations*, London: Stevens & Sons, 1950, 724–5, 732–7.

[4] Cf <http://www.un.org/sc/committees/>. See also the survey of sanctions regimes in Farrall, *UN Sanctions*, Appendix 2.

[5] See, eg, SC Res 661 (1990), 6 August 1990, on Iraq.

[6] *Supplement to an Agenda for Peace*, UN Doc A/50/60–S/1995/1, 3 January 1995, para 70.

[7] See, eg, SC Res 1173 (1998), 12 June 1998, on Angola; more generally D Cortright & G A Lopez (eds), *Smart Sanctions: Targeting Economic Statecraft*, Lanham, MD: Rowman & Littlefield, 2002.

convened to tackle the issue.[8] Because the impact of these relatively light sanctions depends in large part on comprehensive implementation, the Security Council also stepped up its efforts to monitor and control how the measures were applied. This began with the creation of monitoring teams to identify shortcomings and, in some cases, actual violations; involved the establishment of expert groups to advise the Council's sanctions committees on the general design of the measures; and led to broader steps to improve states' capacity to implement their obligations on a practical level.[9] All this went furthest in the area of terrorism where the Council targeted hundreds of individuals and entities and also established, with the Counter-Terrorism Committee (CTC) and the Counter-Terrorism Executive Directorate (CTED), new bodies to help anchor counter-terrorist measures in member states' legal and administrative structures.[10]

As a result, the UN sanctions regime today bears little resemblance to the classical ways in which international law is created and implemented. First, of course, rules are made not by agreement and ratification of the states concerned, but by a fifteen-member body on the basis of majority voting. For most states, this means little influence on the shape of their obligations.[11] Secondly, states' freedom to determine the mode of implementation has become increasingly circumscribed, as the rules have become ever more precise and are concretized further by the sanctions committees and the CTC through monitoring and the development of best practices. What is more, the CTC, in its mission of capacity-building, conveys a distinctive vision of administrative organization as a basis for a state's ability to fulfill its obligations, thus providing a push for 'good governance' reform in many countries.[12] Thirdly, the turn to targeted sanctions has given Security Council

---

[8] See: <http://www.watsoninstitute.org/tfs/CD/sanc.html>.

[9] See Farrall, *UN Sanctions*, 163–80, for a survey of the different bodies created.

[10] See N Krisch, 'The Rise and Fall of Collective Security: Terrorism, US Hegemony, and the Plight of the Security Council' in C Walter et al (eds), *Terrorism as a Challenge for National and International Law*, Berlin/Heidelberg: Springer Verlag, 2004, 879–908; also E Rosand, 'Security Council Resolution 1373, the Counter-Terrorism Committee, and the Fight against Terrorism', *American Journal of International Law* 97 (2003), 333–41; E Rosand, 'The Security Council's Efforts to Monitor the Implementation of Al Qaeda/Taliban Sanctions', *American Journal of International Law* 98 (2004), 745–63.

[11] On the 'hegemonic' character of much of Security Council-made law, J E Alvarez, 'Hegemonic International Law Revisited', *American Journal of International Law* 97 (2003), 873–88.

[12] D Cortright et al, 'Global Cooperation Against Terrorism: Evaluating the Counter-Terrorism Committee' in D Cortright & G A Lopez (eds), *Uniting Against*

action itself an administrative character: individuals are directly affected by a public listing (at least in their reputation); and even insofar as member state implementation is necessary to give measures effect (as is the case for asset freezes and travel bans), states' action is reduced to a subordinate, non-discretionary role in the overall administrative machinery directed by the Council and its committees.[13]

This transformation has significantly reduced the distance between national and international law in this domain, and it has in practice led to an increasing enmeshment between those layers, a point I will return to in the next section. It has also shifted the focus of human rights concerns. The comprehensive sanctions of the 1990s had triggered critique mainly from the angle of economic and social rights, reflected in the fact that the UN Committee on Economic, Social and Cultural Rights issued a General Comment on the issue in 1997.[14] Given the transboundary nature of the problems and the difficult issues of causality and responsibility, the human rights critique faced serious obstacles at the time.[15] The focus shifted with the move to targeted sanctions as their effect on the designated individuals was intentional and more immediate, thus triggering interference with civil rights ranging from the protection of property to the right to privacy and free movement, and often raising concerns about due process and procedural rights.[16] As we will see, this new constellation brought the Security Council into the spotlight of constitutional and administrative lawyers and of domestic courts, normally unconcerned by phenomena beyond the national (or in case of Europe, EU) realm. This new attention is evidence of the growing linkages between the different layers of law and institutions,

---

Terror: Cooperative Nonmilitary Responses to the Global Terrorist Threat, Cambridge, MA: MIT Press, 2007, 23–50 at 37–9.

[13] On the concept of a global administrative space, and on understanding global governance as administration, see B Kingsbury, N Krisch, & R B Stewart, 'The Emergence of Global Administrative Law', *Law & Contemporary Problems* 68:3 (2005), 15–61. On the administrative turn of the Council, see Krisch, 'Rise and Fall'.

[14] UN Committee on Economic, Social and Cultural Rights, *General Comment 8: The relationship between economic sanctions and the respect for economic, social and cultural rights*, UN Doc E/C.12/1997/8, 12 December 1997.

[15] But see W M Reisman & D L Stenvick, 'The Applicability of International Law Standards to United Nations Economic Sanctions Programmes', *European Journal of International Law* 9 (1998), 86–141.

[16] See the discussion of affected rights in P Gutherie, 'Security Council Sanctions and the Protection of Individual Rights', *NYU Annual Survey of American Law* 60 (2004), 491–541 at 499–511.

and it seems to have played a part in the Security Council's growing awareness of, and eventual response to, the human rights critique.

Initially, the Council barely paid attention to those human rights issues. Regarding itself as a political, diplomatic body, it situated its sanctions regimes in the context of international security and intelligence rather than in that of administration and fair procedures.[17] Complaints about its designation of particular individuals, which intensified soon after it added many to its list of Al-Qaeda/Taliban targets after the attacks of 9/11, were thus dealt with in the typical diplomatic fashion of confidential intergovernmental approaches.[18] It took the Council until late 2002 to respond to increasing pressure and court cases in member states to establish a first procedure for delisting individuals.[19] Yet this procedure did not define the relevant standards or offer individuals access to the sanctions committee, and over the next few years, discontent among both non-governmental organizations (NGOs) and governments grew. It found reflection in the report of the UN High Level Panel on Threats, Challenges and Change in 2004,[20] and then also in the World Summit Outcome document in 2005, which called for 'fair and clear procedures' in sanctions administration.[21]

Pressure intensified in 2006 when the UN Secretary-General, a Special Rapporteur of the Commission on Human Rights, and eventually also the General Assembly called for procedural reforms and greater accountability.[22]

---

[17] On this contrast with a focus on transparency, see D Hovell, 'The Deliberative Deficit: Transparency, Access to Information and UN Sanctions' in J Farrall & K Rubenstein (eds), *Sanctions, Accountability and Governance in a Globalised World*, Cambridge: Cambridge University Press, 2009, 92–122.

[18] On an early case, see P Cramér, 'Recent Swedish Experiences with Targeted UN Sanctions: The Erosion of Trust in the Security Council' in E de Wet & A Nollkaemper (eds), *Review of the Security Council by Member States*, Antwerp: Intersentia, 2003, 85–106.

[19] On the developments summarized in this paragraph, see, eg, M Kanetake, 'Enhancing Community Accountability of the Security Council through Pluralistic Structure: The Case of the 1267 Committee', *Max Planck Yearbook of United Nations Law* 12 (2008), 113–75 at 142–64; M Heupel, 'Multilateral sanctions against terror suspects and the violation of due process standards', *International Affairs* 85 (2009), 307–21.

[20] High-level Panel on Threats, Challenges and Change, *A more secure world: our shared responsibility*, UN Doc A/59/565, 2 December 2004, para 152, available at: <http://www.un.org/secureworld/>.

[21] General Assembly Res 60/1, 24 October 2005, para 109.

[22] See Report of the UN Secretary-General, *Uniting against terrorism: recommendations for a global counter-terrorism strategy*, UN Doc A/60/825, 27 April 2006, para 42;

In response, the Security Council acknowledged the need for change, instituted a 'focal point' to which individuals could direct their request for delisting, and clarified some procedural standards.[23] The procedure was further strengthened in 2008,[24] yet still without instituting any form of independent review or a true, effective opportunity for appeal by an individual. The decisions on listing and delisting continued to be taken by consensus in the Sanctions Committee and were not subject to outside scrutiny.[25] Unsurprisingly thus, the human rights critique did not go away, was taken up by the UN Human Rights Committee in the 2008 *Sayadi* case,[26] and vindicated by domestic courts, for example by the European Court of Justice in its famous *Kadi* judgment which I will discuss below in greater detail.[27] An English High Court judge found the procedure did 'not begin to achieve fairness for the person who is listed',[28] and a Canadian federal judge went so far as to state that the situation was 'for a listed person not unlike that of Josef K. in Kafka's *The Trial*, who awakens one morning and, for reasons never revealed to him or the reader, is arrested and prosecuted for an unspecified crime'.[29]

Faced with those challenges and wary of further litigation in courts around the world, especially in Europe, the Security Council responded by delisting further individuals and instituting another round of reforms. It did not go as far as establishing an independent review panel, called for by many states and observers, but instead put into place an Ombudsperson competent to receive delisting requests, discuss them with members of the Sanctions Committee,

---

Report of the Special Rapporteur on the promotion and protection of human rights and fundamental freedoms while countering terrorism, UN Doc A/61/267, 16 August 2006, paras 38–41; General Assembly Res 60/288, *The United Nations Global Counter-Terrorism Strategy*, 20 September 2006, Annex: Plan of action, Part II, para 15.

[23] SC Res 1730 (2006), 19 December 2006; 1735 (2006), 22 December 2006.

[24] SC Res 1822 (2008), 30 June 2008.

[25] The procedure is laid out in the Guidelines of the Committee administering the sanctions against Al-Qaeda and the Taliban (1267 Committee), <http://www.un.org/sc/committees/1267/pdf/1267_guidelines.pdf>.

[26] UN Human Rights Committee, Views concerning Communication no 1472/2006, *Sayadi and Vinck v Belgium*, 22 October 2008, UN Doc CCPR/C/94/D/1472/2006, 29 December 2008.

[27] See Section II.2 below.

[28] England and Wales High Court, Queen's Bench Division, Administrative Court, Judgment of 24 April 2008, *A, K, M, Q & G v HM Treasury* [2008] EWHC 869 (Admin), para 18.

[29] Federal Court of Canada, Judgment of 4 June 2009, *Abousfian Abdelrazik v Minister of Foreign Affairs*, 2009 FC 580, para 53.

inquire into their merits, and present a report to the Committee as a basis for its decision.[30] In the interplay of increasing pressure and gradual concessions, however, this step is unlikely to be the last. Domestic courts, now aware of their influence, continue to press for more. The new UK Supreme Court, for one, 'welcomed' the improvements but still saw them as falling short of providing an effective judicial remedy.[31]

II. SANCTIONS AMID A MULTIPLICITY OF LAWS

The contestation over fair procedures in sanctions administration is part of the broader debate about the relationship of security and human rights that has regained intensity in the wake of the 9/11 attacks.[32] Its peculiarity derives in part from the fact that the different elements of this broader debate are reassembled here as a competition not just of countervailing principles within one legal order, but as a contest between legal orders the relationships between which are far from clear. The different institutions involved face the task not only of defining a substantive position but also of positioning themselves, and the legal order(s) of which they are part, vis-à-vis others, thereby engaging in far-reaching, principled argument. As we will see, different courts have responded to this challenge in very different ways, and quite a few of them have, in one way or another, sought to transcend the classical, dichotomous concepts of monism and dualism and tried to shape a suitable strategy for navigating in a world of plural, but heavily enmeshed, legal orders.

1. The Enmeshment of Laws

As I have pointed out in the introductory chapter, this enmeshment is a pervasive feature of global regulatory governance, triggering conceptualizations such as that of a 'global administrative space'.[33] It is particularly visible in the UN sanctions regime where the classical separation between domestic and international law has come under severe pressure for functional reasons. For not only are Chapter VII measures of the Security Council binding,

---

[30] SC Res 1904 (2009), 17 December 2009. For a discussion of the different reform options, see the *Tenth Report of the Analytical Support and Sanctions Implementation Monitoring Team*, UN Doc S/2009/502, 2 October 2009, paras 34–54.

[31] UK Supreme Court, Judgment of 27 January 2010, *HM Treasury v Mohammed Jabar Ahmed and others* [2010] UKSC 2, paras 78 (Lord Hope), 239 (Lord Mance).

[32] See, eg, B J Goold & L Lazarus (eds), *Security and Human Rights*, Oxford: Hart Publishing, 2007.

[33] See Chapter 1, II, and Kingsbury, Krisch, & Stewart, 'Emergence of GAL'.

they also require speedy implementation. The legislative process, which typically provides the link between international and domestic law by transforming one into the other, is ill-suited to this task—it is usually too slow to give sanctions rapid domestic effect; and it is also too cumbersome for issues that are often seen as technical and administrative in nature. Extending an arms embargo to yet another rebel group or geographic area, including yet another person on a target list, or establishing a travel ban for those responsible for yet another conflict are often matters of course, beyond political controversy once the Security Council has decided on them. But they require immediate impact to be effective, and executive implementation may appear as more adequate to the task.

As a result, the structures and institutions of domestic sanctions implementation have evolved significantly since the early 1990s.[34] Many countries have introduced framework legislation allowing for the executive transformation of Security Council decisions, taking parliaments out of the process or reducing them to an oversight role.[35] In other countries, the same effect is achieved on the basis of delegations contained in existing legislation on foreign trade or immigration.[36] Sometimes, legislation or governmental regulations even provide for the automatic transformation of certain sanctions decisions, as we shall see below in the case of the UK. Taken together, this amounts to a normalization of facilitated sanctions implementation through governmental or administrative bodies, resulting in an increasingly immediate effect of Security Council decisions in the domestic realm.[37]

An impressive example of the resulting maze of legal orders is a recent case in the UK courts, involving individuals hit by different sanctions regimes.[38] In our context, the case of G is the most instructive. Upon request of the UK

[34] See the overview in V Gowlland-Debbas, 'Implementing Sanctions Resolutions in Domestic Law' in V Gowlland-Debbas (ed), *National Implementation of United Nations Sanctions: A Comparative Study*, The Hague: Martinus Nijhoff, 2004, 33–78.

[35] This is the case, eg, in Finland; see M Koskenniemi, P Kaukoranta, & M Björklund, 'Finland' in Gowlland-Debbas, *National Implementation*, 167–94.

[36] This is the case, eg, in Germany; see J A Frowein & N Krisch, 'Germany' in Gowlland-Debbas, *National Implementation*, 233–64.

[37] See Gutherie, 'Security Council Sanctions', 516–18; and the findings in Gowlland-Debbas, 'Implementing Sanctions Resolutions'. The conclusions should not be overstated; most existing studies, for example, focus on European countries, and it is not fully clear to what extent their findings apply beyond Europe.

[38] See England and Wales High Court, *A, K, M, Q & G v HM Treasury*; England and Wales High Court, Judgment of 10 July 2009, *HAY v HM Treasury* [2009] EWHC 1677 (Admin); England and Wales Court of Appeal, Judgment of 30 October 2008,

government, G had been listed by the Security Council's 1267 Committee[39] as suspected of supporting the Taliban or Al-Qaeda. As a result of a remarkable chain of legal instruments, this made him automatically subject to enforcement measures under UK law. These were based on the United Nations Act 1946 which grants the UK government wide implementation powers:

> If...the Security Council of the United Nations call upon His Majesty's Government in the United Kingdom to apply any measures to give effect to any decision of that Council, His Majesty may by Order in Council make such provision as appears to Him necessary or expedient for enabling those measures to be effectively applied...[40]

The government had made use of these far-reaching powers on many occasions and come to act routinely on this basis whenever the Security Council enacted new sanctions.[41] As regards Security Council action against terrorism, it had created an especially tight link. Its Al Qaida and Taliban (United Nations Measures) Order 2006 (AQO) subjected to financial measures every 'designated person', including *ipso facto* all persons listed by the Sanctions Committee, thus granting such listings direct effect in the UK legal order.[42] As a result, after his UN listing, G's bank accounts in the UK were frozen immediately.

When G sought to contest these measures in court, he learned that the AQO provided for judicial review on the merits only against designations by the Treasury, not against those automatically following from Security Council listings. Because of a lack of alternative channels of appeal in the UN context, this would have completely deprived G of meaningful review options. The Court of Appeal decided to reinterpret the AQO, despite its clear language, and make merits review available to G. Both the High Court and the Supreme Court found such a construction impossible and quashed the AQO for lack of effective review mechanisms.

A, K, M, Q & G v HM Treasury [2008] EWCA Civ 1187; UK Supreme Court, *Treasury v Mohammed Jabar Ahmed and others.*

[39] The 1267 Committee—the sanctions committee administering sanctions against these targets—derives its name from SC Res 1267 which first created it; see SC Res 1267 (1999), 15 October 1999.

[40] Section 1(1) United Nations Act 1946.

[41] See C Greenwood, 'United Kingdom' in Gowlland-Debbas, *National Implementation*, 581–604. An 'Order in Council' requires a meeting of the Privy Council; see ibid, 592.

[42] Art 3(1)(b) AQO.

There is no need to examine the (in part quite convoluted) reasoning of the courts in detail, but it is important to highlight how multiple layers of law mattered for their decisions. Domestic and international law were not only intertwined on the sanctions side, they were also tightly linked on the opposite side, that of human rights. For a right to an effective remedy exists in UK law, apart from common law foundations, mainly on the basis of the Human Rights Act (HRA) which incorporates the European Convention on Human Rights (ECHR). In the interpretation of the House of Lords, the HRA does not 'domesticate' the Convention but refers to it as an international law document[43]—implying that international legal limits to Convention rights are transposed into UK law too. This also applies to the limits imposed by the UN Charter and especially its Article 103 which provides that in case of conflict, obligations under the Charter—including those created by the Security Council on the basis of its delegated powers—prevail over other international agreements. Thus, insofar as sanctions measures conflict with rights under the ECHR, the former enjoy primacy—and not only under international law, but because of the linkages, also as a matter of UK law.

Both the High Court and the Court of Appeal recognized this, but did not for this reason disregard Convention rights altogether. For the House of Lords had held in a previous judgment concerning detention in Iraq that, despite Article 103, such conflicts should as far as possible be resolved by reconciliation—by attempts at interpreting Security Council resolutions in a rights-friendly way and by using discretion in implementation in accordance with the ECHR.[44] In the present case, the lower courts regarded such a reconciliation as possible: the measures could be examined on the merits; only the remedy needed to be limited to avoid conflict. If the court found the complaint justified, it could thus not order the government to lift the asset freeze; it could only require it to pursue delisting in the sanctions committee.[45]

I have presented this case to highlight the entanglement of various layers of law. G's asset freeze is the result of a Security Council determination imported automatically into UK law and—through a designation by the European Commission—also into EU (and consequently domestic) law. And his remedies against it are based on a mélange of the common law, the UK

---

[43] See House of Lords, Judgment of 17 June 2004, *R v Special Adjudicator, ex parte Ullah*, [2004] UKHL 26, para 20. See also the discussion in Chapter 4, II.2.

[44] House of Lords, Judgment of 12 December 2007, *R (Al Jeddah) v Defence Secretary* [2007] UKHL 58, para 39 (Lord Bingham).

[45] High Court, *A, K, M, Q & G v HM Treasury*, paras 34–6; Court of Appeal, *A, K, M, Q & G v HM Treasury*, paras 116–19.

Human Rights Act and the ECHR, though these again oscillate between domestic and international law and find their limits in the primacy of the UN Charter (though ultimately only in the sovereignty of the UK parliament). The High Court and Court of Appeal grappled hard to structure their argument, and the 'conciliation' solution is certainly an attempt not to press the issues of principle—of hierarchies and distinctions between legal orders—too hard. This is typical English judicial style, but it also reflects the intricacies of the matter and a particular caution of the courts. They could have found in favour of merits-based judicial review also on the basis of the common law alone—in fact, much of the argument before the court turned on this issue. This would have avoided the difficulties with international law caused by the reliance on the HRA and the ECHR.

It is this common law course that the UK Supreme Court ultimately embarked upon. It recognized the limitations on HRA arguments because of Article 103 and decided not to address them pending clarification of the matter by the Grand Chamber of the European Court of Human Rights. Instead, it founded its judgment primarily on the common law principle of legality, which for serious interferences with certain rights requires a basis in parliamentary statute. In the view of the Supreme Court, the United Nations Act 1946 was not specific enough to provide such a basis; the AQO thus had to be quashed.

Though important for stressing (and clarifying) separation of powers issues, the Supreme Court judgment largely avoids the difficult issues at the intersection of the different layers of law. It decides the case on narrow grounds, in a minimalist fashion,[46] and its main effect is to move the proceedings a step back, forcing the government to secure a more explicit legislative grounding. The government did so just two weeks after the judgment, at least in temporary fashion, and thus avoided non-compliance with UN resolutions.[47] But as the legislation merely re-enacts the orders quashed by the court, it raises the same substantive questions about the protection of rights and judicial review—questions left open by the Supreme Court, to be addressed in future adjudication. The 2010 judgment is so far little more than a warning shot.

Overall, thus, the UK courts have taken a cautious approach. They decided not to adopt the confrontational course of insisting on the supremacy of domestic rights which, as we shall see shortly, was taken by the European Court of Justice (ECJ). They instead either postponed a decision on the substantive issues (as the Supreme Court did) or situated their solution in the

---

[46] On minimalism in pluralist adjudication, see Chapter 8, III.1.

[47] Terrorist Asset-Freezing (Temporary Provisions) Act 2010, 10 February 2010.

midst of a pluralist web of legal orders. They thus acted more in the spirit the ECJ's Advocate-General, Miguel Maduro, had advocated in his opinion in the *Kadi* case:

> In an increasingly interdependent world, different legal orders will have to endeavour to accommodate each other's jurisdictional claims. As a result, the [ECJ] cannot always assert a monopoly on determining how certain fundamental interests ought to be reconciled.[48]

The enmeshment of different legal orders does not do away with their distinctive natures: they continue to rely on different sources, *Grundnormen*, and substantive principles. From a theoretical perspective, all those outside norms are not a necessary, only a contingent part of the UK's legal order— the UK could have refrained from an automaticity in listing and could have insisted on its autonomy in determining who is sanctioned and when. In practice, though, these options were hardly real in today's interwoven legal and political structure. Just as monism does not capture the distinctness of the parts of that order, dualism overstates their separation. What is far more interesting, then, are the efforts at coordination and distancing that characterize their relationships. The winding argument, the avoidance of statements of principle, and the quest for reconciliation we have observed in the UK courts is a reflection of precisely such an effort. It is the search for a judicial voice in a new, pluralist context.

2. Pluralism and Principle in the Judicial Response to Sanctions

Other courts have adopted a more principled stance on the structural questions involved. I cannot analyse all the relevant jurisprudence in detail here[49] and will instead focus on two decisions from the EU context that exemplify the opposing positions and help clarify the difficulties when courts undertake the task of determining the relationship between the different layers of law in a systematic way. They have also attracted the strongest political

---

[48] European Court of Justice, Opinion of Advocate-General Poiares Maduro, 16 January 2008, C-402/05, *Kadi*, para 44.

[49] See A Tzanakopoulos, 'Domestic Court Reactions to UN Security Council Sanctions' in A Reinisch (ed), *Challenging Acts of International Organizations Before National Courts*, Oxford: Oxford University Press, 2010, forthcoming, available at: <http://ssrn.com/abstract=1480184>. On litigated cases, see the reports of the 1267 Committee's monitoring team, available at: <http://www.un.org/sc/committees/1267/monitoringteam.shtml>; for example, the Ninth Report, UN Doc S/2009/245, 13 May 2009, Annex I.

attention, including by the 1267 Committee's Monitoring Team,[50] and are thus worth analysing in some detail.

The contrasting judgments stem from the same proceedings in the EU courts, brought by, among others, Yassin Abdullah Kadi, a Saudi businessman whose European assets had been frozen following his listing by the 1267 Committee soon after the 9/11 attacks. As I have mentioned above, the transformation of Security Council decisions into EU law is not automatic; it requires a Commission regulation, which in Mr Kadi's case was adopted two days after the UN decision.[51] This regulation, together with the Council regulation on which it was based, formed the object of Mr Kadi's challenge in the European courts; he argued that he had been listed mistakenly, had no effective way of appealing this decision on the international level, and that his rights to a fair hearing and to effective review as well as his property rights were infringed.

The European Court of First Instance (CFI) approached the issue from a largely monist angle.[52] Because it constructs a comprehensive, hierarchically ordered system of which EU law is a part, it can also be characterized as a 'constitutionalist' approach.[53] For the CFI, even though the EU is not a member of the UN, the EC Treaty had to be read as limited by member states' obligations under the UN Charter. This followed from both general international law, which through Article 103 of the UN Charter established a primacy of the Charter over other obligations, and from the EC Treaty itself, which in Article 307 provides that pre-existing rights and obligations of members under international agreements shall not be affected by the Treaty's entry into force.[54] Moreover, the EU was now exercising powers previously exercised by member states and had entered into their obligations in this respect. The Court thus found

> first, that the Community may not infringe the obligations imposed on its Member States by the Charter of the United Nations or impede their performance and, second, that in the exercise of its powers it is bound, by the very

---

[50] See especially the Ninth Report, paras 19–23, 27.

[51] Commission Regulation (EC) No 2062/2001, 19 October 2001, *Official Journal EU* 2001, L 277/25. For the general framework of UN sanctions implementation in the EU, see D Bethlehem, 'The European Union' in Gowlland-Debbas, *National Implementation*, 123–65.

[52] CFI, Judgment of 21 September 2005, T-315/01, *Kadi*.

[53] See G de Búrca, 'The European Court of Justice and the International Legal Order after *Kadi*', *Jean Monnet Working Paper* 01/09, <http://www.jeanmonnetpro­gram.org/papers/09/090101.html>, 45.

[54] CFI, *Kadi*, paras 181–97.

Treaty by which it was established, to adopt all the measures necessary to enable its Member States to fulfil those obligations.[55]

The hierarchy of norms under international law thus continued in EU law, and the CFI regarded an exercise of judicial review powers as contrary to the norms of UN law which enjoyed primacy. It therefore rejected the claim of the applicant that it should apply EU fundamental rights standards to the Commission's listing decision. However, it allowed for limited judicial review in order to establish whether the listing decision by the Security Council contravened higher norms of international law, namely *ius cogens*—this was possible in the Court's view because peremptory norms of international law also limited Security Council powers, and Security Council resolutions that violated them could accordingly not bind the EU or its member states so that the initial rationale against judicial review would no longer apply. Even though the CFI took a very generous view of what norms *ius cogens* encompassed, it eventually rejected the applicant's claims.

The recourse to peremptory norms and their extensive interpretation may have been a warning shot to the Security Council, indicating that despite the limited ambit of judicial review European courts might decide to intervene at some point.[56] But as with a largely parallel judgment by the Swiss Federal Court,[57] this threat was widely regarded as weak and the decision as an abdication of judicial power in the face of sanctions decisions of the Security Council.[58] This challenged some common alliances—human rights activists, typically much in favour of an internationalist, constitutionalist approach of the kind the CFI defended, were now very critical of that general stance, while those keen on security interests, usually more

---

[55] ibid, para 204.

[56] C Tomuschat, note on *Kadi*, *Common Market Law Review* 43 (2006), 537–51 at 551, observes that under the cover of *ius cogens* the CFI 'resorted to applying to their full extent the standards evolved in the practice of the Community's judicial bodies'.

[57] Schweizerisches Bundesgericht, Judgment of 14 November 2007, 1A.45/2007, *Nada v SECO, Staatssekretariat für Wirtschaft*, available at: <http://www.bger.ch/fr/index/jurisdiction/jurisdiction-inherit-template/jurisdiction-recht/jurisdiction-recht-urteile2000.htm>.

[58] See, eg, P Eeckhout, 'Community Terrorism Listings, Fundamental Rights, and UN Security Council Resolutions: In Search of the Right Fit', *European Constitutional Law Review* 3 (2007), 183–206; J Almqvist, 'A Human Rights Critique of European Judicial Review: Counter-Terrorism Sanctions', *International and Comparative Law Quarterly* 57 (2008), 303–31 at 319–26.

nationally minded, grew fonder of an international law that played into their hands.[59]

Apart from this reconfiguration, the CFI decision follows conceptually predictable lines—in its clear, integrated construction of the global legal order it takes a largely monist turn, without grappling much with the tensions between different parts of the order or efforts at reconciling conflicting substantive rules. A greater awareness of these tensions can be found in the appeals judgment by the ECJ, a judgment that has sometimes been described as epitomizing a pluralist vision.[60] I will return later to the question whether it can indeed be described in these terms. Pluralism certainly was an explicit theme in the opinion of the ECJ's Advocate-General—unsurprisingly, as Miguel Maduro had long been a protagonist of pluralist, 'counterpunctual' conceptions of the European legal order.[61] In this opinion, however, pluralist sensitivities—as in the passage quoted in the previous section—do not engender conclusions different from those to be expected in a classical dualist setting. For Maduro gives pride of place to fundamental rights under European law and relegates international law to a place on the outside, largely irrelevant for decision-making. This is, as he emphasizes, because the Security Council decisions in question are out of sync with European understandings of rights:

> the Court cannot, in deference to the views of...institutions [such as the Security Council], turn its back on the fundamental values that lie at the basis of the Community legal order and which it has the duty to protect. Respect for other institutions is meaningful only if it can be built on a shared understanding of these values and on a mutual commitment to protect them.[62]

In the end, this simply reiterates the dualist position:

> The relationship between international law and the Community legal order is governed by the Community legal order itself, and international law can

---

[59] On some of those tensions, see A Gattini, note on *Kadi and Al Barakaat*, *Common Market Law Review* 46 (2009), 213–39 at 213–14.

[60] de Búrca, 'ECJ and International Legal Order', 45; D Halberstam & E Stein, 'The United Nations, the European Union, and the King of Sweden: Economic Sanctions and Individual Rights in a Plural World Order', *Common Market Law Review* 46 (2009), 13–72 at 58–61.

[61] M Poiares Maduro, 'Europe and the Constitution: What if This is as Good as it Gets?' in J H H Weiler & M Wind (eds), *European Constitutionalism Beyond the State*, Cambridge: Cambridge University Press, 2003, 74–102; M Poiares Maduro, 'Contrapunctual Law: Europe's Constitutional Pluralism in Action' in N Walker (ed), *Sovereignty in Transition*, Oxford: Hart Publishing, 2003, 501–38.

[62] Opinion of the Advocate-General, *Kadi*, para 44.

permeate that legal order only under the conditions set by the constitutional principles of the Community.[63]

The freeze of Mr Kadi's assets in the EU is consequently assessed on the basis of the same criteria that would have been applied had no Security Council measure preceded it—an entirely 'domestic' solution.

The judgment of the ECJ's Grand Chamber largely follows in this track, even if it is less explicit in its theoretical choices.[64] It draws a clear dividing line between EU law and international law, stressing the autonomy of the EU legal order in determining which international legal rules enter that order and at what place in the hierarchy of norms. The ECJ describes international law as important within the EU, for example as binding EU institutions in the exercise of their powers[65] and as possibly even trumping primary law in certain cases.[66] But it leaves no doubt that under no circumstances will international rules affect the fundamental, constitutional pillars of EU law:

> Those provisions [on international law as part of EU law] cannot . . . be understood to authorise any derogation from the principles of liberty, democracy and respect for human rights and fundamental freedoms enshrined in Article 6(1) EU as a foundation of the Union.[67]

The Court thus acts—as it had been invited to do by the Advocate-General[68]—as a constitutional court, protecting the core of European law from internal and external challenge. This becomes clearest in the summarizing paragraph:

> [T]he review by the Court of the validity of any Community measure in the light of fundamental rights must be considered to be the expression, in a community based on the rule of law, of a constitutional guarantee stemming from the EC Treaty as an autonomous legal system which is not to be prejudiced by an international agreement.[69]

The ECJ thus claims for itself the power to 'ensure the review, in principle the full review'[70] of the acts that give the Security Council decisions effect, and

---

[63] ibid, para 24.

[64] ECJ, Grand Chamber, Judgment of 3 September 2008, C-402/05 P & 415/15 P, *Kadi and Al-Barakaat v Council of the European Union*.

[65] ibid, para 291.

[66] ibid, para 301.

[67] ibid, para 303.

[68] Opinion of the Advocate-General, *Kadi and Al-Barakaat*, para 37.

[69] ECJ, *Kadi and Al-Barakaat*, para 316.

[70] ibid, para 326.

it softens the resulting blow to the international system only by emphasizing that the effect of its judgments are limited to the European legal order and do 'not entail any challenge to the primacy of [the Security Council] resolution in international law'.[71] The two spheres are thus neatly divided, linked only by certain provisions of EU law that open it up to the outside world. Just as under many national constitutions, international law thus imported enters the domestic sphere below the constitutional level, trumping ordinary legislation, not constitutional guarantees.[72]

Unlike many constitutional courts, though, the ECJ leaves unclear whether and to what extent European standards of rights protection may be modified for the sake of international cooperation. Ever since the German Constitutional Court's first *Solange* judgment,[73] it has become a typical topos in constitutional adjudication to argue that insisting on full compliance of international institutions with the constitutional rules of *all* member states would unduly inhibit cooperative efforts, and that consequently domestic constitutions should be read as allowing for some flexibility. This approach has also been adopted by the European Court of Human Rights (ECtHR) which in a series of judgments has insisted that member states cannot evade their human rights obligations by transferring powers to international institutions, but that they do not have to ensure full compliance of these institutions with the ECHR, only a standard of 'equivalent protection'. Where such equivalent protection is generally assured, the ECtHR would only exercise limited scrutiny of the particular acts of the institution in question—as it has accepted to do, for example, vis-à-vis the European Space Agency and the European Union itself, as we have seen in the discussion of the *Bosphorus* judgment in Chapter 4.[74]

The ECJ's stance towards the Security Council shows traces of such an approach, but no explicit endorsement. The Court states, for example, that:

> the existence, within that United Nations system, of the re-examination procedure before the Sanctions Committee...cannot give rise to generalised immunity from jurisdiction within the internal legal order of the Community.... [S]uch immunity, constituting a significant derogation from the scheme of judicial protection of fundamental rights laid down by the EC

---

[71] ibid, para 288.

[72] ibid, paras 307–8.

[73] Bundesverfassungsgericht, Judgment of 29 January 1974, BVerfGE 37, 271, *Solange I*.

[74] ECtHR (Grand Chamber), Judgment of 18 February 1999, *Waite & Kennedy v Germany*; ECtHR (Grand Chamber), Judgment of 30 June 2005, *Bosphorus Hava Yolları Turizm v Ireland*. See also Chapter 4, II.1.

Treaty, appears unjustified, for clearly that re-examination procedure does not offer the guarantees of judicial protection.[75]

It then goes on to explain the shortcomings of the Sanctions Committee listing process, but it leaves unspecified what would have been the consequence of a fairer procedure. Would it have given rise to a 'generalized immunity'? To a more limited level of scrutiny? And what level of rights protection would have triggered such a consequence—full compliance with EU fundamental rights, or some adjusted standard such as 'equivalent protection'?

A judgment is not a scholarly treatise and one should not expect too much elaboration on theoretical questions that are not immediately necessary for deciding the case at hand. Commentators disagree on how to interpret the Court's 'somewhat cryptic'[76] statements: some believe they indicate a *Solange*-style approach;[77] others see them as rejecting it.[78] It is probably best to understand them as deliberately vague, leaving open the question of whether, and under what conditions, the Court may in the future practise deference to the Security Council or other international institutions with binding powers.

Apart from this point, though, the ECJ's approach in *Kadi* is entirely domestic—as in the case of the Advocate-General's opinion, the result does not seem any different from what it would have been had an isolated EU measure been challenged.[79] It is not a strictly dualist stance because in the reading of the Court, certain obligations under international law form part of the European legal order and even trump secondary Community law. But it is clear that the impact of international law is controlled solely by EU law itself, and insofar as EU law does not import it or imposes limits on its application, international law is of no relevance to the Court. On a theoretical level, this is not unlike what we have found to be the situation in the UK. But in their judicial approaches, the ECJ and the UK courts are worlds apart: while the latter actively seek (or, in the Supreme Court's case, allow for) ways to accommodate the positions of different layers of law, the former insists on the supremacy of European law in its sphere of jurisdiction, and

---

[75] ECJ, *Kadi and Al-Barakaat*, paras 321–2.

[76] Halberstam & Stein, 'UN, EU, and the King of Sweden', 60.

[77] P Eeckhout, 'Kadi and Al Barakaat: Luxembourg is not Texas—or Washington DC', *EJIL:Talk!*, 25 February 2009, at: <http://www.ejiltalk.org/kadi-and-al-barakaat-luxembourg-is-not-texas-or-washington-dc/>.

[78] Halberstam & Stein, 'UN, EU, and the King of Sweden', 60–1; Gattini, note on *Kadi and Al Barakaat*, at 234–5.

[79] J H H Weiler, 'Editorial', *European Journal of International Law* 19 (2008), 895–9 at 895–6.

the interwovenness of the parts of the global legal order does not really enter the picture.[80]

The ECJ's judgment nevertheless fits into an overall pluralist structure, one that is characterized by the coexistence of different legal orders, all with their own foundational norms and substantive commitments.[81] For it is typical for pluralism that relations with other orders are assessed and governed by each order itself—*how* they are governed may then vary widely.[82] The ECJ's stance may be characterized as one of distance, that of the UK courts as one of greater proximity. All of them—unlike the CFI that tried to construct EU law and international law as part of one, overarching legal order with clear hierarchies and conflict rules—devise frameworks that interrelate foundational difference with practical interaction among different orders. Their strategies for this differ, and they may indeed be *strategies*: attempts at influencing the evolution of other orders. Yet these strategies are embedded in broader understandings of who should enjoy ultimate supremacy and how far cooperation with the outside should go.

3. Europe's Internal Pluralism

The discussion so far has made it seem as if international law were the only 'outside' the ECJ needed to position itself towards. It was certainly the only explicit one in *Kadi*. But in the background—both practically and theoretically—loomed others that could also have created difficulties for the court: domestic constitutional orders. As Jo Murkens has highlighted, the strong insistence on fundamental rights and on the autonomy of EU law can be understood as an attempt by the ECJ to ward off potential challenges by national courts. For had it let the contested EU regulation stand, domestic constitutional courts may have seen it as their duty to intervene and protect the human rights anchored in their constitutions, challenging the supremacy of European law in the process.[83]

This was no merely academic risk; after all, the ECJ has been under the supervision of domestic courts ever since the German Constitutional Court, in the above-mentioned *Solange* judgment of 1974, announced that it would

---

[80] See also the critique of a missing attempt at interjurisdictional dialogue in Halberstam & Stein, 'UN, EU, and the King of Sweden', 61–8; Gattini, note on *Kadi and Al Barakaat*, 224–35.

[81] See the discussion in de Búrca, 'ECJ and International Legal Order', 45–55.

[82] See Chapter 3, I and III.3 and Chapter 8, III.

[83] J Murkens, 'Countering Anti-Constitutional Argument: The Reasons for the European Court of Justice's Decision in *Kadi and Al Barakaat*', *Cambridge Yearbook of European Legal Studies* 11 (2009), 15–51 at 43–50.

scrutinize European Community acts for fundamental rights violations unless the EC developed a satisfactory system of human rights protection.[84] Twelve years later, the German court recognized the progress the ECJ had achieved and retreated to a role in the background, without however relinquishing its right to resume closer scrutiny should the situation change.[85] And from time to time, it has fired warning shots, also outside the area of fundamental rights, to rein the EU in when it appeared to have gone too far—the notorious *Maastricht* judgment is only the most prominent among them.[86]

The German court was not alone with this stance; other constitutional courts followed suit and reinforced the challenge to the ECJ.[87] The conflict was, of course, about much more than the correct interpretation of rights—it was about who was entitled to decide on the right interpretation (national or European judges) and what legal order was ultimately controlling (national or European). For the national courts, EU law derived its foundation from the various national legal orders of member states and had not been able to cut this umbilical cord; it was up to the member states to define the conditions and limits for EU competences and for national courts to police that these limits, contained in national constitutions and in the treaties by which powers had been transferred, were respected.

From this perspective, the supremacy of European law, already claimed by the ECJ in the 1960s, had to appear as conditional. This did not change when the 2004 draft constitutional treaty sought to anchor supremacy explicitly.[88] The treaty left some room for the argument that the supremacy

---

[84] See Bundesverfassungsgericht, *Solange I*.

[85] Bundesverfassungsgericht, Judgment of 22 October 1986, BVerfGE 73, 339, *Solange II*.

[86] See Bundesverfassungsgericht, Judgment of 12 October 1993, *Maastricht*, BVerfGE 89, 155; Judgment of 18 July 2005, *European Arrest Warrant*, BVerfGE 113, 273; Judgment of 30 June 2009, 2 BvE 2/08 et al, *Lisbon Treaty*.

[87] See A-M Slaughter, A Stone Sweet, & J H H Weiler (eds), *The European Court and National Courts: Doctrine and Jurisprudence*, Oxford: Hart Publishing, 1997; F C Mayer, *Kompetenzüberschreitung und Letztentscheidung*, Munich: C H Beck, 2000, 140–259. On recent cases, see W Sadurski, '"Solange, Chapter 3": Constitutional Courts in Central Europe—Democracy—European Union', *European Law Journal* 14 (2008), 1–35; J Baquero Cruz, 'The Legacy of the Maastricht-Urteil and the Pluralist Movement', *European Law Journal* 14 (2008), 389–422 at 391–403.

[88] Art I-6 of the Treaty establishing a Constitution for Europe, *Official Journal EU*, C 310/1, 16 December 2004, read: 'The Constitution and law adopted by the institutions of the Union in exercising competences conferred on it shall have primacy over the law of the Member States'.

clause only applied to the ordinary law of member states, not to their constitutions. And because of an additional declaration to the effect that the clause merely reflected the jurisprudence of the ECJ, it was unclear to what extent it could be interpreted as a major element of change.[89] Doubts in this respect were confirmed when both the French *Conseil constitutionnel* and the Spanish *Tribunal Constitucional* ruled that, even under the Constitutional Treaty, EU law remained subject to national constitutional law and that the supremacy clause was only of limited scope.[90] This position was reinforced when, after the failure of the constitutional treaty, a series of highest national courts fired warning shots by challenging the legislation implementing the European arrest warrant.[91] The Lisbon Treaty, then, does not contain a supremacy clause; it is only accompanied by a declaration that refers to the settled case law on the primacy of EU law.[92] The treaty thus explicitly does not move beyond the status quo.[93]

Awareness had already risen in the 1990s, especially after the German Constitutional Court's *Maastricht* judgment, of the fact that the opposing

---

[89] Declaration No 1 on Article I-6, *Official Journal EU*, C 310/1, 16 December 2004, 428. For the view that the supremacy clause left the situation unchanged, see A Weber, 'Zur föderalen Struktur der Europäischen Union im Entwurf des Europäischen Verfassungsvertrags', *Europarecht* 39 (2004), 841–56; G Beck, 'The Problem of *Kompetenz-Kompetenz*: A Conflict between Right and Right in Which There is No *Praetor*', *European Law Review* 30 (2005), 42–67. For the opposite position, see M Kumm & V Ferreres Comella, 'The Primacy Clause of the Constitutional Treaty and the Future of Constitutional Conflict in the European Union' in J H H Weiler & C Eisgruber (eds), 'Altneuland: The EU Constitution in a Contextual Perspective', *Jean Monnet Working Paper* 5/04, at: <http://www.jean-monnetprogram.org/papers/04/040501-15.html>.

[90] Tribunal Constitucional, Judgment of 13 December 2004, DTC 1/2004, part II, sections 3–4; Conseil constitutionnel, Decision of 19 November 2004, no 2004-505 DC, para 10-3. On the latter, see F C Mayer, 'Europarecht als französisches Verfassungsrecht', *Europarecht* 39 (2004), 925–36. For a similar argument, see V Röben, 'Constitutionalism of the European Union after the Draft Constitutional Treaty: How Much Hierarchy?', *Columbia Journal of European Law* 10 (2004), S339–77.

[91] See J Komárek, 'European Constitutionalism and the European Arrest Warrant: In Search of the Limits of "Contrapunctual Principles"', *Common Market Law Review* 44 (2007), 9–40.

[92] Declaration no 17 annexed to the Lisbon Treaty, *Official Journal EU* 2008, C 115/344.

[93] See S Griller, 'Is this a Constitution? Remarks on a Contested Concept' in S Griller & J Ziller (eds), *The Lisbon Treaty: EU Constitutionalism without a Constitutional Treaty?*, Vienna: Springer Verlag, 2008, 21–56 at 46–50.

positions on supremacy were not provisional, accidental, or merely strategic but reflected fundamental convictions of the different courts involved—convictions that also had a basis in popular attitudes to the European Union.[94] As I have mentioned in Chapter 3, it was Neil MacCormick who sought to capture this overall picture by understanding the conflicting views as positions that, in the contexts within which the institutions operated, were entirely rational.[95] The conflict was thus not merely about interpretation within one legal order, it reflected a clash between different systems with different starting points. It was thus also not amenable to a legal solution, for there was no independent standpoint that could have provided a decision—there were only the competing, fundamentally diverging perspectives of the different systems, which could at most be pragmatically bridged for the solution of concrete problems. The overall structure was thus pluralist.

MacCormick's assessment later underwent some change, but his initial conception still proved highly influential.[96] It has provided a counterpart to interpretations of EU law in constitutional, hierarchically ordered terms on the one hand, and to understandings in a classical international law framework on the other. These have significant downsides: the latter cannot quite capture the level of integration the European legal order has achieved; the former, constitutional reading downplays the fundamental tension between the supremacy claims of the competing levels, and ignores the absence of an accepted, overarching frame to resolve it. MacCormick's later view came in fact close to such a constitutional interpretation, understanding international law as the frame within which national and EU law interacted.[97] But this supposed frame was heavily contested itself: one key element in the dispute over supremacy was whether or not EU law had cut the link to its international law origins—and to the sovereignty of member states these origins implied.

[94] See N Krisch, 'Die Vielheit der europäischen Verfassung' in K Groh et al (eds), *Die Europäische Verfassung–Verfassungen in Europa*, Baden-Baden: Nomos, 2005, 61–90 at 71–9, on pluralism and social attitudes in the EU.

[95] See Chapter 3, I and N MacCormick, 'Beyond the Sovereign State', *Modern Law Review* 56 (1993), 1–18; N MacCormick, 'The Maastricht-Urteil: Sovereignty Now', *European Law Journal* 1 (1995), 259–66.

[96] See, eg, J Shaw, 'Postnational Constitutionalism in the European Union', *Journal of European Public Policy* 6 (1999), 579–97; N Walker, 'The Idea of Constitutional Pluralism', *Modern Law Review* 65 (2002), 317–59; Poiares Maduro, 'Europe and the Constitution' and 'Contrapunctual Law'; also the collected essays in Walker, *Sovereignty in Transition*; Weiler & Wind, *European Constitutionalism*.

[97] N MacCormick, 'Risking Constitutional Collision in Europe?', *Oxford Journal of Legal Studies* 18 (1998), 517–32.

The pluralist reading of European law has attracted much normative critique, especially from a rule-of-law perspective, which I will return to in Chapter 8. In analytical terms, however, critics of pluralism have had less resonance, and they have had difficulties integrating the supremacy contest, with its multiplicity of systemic perspectives, into alternative frameworks.[98] For example, the attempt to rationalize it as a form of 'civil disobedience' on the part of national courts[99] is not overly plausible when it is in fact the ECJ that the national courts accuse of disobedience.

The value of the pluralist interpretation becomes even clearer when the European example is situated in the broader global context, as we have seen in this chapter. For the contestation between national law, European law and both security and human rights regimes under international law can hardly be captured in the well-ordered terms constitutionalist frameworks of whatever kind are built upon. Hierarchies are here even more contested than in the regional context, and Europe's internal pluralism (which of course also extends to the pluralism of its human rights regime, as the previous chapter has shown) then becomes a piece in a broader transnational mosaic,[100] in the interplay between radically diverging visions of what order is ultimately controlling. And just like in Europe, the global pluralist structure provides the backdrop to a strategic positioning of actors—courts and political bodies—seeking to influence each other and ward off fundamental challenges.

III. PLURALISM VS EFFECTIVENESS IN SECURITY GOVERNANCE?

Pluralism may be attractive as an account of the current structure of postnational governance, in Europe and beyond, but it still faces serious normative concerns, and in particular unease about its ability to secure stability and effectiveness. These need not always pose problems, as we have seen in the previous chapter on European human rights, but in that case stability might simply have been a result of benign circumstances. The present chapter provides a harder test: international security cooperation operates in far less favourable conditions than the European human rights regime, especially as regards the homogeneity of the countries at its core.

---

[98] See also N W Barber, 'Legal Pluralism and the European Union', *European Law Journal* 12 (2006), 306–29 at 323–7.

[99] Baquero Cruz, 'Legacy of the Maastricht-Urteil', 416–17.

[100] I borrow the image of a mosaic from Neil Walker; see, eg, N Walker, 'Beyond Boundary Disputes and Basic Grids: Mapping the Global Disorder of Normative Orders', *International Journal of Constitutional Law* 6 (2008), 373–96 at 388.

1. The Security Council's Authority in a Pluralist Order

Because the Security Council's authority rests on relatively weak pillars, the international security regime is highly vulnerable to destabilizing factors. In the case of sanctions against terrorism, the Council benefits from the support—and enforcement efforts—of the United States, but this support alone does not guarantee compliance by other states; in fact, too close an alignment with the powerful might be harmful to the Council's efforts to win acceptance from the rest of the international community.[101] This acceptance, as far as it goes,[102] can most plausibly be explained on a rationalist basis as a function of the benefits the Security Council provides.[103] On the one hand, it helps solve cooperation problems on urgent security issues, by establishing a focal point for the terms of cooperation and by enforcing those terms and preventing defection.[104] That this should be the task of the Council and not some other institutional arrangement may be due to path-dependence and a lack of realistic alternatives, but it is possibly due also to the procedural benefits many states derive from it compared to more informal, ad hoc means of coordination. Unlike less institutionalized options, the Security Council provides at least some restraint on the most powerful states: by its more inclusive membership, by the modest degree of transparency it offers, and perhaps also by a demand for justifiying security policies in its midst.[105] Despite the inequalities in composition and voting power, most states derive advantages (however modest) from the Council's centrality in the global security regime.

The resulting authority of the Council is thin; it is subject to a recalculation of interests in every single case. Some governments may have developed

---

[101] Cf K W Abbott & D Snidal, 'Why States Act through Formal International Organizations', *Journal of Conflict Resolution* 42 (1998), 3–32 at 18–19.

[102] On the expansion of the Council's authority in recent decades, see B Cronin & I Hurd (eds), *The UN Security Council and the Politics of International Authority*, London: Routledge, 2008.

[103] N Krisch, 'The Security Council and the Great Powers' in Lowe et al, *Security Council and War,* 133–53 at 145–7.

[104] This aspect is emphasized by E Voeten, 'The Political Origins of the UN Security Council's Ability to Legitimize the Use of Force', *International Organization* 59 (2005), 527–57.

[105] On the latter, see the (overly idealistic) account of I Johnstone, 'Security Council Deliberations: The Power of the Better Argument', *European Journal of International Law* 14 (2003), 437–80. See also G J Ikenberry, *After Victory: Institutions, Strategic Restraint, and the Rebuilding of Order After Major Wars*, Princeton, NJ: Princeton University Press, 2001, for a broader account of institution-building as stabilizing self-restraint by great powers.

a habit of implementing Security Council decisions, but many have not; and there is uneven resonance among publics for the proposition that Council decisions ought to be generally obeyed.[106] In many sanctions regimes, even reporting duties are only followed reluctantly, and further obligations are implemented unevenly. If the Council possesses anything resembling legitimacy—a generalized acceptance stemming from a sense of appropriateness—it is very fragile.[107]

Pluralism might weaken the authority of the Council further. By maintaining a plurality of parallel legal orders, it seems to undermine the hierarchy the UN Charter establishes and to open up paths to justify noncompliance. If this facilitates violations of Council decisions, it could set in motion a cascade of further violations—too many defections are likely to undercut the utility of the regime even for those willing to cooperate. And as it also allows space for alternative normative frameworks, it might make attempts at delegitimation easier—and may damage what little legitimacy the Security Council enjoys.

Such effects are indeed visible in our context. Reliable data about compliance rates are not available, but there is impressionistic evidence about attitudes towards the global security regime. For example, the 1267 Committee's monitoring team as well as outside observers have noted an increasing reluctance of governments to propose new names for inclusion in the sanctions list, and more generally a dwindling of support.[108] This may stem from a lack of trust in the effectiveness of the regime, but it may also be due to

---

[106] In a 2007 poll, sixteen publics around the world were asked whether their governments 'should be more willing to make decisions within the United Nations even if this means that [the respective country] will sometimes have to go along with a policy that is not its first choice'. Majorities agreed in four countries, pluralities in six; pluralities disagreed in three countries, a majority in one territory. Two countries were divided. See WorldPublicOpinion.org, 'World Publics Favor New Powers for the UN', 9 May 2007, <http://www.worldpublicopinion.org/pipa/articles/btunitednationsra/355.php?lb=btun&pnt=355&nid=&id=>.

[107] See also Krisch, 'Security Council and Great Powers', 146–7. For an example for contestations over legitimacy, see I Hurd, 'The Strategic Use of Liberal Internationalism: Libya and the UN Sanctions, 1992–2003', *International Organization* 59 (2005), 495–526. For a broader account of the politics of legitimacy at the Council, see I Hurd, *After Anarchy: Legitimacy and Power in the UN Security Council*, Princeton, NJ: Princeton University Press, 2007.

[108] See the *Seventh Report* of the Monitoring Team, UN Doc S/2007/677, 29 November 2007, paras 25–6; C Whitlock, 'Terrorism Financing Blacklist at Risk', *Washington Post*, 2 November 2008, <http://globalpolicy.org/component/content/article/178/33243.html>.

delegitimating effects[109]—many governments had raised concerns about the lack of procedural guarantees in the listing and delisting process.[110] The monitoring team closely observes legal challenges to the sanctions regime, and after the ECJ's judgment in *Kadi*, it feared that other courts might follow suit. Its coordinator even described the court's stance as 'a major challenge to the use of sanctions as an international counterterrorism tool'.[111]

2. Destabilizing Pluralism?

Whether those adverse effects for the overall regime are due to the pluralist structure, though, may be doubted. First, possibilities for judicial resistance do not arise solely in a pluralist order; they are also present in constitutional settings. Courts could have found the sanctions regime wanting even on the basis of a pre-eminence of international law and the UN Charter. They could have taken the reconciliation approach of the lower English courts further and interpreted Security Council resolutions in conformity with the Charter's emphasis on human rights in its purposes and principles. This would have posed a limit on the 1267 Committee's use of its delegated powers when establishing procedural guidelines.[112] Courts could also have focused on the remaining discretion of governments—as the UN Human Rights Committee (HRC) did when, in late 2008, it found that Belgium had violated the International Covenant on Civil and Political Rights in the *Sayadi* case. In the HRC's view, Belgium had enjoyed considerable freedom in deciding whom to put forward for listing, and its listing proposal, combined with later enforcement measures, triggered the government's responsibility under the Covenant.[113]

---

[109] See Heupel, 'Multilateral Sanctions', 311–12; and the *Ninth Report* of the Monitoring Team, para 16: 'several factors have undermined . . . effective implementation: some States lack the capacity to introduce and enforce the measures; some regard its targets as of marginal national relevance; some grant it a low priority because they believe it ineffective, and some have questioned its legitimacy'.

[110] See the report of the 1267 Committee, UN Doc S/2005/761, 6 December 2005, Annex, para 37.

[111] R Barrett, 'Al-Qaeda and Taliban Sanctions Threatened', *PolicyWatch* 1409, <http://www.washingtoninstitute.org/templateC05.php?CID=2935>.

[112] On further possible arguments regarding human rights limits of Chapter VII action, see J A Frowein & N Krisch, 'Introduction to Chapter VII' in Simma et al, *United Nations Charter*, 701–16 at 710–12; Frowein & Krisch, 'Article 41', 745–6. For a cautious view, see J E Alvarez, 'The Security Council's War on Terrorism: Problems and Policy Options' in de Wet & Nollkaemper, *Review of the Security Council*, 119–45 at 123–35.

[113] UN Human Rights Committee, *Sayadi and Vinck*.

Secondly, resistance by courts in a pluralist setting does not need to lead to non-compliance. This has been obvious in the judgments of the English Court of Appeal—which limited potential remedies to the pursuit of delisting requests by the government—and the UK Supreme Court, which only insisted that parliament, rather than the executive, provide the legal basis. Because of an immediate legislative reaction, non-compliance did not become a serious issue.[114] The same is true for the ECJ. The *Kadi* decision did not ask the EU organs to violate sanctions obligations; it only required them to establish a procedure through which targeted individuals could make their views heard and potentially contest a decision to place them under sanctions.[115] In the case at hand, Mr Kadi was subsequently offered such a hearing; as could be expected, the Commission did not change its views and renewed his listing soon after.[116] The EU's broader response to the judgment does not go any further: the amended European listing procedure only provides for a communication of the reasons as well as an opportunity for the affected individial or entity to file observations, resulting in a review by the Commission of its decision.[117] Whether this will be sufficient in the eyes of the courts remains to be seen; Mr Kadi has already challenged the Commission's relisting decision in the European courts.[118]

This response by the EU's political bodies has been criticized as half-hearted, but it is not clear that the ECJ had required more from them, and we also do not know whether in the future European courts will subject the merits of future listing decisions to particularly strict scrutiny.[119] Thus, even though it came with much fanfare and broad assertions of principle, the *Kadi* judgment's actual consequences may be less far-reaching. This would fit with the split between principle and pragmatism we have observed in courts' positions in the previous chapter, and it also corresponds with the general observation that courts rarely mount serious challenges to the

---

[114] See Section II.1 above.

[115] ECJ, *Kadi and Al Barakaat*, para 348.

[116] Commission Regulation (EC) 1190/2008, 28 November 2008, *Official Journal EU* 2008, L 322/25.

[117] Council Regulation (EU) No 1286/2009, 22 December 2009, *Official Journal EU* 2009, L 346/42, Art 7a.

[118] See D Hovell, 'A House of Kadis? Recent Challenges to the UN Sanctions Regime and the Continuing Response to the ECJ Decision in Kadi', *EJIL:Talk!*, 7 July 2009, <http://www.ejiltalk.org/a-house-of-kadis-recent-challenges-to-the-un-sanctions-regime-and-the-continuing-response-to-the-ecj-decision-in-kadi/>.

[119] On different possible levels of scrutiny, see Alvarez, 'The Security Council's War on Terrorism', 138–40.

political branches in areas as sensitive as security and foreign affairs.[120] If they have done so increasingly in recent times, this may have been a reaction to greater transnational cooperation among executives and the result of increased coordination among courts from different countries in checking them.[121] In this case, too, the ECJ did not make a solitary move—as mentioned above, its position formed part of a mounting critique from different directions. Institutionally, it might have gone further than earlier challenges; but as a matter of substance, it gave expression to a point of view shared by many UN members and especially by European governments, which had raised the issue consistently in the Security Council.[122] This is unlikely to be accidental—courts typically respond to public opinion in one way or the other.[123] Insofar as pluralism favours challenges by courts, these challenges are thus unlikely to be too frequent.[124] They are likely to arise (and to be effective) mainly when they are part of a broader web of normative critiques—critiques that pose a challenge to the global security regime in any case, regardless of the institutional structure.[125]

The pluralist structure may thus be seen as a reflection of underlying problems rather than the problem itself. This is also suggested by the fact that where hierarchical structures are formally available, they are typically left unused. In the counter-terrorism context, this is most obvious in

[120] See E Benvenisti, 'Judicial Misgivings Regarding the Application of International Law: An Analysis of Attitudes of National Courts', *European Journal of International Law* 4 (1993), 159–83.

[121] E Benvenisti, 'Reclaiming Democracy: The Strategic Uses of Foreign and International Law by National Courts', *American Journal of International Law* 102 (2008), 241–74.

[122] See, eg, UN Doc S/PV.5474 and S/PV/5474 (Resumption 1), 22 June 2006; R Foot, 'The United Nations, Counter Terrorism, and Human Rights: Institutional Adaptation and Embedded Ideas', *Human Rights Quarterly* 29 (2007), 489–514 at 504–5. See also Section I above on institutional initiatives.

[123] Cf, eg, R A Dahl, 'Decision-Making in a Democracy: The Supreme Court as a National Policy-Maker', *Journal of Public Law* 6 (1957), 279–95; G Vanberg, *The Politics of Constitutional Review in Germany*, Cambridge: Cambridge University Press, 2005.

[124] See E de Wet & A Nollkaemper, 'Review of Security Council Decisions by National Courts', *German Yearbook of International Law* 45 (2002), 166–202, also on conditions for review by national courts that may help to mitigate the risk of friction.

[125] On alternative policy options for expressing the normative concerns in this context, see Alvarez, 'The Security Council's War on Terrorism', 140–4.

the Security Council's approach to the implementation of Resolution 1373 (2001), which had established general obligations of member states soon after the attacks of 9/11. The resolution was unprecedented in its assertion of legislative authority beyond a particular country or situation,[126] but its implementation followed far less hierarchical lines.[127] Even though coercive means were at the disposal of the Security Council, its Counter-Terrorism Committee deliberately adopted a cautious, cooperative approach. It monitors implementation progress on the basis of member state reports, seeks to detect areas where they require assistance with capacity-building, and has defined best practices for applying the vague norms contained in the original resolution. It has not taken up suggestions to use more confrontational means, such as 'naming and shaming' non-complying states, apparently (at least in part) out of concern that this might undermine the generally positive attitude of member states towards implementation.[128]

The approach to implementation in the Al-Qaeda/Taliban context has been somewhat less cautious—necessarily so, as implementation requirements are more concrete and failure to comply can easily lead to gaps that undermine the sanctions more broadly, especially as regards asset freezes. Yet here, too, the Security Council has avoided open confrontation. The first monitoring team of the 1267 Committee, for example, stirred controversy for its 'naming and shaming' attitude and was soon replaced by the current, so-called Analytical Support and Sanctions Monitoring Team.[129] And here, too, a main focus is on capacity-building and the solution of technical obstacles to implementation, rather than on identifying deliberate violations.[130]

The Council committees have been criticized for this non-confrontational stance,[131] but it brings into relief the political constraints they face. Even where hierarchical tools exist, normative and prudential reasons as well as

---

[126] eg, P C Szasz, 'The Security Council Starts Legislating', *American Journal of International Law* 96 (2002), 901–5.

[127] M Heupel, 'Combining Hierarchical and Soft Modes of Governance: The UN Security Council's Approach to Terrorism and Weapons of Mass Destruction Proliferation after 9/11', *Cooperation and Conflict* 43 (2008), 7–29; see also I Johnstone, 'The Security Council as Legislature' in Cronin & Hurd, *UN Security Council*, 80–104 at 90–2.

[128] See Heupel, 'Hierarchical and Soft Modes', 20, 22; Cortright et al, 'Global Cooperation', 25, 33, 46.

[129] Cortright et al, 'Global Cooperation', 42.

[130] See, eg, the focus in the *Eighth and Ninth Reports* of the Monitoring Team.

[131] E Rosand & A Millar, 'Strengthening International Law and Global Cooperation' in Cortright & Lopez, *Uniting Against Terror*, 51–82 at 71–2; see also Cortright et al, 'Global Cooperation', 46.

disagreements within the Council seriously limit their utility. In a highly diverse polity, cooperative network governance seems to be preferred over hierarchical approaches, regardless of formal institutional possibilities.[132] Pluralism is an institutional expression of that accommodative stance, and an order along constitutional, hierarchical lines might not be more effective in practice as long as it does not resonate better with the shape of the global polity. The real obstacles to stable and effective cooperation here are political and societal, not institutional.

3. Pluralism and Regime Design

Overcoming the obstacles to stability is not easy in any global institutional setting, but a pluralist order may have certain advantages in this respect. We have just seen the risks of friction in the international security regime if hierarchical tools are actually used; pluralism's push for accommodation may reduce this risk somewhat.

Change

A pluralist order might also help to tackle the challenge of institutional change. In classical international law, change faces high hurdles because of widespread unanimity requirements; replacing it with more effective, majoritarian amendment processes, however, would provoke not only political resistance but also raise normative concerns. Requiring all states' consent to change may be impractical, but ignoring states' objections risks neglecting their well-grounded claim for political autonomy.[133] In Chapter 3 I argued that pluralism helps steer a middle course between those positions—one that does not grant ultimate authority to any collective or process, but can help bring the competing visions into an informal balance.[134] In the sanctions example we can observe how this might work in practice. Litigation in member states and in the EU courts has very likely contributed to the procedural improvements in the listing process and may well instigate further change.[135] But it is not formally relevant to the Security Council and cannot *determine* the outcome; the practical result is one of (limited) convergence on the observance of certain due process standards.

---

[132] See also the comparison with the EU's Open Method of Coordination in Heupel, 'Hierarchical and Soft Modes', 23.

[133] See also B Kingsbury, 'Sovereignty and Inequality', *European Journal of International Law* 9 (1998), 599–625.

[134] See Chapter 3, II.3 and III.

[135] Heupel, 'Multilateral Sanctions', 320.

This accommodation is not an arbitrary process: as we have seen, the impact of a challenge depends on a number of political conditions, including the weight of the underlying normative concerns in the polity from which they emanate and the extent to which they are shared more broadly in the international community. Litigation around sanctions received attention because it was part of a broader movement for change. This has been similar in the development of pluralism within the EU: the rights challenge launched by the German Constitutional Court against the ECJ reflected mounting concerns over a lack of fundamental rights protection in the ever more powerful European Communities, and as it was supported by political initiatives as well as courts in other countries, it helped drive institutional change. Such change would not have been impossible in a constitutionalist order, yet pluralism facilitated it by allowing recourse to normative resources that had broad resonance politically but only particularistic status legally: rights guarantees contained in member state constitutions. Pluralism, unlike constitutionalism, allowed for the full mobilization of this resource as a legal, not only political tool.

Signals

If pluralism opens up avenues for change, it might also enhance regime design in other ways. For example, it may allow for more reliable information about preferences and their strength.[136] In global regulatory regimes, signalling is typically limited to the positions of governments and often occurs only at the stage of regime design. Governments not taking part in the design process as well as other actors are largely excluded, and the classical processes of international law and organization allow for less signalling at later stages in the life of a regime. This is especially true when later decisions are taken by bodies with limited membership. As the regime changes, though, it risks becoming unstable if it clashes with strong preferences of excluded actors. This is particularly likely if it goes against entrenched positions of certain domestic actors. The standpoint of domestic parliaments, courts, interest groups, or societies more broadly will remain highly relevant in powerful states that can employ two-level games to their advantage. In most countries, though, they will matter far less in foreign policy decision-making than in the course of domestic politics. As global regimes impact further on internal affairs, this will cause increasing friction as these actors see themselves being sidelined and may seek to undermine global

---

[136] On information supply as a central element in the demand for international regimes, see R O Keohane, 'The Demand for International Regimes', *International Organization* 36 (1982), 325–55 at 343–5.

decisions.[137] A pluralist order might then be a vehicle for institutionalized signalling of the weight of their interests or values.[138]

I will return to this issue more fully in Chapter 7, but the present case presents a good example. As we have seen, procedural safeguards in sanctions administration were an important issue for a number of states, and they brought it up repeatedly in the Security Council and pushed it as part of processes of sanctions improvement. On the international level, they could not press the issue too hard if they wanted to be seen as committed to the overall sanctions regime; and because of the decision-making practices in the Council, they did not manage to achieve decisive successes there.[139] The degree of entrenchment the underlying values enjoyed domestically—their constitutional status—could not be brought to bear in this international process, but the actors charged with defending them domestically—mainly courts—took up the challenge. The pluralist setting facilitated this because, unlike a constitutionalist order, it allowed for a primary emphasis on domestic values and rules.

One might not find this result satisfactory, and one would certainly not want all domestically entrenched interests to have a decisive impact on the global level; otherwise, cooperation would be seriously hampered. But as the global and the domestic planes are ever further entangled, there is a distinct need for processes by which the guiding values of both can communicate with each other. I have discussed this challenge already in Chapter 1. Moreover, as I have noted earlier in the present chapter, there are serious political constraints on courts' assertions of overriding interests, which will typically limit them to exceptional cases. But when these constraints are overcome and a certain value has sufficient resonance to ground a judicial challenge, one can usually assume that the international regime has an interest in taking note of it—it is typically a signal of a broader problem for the regime, an indicator of a resistance that might spread further and cause significant friction.

Power

Even if this is true, such opportunities for institutional resistance may be distributed too asymmetrically to make pluralism an attractive option.

---

[137] See M Zürn, 'Global Governance and Legitimacy Problems', *Government & Opposition* 39 (2004), 260–87 at 283–4, on national resistance to executive multilateralism.

[138] For a similar argument in the context of global trade, see also M A Pollack & G C Shaffer, *When Cooperation Fails: The International Law and Politics of Genetically Modified Foods*, Oxford: Oxford University Press, 2009, 176.

[139] See Heupel, 'Multilateral Sanctions', 313–14.

Eyal Benvenisti and George Downs suggest that powerful states can typically make better use of the structures and tools of a fragmented order, for example by forum-shopping between competing regimes.[140] I will take this challenge up in greater detail in Chapter 7; suffice it to note here that in the present context, which is primarily about the heterarchical relations between domestic, regional, and global levels of governance, this conclusion is not so easily drawn. Judicial challenges naturally have a greater impact when they originate from powerful states, and it is not accidental that it was an attack from a court of the EU, one of the world's most influential players, that received the greatest attention in the UN. Likewise, in the pluralist interplay about rights within the European Union, the most influential domestic player has been the constitutional court of Germany—not exactly a negligible force in EU politics. Yet in the sanctions context, litigation in other countries has gone far from unnoticed, and challenges in a number of countries—especially in Turkey and Pakistan—have been followed with a keen interest, even if none of them have ultimately been successful so far.[141] Moreover, the ECJ's move was embedded in a political process that reached well beyond Europe—a number of other countries, among them Mexico and Brazil, had prominently pursued the cause of procedural safeguards[142], and the 1267 Committee noted in 2005 that more than fifty countries had voiced similar concerns about the listing process.[143] And those European countries that were most vocal about the issue—Germany, Sweden, and Switzerland—are not (all) among the strongest players in or around the Security Council.

The pluralist interaction in this case presented an indirect challenge to the dominant Council members—the US, Russia, and China—who had sought to preserve the Council's unfettered discretion in security affairs. Rather than preventing alliances from being formed,[144] it allowed for the creation of coalitions excluded in the formal, institutional setting of the Security Council. A pluralist order may not be free from problems of power; but as

---

[140] E Benvenisti & G W Downs, 'The Empire's New Clothes: Political Economy and the Fragmentation of International Law', *Stanford Law Review* 60 (2007), 595–631.

[141] See the annexes on instances of litigation in the reports of the Monitoring Team, available at: <http://www.un.org/sc/committees/1267/monitoringteam. shtml>.

[142] Foot, 'UN, Counter Terrorism, and Human Rights', 501–10.

[143] See the report of the 1267 Committee, UN Doc S/2005/761, 6 December 2005, Annex.

[144] Which Benvenisti & Downs, 'Empire's New Clothes', see as a central downside of fragmented orders.

we can see here, it can at times serve as a counterweight to institutionalized dominance.

IV. CONCLUSION

There is little doubt that in an ideal world constitutionalism would be the best option for structuring global law. It would provide us with a reasoned framework in which different institutions would fulfil important collective functions within the bounds of clearly delimited competences. Common values would be given expression in constitutional guarantees, to be enforced by courts on different levels. This would not eliminate conflicts, but it would channel them into civilized, institutional mechanisms and often into legal solutions, aspiring to coherence and justification and eschewing the vagaries of politics.

Yet the world is not ideal, and our models of order have to cope with the actual constraints politics and social structures on the global level impose on us. It may not quite be the world of devils Immanuel Kant wanted to make his proposals fit for,[145] but it is still one in which radical disagreement and enormous power differentials are central features. In this context, justice and stability are not easily achieved, or even approximated; and institutional structures will not be able to make more than a limited contribution to their pursuit. Our models of order will always be non-ideal, and rather than measuring them against ideal standards, we will have to compare actually available alternatives, knowing that the best will be the one with the least flaws.

This chapter has tried to illuminate what structures emerge and how they fare in the conditions of global politics using the example of the UN sanctions regime and the struggle over due process guarantees in it. This is not as benign a case as the one in the previous chapter; on the contrary, it epitomizes the extent of the political challenges on the global level. These challenges are here encapsulated in the tension between a strong interest in effective security cooperation and the far-reaching disagreements among countries and institutions about the right balance between security concerns and the protection of fundamental rights.

As we have seen, this tension has led to a characteristic process of approximation and distancing between various layers of law and politics. The imperative of security cooperation has brought these layers closer together, creating an enmeshment of legal orders in the shaping and implementation of the

---

[145] I Kant, 'Zum ewigen Frieden: Ein philosophischer Entwurf' in I Kant, *Schriften zur Anthropologie, Geschichtsphilosophie, Politik und Pädagogik I* (Werkausgabe, vol XI; W Weischedel, ed), Frankfurt am Main: Suhrkamp Verlag, 1993, 191–251 at 224.

sanctions regime. But the differences in values have also led to attempts to re-establish greater distance between the layers and thus a certain degree of political autonomy. The resulting maze is best characterized neither as monist or dualist but as pluralist—as deeply entangled yet not integrated into one coherent whole. Within that framework, there is space for widely diverging conceptions of the shape of this entanglement, as we have seen in the approaches of the lower English courts, on the one hand, and the European Court of Justice, on the other. While the UK courts framed their challenge to the overall sanctions regime as an attempt at reconciling the countervailing approaches of the different levels of law, the ECJ conceived its challenge as based solely on the European legal order, thus insisting on distance in the face of ever greater enmeshment.

Neither of these approaches may appear satisfying from a constitutionalist perspective, but they pose fewer problems than is usually assumed. As we have seen, the problems with stability and effectiveness, which the UN sanctions regime undoubtedly has, stem from political and societal conditions pluralist and constitutionalist orders face alike—conditions that in most circumstances favour networked, cooperative approaches over hierarchical decision-making styles. Pluralism also has distinct advantages: it opens up avenues for change that otherwise do not exist and are difficult, if not impossible, to establish. And it allows for institutionalized signals about actual and potential resistance that any regime must be interested in receiving in order to ensure its longer term stability.

Pluralism is not without flaws, but its openness and contestatory elements perform important functions in today's global order. We have arrived at a point where political and functional needs bar a return to the old order of international law in which difference was processed through consent-based law-making and strictly domestic mechanisms of implementation. Yet difference remains strong, and pluralism's open architecture helps bridge it to some extent. It helps to bring the diverging viewpoints, the universal and the many particulars, into communication—without, however, favouring one over the other or even seeking to merge all of them into one.

6

Pluralism in Postnational Risk Regulation

The dispute over UN sanctions, the focus of the previous chapter, is mostly about the place of rights in global security policies, but it is also about *which* rights, *which* law, should ultimately limit Security Council action. As we have seen, the European Court of Justice (ECJ) insisted on the primacy of European standards of rights, thereby rejecting the emphasis of the Court of First Instance (CFI) on universal rights, circumscribed as these were by the superiority of the UN Charter.

The competition between different levels of law is also a competition between different collectives' rights to make law, between competing claims for law-making authority. The contested locus of ultimate authority is, as we have seen in Chapter 2, at the core of my normative defence of a pluralist order, and it has been an important—though perhaps less visible—factor in the case studies of the two previous chapters. The practical salience of this contestation for the creation of pluralist structures is more apparent in the dispute over genetically modified organisms (GMOs) and international trade, which has absorbed the energy of trade negotiators and regulators since the mid-1990s, with little hope for resolution at any time soon. As we shall see, the serious obstacles to dispute resolution in this case stem, in large part, from entrenched positions not only on the substance of the matter, but also on the appropriate site of governance.

By analysing this dispute, I hope also to shed light on a number of further themes that have emerged at different points in my discussion of a pluralist postnational order so far. One of them is the breadth of the phenomenon: the complex regime of risk regulation that connects GMO issues with food safety and environmental matters, is yet another example of how pervasive pluralist structures have become in central areas of global governance. Another important theme is that of stability: here, the GMO dispute appears as a particularly hard case, as an example of 'when cooperation fails'.[1] Yet

---

[1] Thus the title of M A Pollack & G C Shaffer, *When Cooperation Fails: The International Law and Politics of Genetically Modified Foods*, Oxford: Oxford University Press, 2009.

the assessment may not have to be that gloomy—there are many points of convergence around GMOs and much evidence of successful cooperation in the broader regime complex on sanitary and phytosanitary regulation. Moreover, it is doubtful whether failures of cooperation in this context should indeed be attributed to the pluralism of governance arrangements, or whether their causes lie elsewhere.

This chapter proceeds in four steps. It first sketches the contours of the substantive disputes over GMOs and their institutional expression in different sites of governance (Section I). It then outlines the legal pluralism at work here, in both a horizontal and a vertical dimension (Section II). The chapter goes on to analyse the competition between different visions of the right polity for determining the issues at stake, and how this competition has shaped the pluralism of the governance structure (Section III). In a last step, it considers the extent to which this pluralism has been of a disruptive or a stabilizing nature—the extent to which it may have hindered or helped cooperation in this area (Section IV).

I. THE GMO DISPUTE

In the GMO dispute, two fundamentally opposed approaches confront each other, and both respond to deeply held convictions about risk, nature, and scientific progress.[2] On the one hand, the 'permissive' approach that is today dominant in the United States sees restrictions on the production, sale, and use of foodstuffs as justified only when there are scientifically proven risks for human health, the environment, or other important goods. Absent such proof, the production, sale, and use of food and feed is free, and since for many products that contain GMOs or have been produced on the basis of GMOs risk assessments have not revealed ascertainably higher risks than for other products, restrictions are not warranted under this approach.

On the other hand, the 'precautionary' approach that is largely favoured in Europe (although with significant differences amongst countries[3]) emphasizes the scientific uncertainty that even thorough risk assessments

---

[2] I can only provide a brief sketch of a huge issue here. On the two general approaches, see D Vogel, 'The Politics of Risk Regulation in Europe and the United States', *Yearbook of European Environmental Law* 3 (2003), 1–43; Pollack & Shaffer, *When Cooperation Fails*, ch 2. For a cautionary note on the differences between the US and Europe, see J B Wiener & M D Rogers, 'Comparing Precaution in the United States and Europe', *Journal of Risk Research* 5 (2002), 317–49.

[3] On the contestation around food safety issues in Europe itself, see C Ansell & D Vogel (eds), *What's the Beef? The Contested Governance of European Food Safety*, Cambridge, MA: MIT Press, 2006.

leave and insists that in situations of uncertainty and potentially serious risks, one should err on the side of caution. Since the consequences for public health and the environment for products containing or based on GMOs cannot be fully determined—in part because of the short time that has so far been available for testing and in part because testing is usually limited to small contexts and does not extend to entire ecosystems—the precautionary approach tends to restrict the production, sale, and use of such products significantly. Regulatory approvals of the production and sale of such products have accordingly been very limited in Europe; for several years, EU institutions even operated a de facto moratorium on new applications, and a number of EU member states continue to reject the use of GM products on their territories.

On a more general level, the competing approaches reflect divergent attitudes towards risk in scientific progress and in particular to alterations of nature and its potential consequences. But in the case of the EU, the more cautious approach also stems from recent experiences in the area of food safety, in particular the BSE scandal, as well as concerns about the effect of a shift towards GMO food and feed for the agricultural landscape. This may be connected with a desire to shield the relatively small European agricultural businesses from the pressures for stronger industrialization that GMO agriculture and competition with large-scale American farms would bring. But even though on both sides of the Atlantic regulatory approaches are certainly influenced by economic interests and are also due to institutional structures and path-dependence,[4] they have far deeper social roots. In Europe, a majority of citizens has consistently declared its opposition to the use of GMOs, while in the US, majorities or pluralities favour genetic engineering for particular purposes or for the commercial use of GM products more broadly.[5]

These two approaches clash over questions of global trade. US exports of agricultural products containing or based on GMOs to Europe are severely limited by stringent EU rules, and exports to developing countries are often hampered because of the wish of these countries to export agricultural products to Europe, which is more difficult with GMOs in the food chain.

---

[4] The importance of this latter point is highlighted by Pollack & Shaffer, *When Cooperation Fails*, 72–3.

[5] Cf D W Drezner, *All Politics is Global: Explaining International Regulatory Regimes*, Princeton, NJ: Princeton University Press, 2007, 156–8; Pollack & Shaffer, *When Cooperation Fails*, 73–5. For more recent data on Europe, see also the Special Eurobarometer 295, 'Attitudes of European Citizens towards the Environment', March 2008, <http://ec.europa.eu/public_opinion/archives/ebs/ebs_295_en.pdf>, 65.

Accordingly, the contest between the two approaches takes place mostly in trade-related institutions and involves many more players than just the US and the EU.

Initially, regulatory cooperation on GMO matters had been rather effective, taking place in bodies of a largely technical character, most importantly within the Organisation for Economic Co-Operation and Development (OECD) and the Codex Alimentarius Commission (CAC), a standard-setting organization in the area of food safety set up by the UN's Food and Agriculture Organization (FAO) and the World Health Organization (WHO) in 1962.[6] Cooperation ran into difficulties, though, when in the mid-1990s the issue became increasingly politicized in Europe, positions became more entrenched and disagreement could no longer be treated as merely technical.[7] By that time, however, regulatory efforts, especially those of the Codex, had become embedded in the new World Trade Organization (WTO) framework, especially through the Agreement on the Application of Sanitary and Phytosanitary Measures (SPS Agreement)—a treaty that, unlike most other texts of the Uruguay Round, had been accorded relatively low priority and was negotiated quite speedily, largely by technical experts and without much fundamental controversy.[8] The SPS Agreement grants the Codex Alimentarius Commission, among a few other standard-setting bodies, an elevated role in that its standards enjoy particular weight in determining whether national measures are in conformity with the agreement. States can establish more exacting conditions than those contained in Codex standards, but only if they can provide a justification based upon a scientific risk assessment of the products in question.[9]

---

[6] On the CAC, see WHO/FAO, *Understanding the Codex Alimentarius*, 2005, at <http://www.fao.org/docrep/008/y7867e/y7867e00.htm>.

[7] On the trajectory of regulatory cooperation on GMOs, see Pollack & Shaffer, *When Cooperation Fails*, ch 2.

[8] Drezner, *All Politics is Global*, 161–3; T Büthe, 'The Globalization of Health and Safety Standards: Delegation of Regulatory Authority in the SPS Agreement of the 1994 Agreement Establishing the World Trade Organization', *Law & Contemporary Problems* 71 (Winter 2008), 219–55 at 238–55; G Skogstad, 'The WTO and Food Safety Regulatory Policy Innovation in the European Union', *Journal of Common Market Studies* 39 (2001), 485–505 at 492–4.

[9] SPS Agreement Art 3; the text of the Agreement is at: <http://www.wto. org/english/tratop_e/sps_e/spsagr_e.htm>. See also J Scott, *The WTO Agreement on Sanitary and Phytosanitary Measures*, Oxford: Oxford University Press, 2007, ch 7.

This emphasis on science,[10] initially agreeable to all sides, soon came to haunt the Europeans. Their increasingly precautionary approach seemed to be in tension with this emphasis, and in the late 1990s it came under scrutiny in the WTO framework, especially in the *Beef Hormones* case. The EU had banned the import and sale of meat derived from hormonally treated farm animals, thus limiting the export prospects of (especially) American meat producers significantly, and it had done so well beyond the restrictions provided for in Codex standards. The argument that this was justified as a matter of precaution was, however, not accepted; the WTO Appellate Body saw those measures as lacking a sufficient basis in scientific assessments of the risks the hormones actually posed.[11]

This finding did not automatically doom the EU's GMO measures—after all, the Appellate Body has at times left considerable scope for national regulation in public health and environmental matters, and it has indicated that a precautionary approach may find wider application than just for the provisional measures for which it is explicitly admitted in the SPS Agreement.[12] Some commentators thus believe a good case can be made for the conformity of European GMO policies with the Agreement.[13] Yet on a number of other occasions, the Appellate Body has rejected arguments from precaution and found restrictive measures to violate WTO law.[14] Quite understandably

---

[10]   On the dominant role of science in the SPS Agreement and WTO decisions, see J Peel, 'Risk Regulation under the WTO SPS Agreement: Science as an International Normative Yardstick?', *Jean Monnet Working Paper* 02/04, available at: <http://www.jeanmonnetprogram.org/papers/04/040201.html>.

[11]   WTO Appellate Body, Report of 16 January 1998, WT/DS26/AB/R & WT/DS48/AB/R, *EC Measures Concerning Meat and Meat Products* (hereinafter: *Beef Hormones*). See also the Appellate Body's Report of 16 October 2008, WT/DS/320/AB/R, *Continued Suspension of Obligations in the EC-Hormones Dispute*.

[12]   See only R Howse, 'The WHO/WTO Study on Trade and Public Health: A Critical Assessment', *Risk Analysis* 24 (2004), 501–7.

[13]   eg, R Howse & P C Mavroidis, 'Europe's Evolving Regulatory Strategy for GMOs–The Issue of Consistency with WTO Law: Of Kine and Brine', *Fordham International Law Journal* 24 (2000), 317–70; A A Ostrovsky, 'The New Codex Alimentarius Commission Standards for Food Created with Modern Biotechnology: Implications for the EC GMO Framework's Compliance with the SPS Agreement', *Michigan Journal of International Law* 25 (2004), 813–43.

[14]   Precautionary considerations are explicitly allowed only with respect to provisional measures in situations of insufficient scientific evidence; see SPS Agreement Art 5.7. For the cases, see WTO Appellate Body, *Beef Hormones*; Report of 20 October 1998, WT/DS18/AB/R, *Australia–Measures Affecting Importation of Salmon*; Report of 22 February 1999, WT/DS76/AB/R, *Japan–Measures Affecting Agricultural Products*; Report of 26 November 2003, WT/DS245/AB/R, *Japan–Measures Affecting*

then, Europeans came to see the SPS jurisprudence as likely to pose a challenge to their regulatory approach vis-à-vis GM products, and they looked for strategies to change or destabilize it.

A crucial part of these strategies was the Biosafety Protocol.[15] Negotiated in the framework of the Convention on Biodiversity (CBD) and thus a part of the Rio Process on environmental protection, it represented an attempt at establishing a counterweight to WTO rules. The route via the CBD appeared promising because of its greater membership compared to the WTO and the resulting stronger role of developing countries, many of whom were sceptical towards GMO foods and feeds. Moreover, as the US was not a party to the CBD, it could take part in the negotiations only as an observer. In the end, this did not relegate it to a secondary role—the US played a major part in the process, largely as a member of the 'Miami Group' of countries with an interest in the export of GMO products, and it managed to limit significantly the EU's ability to draft a treaty along the lines of its regulatory vision. Still, the eventual Protocol places emphasis on the 'Advance Informed Agreement' of countries importing GMO products that are to be released into the environment[16] and, besides its requirement of a scientific risk assessment as a basis for the importing decision, the Protocol makes several references to precautionary measures.[17] It states in particular that a lack of scientific certainty shall not prevent a party from taking measures to avoid or minimize potential adverse effects of GMOs to be imported as food or feed.[18] It is thus relatively close to European approaches to GMOs,[19] and commentators believed that, as an 'international standard', it could potentially have an impact on decision-making under the SPS Agreement similar to that of

---

the *Importation of Apples*. For a good overview of the first three cases, see D G Victor, 'The Sanitary and Phytosanitary Agreement of the World Trade Organization: An Assessment After Five Years', *NYU Journal of International Law and Politics* 32 (2000) 865–937 at 895–913.

[15] Cartagena Protocol on Biosafety, <http://www.cbd.int/biosafety/>. On the protocol and its negotiation, see C Bail, R Falkner, & H Marquard (eds), *The Cartagena Protocol on Biosafety: Reconciling Trade in Biotechnology with Environment and Development*, London: Earthscan, 2002; M Böckenförde, *Grüne Gentechnik und Welthandel: Das Biosafety-Protokoll und seine Auswirkungen auf das Regime der WTO*, Heidelberg: Springer Verlag, 2004, 118–240.

[16] Biosafety Protocol Art 7.

[17] See especially the Biosafety Protocol, Preamble and Art 1.

[18] Biosafety Protocol Art 11 para 8.

[19] R Falkner, 'Regulating Biotech Trade: the Cartagena Protocol on Biosafety', *International Affairs* 76 (2000), 299–313 at 301–2, 313; Böckenförde, *Grüne Gentechnik*, 140–4.

Codex Alimentarius standards.[20] The ultimate relationship with WTO law is left unclear in the Protocol itself. After long negotiations, the Biosafety Protocol addresses the issue in two contradictory clauses in the preamble: one emphasizes that the Protocol is not intended to change rights and obligations under other agreements, while the other insists that this proviso is not meant to subordinate the Protocol to other agreements.[21]

The negotiations on the Biosafety Protocol operated in the shadow of the US threat to initiate WTO proceedings if the EU failed to relent on the issue, as did efforts of the EU to reform its approval system for GMO products. Limited as they were, these hardly assuaged the American side, and attempts at creating greater regulatory convergence—in both the OECD and Codex—also floundered because of the distance between the positions.[22] US efforts to negotiate the issue within the WTO context failed as Europeans preferred the CBD forum.[23] Against the background of such entrenched viewpoints, the US eventually acted upon their threat and brought a case before the Dispute Settlement Body in 2003.[24]

More than three years later, the Panel finally presented a report running to more than a thousand pages—even by WTO standards a massive document.[25] It ruled in favour of the US, but because of the limited scope of the proceedings and the narrow basis of the Panel's reasoning, the report has come to be seen as leaving most crucial issues open.[26] Because of the way the US had framed their application, the Panel did not make a pronouncement on the EU's regulatory system but limited itself to the de facto moratorium on approvals and the safeguard bans of a number of individual EU

---

[20] See Howse & Mavroidis, 'Europe's Evolving Regulatory Strategy', 354–70; see also L Boisson de Chazournes & M M Mbengue, 'GMOs and Trade: Issues at Stake in the EC Biotech Dispute', *Review of European Community and International Environmental Law* 13 (2004), 289–305 at 297–303; Böckenförde, *Grüne Gentechnik*, 333–6.

[21] See S Safrin, 'Treaties in Collision? The Biosafety Protocol and the World Trade Organization Agreements', *American Journal of International Law* 96 (2002), 606–28 at 614–28; also Falkner, 'Regulating Biotech Trade', 309–10. On the wording of these clauses and their interpretation, see Section II.1 below.

[22] Pollack & Shaffer, *When Cooperation Fails*, 58–68, 142–5, 168–74, 237–45.

[23] Falkner, 'Regulating Biotech Trade', 305.

[24] Pollack & Shaffer, *When Cooperation Fails*, 179–82; Drezner, *All Politics is Global*, 165–70.

[25] WTO Panel, Report of 29 September 2006, WT/DS291/R, *European Communities–Measures Affecting the Approval and Marketing of Biotech Products* (hereinafter: *Biotech*).

[26] Pollack & Shaffer, *When Cooperation Fails*, ch 5.

member states. It was clear on the substantive incompatibility of the latter with the SPS Agreement for lack of a rational relation with the risk assessments available. Its stance on the former was more circumscribed: it found the EU's moratorium to be in violation of the Agreement, but only because it represented an 'undue delay' in deciding on applications. The Panel notably avoided any pronouncement on whether the EU position had a sufficient scientific basis.[27] And in its consideration of member state measures, it pointed out that there would be room for precautionary considerations if a risk assessment indicated 'uncertainties or constraints' in its evaluation.[28]

Though favouring the US in the result, this leaves open the possibility that the European regulation of GMOs may be in (or could relatively easily be brought into) conformity with SPS rules.[29] Despite a number of principled statements on the interpretation of the SPS Agreement,[30] the Panel's report as a whole has a rather circumscribed character, avoiding broad statements wherever possible and founding its eventual conclusions on the narrowest grounds available. It brackets the key areas of disagreement between the parties, just as they have been left out by regulatory bodies for want of common ground.[31] The dispute thus continues. Certainly, the EU claims to have ended its moratorium: since 2004, it has begun to process (and sometimes approve) applications, though in the US view still at too slow a pace and in too small a number. Efforts by the European Commission to remove the national safeguard bans have so far—despite the clear findings of violation by the Panel in this respect, and parallel assessments by the European Food Safety Authority—met with sustained resistance amongst member states and in the Council of Ministers. Given the strength of adverse public opinion

---

[27] See the summary of the findings in WTO Panel, *Biotech*, paras 8.2–8.10.

[28] WTO Panel, *Biotech*, paras 7.3065, 7.3244–7.3245.

[29] Pollack & Shaffer, *When Cooperation Fails*, 196–7.

[30] Some of these have been the subject of pronounced critique; see, eg, J Peel, 'A GMO by Any Other Name . . . Might be an SPS Risk!: Implications of Expanding the Scope of the WTO *Sanitary and Phytosanitary Measures Agreement*', *European Journal of International Law* 17 (2006), 1009–31; M A Young, 'The WTO's Use of Relevant Rules of International Law: An Analysis of the *Biotech* Case', *International and Comparative Law Quarterly* 56 (2007), 907–30; R L Howse & H Horn, 'European Communities–Measures Affecting the Approval and Marketing of Biotech Products', *World Trade Review* 8 (2009), 49–83.

[31] See Pollack & Shaffer, *When Cooperation Fails*, ch 6; C Joerges, 'Conflict of Laws as Constitutional Form: Reflections on International Trade Law and the *Biotech* Panel Report', *RECON Online Working Paper* 2007/03, 9–13, available at: <http://www.reconproject.eu/main.php/RECON_wp_0703.pdf?fileitem=5456959>.

in Europe and the concomitant risk of further antagonism, the US has also suspended its WTO proceedings to gain authority for retaliatory sanctions in response to the continued non-compliance by EU member states—though only provisionally; as it points out, to give the EU the 'opportunity to demonstrate meaningful progress'.[32] This somewhat mirrors the situation in the dispute about beef hormones, in which the US and the EU have concluded a Memorandum of Understanding to bracket and bypass the most contested issues.[33]

II. THE GMO DISPUTE IN A PLURALIST ORDER

So far, I have told the story of the GMO dispute largely as one of regulatory conflict, adjudication, and non-compliance, situated mainly between two actors and channelled through a variety of institutions. Yet it is also a story of an ever more visible legal pluralism and its driving force—the competition of different collectives for ultimate law-making authority.

1. Horizontal Pluralism in the Global Food Safety Regime Complex

The pluralism on show in this example has two dimensions, one vertical and the other horizontal. I have already touched upon the latter in the description of the creation of the Biosafety Protocol and its ambiguous rules on its relationship with WTO law. But is this an instance of pluralism or perhaps simply another case of conflicting treaty obligations, to be solved according to the classical rules of international law?

In the eyes of the Panel in the *Biotech* case, it is certainly the latter. The Panel framed the issue, understandably, from the perspective of WTO law and mainly asked whether and how, under standard international law rules, the provisions of the Biosafety Protocol mattered to the interpretation of the SPS Agreement. Using the Vienna Convention on the Law of Treaties (VCLT), it came to the conclusion that the Protocol did not have to be taken into account as long as some parties to the dispute were not parties to it.[34]

---

[32] Cf Pollack & Shaffer, *When Cooperation Fails*, 227.

[33] Memorandum of Understanding between the United States of America and the European Commission Regarding the Importation of Beef from Animals not Treated with Certain Growth-Promoting Hormones, available at: <http://www.ustr.gov/sites/default/files/asset_upload_file254_15654.pdf>; see Office of the United States Trade Representative, 'Implementation of the US-EC Beef Hormones Memorandum of Understanding', *US Federal Register* 74:155 (2009), 13 August 2009, 40864–5.

[34] WTO Panel, *Biotech*, para 7.75. For an insightful discussion, see Young, 'The WTO's Use'.

This conclusion appeared to differ in tone (though perhaps not in result) from previous uses of other international agreements by the WTO Appellate Body which had emphasized that WTO law should not be read 'in clinical isolation from public international law'.[35] But it is unexceptional given the wording of the VCLT, which provides for an interpretive effect of 'any relevant rules of international law applicable in the relations between the parties';[36] in the case of the Biosafety Protocol, it was simply not 'applicable' between the parties as not all of them were bound by it. The Panel also offered some further reasoning for why this was an adequate solution:

> Indeed, it is not apparent why a sovereign State would agree to a mandatory rule of treaty interpretation which could have as a consequence that the interpretation of a treaty to which that State is a party is affected by other rules of international law which that State has decided not to accept.[37]

On the basis of state voluntarism, this is a plausible consideration. In this particular case, it left little space for using the Biosafety Protocol: the Protocol certainly could not serve as a mandatory tool to interpret the SPS Agreement; its only role could be that of helping to illuminate the 'ordinary meaning' of the terms of the Agreement.[38] This accorded the Protocol a role akin to that of dictionaries—sometimes useful, but only taken into account if the Panel so wished or considered appropriate. Ultimately, the Panel 'did not find it necessary or appropriate to rely on these particular provisions [of the Biosafety Protocol] in interpreting the WTO agreements at issue in this dispute'.[39]

This approach preserves the autonomy and flexibility of the WTO in deciding on how to respond to other international legal rules, and it is in line with the typical response of many international lawyers to what they perceive as an increasing 'fragmentation' of the international legal order.[40]

---

[35] WTO Appellate Body, Report of 20 May 1996, WT/DS2/AB/R, *United States– Standards of Reformulated and Conventional Gasoline*, 16. See also Howse & Horn, 'European Communities', 60–2; and the survey in ILC, Report of the Study Group (finalized by Martti Koskenniemi), *Fragmentation of International Law: Difficulties arising from the Diversification and Expansion of International Law*, UN Doc A/CN.4/L.682, 13 April 2006, paras 165–71, 443–50.

[36] Vienna Convention on the Law of Treaties, Art 31 para 3(c).

[37] WTO Panel, *Biotech*, para 7.71.

[38] ibid, paras 7.92–7.95.

[39] ibid, para 7.95.

[40] From what is by now a vast literature on the topic, see, eg, M Koskenniemi & P Leino, 'Fragmentation of International Law. Postmodern Anxieties?', *Leiden Journal of International Law* 15 (2002), 553–79; M Craven, 'Unity, Diversity and

Expressed through a proliferation of treaties and regimes, institutions as well as courts and quasi-courts, this fragmentation not only appears as the flipside of the growth in strength and breadth of international law, but also seems to pose a threat to its unity and coherence. After a period of unease, however, many international lawyers found they could address the resulting problems by applying the classical rules governing treaty interpretation and conflicting obligations.[41] This path was taken, most prominently, by the UN International Law Commission (ILC), which spelled out in much detail how the rules of VCLT on interpretation and norm conflicts, such as *lex specialis*, *lex posterior* etc, applied to the multiplicity of rules governing many issue areas in global governance.[42] In the view of this eminent body, there was little new under the sun. Conflicts between obligations had always existed and were the logical result of an order of sovereigns:

> Because of the spontaneous, decentralized and unhierarchical nature of international law-making—law-making by custom and by treaty—lawyers have always had to deal with heterogeneous materials at different levels of generality and with different normative force.[43]

If today the focus had shifted from inter-sovereign to inter-regime conflicts, international law, with its ideals of 'system' and 'systemic integration', retained the moderating impetus that had characterized it all along and could provide, or develop, collision rules to avoid incoherence and friction.[44]

Yet the harmonizing effects of an international law thus understood have limits, and the report of the ILC's study group, as finalized by its chairman, Martti Koskenniemi, acknowledged as much: many normative conflicts, expressions of diverging preferences and values rather than merely technical mistakes, 'require a legislative, not a legal-technical response'.[45] The development of interpretation and conflict rules can hardly deliver as much, and

---

the Fragmentation of International Law', *Finnish Yearbook of International Law* 14 (2003), 3–34.

[41] See, eg, P-M Dupuy, 'L'unité de l'ordre juridique international', *Recueil des cours de l'Académie du droit international* 297 (2003), 9–489. With a particular focus on the WTO, see, eg, J Pauwelyn, *Conflict of Norms in Public International Law*, Cambridge: Cambridge University Press, 2003, chs 5–7.

[42] See ILC, 'Conclusions of the Work of the Study Group on the Fragmentation of International Law', *Report of the International Law Commission on the Work of its Fifty-eighth Session (2006)*, UN Doc A/61/10, paras 241–51; Report of the Study Group, *Fragmentation*.

[43] Report of the Study Group, *Fragmentation*, para 486.

[44] ILC, 'Conclusions', nos 1, 4; Report of the Study Group, *Fragmentation*, paras 487, 489, 493.

[45] Report of the Study Group, *Fragmentation*, para 484.

in their current form, they also have intrinsic limits. For those rules focus on inconsistent norms between the same states: it is then that the interpretive tools of the Vienna Convention, or rules on *lex specialis* and *lex posterior*, have some bite. They do not, however, resolve conflicts between obligations that are owed to different parties. The formal solution here is clear: the addressee of the obligations has to fulfil both, and if this is impossible, it will incur responsibility—including financial liability—for falling foul of at least one of them.

If this may be a sensible solution in a contractual framework, it becomes more problematic if one emphasizes the legislative aspects of the rules in question.[46] The unresolved parallelism of individual obligations, mitigated by potential monetary compensation, then turns into a largely unmediated competition of regulatory, legislative programmes. And this is far from a rare occurrence: wherever regimes have a great number of parties, identity of membership—the precondition for the operation of collision rules—is likely to be elusive. In the WTO context, hardly any agreement will have all WTO members as parties.[47] Beyond this, and even when there is identity of membership, collision rules—typically conceived as giving expression to some underlying will of the parties—will often be doomed to failure.[48] A rival regime may have its main purpose in counteracting a previous set of rules; amending those rules in the ordinary procedure is typically too cumbersome and will often require unanimity. As we have seen, the GMO case is a prime example of such a counteracting strategy, and the Biosafety Protocol's own collision rules reflect best the unavailability of a common will of states to resolve its tension with the SPS Agreement.[49] Little could be deduced from preambular clauses such as the following:

---

[46] I use 'contractual' to refer to the reciprocal obligations of states under a treaty they are parties to, and 'legislative' to emphasize the broader, norm-generating character of multilateral treaties. A similar focus can be found in N Matz, *Wege zur Koordinierung völkerrechtlicher Verträge*, Heidelberg: Springer Verlag, 2005, chs 7–9. See also the mention of the 'legislative ethos' of many multilateral efforts in Report of the Study Group, *Fragmentation*, para 471.

[47] Identity of the parties may in fact be impossible as the WTO has granted membership to a number of non-sovereign entities, such as Hong Kong, that would not be able to join other treaties. I am grateful to Andrew Lang for drawing my attention to this fact.

[48] See also Matz, *Wege zur Koordinierung*, 336–9.

[49] For another example, see C B Graber, 'The New UNESCO Convention on Cultural Diversity: A Counterbalance to the WTO?', *Journal of International Economic Law* 9 (2006), 553–74; H Ruiz-Fabri, 'Jeux dans la fragmentation: La Convention sur la promotion et la protection de la diversité des expressions culturelles', *Revue générale de droit international public* 111 (2007), 43–87.

Recognizing that trade and environment agreements should be mutually supportive with a view to achieving sustainable development,

Emphasizing that this Protocol shall not be interpreted as implying a change in the rights and obligations of a Party under any existing international agreements,

Understanding that the above recital is not intended to subordinate this Protocol to other international agreements . . . [50]

The relationship between the agreements hangs in the balance here, and the classical tools of international law soon run out.[51] Just like the Biosafety Protocol, WTO law claims for itself the right to define its status vis-à-vis other regimes: we have seen this in the Panel Report in *Biotech*, but it is also on display in the decisions of the Appellate Body which refers quite frequently to other international legal rules, but does not necessarily accord them much interpretive weight.[52]

The result is a regime complex with a multiplicity of interacting sites of governance, each of which insists on determining its relationship with the outside.[53] This is reminiscent of an account based upon systems theory,[54] and it shows how thin the framework of international law has become—how little impact its integrating, 'systemic' impetus now has. This all the more as the contestation I have described is not only a contestation about the application of particular rules, but also, as we shall see below, one about the structure and scope of the polity—a contestation about fundamentals, expressed in a pluralist legal order.

2. Vertical Pluralism: National Law, European Law, WTO Law

The picture is similar in the vertical dimension: between WTO law and regional or national legal systems. This relationship is generally characterized by a distance as a matter of principle—and is one that is typically greater

---

[50] Biosafety Protocol, Preamble.

[51] See n 21 above.

[52] See, eg, WTO Appellate Body, Report of 13 July 1998, WT/DS69/AB/R, *EC–Measures Affecting the Importation of Certain Poultry Products*, para 83. See also the Report of the Study Group, *Fragmentation*, para 445.

[53] On the concept of a regime complex, see K Raustiala & D G Victor, 'The Regime Complex for Plant Genetic Resources', *International Organization* 58 (2004), 277–309 at 295–305; on the notion of 'sites of governance', see F Snyder, 'Governing Economic Globalisation: Global Legal Pluralism and European Law', *European Law Journal* 5 (1999), 334–74.

[54] For such an account, see A Fischer-Lescano & G Teubner, *Regime-Kollisionen: Zur Fragmentierung des globalen Rechts*, Frankfurt am Main: Suhrkamp Verlag, 2006.

than is the case for other norms of international law. This is particularly noticeable in the United States: when approving the WTO Agreements, the Congress emphatically excluded any form of reliance on them in the courts, providing that

> [n]o provision of any of the Uruguay Round Agreements . . . that is inconsistent with any law of the United States shall have effect

and that

> [n]o person other than the United States . . . may challenge . . . any action or inaction by any department, agency, or other instrumentality of the United States . . . on the ground that such action or inaction is inconsistent with such agreement.[55]

Even if international agreements are today often denied self-executing character by the US upon ratification, this denial in the case of WTO law is exceptionally clear and pronounced and has also led to a particular hesitancy amongst the courts to use WTO law, even as an interpretative device.[56]

In our context of greater interest is the position of the EU, the receiving end of WTO disciplines in this case. Politically, the Council of the EU positioned itself in a similar way to the US Congress, stating that the WTO Agreements are 'not susceptible to being directly invoked in Community or Member State courts'.[57] But this was only part of the preamble of the Council's decision to conclude the agreements, and it certainly has not hindered ample speculation about the status of WTO law in EU law, both within and outside the courts. This speculation was fuelled by the ECJ's position on the status of the General Agreement on Tariffs and Trade (GATT 1947). The ECJ has traditionally been relatively open to international law, recognizing its potential direct effect in the EC legal order from early on.[58] The GATT was an outlier from the beginning: in the 1972 *International Fruit Company* decision, the Court had already found it not to be 'capable of conferring on citizens of

---

[55] United States Uruguay Round Agreement Act, 19 USC §3512, (a)(1) and (c)(1).

[56] See A Davies, 'Connecting or Compartmentalizing the WTO and United States Legal Systems? The Role of the *Charming Betsy* Canon', *Journal of International Economic Law* 10 (2007), 117–49.

[57] Council Decision 94/800 of 22 December 1994 concerning the conclusion on behalf of the European Community, as regards matters within its competence, of the agreements reached in the Uruguay Round multilateral negotiations (1986–1994), Official Journal L336/1, 23 December 1994.

[58] See P P Craig & G de Búrca, *EU Law: Text, Cases, and Materials*, 4th edn, Oxford: Oxford University Press, 2008, 202–13. See also the discussion in Chapter 4, II.1 and Chapter 5, II.2.

the Community rights which they can invoke before the courts'. This was chiefly due to the great flexibility of the GATT's provisions, the possibilities of derogation, and the power of unilateral withdrawal from its obligations.[59] The creation of the WTO raised doubts about this stance, primarily because the 'great flexibility' was to be significantly reduced by the advent of the new, far more powerful dispute-settlement mechanism. Yet hopes for a change in direction were thwarted in successive steps: in 1999, in *Portugal v Council*, the ECJ rejected the idea that the new institutional set-up of the WTO made a difference to the status of the GATT in EU law;[60] in later decisions, it also denied direct effect to other WTO agreements, such as the Agreement on Trade Related Aspects of Intellectual Property Rights (TRIPS Agreement) and the Agreement on Technical Barriers to Trade (TBT Agreement);[61] it held that the existence of clear rulings by the WTO Dispute Settlement Body did not change the situation;[62] and it rejected claims of damages based on non-compliance with such rulings.[63] Holding expressly that

> [a]s regards...the WTO agreements, it is settled case-law that, given their nature and structure, those agreements are not in principle among the rules in the light of which the Court is to review the legality of measures adopted by the Community institutions,[64]

the ECJ firmly closed the door on all attempts to reduce the distance that exists between EU law and WTO law as a matter of principle.

The Court, however, did recognize exceptions to this strict separation notably in two circumstances: when EU law makes 'clear reference' to WTO law, or when it seeks to transpose a particular part of it into the EU legal order. In these cases, an EU act can be invalidated if found incompatible with WTO law.[65] Moreover, the Court frequently uses the tool of treaty-consistent

---

[59] ECJ, Judgment of 12 December 1972, 21–24/72, *International Fruit Company*, [1972] ECR 1219.

[60] ECJ, Judgment of 23 November 1999, C-149/96, *Portugal v Council* [1999] ECR I-8395, paras 36–47.

[61] ECJ, Judgment of 14 December 2000, C-300/98 & C-392/98, *Dior* [2000] ECR I-11307, paras 42–4; Judgment of 12 March 2002, C-27/00 & C-122/00, *Omega Air* [2002] ECR I-02569, paras 85–97.

[62] ECJ, Judgment of 9 September 2008, C-120/06 & C-121/06, *FIAMM and Fedon* [2008] ECR I-06513, paras 125–33.

[63] ECJ, *FIAMM and Fedon*, paras 120–4.

[64] ECJ, *FIAMM and Fedon*, para 111.

[65] See, eg, ECJ, *Portugal v Council*, para 49; see also P J Kuijper & M Bronckers, 'WTO Law in the European Court of Justice', *Common Market Law Review* 42 (2005), 1313–55 at 1323–8.

interpretation to read EU law in the light of international law, and also of WTO law. Using these mechanisms, the European courts have drawn upon WTO law in hundreds of cases and established an extensive jurisprudence on it.[66] As I will discuss in some greater detail below, the separation in principle has thus not hindered an engagement in practice.

What is clear, though, is that the separation alters the spirit of engagement. The EC Treaty's clear statement that international '[a]greements ... shall be binding on the institutions of the Community and on Member States'[67] and the ECJ's deduction that 'those agreements have primacy over secondary Community legislation'[68] seemed to imply an unconditional subjection of most EU law, a hierarchy in favour of international legal rules, and a tight connection between the two legal orders. The ECJ's stance towards WTO law effects a shift towards a more subtle form of interaction, one in which the Court enjoys far greater flexibility. In this setting, international rules can no longer be directly invoked by private parties, and they rarely allow challenges to the validity of EU legislation. Yet the two exceptions sketched above and the tool of treaty-consistent interpretation grant the courts sufficient leeway to use WTO law when they see fit. For example, they have reviewed EU anti-dumping legislation on the basis of WTO rules,[69] interpreted the EC Customs Code in line with the WTO Agreement on Rules of Origin,[70] and used the TRIPS Agreement to construe national trademark law.[71] Yet in other areas, the ECJ has stood aside. This is especially so in cases with high salience: for example, on the strongly politicized issues of the EU's banana market[72] and the ban on the import of hormonally treated

---

[66] F Snyder, 'The Gatekeepers: The European Courts and WTO Law', *Common Market Law Review* 40 (2003), 313–67; M Bronckers, 'From "Direct Effect" to "Muted Dialogue": Recent Developments in the European Courts' Case Law on the WTO and Beyond', *Journal of International Economic Law* 11 (2008), 885–98.

[67] EC Treaty Art 300(7), now Treaty on the Functioning of the European Union Art 216 (2).

[68] See, eg, ECJ, Judgment of 10 January 2006, C-344/04, *IATA* [2006] ECR I-00403, para 35.

[69] eg, ECJ, Judgment of 9 January 2003, C-76/00 P, *Petrotub and Republica v Council* [2003] ECR I-79.

[70] ECJ, Judgment of 8 March 2007, 447/05 & C-448/05, *Thomson Multimedia and Vestel France* [2007] ECR I-04307, paras 29–30.

[71] ECJ, Judgment of 16 November 2004, C-245/02, *Anheuser Busch v Budvar* [2004] ECR I-10989.

[72] ECJ, Order of 2 May 2001, C-307/99, *OGT Fruchthandelsgesellschaft* [2001] ECR I-3159, paras 24–31; ECJ, *FIAMM and Fedon*.

meat,[73] the Court simply referred to its general line and refused to consider the respective WTO rulings.

One consequence of this stance is obviously a stronger role of the political institutions in the EU. The domestic impact of the WTO Agreements now depends upon them to a much larger extent than in the case of automatic direct effect, and this also allows them to deny any impact—an option that was specifically contemplated by the ECJ. One of the central considerations of the Court in *Portugal v Council* was the preservation of the freedom of the political organs in dealing with the EU's trading partners. Political options, the ECJ argued, would be unduly restricted if, through the operation of direct effect, the political organs could no longer refuse compliance with WTO rulings and seek a negotiated solution for an issue.[74] This consideration was, of course, bolstered by the fact that other major parties, such as the US, had not provided for direct effect either.[75] Unilaterally renouncing the option of non-compliance would have seemed to weaken the EU's hand in international trade disputes considerably.

Another reason for insisting on the distance between EU and WTO law was probably the depth and precision of the latter's impact.[76] The GMO case has provided an example for how the SPS Agreement structures domestic policy choices, but WTO law reaches out into many other issue areas. The resulting impact is broad, but because of the indeterminacy and openness of the agreements it would normally have left domestic courts—even in the case of direct effect—a considerable freedom of interpretation and space for the determination of potential forms of compliance. With the increasing concretization of the rules through an ever more active dispute-settlement mechanism, however, this freedom has been heavily curtailed—indeterminacy no longer provides the buffer between the different layers of law that it had provided before. In this light, it is understandable that the ECJ sought to reclaim some of the EU's autonomy from an ever more tightly judicialized WTO legal order.

Such an account is all the more plausible in this case as the other areas in which the ECJ has distanced EU law from international law are likewise characterized by a high degree of legalization and institutionalized concretization. We have already encountered two of them in the previous chapters.

---

[73] ECJ, Judgment of 30 September 2003, C-93/02 P, *Biret International*, [2003] ECR I-10497, paras 51–65; see also A Thies, 'Biret and Beyond: The Status of WTO Rulings in EC Law', *Common Market Law Review* 41 (2004), 1661–82.

[74] ECJ, *Portugal v Council*, paras 40, 46.

[75] ibid, para 43.

[76] Snyder, 'Gatekeepers', 333; Bronckers, 'Direct Effect to Muted Dialogue', 887.

One of them concerns the relationship with European human rights law where the ECJ has insisted on its discretion to decide whether or not to follow judgments of the European Court of Human Rights.[77] The other relates to the UN Security Council: as we have seen, the Court insisted in *Kadi* on the autonomy of the EU legal order and the ensuing dominance of *European* standards of procedural protection vis-à-vis the designation of individuals as terrorist subjects by the UN sanctions committees.[78] A third area is that of the law of the sea: here, the ECJ ruled in the *Intertanko* case—decided only three months before *Kadi*—that the UN Convention on the Law of the Sea (UNCLOS) operated exclusively in the intergovernmental realm, did not create individual rights, and was, as a result, not directly applicable in the EU legal order.[79] UNCLOS, like the WTO Agreements, has often been heralded as an example of the increasing legalization—and especially judicialization—of international affairs: the International Tribunal for the Law of the Sea, even though it does not at present attract a great number of cases, certainly represents an important element in the move towards dispute settlement by permanent judicial institutions.[80] The ECJ's response to this move is to distance EU law more effectively. This may appear as a step backwards, but it may also be seen as trying to re-establish the *marge de manoeuvre* that courts had enjoyed in the older, more imprecise international legal order. Seen in this light, the creation of distance through a pluralist order appears as a countertendency to the increasing legalization of postnational politics.

III. A PLURALISM OF COMPETING COLLECTIVES

This pluralism—which also includes that *within* Europe[81]—is not only a legal, technical affair, but is also based on intense social contestation about the locus of authority and the right collective for decision-making on matters of food safety and the environment. Such contestation is at the heart of the normative argument for pluralism developed in Chapter 3. Here we can

---

[77] See Chapter 4, II.1.

[78] ECJ (Grand Chamber), Judgment of 3 September 2008, C-402/05 P & 415/05 P, *Kadi and Al Barakaat* [2008] ECR I-06351. See Chapter 5, II.2.

[79] ECJ, Judgment of 3 June 2008, C-308/06, *Intertanko* [2008] ECR I-04057, paras 64–5.

[80] On the general trend, see, eg, J Goldstein et al (eds), *Legalization and World Politics*, Cambridge, MA: MIT Press, 2001; Société française pour le droit international (ed), *La juridictionnalisation du droit international*, Paris: Pedone, 2003.

[81] See Chapter 5, II.3.

observe more specifically how the two phenomena relate to each other in a concrete case.

The contestation about the right collective is most clearly on display in the competition between the SPS Agreement and the Biosafety Protocol for leadership on the issue of GMOs. As mentioned before, the Protocol was an attempt to establish a counterweight to WTO rules, and it was also driven by a desire to rebalance participation in international rule-making and make it more inclusive. This may seem counterintuitive, given that the WTO and the Biosafety Protocol (as of May 2009) both have 153 parties.[82] It becomes easier to grasp when we look at the number of countries participating in the negotiations: in the Uruguay Round that led to the creation of the WTO, overall participation reached 123 countries.[83] Negotiations on the Biosafety Protocol were open to all 175 states that had joined the Biodiversity Convention by early 1999,[84] plus a number of observers (sometimes, as in the case of the US, very active ones).

Sheer numbers, however, hardly reflect all the imbalances. One such imbalance concerned the paradigms of negotiation, which in the case of the WTO largely followed the logic of trade, as trade officials were typically at the helm of negotiations, although on some issues—including SPS negotiations—ministries of agriculture were equally involved. The Biosafety Protocol, in contrast, because it was part of the Rio process, was largely driven by officials from environmental ministries who shared quite a different worldview.[85] Yet more importantly, the negotiations on the Protocol were strongly influenced by developing countries gathered in the powerful 'Like-Minded Group'. Many of them had difficulties establishing domestic rules on GMO matters, often for lack of expertise and capacity, and thus had a particular interest in harmonized—and relatively strong—regulation.[86] The Uruguay Round and the negotiations on the SPS Agreement were to a much greater extent dominated by OECD countries, especially by the US and the EU.[87]

---

[82] As of 19 May 2009; see: <http://www.wto.org/english/thewto_e/whatis_e/ tif_e/org6_e.htm>; <http://www.cbd.int/biosafety/signinglist.shtml>.

[83] See: <http://www.wto.org/english/thewto_e/whatis_e/tif_e/fact4_e.htm>; Büthe, 'Globalization of Health and Safety Standards', 241.

[84] See: <http://www.cbd.int/convention/parties/list/>.

[85] Pollack & Shaffer, *When Cooperation Fails*, 135–6, 157; see also Büthe, 'Globalization of Health and Safety Standards', 241–2, 252, on the SPS negotiations.

[86] Böckenförde, *Grüne Gentechnik*, 140–2.

[87] See generally J H Barton, J L Goldstein, T E Josling, & R H Steinberg, *The Evolution of the Trade Regime: Politics, Law, and Economics of the GATT and the WTO,*

In its submissions in the *Biotech* case, the EU relied heavily on the argument of greater inclusiveness. It used it in a general way to question the appropriateness of the WTO as a forum for deciding on GMO issues, stating that:

> it is not the function of the *WTO Agreement* to allow one group of countries to impose its values on another group. Nor is it the purpose of the *WTO Agreement* to trump the other relevant rules of international law which permit—or even require—a prudent and precautionary approach. There is a serious question as to whether the WTO is the appropriate international forum for resolving all the GMO issues that the Complainants have raised in these cases.[88]

More specifically, the argument about the right collective for rule-making on the issue found reflection in the EU position on the role of other international agreements in the proceedings, and in particular in the interpretation of WTO law by the Panel. In the view of the EU,

> the issues faced by the Panel have to be taken in their broader context. That context includes other relevant international instruments, which *reflect the view of the international community* as to the appropriate way to proceed on decision-making in relation to GMOs and GM products.... [A] failure by the Panel to have regard to this broader context will risk undermining the legitimacy of the WTO system. The Panel should therefore not accede to the Complainants' arguments that this case may be decided in 'clinical isolation' from the rules of public international law more generally.[89]

For the EU, it was thus the 'international community', rather than a particular faction of it, that was called upon to determine the issue, and its views could be gauged better by considering the entirety of global regulatory approaches, including the Biosafety Protocol, even if the complainants were not parties to it. Yet the invocation of the international community is not the sole, and perhaps not even the decisive, element of the EU position: for as becomes clear from the beginning of the first quote, the EU also insists

Princeton, NJ: Princeton University Press, 2006, 62–7; on the SPS negotiations, Büthe, 'Globalization of Health and Safety Standards', 244–5.

[88] European Communities, First Written Submission in *EC–Measures Affecting the Approval and Marketing of Biotech Products*, 17 May 2004, at: <http://trade.ec.europa.eu/doclib/docs/2004/june/tradoc_117687.pdf>, para 10.

[89] European Communities, Second Written Submission in *EC–Measures Affecting the Approval and Marketing of Biotech Products*, 19 July 2004, at: <http://trade.ec.europa.eu/doclib/docs/2005/february/tradoc_121552.pdf>, para 8 (emphasis added).

on the freedom of states from imposition by others—a classical sovereignty theme. This is better reflected in a further statement:

> it cannot be right that the Complainants should be allowed to impose their approach on the European Communities, or indeed on any other countries, and to do so through the WTO. Even less so at a time when countries around the world are still trying to clarify the balance between risks and benefits.[90]

How those two aspects—sovereignty and international community—relate, is not immediately clear. We may understand them as resisting the idea that the SPS Agreement disposed of the issue of GMOs, and as insisting that the issue should be determined either by each state for itself or by a broader international community, but not by the group of states represented in the WTO or by its Dispute Settlement Body.

As we have seen above, the WTO Panel disagreed and approached the issue from the narrower, and more formal angle of the SPS Agreement alone. For the Panel, too, this was a consequence of a principled stance on which collective should have the final say on the issue. I have already quoted the passage in which the Panel pointed out that the EU's broader approach could hardly be reconciled with state sovereignty: in its view, a state could only be affected by those obligations it had agreed to undertake.[91] This reflects a standard state-voluntarist position, although it is less clear how useful it is as a guide for the work of the Dispute Settlement Body. After all, the Dispute Settlement Body's task is not only that of restating what states have already agreed to, but also—as with all judicial bodies—of the active, progressive development of those (invariably indeterminate) commitments. The reference to consent as an expression of state sovereignty, backward-looking as it is, hardly helps to shed light on what norms and whose views should guide this creative, forward-looking work. The Panel's rejection of external guidance may even be seen as turning the emphasis on sovereignty on its head: it opens up greater space for a transnational body—the Panel itself—to fill the gaps in the WTO Agreements, thus creating precisely the risk to states' freedom from external imposition the Europeans had warned against.

These ambiguities around the meaning of sovereignty, and especially the EU position on it, lead us into another debate about the locus of authority in which the pluralist legal structure is embedded. This debate centres on the idea of 'food sovereignty', a term typically understood as 'the right of peoples and sovereign states to democratically determine their own agricultural and

---

[90] European Communities, First Written Submission, para 2.

[91] See text at n 37 above.

food policies.'[92] The notion has found strong resonance especially in developing countries as an attempt at reclaiming decision-making power over the production and importation of food, and at keeping the influence of international rules and markets at bay. Originating in the sphere of non-governmental organizations (NGOs) such as the *Via Campesina* international peasant movement,[93] it has inspired numerous civil society groups[94] and has entered the vocabulary of intergovernmental fora as well.[95] Moreover, it has found legislative reflection in Venezuela and has been included in the new constitution of Ecuador.[96]

Beyond that immediate impact, the term provides a link to a host of normative claims about sites of governance on food. Within the EU, for example, the contestation about GMOs has triggered a variety of initiatives for a greater local impact on the extent of cultivation of GM crops. Based upon an Austrian initiative, hundreds of European municipalities and regions have formed a network of 'GMO-free regions', rejecting the cultivation of GM crops on their territories.[97] As evidenced by its 2008 conference on 'Food and Democracy', a central goal of this campaign is to re-establish the possibility for local or national democratic determination of GMO cultivation and sale, and it is clearly directed against European (and global) rule-making on the issue. Some regions' efforts in this direction have openly clashed with EU law: Upper Austria (Oberösterreich), for example, saw its GMO ban rejected by the European Commission, took the case to the courts, but

---

[92] International Assessment of Agricultural Knowledge, Science and Technology for Development (IAASTD), *Summary for Decision-Makers*, 2008, at: <http://www.agassessment.org/docs/IAASTD_GLOBAL_SDM_JAN_2008.pdf>, 15. See also the definition in the Nyéléni Declaration of the Forum for Food Sovereignty, at: <http://www.foodsovereignty.org/public/new_attached/49_Declaration_of_Nyeleni.pdf> ('Food sovereignty is the right of peoples to healthy and culturally appropriate food produced through ecologically sound and sustainable methods, and their right to define their own food and agriculture systems').

[93] See <http://viacampesina.org/main_en/index.php>.

[94] See, eg, the International Planning Committee Food Sovereignty, at: <http://www.foodsovereignty.org/new/>.

[95] See IAASTD, *Summary*.

[96] On Ecuador, see Art 13 of the 2008 Constitution, at: <http://issuu.com/restrella/docs/constitucion_del_ecuador>; on Venezuela, see the decree of 31 July 2008 establishing the Ley Orgánica de Seguridad y Soberanía Agroalimentaria, at: <http://www.rnv.gov.ve/noticias/index.php?s=b2c8b83055482f5ea1b0c8631a3dd973&act=Attach&type=post&id=post-29-1217897618.ibf>.

[97] See: <http://www.gmo-free-regions.org>.

lost eventually.[98] Otherwise however, as we have seen above, Commission efforts to remove national safeguard bans have so far largely failed because of the degree of resistance from member states. Calls for renationalizing decision-making rights on this matter have become louder—and have found increasing acceptance even within the Commission.[99]

Such moves resonate with significant parts of the population: in a 2005 European survey on biotechnology, 32 per cent of respondents said they wanted the governance of science and technology to be based primarily on moral and ethical considerations rather than on scientific evidence. Additionally, 24 per cent wanted the general public, not experts, to have the main influence on decision-making.[100] These may be minorities—after all, 59 per cent of respondents favoured decision-making by experts on the basis of scientific evidence—but they are sizeable enough to sustain resistance to a delegation of powers detached from local and national democratic influence. With the greater salience of the issue, approval ratings of the European regulation of biotechnology have declined, while those of national regulation are on the increase.[101]

The greater politicization of the cultivation and trade of GM products has thus removed the issue from the realm of the technical and has placed the question of the appropriate sites of governance—and of their interplay—squarely back into the public debate. As we can observe from the sketch above, different visions clash here, and democratic depth and inclusiveness stand in tension with each other as well as with instrumental considerations stemming from the need for (relatively) harmonized rules in international trade. This may be unsurprising as it mirrors the broader strands of thought explored in Chapter 3. Yet it is remarkable as an example of how this normative contestation feeds into, and sustains, the systemic pluralism between

---

[98] CFI, Judgment of 5 October 2005, T-366/03, *Land Oberösterreich and Austria v Commission* [2005] ECR II-04005; ECJ, Judgment of 13 September 2007, C-439/05 P, *Land Oberösterreich and Austria v Commission* [2007] ECR I-07141.

[99] See, eg, the statement by the Austrian minister of agriculture, at: <http://www.news.at/articles/0910/15/235678/minister-berlakovich-eu-stirn-gen-mais-verbot-laender>; J M Barroso, *Political Guidelines for the Next Commission*, 39, at: <http://ec.europa.eu/commission_2010-2014/president/pdf/press_20090903_en.pdf>.

[100] Special Eurobarometer, 'Europeans and Biotechnology in 2005: Patterns and Trends', July 2006, at: <http://ec.europa.eu/public_opinion/archives/ebs/ebs_244b_en.pdf>, 42–3.

[101] ibid, 46. Between 2002 and 2005, the 'trust surplus'—the difference between positive and negative assessments—for European regulation decreased from 48 to 42, while that for national regulation increased from 27 to 33.

the different legal orders at play here. Claims for ultimate authority of the local, national, or European polities clash with each other and with those who want to situate that authority in a WTO framework or in a broader 'international community'. In the GMO dispute, social and political contestation about the right collective—ultimately arguments about the scope and structure of a democratic polity and its jurisdiction—very visibly conditions the pluralist structure of governance.

IV. DISRUPTIVE PLURALISM?

The story of the GMO dispute may be an instance of pluralism, and also one of intense competition for authority by different collectives, but at first sight it does not appear as an example of a particularly stable, or commendable, form of cooperation. Quite the opposite: the story of a breakdown of cooperation because of contestation and institutional fragmentation. A leading book on the issue bears the telling title *When Cooperation Fails*.[102]

Upon closer inspection, though, this characterization appears as excessively gloomy, and it certainly is if we consider the broader picture of transnational food safety, environmental, and trade regulation. As I will try to show in this section, the contestation over GM food and feed signals the limits of what transnational regulation can aspire to, but it is also evidence of how much cooperation can be achieved in spite of deep-seated disagreement.

The outcome of the GMO dispute so far is naturally frustrating for proponents of GM products, and it often seems simply to reflect a non-cooperative stance of the EU. As I have sketched above, early on during the WTO proceedings, the EU again started to process applications to import GM food and grow GM crops, but the number of decisions taken is still low, and every new one encounters resistance from national governments.[103] Moreover, member states maintain domestic bans on certain products and reject Commission efforts to remove them. Much of this dispute centres on whether Monsanto's genetically modified MON810 corn can be cultivated. Already approved by the EU in 1998, it is subject to bans in several member

---

[102] Pollack & Shaffer, *When Cooperation Fails*.

[103] See, eg, J Smith, 'EU Clashes on Authorizing Monsanto GM Soybean', Reuters, 19 November 2008, <http://uk.reuters.com/article/environmentNews/idUK-TRE4AI71C20081119>; Reuters, 'EU Approves Genetically Modified Soybean for Import', 4 December 2008, <http://uk.reuters.com/article/environment-News/idUKTRE4B33GO20081204>; P Harrison, 'EU Meeting on GM Maize ends in Deadlock', Reuters, 25 February 2009, <http://uk.reuters.com/article/behindTheScenes/idUKTRE51O57320090225>; BBC Online, 'GM Potato Cleared for EU Farming', 2 March 2010, <http://news.bbc.co.uk/2/hi/8545503.stm>.

states, and in February and March 2009, large majorities of member states voted down Commission proposals to lift these bans, despite positive assessments of the crop's safety by the European Food Safety Agency (EFSA) and other bodies.[104] Emboldened by this political mood, in the spring of 2009 Luxembourg and Germany joined in with their own bans.[105] And domestic courts have largely refused to interfere with those decisions.[106]

Yet there are also signs of cooperation and convergence, especially on a systemic level. EU courts, for instance, have adjusted their jurisprudence on precautionary measures in a way that comes very close to what the SPS Agreement requires.[107] As Joanne Scott notes,

> [t]he WTO Agreement may not have a direct effect in Community law, but it enjoys a significant, if still uncertain, capacity to influence strongly the interpretation of this body of law.[108]

This may not only be true for the area of GMOs, but for public health issues more broadly,[109] and probably quite generally for other areas covered by WTO rules. The European courts may not always be explicit about it, and they may maintain their role as 'gatekeepers' at the door of EU law, but in substance they have come to integrate WTO law into their jurisprudence

[104] P Harrison, 'EU Upholds Austria, Hungary Right to Ban GM Crops', Reuters, 2 March 2009, <http://uk.reuters.com/article/environmentNews/idUKTRE5212OL20090302>.

[105] See ICTSD, 'Luxembourg to Ban GM Maize Cultivation', *Bridges Trade BioRes* 9:6, 3 April 2009, <http://ictsd.net/i/news/biores/44622/>; Deutsche Welle, 'Germany to Ban US Biotech Giant's Genetically Modified Corn Strain', 14 April 2009, <http://www.dw-world.de/dw/article/0,,4176790,00.html>.

[106] See, eg, on France, Conseil d'Etat, juge de référés, Order of 19 March 2008, no 313547, available at: <http://www.legifrance.gouv.fr>; on Germany, Oberverwaltungsgericht Lüneburg, Order of 28 May 2009, 13 ME 76/09, available at: <http://www.dbovg.niedersachsen.de/index.asp>. But see GMO Compass, 'Italian Court Gives GM Go-ahead', 5 February 2010, <http://www.gmo-compass.org/eng/news/487.docu.html>.

[107] J Scott, 'European Regulation of GMOs and the WTO', *Columbia Journal of European Law* 9 (2003), 213–39 at 223, 228–9, 233; see also A Alemanno, *Trade in Food: Regulatory and Judicial Approaches in the EC and the WTO*, London: Cameron May, 2007, 145.

[108] Scott, 'European Regulation', 223.

[109] See the (somewhat preliminary) assessment in M Slotboom, 'Do Public Health Measures Receive Similar Treatment in European Community and World Trade Organization Law?', *Journal of World Trade* 37 (2003), 553–96 at 594.

almost as a matter of routine.[110] This has led to a situation in which, in Francis Snyder's words, '[t]ogether, clear reference, transposition and consistent interpretation may prove nearly as effective as direct effect in integrating WTO law into EC law'.[111] As regards GMOs, the ECJ certainly has not been too cautious: it has not hesitated in finding member state resistance in violation of EU law, and it has even imposed a substantial fine on France for its delayed implementation of Community legislation.[112]

On the other hand, WTO jurisprudence has not been deaf to calls to give precaution greater weight in assessing the legality of SPS measures. Even if the outcomes of proceedings sometimes suggest the contrary, the Appellate Body has—at least in principle—opened doors in this direction,[113] and the Panel in the *Biotech* case has, as we have seen, also refrained from rejecting the European approach outright. Not only did it decide on a narrow basis, thus leaving a substantive assessment for future cases, but it also indicated to the EU how to pursue its approach in conformity with the SPS Agreement. As mentioned above, the Panel pointed out that if a risk assessment produced 'uncertainties or constraints' in its evaluation, restrictive measures by member states may be admissible.[114] In a clarifying letter, it reaffirmed that its findings did not restrain the freedom of the parties to act on new scientific evidence:

> Particularly if the new or additional scientific evidence provides grounds for considering that the use or consumption of a product might constitute a risk to human health and/or the environment, a Member might need expeditiously to re-assess the risks to human health and/or the environment.[115]

Both the ECJ and the WTO Panel insist on the autonomous interpretation of their respective bodies of law—a typical feature of the interaction of courts in a pluralist setting, as we have already seen in previous chapters. But this autonomous stance does not hinder mutual awareness and consideration of the position and jurisprudence of each other—a form of 'muted

---

[110] Snyder, 'Gatekeepers'. See also Bronckers, 'Direct Effect to Muted Dialogue'; A Antoniadis, 'The European Union and WTO Law: A Nexus of Reactive, Coactive, and Proactive Approaches', *World Trade Review* 6 (2007), 45–87 at 65–74.

[111] Snyder, 'Gatekeepers', 362.

[112] ECJ, Judgment of 9 December 2008, C-121/07, *Commission v France* [2008] ECR I-09159.

[113] See Howse, 'WHO/WTO Study'; Peel, 'Risk Regulation', at 53–86.

[114] See n 28 above.

[115] WTO Panel, *Biotech*, WTO Doc WT/DS291/R/Add.9, 29 September 2006, K-2.

dialogue', as one commentator has called it.[116] After all, the legitimacy of both institutions is relatively fragile, and they depend on cooperative relations to avoid serious challenges[117]—in a similar way as courts in the European human rights context needed each other to bolster their own authority.[118] Yet in the GMO context, the full extent of dialogue and exchange only becomes visible when the view is broadened beyond the realm of judicial actors. One effect of the courts' reluctance to engage—by denying WTO law direct effect in the ECJ's case, and by refraining from deciding upon substance in that of the WTO Panel—is to strengthen further the central role of political, regulatory institutions in the interaction between the different sites of governance.

EU regulation on GMOs has borne the stamp of WTO influence since at least the early 2000s—a time when the de facto moratorium on approvals of GM products was in full operation. The new legislation on the issue, adopted between 2001 and 2003,[119] reflects the approach of the SPS Agreement in many key areas, especially in the formulation of the precautionary principle, the acceptance that restrictions on the import, cultivation, and sale of products need to be based on a thorough, science-based risk assessment—and in its creation of a separate agency, EFSA, for that purpose.[120]

This reflects a broader trend towards convergence in risk regulation, triggered to a significant extent by SPS rules. European policy in this area before the Uruguay Round was characterized by a parallelism of scientific and social/cultural concerns and by a mediated policy style that integrated decision-making on how much risk a certain product or process posed and what consequences to draw from that risk.[121] The former issue was important to European negotiators on the SPS Agreement: they sought to include 'other concerns' than science as justification for trade-restrictive measures, partly in order to shield the European ban on hormonally treated beef from WTO challenge. But the EC found itself with few allies and had to give in if negotiations were to continue—it was keen on a successful conclusion because it

---

[116] Bronckers, 'Direct Effect to Muted Dialogue'.

[117] See the account of the *Biotech* report in Pollack & Shaffer, *When Cooperation Fails*, 220–4.

[118] See Chapter 4, II and III.2.

[119] EC Directive No 2001/18/EC, 12 March 2001, *Official Journal EU*, L 106/1, 17 April 2001; Regulations (EC) No 1829/2003 and 1830/2003, 22 September 2003, Official Journal L268/1 and 268/24, 18 October 2003.

[120] See Scott, 'European Regulation'; see also Pollack & Shaffer, *When Cooperation Fails*, 237–45, 260–1.

[121] Skogstad, 'Food Safety Regulatory Policy Innovation', 488–92.

sought to reduce obstacles to its own market access in other countries and did not want to see this relatively low-priority issue threaten negotiations on other, more central parts of the Uruguay Round.[122] As a result, SPS rules came to require significant adjustment from Europe—adjustment at a time when the food safety scandals of the 1990s had raised the political hurdles for liberalization substantially. The EU consequently tried to renegotiate the SPS Agreement but was met with resistance by the US.[123] Despite these problems with the agreement, though, we can observe far-reaching convergence on both principles and processes around the SPS approach.[124] The EU has centred its new food safety regulation on scientific risk assessment as the key element, and it has also institutionally separated that risk assessment from the risk management that is performed by political bodies—while EFSA performs the former, the latter is undertaken in the Comitology system.[125]

Yet actual convergence on food safety at the global level goes much further than this and extends to detailed standards as well. For example, since the 1990s a large number of states have adopted the Hazard Analysis and Critical Control Point (HACCP) system, which requires identification of critical control points and development of procedures for monitoring controls.[126] The range of still-existing differences between countries in this respect has been further narrowed by a template for HACCP that has been elaborated by the Codex Alimentarius Commission.[127] Codex has also

---

[122] Skogstad, 'Food Safety Regulatory Policy Innovation', 492–4; Drezner, *All Politics is Global*, 162–3. But see also the somewhat different account in Büthe, 'Globalization of Health and Safety Standards', 238–50.

[123] Drezner, *All Politics is Global*, 163.

[124] See D Roberts, 'Preliminary Assessment of the Effects of the WTO Agreement on Sanitary and Phytosanitary Measures', *Journal of International Economic Law* 1 (1998), 377–405 at 396–8; D Roberts & L Unnevehr, 'Resolving Trade Disputes Arising from Trends in Food Safety Regulation: The Role of the Multilateral Governance Framework', *World Trade Review* 4 (2005), 469–97 at 470–5; see also Slotboom, 'Public Health Measures', 593–5.

[125] Skogstad, 'Food Safety Regulatory Policy Innovation', 497–501. It is the risk management process—a rather byzantine interplay between Commission and member states in an elaborate committee structure—that often produces outcomes with little relation to scientific findings, allowing member states to block approvals even if EFSA has not found a significant risk. See Pollack & Shaffer, *When Cooperation Fails*, 245–60.

[126] Roberts & Unnevehr, 'Resolving Trade Disputes', 474.

[127] See Codex Doc CAC/RCP 1, Recommended International Code of Practice—General Principles of Food Hygiene, 1969, last revised 2003, <http://www.codexalimentarius.net/web/more_info.jsp?id_sta=23>; see Roberts & Unnevehr, 'Resolving Trade Disputes', 492.

developed a great number of other standards pertaining to both the process and substance of food safety regulation—ranging from guidelines for
equivalence assessments between countries[128] to a code of practice for the
prevention and reduction of aflatoxin contamination in tree nuts,[129] to
standards for oranges, dairy fat spreads, and camembert cheese—altogether
more than 3,000 standards.[130] These are of course not binding, and member states can and do deviate from them, but both the weight assigned to
them by the SPS Agreement and the commitment associated with consensus
decision-making in Codex make them influential factors in domestic food
safety regulation.[131] They often address controversial issues: for example,
the above-mentioned code of practice concerns an issue—aflatoxin levels—
that had led to significant friction between the EU and its trading partners in
the late 1990s.[132] Since then, Codex has managed to adopt a range of guidelines on the issue.[133]

Cooperation and convergence are also facilitated within the WTO itself,
where much of the work is not as fraught with friction as the widespread

[128] Codex Doc CAC/GL 53, Guidelines on the Judgement of Equivalence of
Sanitary Measures Associated with Food Inspection and Certification Systems,
2003, revised 2008, <http://www.codexalimentarius.net/web/more_info.
jsp?id_sta=10047>.

[129] Codex Doc CAC/RCP 59, Code of Practice for the Prevention and Reduction
of Aflatoxin Contamination in Tree Nuts, 2005, <http://www.codexalimentarius.
net/web/more_info.jsp?id_sta=10221>.

[130] Standards are available at: <http://www.codexalimentarius.net/web/stand-
ard_list.do?lang=en>. On the activity of the Codex, see F Veggeland & S O Borgen,
'Negotiating International Food Standards: The World Trade Organization's
Impact on the Codex Alimentarius Commission', *Governance* 18 (2005), 675–708 at
676; see also Pollack & Shaffer, *When Cooperation Fails*, 164.

[131] See the assessment of the importance of Codex standards by governments
in *Report of the Evaluation of the Codex Alimentarius and other FAO and WHO Food
Standards Work*, 15 November 2002, at: <http://www.who.int/foodsafety/codex/
eval_report/en/index.html>, paras 56–9. Another indicator of their importance
is the level of resources invested in them and the degree of participation in meet-
ings. Participation has increased significantly over the last twenty years and
yet again reached record levels in 2008; see Veggeland & Borgen, 'Negotiating
Food Standards', 687–9; Report of the US Delegate, 31st Session of the Codex
Alimentarius Commission, 2008.

[132] See Roberts & Unnevehr, 'Resolving Trade Disputes', 486–7.

[133] See also the codes of practice on peanuts (Codex Doc CAC/RCP 55, 2004,
<http://www.codexalimentarius.net/web/more_info.jsp?id_sta=10084>) and
dried figs (Codex Doc CAC/RCP 65, 2008, <http://www.codexalimentarius.net/
web/more_info.jsp?id_sta=11025>).

focus on the dispute-settlement mechanism in scholarship and the media suggests. This is in large part due to the more informal and cooperative approach to problem-solving in the SPS Committee, where member states notify the Committee of their SPS measures and others can lodge complaints against them.[134] In this forum, many problems can be detected and raised early: from 1995 to 2008, more than 7,500 SPS measures were notified to the Committee, and 277 'specific trade concerns' were raised.[135] A significant number of these concerns—about one-third—was wholly or partially resolved, through broader information, better mutual understanding, capacity-building, and/or the adjustment or withdrawal of the measures in question.[136] Moreover, cooperation in the Committee helps to concretize rules and align normative expectations so that member states can anticipate, avoid, or solve potential problems early on.[137] For example, EU safeguard measures restricting imports from a number of African countries following a cholera outbreak were questioned in the SPS Committee by Tanzania. Partly due to interventions by the observer representative of the WHO, the EU recognized that the actual risk of cholera transmission from food imports was very low and therefore withdrew the measures. The debate settled the particular dispute, but it also helped shape member states' views on the appropriate standards for the matter along the lines of WHO guidance.[138] In another example, a dispute over HACCP requirements by the Philippines, brought up by Canada, led to extensive debate among Committee members and helped them to elaborate a common approach to what HACCP implied—beyond the solution of the particular dispute in which the Philippines deferred implementation of its policy indefinitely.[139]

These examples signal a relatively high degree of cooperation and policy convergence in an area that has become heavily politicized in the last twenty years. This is noteworthy but should not conceal the limits of cooperation. Regarding those issues where positions are far apart, heavily entrenched,

---

[134] See Scott, *SPS Agreement*, ch 2.

[135] WTO Doc.G/SPS/GEN/887/Rev.1, 6 February 2009, paras 25, 66.

[136] WTO Doc G/SPS/GEN/204/Rev.9, 5 February 2009, paras 8, 10; G/SPS/GEN/204/Rev.9/Add.3, 6 February 2009. As this report by the WTO Secretariat notes, some solved cases may not have been reported. See also Scott, *SPS Agreement*, 50–60; Roberts & Unnevehr, 'Resolving Trade Disputes', 480–2, 493.

[137] Scott, *SPS Agreement*, 50–60, 69–74. For a broader analysis of functions of information exchange and norm elaboration in WTO non-judicial governance, see A Lang & J Scott, 'The Hidden World of WTO Governance', *European Journal of International Law* 20 (2009), 575–614.

[138] Scott, *SPS Agreement*, 53–4.

[139] ibid, 54–5.

and enjoy considerable support on both sides, cooperative successes have often been elusive. This is true in the Codex Commission for the debates on the role of precaution and of 'other legitimate factors' in food safety risk management in general. On both issues, Codex has managed to produce compromise documents, but they are very vague and bracket, rather than resolve, the conflict.[140] The most intransigent problems, however, are related to biotechnology in particular: on issues such as labelling and traceability in GM products, common ground could not be found within Codex.[141] This does not imply, though, that no progress at all has been achieved on GMO-related issues.[142] In 2003, Codex managed to agree on *Principles and Guidelines on Foods Derived from Biotechnology*, which contain three sets of norms on risk assessment and food safety analysis for GM foods.[143] The task force that had prepared these documents was judged a success,[144] had its mandate extended, and managed to agree upon a number of further documents, especially risk assessment in particular areas.[145]

The overall picture of global regulatory cooperation on food safety and related SPS matters is thus not as bleak as it is sometimes made out to be. Although the area may be characterized as one of fundamentally 'contested governance',[146] cooperation is routine and both broad and relatively deep, and even on GMO issues, we can observe significant regulatory successes.

---

[140] See S Poli, 'The European Community and the Adoption of International Food Standards within the Codex Alimentarius Commission', *European Law Journal* 10 (2004), 613–30 at 619–25; Veggeland & Borgen, 'Negotiating Food Standards', 694–7.

[141] See Poli, 'Adoption of International Food Standards', 626–9; Pollack & Shaffer, *When Cooperation Fails*, 170–1.

[142] See Pollack & Shaffer, *When Cooperation Fails*, 166–8.

[143] Codex Doc CAC/GL 44, Principles for the Risk Analysis of Foods Derived from Modern Biotechnology, 2003, revised 2008; CAC/GL 45, Guideline for the Conduct of Food Safety Assessment of Foods Derived from Recombinant-DNA Plants, 2003, revised 2008; CAC/GL 46, Guideline for the Conduct of Food Safety Assessment of Foods Produced Using Recombinant-DNA Microorganisms, 2003, all available at: <http://www.codexalimentarius.net/web/standard_list.do?lang=en>. See also Ostrovsky, 'New CAC Standards', 818–21.

[144] *Report of the Evaluation of the CAC*, para 69, box 2.

[145] See Report of the US Delegate, 7th Session of the Codex ad hoc Intergovernmental Task Force on Foods Derived From Biotechnology, 24–8 September 2007, Chiba, Japan, at: <http://www.fsis.usda.gov/Regulations_&_Policies/Delegate_Report_7FBT/index.asp>.

[146] C Ansell & D Vogel, 'The Contested Governance of European Food Safety Regulation' in Ansell & Vogel, *What's the Beef?*, 3–32 at 10–12.

Yet there are limits: as we have seen, efforts at cooperation have led to unsatisfactory results, or have failed outright, on issues of a particularly high domestic salience.[147] And they have certainly been less successful in matters with entrenched positions of important societal actors than in those arising anew.[148]

V. CONCLUSION

Are these limits of cooperation the product of the pluralist governance structure that I have described above? Pollack and Shaffer suggest as much when they point to the difficulties that arise from the competition between, and forum-shopping for, the multiple regulatory sites at play.[149] Yet they are quick to acknowledge that this multiplicity itself is not so much the cause as the effect of 'underlying differences among states and social constituencies in a diverse, pluralist world'.[150] Could then a more tightly integrated, hierarchically organized, 'constitutionalist' structure have helped to overcome the difficulties of cooperation? In a formal sense yes: it might have assigned decision-making rights to particular institutions, thus potentially breaking the deadlock that has arisen in more informal, consensual settings, such as Codex. Yet there are reasons to doubt that such powers would eventually have made a significant difference. Just as in the context of the UN sanctions regime,[151] here too institutions with unilateral decision-making powers have been hesitant to exercise them. The WTO Panel in *Biotech* has refrained from any but the narrowest findings against the EU, and the EU Commission has been very cautious in pressing GMO issues on member states even when it had the formal basis to do so. In both cases, this hesitation is probably linked to concerns about legitimacy: those institutions would overstretch their normative resources and would thus undermine their position in the long term.[152]

---

[147]   See Pollack & Shaffer, *When Cooperation Fails*, 280–5; also (on the beef hormones dispute) S Princen, 'EC Compliance with WTO Law: The Interplay of Law and Politics', *European Journal of International Law* 15 (2004), 555–74 at 570.

[148]   Princen, 'EC Compliance', 572–3; A R Young & P Holmes, 'Protection or Protectionism? EU Food Safety and the WTO' in Ansell & Vogel, *What's the Beef?*, 281–305 at 298, 303.

[149]   Pollack & Shaffer, *When Cooperation Fails*, 175, 284–6.

[150]   ibid, 176.

[151]   See Chapter 5, III.2.

[152]   On the WTO, see text at n 117 above; on the need for a mediative policy style in the EU, see G Skogstad, 'Regulating Food Safety Risks in the European Union: A Comparative Perspective' in Ansell & Vogel, *What's the Beef?*, 213–36 at 219–20.

This brings us back to the societal factors that condition postnational governance—an issue central to the argument in Chapters 2 and 3 and one I will pursue further in the next chapter. The structure underlying the regulatory conflict over GMO products has been likened to a collaboration game of a battle of the sexes type—one in which cooperation would be pareto-improving, but where distributive costs are so high as to render agreement impossible.[153] Framing the problem in these terms, however, suggests solutions that are actually unavailable, for normally distributive costs could be overcome by side-payments if the eventual outcome remained pareto-optimal. This would probably be the case here: one could well imagine the US paying off the EU for some of the adjustment costs it would bear when switching to a more GMO-friendly regime. However, this has not happened, and it is also unlikely to happen—because significant constituencies within the EU regard the issue as one of culture and values: as an issue with an absolute baseline, not to be traded off against other gains. This points to the non-exchangeable character of the goods involved here, and it suggests that the costs of cooperation simply outweigh its benefits, making a stable equilibrium impossible to achieve.[154]

Moreover, as we have seen, because the issue has such political salience, it is also seen by many as one that is not amenable to technical, delegated decision-making, but as one that is properly subject to democratic determination—in the local or (at most) national realm. On GMOs, therefore, we face an entrenchment not only of a substantive, but also a jurisdictional position—a position on the relevant polity. Creating a more 'constitutionalist' legal and governance structure—one that assigns decision-making rights at a higher level and thus allows for effective coordination—may force actors to cooperate, but it would conflict with the views of important sections of the population and would probably create significant resistance, potentially threatening the institutional structure itself. In this situation, a pluralist order may be the most prudent option. Leaving issues of principle and hierarchies undecided may allow space for pragmatic solutions on issues that are less fraught and might provide a safety valve when one or the other site of governance overreaches.

Pluralism may thus have advantages over constitutionalist approaches as regards cooperation in circumstances of strong and principled disagreement, as we have encountered them in the GMO context. Facilitating cooperation, however, is not the sole yardstick by which we should measure a pluralist vision—other standards, such as democracy and the rule of law,

---

[153] Pollack & Shaffer, *When Cooperation Fails*, 117–30, 285.

[154] See also Drezner, *All Politics is Global*, 210.

have to come into the equation too. Perhaps most importantly, we also need to ask whether the cooperation that results from a pluralist structure is not only effective but also fair. Doubts may arise here from the relative absence of developing countries from the accounts in the case studies of this and the previous chapters—in both the UN sanctions and the GMO contexts, developing countries seemed to play only a limited role, and we need to inquire more carefully into whether this was due to the pluralist setting in which the controversies unfolded or could be attributed to other factors equally relevant in a constitutionalist order. The two chapters that follow will thus broaden our view again and consider such broader questions—of fairness, power, democracy, and the rule of law—in a cross-cutting fashion, alongside a deeper analysis of how pluralism affects the prospects of cooperation in postnational politics.

PART III

PLURALISM'S VIRTUES (AND VICES)

7

Cooperation and Power in a Pluralist World

The pluralist postnational order, as we have encountered it in the last three chapters, appears like a rugged, mountaineous terrain: highly uneven, difficult to get a grasp of, and certainly not formed according to neat and clear principles. It is a far cry from the hope for an order based on reason along constitutionalist lines—much of it seems due to 'accident and force' and not the 'reflection and choice' Alexander Hamilton saw in the (American) constitutional project.[1]

And yet, this pluralism has not caused as many problems as one might have feared. In most of the cases we looked at it led to irritations on particularly salient issues but did not hamper the smooth, day-to-day functioning of the regimes in question. Yet our choice of cases was not representative; it was merely meant to provide a start in the inquiry into the empirics of pluralism. And it was meant to produce insights on the questions that had been left hanging in the normative engagement in Chapter 3. In that chapter, I made a case for pluralism based on its ability to accommodate competing choices and loyalties for different collectives in the postnational space. But a number of concerns remained: regarding pluralism's stability, its vulnerability to capture by powerful actors, its democratic credentials, and its relationship with the rule of law.[2] It is to these issues that I return in this final part of the book. Concerns about democracy and the rule of law will be the subject of the next chapter, while the present one focuses on questions of stability and power.

I begin this latter inquiry by sketching the shape of the postnational pluralist order with a more systematic intention than in the pointillistic approaches of the case studies (Section I). Understanding the contexts in which pluralism becomes most visible and some of the driving forces behind it will then help us tackle the further questions about stable cooperation and power that are at the core of this chapter (in Sections II and III). The analysis of these

---

[1] A Hamilton, J Madison, & J Jay, *The Federalist Papers* (L Goldman, ed), Oxford: Oxford University Press, 2008, 11 (A Hamilton, *Federalist* no 1).

[2] See Chapter 3, III and IV.

issues seeks to connect insights from the case studies and related inquiries with broader literatures on governance in the postnational space. Given the limited empirical basis, this is more of a stocktaking than a definitive assessment of the vices and virtues of pluralism as a model of postnational order. It should help us gain a clearer understanding of the processes at work and develop hypotheses about the potential for (and limits of) cooperation such an order entails—hypotheses that might be used, confirmed, or refuted, in future studies of the phenonemon.

This endeavour does not operate in an ideal world. Structures of governance have to fit the society in which they operate, and the make-up of 'postnational society' makes demands on them that we do not typically find in domestic contexts; its radical diversity is only the most prominent among them.[3] When thinking about pluralism, we should thus be careful to evaluate it in comparison not to an idealized alternative, but to how other models of order would (or do) fare in a similar context. Throughout this book, I have focused on the constitutionalist alternative because it represents an antithetical yet equally coherent response to the demise of the classical, intergovernmental paradigm of law and politics beyond the state. Both—pluralism and constitutionalism—acknowledge that we have to theorize the global legal order as a whole, not just distinct parts of it; but they differ in whether or not the new order does (and should) rely on an overarching legal frame to structure it. Both competing models offer only broad frames which can be filled by very different institutional arrangements; they do not represent prescriptions for all facets of global regulation. But contrasting them can provide greater clarity about the implications of a fundamental structural choice that may then guide us in analysing, and constructing, the institutions of postnational governance in greater detail.

I. THE SHAPE OF POSTNATIONAL PLURALISM

Before engaging in a more detailed assessment, we should pause for a moment and consider the commonalities and differences of the various phenomena that have gone under the name of pluralism in the preceding chapters. All of them were broadly heterarchical in character, but the element of heterarchy expressed itself quite differently in the context of European human rights, UN sanctions, or global risk regulation.

The central thread running through these cases is the one highlighted in Chapter 3: a genuinely *legal* form of heterarchy in which various claims to supremacy compete. I have not been interested in the (merely) political competition for influence nor in forms of institutional pluralism within a shared legal frame of reference. Instead, I have drawn upon characterizations first

---

[3] See Chapter 2, III.2.

developed in legal anthropology and later applied to the European Union,[4] and I have tried to show how they can help us capture developments that reach well beyond the EU into broader regional and global settings typically conceived through the separate lenses of domestic and international law. The case studies are too few to allow for broad generalizations; but they indicate that pluralist structures are prevalent in a number of key areas of European and global governance. And they reveal a number of common traits that can help us understand the conditions and logic of pluralist orders.

Contexts

The instances of pluralism observed here were typically related to the rise in importance of particular international institutions—the European Court of Human Rights (ECtHR) in Chapter 4, the UN Security Council in Chapter 5, and the World Trade Organization (WTO) Dispute Settlement Body in Chapter 6. This reflects, on the one hand, the claim developed in the introductory chapter that the emergence of 'postnational law' is closely linked to particularly strong forms of trans- and international cooperation; it is here that the blurred line between domestic and international law becomes most acute and that new conceptualizations are needed.[5] On the other hand, strong institutions crystallize the supremacy claims that enter the heterarchical competition: outside institutional frameworks, such claims will often remain inarticulated; it is only through concrete and specific demands that a confrontation of claims become visible. Many articulations of pluralism—including those analysed here, but also, for example, in the EU—arise out of contexts of close integration; indeed, they typically reflect processes of resistance to the rise of regional or global institutions and their increasing impact.

If pluralism is most visible in tight institutional settings, it is not necessarily limited to them. This already follows from the way in which assertions of supremacy are usually framed: with the exception of the particular case of the EU, courts typically make claims not for particular contexts but for the relationship between domestic (or regional) and international law in general. The German Constitutional Court's response to the ECtHR is a case in point, as is the stance of the European Court of Justice (ECJ) on UN and WTO law (even if the latter is based on a variation of the general rule). International and domestic law have long coexisted with diverging visions of hierarchy—in the classical dualist order, national constitutions insisted on governing the relationship, while international law rejected arguments from

---

[4] See Chapter 3, I.

[5] See Chapter 1, II.

domestic law as justifications for non-compliance. As this coexistence in separate spheres comes under increasing pressure from growing interlinkages, the competing rules on the relationship are increasingly in tension with one another. This tension may not come to the surface as long as conflicts do not flare up in institutional settings; rival actors may instead frame divergence as interpretation of the respectively other (underspecified) layer of law. Contests about the meaning of human rights under the UN Covenants are a case in point.[6] In such instances, undecided hierarchies are not in the foreground—they provide the backdrop to processes of legal interpretation in the different sites.

The same holds true for the increasingly dense cooperation in government networks, which largely uses 'soft' instruments and thus escapes the field of 'hard' law.[7] Because of the prevailing informality, hierarchies are unarticulated here; cooperation relies on consensus and non-binding commitments that leave all actors formally free. This is typically interpreted as leaving national sovereignty unaffected; indeed, as bolstering it in certain respects.[8] Yet this is only true as long as network governance takes place in the shadow of *only* national supremacy claims; the situation is more ambivalent when a network is situated among *competing* claims. This is the case, for example, in the EU where government networks—typically in the form of the Open Method of Coordination (OMC)—have become a mainstay of 'new governance'.[9] They have emerged in issue areas such as employment, social policy, and education, in which member states were unwilling to transfer stronger formal powers to EU organs. That far, they do indeed protect national supremacy claims. But they have also been established to ward off attempts by EU bodies to extend their powers into these areas, which in the context of dynamic treaty interpretation by the European Commission and the ECJ may have been a real possibility. From this angle, the emergence of network governance appears as a bridge between different supremacy

---

[6] See, eg, H J Steiner, P Alston, & R Goodman, *International Human Rights in Context*, 3rd edn, Oxford: Oxford University Press, 2007, chs 12 and 13.

[7] Cf A-M Slaughter, *A New World Order*, Princeton, NJ: Princeton University Press, 2004; K Raustiala, 'The Architecture of International Cooperation: Transgovernmental Networks and the Future of International Law', *Virginia Journal of International Law* 43 (2002), 1–92.

[8] Slaughter, *A New World Order*, 269.

[9] See A Jordan & A Schout (eds), *The Coordination of the European Union*, Oxford: Oxford University Press, 2006; G de Búrca & J Scott (eds), *Law and New Governance in the EU and the US*, Oxford: Hart Publishing, 2006; C F Sabel & J Zeitlin (eds), *Experimentalist Governance in the European Union: Towards a New Architecture*, Oxford: Oxford University Press, 2010.

claims; one that allows for cooperation while leaving the issue of principle in the balance.[10] As in UN sanctions administration and global food safety regulation, the turn to networks may then be interpreted as yet another pragmatic tool to steer clear of contested supremacy claims in a pluralist order.

Time

Rival assertions of supremacy claims often follow a strong institutionalization beyond the state, but typically they result less from the *establishment* of such authority than from its *change*. National courts came to contest the ECtHR's authority when it had grown more influential and encompassing in scope; European courts challenged the UN Security Council at a point when it had morphed from occasional intervenor to detailed regulator in security affairs. And the challenge to WTO authority arose when WTO jurisprudence had filled the Agreement on the Application of Sanitary and Phytosanitary Measures (SPS Agreement) with a meaning not necessarily anticipated at the moment of its creation. Likewise, the articulation of national supremacy claims vis-à-vis the European Community was a response to its increasingly immediate impact on national law and policy, created through the doctrines of primacy and direct effect by the ECJ.[11]

At the same time, as we have seen, most of these instances of contestation were not the endpoint of a process, but moves in a continuum of regime change, designed to influence other actors rather than settle an issue once and for all. The result of such strategic moves has in most cases been some form of mutual accommodation of the different actors and layers in a regime. In a related context, that of essential medicines and trade related aspects of intellectual property rights (TRIPS), Larry Helfer has described the dynamic as one of 'regime shifting': as an 'iterative, longer-term strategy that seeks to create outcomes that have feedback effects in other venues'.[12]

This helps us understand the relevant trajectories, and it suggests that in order to grasp the processes in their entirety, we have to take into view creation and implementation not as separate but as intimately connected

---

[10] See also D M Trubek & L G Trubek, 'Hard and Soft Law in the Construction of Social Europe: The Role of the Open Method of Coordination', *European Law Journal* 11 (2005), 343–64 at 346–7.

[11] See A Stone Sweet, *The Judicial Construction of Europe*, Oxford: Oxford University Press, 2004, 81–91.

[12] L R Helfer, 'Regime Shifting in the International Intellectual Property System', *Perspectives on Politics* 7 (2009), 39–44 at 39.

elements in the development of a regime.[13] This is not new to international lawyers who have long understood the making of international law as a process involving customary elements as well as the 'subsequent practice' under international agreements. However, the debate about 'compliance'—long central to explorations at the intersection of international law and international relations scholarship—has often taken the existence of stable, predetermined rules as a given.[14] Likewise, much theorizing about the *creation* of international regimes has focused on how states arrive at formulating terms of agreement (which may then be subject to implementation and enforcement).[15] Both perspectives have paid less attention to the feedback effects from implementation to regime design—feedback effects that are likely to follow a different logic than the initial creation of a regime: new actors may be mobilized and previous participants may see their participation in a new light. The trajectory of the SPS Agreement is a good example: initially seen by the negotiating governments as a technical matter, largely to be left to experts, its growth in importance through shifts in the politial context as well as its interpretation by WTO bodies activated other constituencies within governments and mobilized domestic actors—industry, civil society—that previously had paid little attention.[16] This accords with broader accounts of a greater (domestic) politicization as a result of higher legalization and institutionalization.[17] The assertion of rival supremacy claims appears as a direct result of this change in the structure of actors.

[13] See also K Raustiala & D G Victor, 'The Regime Complex of Plant Genetic Resources', *International Organization* 58 (2004), 277–309 at 302–5; K J Alter & S Meunier, 'The Politics of International Regime Complexity', *Perspectives on Politics* 7 (2009), 13–24 at 15–16.

[14] See the discussion in B Kingsbury, 'The Concept of Compliance as a Function of Competing Conceptions of International Law', *Michigan Journal of International Law* 19 (1998), 345–72.

[15] See, eg, R O Keohane, *After Hegemony: Cooperation and Discord in the World Political Economy*, Princeton, NJ: Princeton University Press, 1984, chs 4–7; B Koremenos, C Lipson, & D Snidal (eds), *The Rational Design of International Institutions*, Cambridge, MA: MIT Press, 2004.

[16] See Chapter 6, I.

[17] J Goldstein & L L Martin, 'Legalization, Trade Liberalization and Domestic Politics: A Cautionary Note', *International Organization* 54 (2000), 603–32; M Zürn et al, 'Politische Ordnungsbildung wider Willen', *Zeitschrift für internationale Beziehungen* 14 (2007), 129–64 at 149–58.

Directions

The most typical direction of pluralist conflicts throughout the case studies has been what in Chapter 6 I have termed 'vertical'—a competition between lower level and higher level actors. Thus, we have encountered the interaction between national courts and the ECtHR; European courts and the UN Security Council; and again European courts and the WTO. Yet we have also detected pluralism in the 'horizontal' dimension—as between different actors operating on the same level, such as EU courts and the ECtHR and the Biosafety Protocol regime and WTO dispute settlement. This latter aspect evokes the perennial debate about the fragmentation of international law into multiple, potentially self-contained, regimes,[18] but it also links to the literature about regime complexes in international relations.[19]

Whether the contrast between the 'vertical' and 'horizontal' dimensions is ultimately useful may be doubted. In the first place, the image of levels with its association of super- and subordination does not sit well with the idea of a heterarchical order in which hierarchies are precisely *not* settled. More substantively, we may understand both vertical and horizontal conflicts as expressions of a competition among constituencies—as rival claims of different societal groups that might be nested in one another, overlap, or be altogether separate. Because of the strength of national loyalties, one of these collectives will often be the national one, and it will typically contest supremacy claims of broader constituencies. Yet such contests can just as well arise between differently assembled collectives in a global setting— such as those around the WTO (trade-minded, with a strong role for both the US and Europe) and the Biosafety Protocol (more environmentally minded, with a strong role for Europe and a number of developing countries, but a lesser one for the US). Or those of the more homogeneous, more closely integrated European Union vis-à-vis the wider, looser group of states party to the European Convention on Human Rights.

The dichotomy of 'vertical' and 'horizontal' may then have little explanatory force; we will have to look in greater detail at the shape of the competing collectives and the driving forces behind their claims. Some of these claims will be stable and deeply rooted, others will stem from collectives assembled ad hoc for a particular purpose or around a particular issue. The

---

[18] See, eg, M Koskenniemi & P Leino, 'Fragmentation of International Law? Postmodern Anxieties', *Leiden Journal of International Law* 15 (2002), 553–79; B Simma & D Pulkowski, 'Of Planets and the Universe: Self-contained Regimes in International Law', *European Journal of International Law* 17 (2006), 483–529.

[19] Raustiala & Victor, 'Regime Complex'; Alter & Meunier, 'Regime Complexity'.

dynamics between them will depend in large part on the material and ideational resources the different constituencies can muster, but not necessarily on the direction (vertical or horizontal) of their interplay.

Modes of Action

A better understanding of these dynamics requires us to develop some basic assumptions about the logic of action behind the processes we are observing. One influential attempt at doing so in the context of 'regime collisions' in global law is that of Andreas Fischer-Lescano and Gunther Teubner.[20] They draw on systems theory to argue that inter-regime conflicts flow from the diverging rationalities of social subsystems, and that the fragmentation of global law results from law's response to the divergence in its environment.[21] Whatever one's general sympathies for their theoretical premises, their application to postnational governance is likely to obscure rather than illuminate the processes at work. For as we have seen in the example of the dispute over genetically modified organisms (GMO) in Chapter 6, rival supremacy claims do not necessarily flow from differentiated systems already in place; the regimes they emerge from may instead be constructed and developed precisely with the aim of countering another regime—by actors who, rather than being caught in the overwhelming rationality of a social system, pursue their own interests through the institutional structures that best suit them. The attempt to establish the Biosafety Protocol (BSP) is a case in point, and the notion of a 'strategic inconsistency' created in this way captures much of this dynamic.[22]

Emphasizing the strategic element here is meant to highlight the agency of the actors involved, not to suggest that they are solely strategically oriented. They may well follow ideational motivations as well, and argumentative logics may complement bargaining modes of interaction.[23] The case studies suggest that varying logics are at work. On the one hand, the forum-shopping we have seen in the GMO case was rational: the selection of the regulatory venue by both the US and the EU followed a calculation

---

[20] A Fischer-Lescano & G Teubner, *Regime-Kollisionen: Zur Fragmentierung des globalen Rechts*, Frankfurt am Main: Suhrkamp Verlag, 2006.

[21] ibid, chs 3 and 4.

[22] Raustiala & Victor, 'Regime Complex', 301.

[23] On the different logics, see T Risse, '"Let's Argue!": Communicative Action in World Politics', *International Organization* 54 (2000), 1–39; H Müller, 'Arguing, Bargaining and All That: Communicative Action, Rationalist Theory and the Logic of Appropriateness in International Relations', *European Journal of International Relations* 10 (2004), 395–435.

of where they would find most support for their positions. Yet the desired outcome had an argumentative element: by mobilizing certain fora, the different actors hoped to create argumentative resources that would influence action in others. This was most obvious in the negotiations over the BSP—the resources invested here by the EU and the US were based to some extent on the hope to create (or limit) influence on the WTO and its dispute-settlement mechanism. This may have been an attempt to signal widespread resistance to a potentially adverse finding in the WTO. But as judicial actors are typically driven (at least in part) by non-strategic considerations,[24] we should understand those investments also as designed to alter the interpretative space the WTO Panel operated in.

The particular combination of strategic and argumentative elements suggested here is due to the *legal* environment in which the inter-regime contestation was embedded. This setting also conditioned argumentative action in another way: as law privileges generalizable argument, claims about hierarchies and the locus of decision-making addressed at actors in the legal system usually have to take an abstract form that makes them applicable to other situations as well. This can 'trap' actors in their arguments: in a future dispute, they will only be able to depart from their general position at some cost.[25] Anticipating such entrapment is likely to lengthen the shadow of the future in the development of policies and strategies; publically defended positions need to be advantageous not only for the dispute at hand but also for future cases and other issue areas. In this sense, the legal context provides linkages across issues and time.[26] These linkages are not necessarily very tight; even in a judicial setting, generalization is only necessary up to a point. As we have seen in the analysis of the ECtHR and also in the stance of UK courts on UN sanctions, courts have manifold tools to get around issues of principle and hierarchy.[27] And states may well choose to bear the costs for limiting general claims in their arguments; the EU's inconsistencies as to the appropriate level of decision-making on GMOs are a case in point.[28]

---

[24] See the discussion in Chapter 4, III.2

[25] See T Risse, 'Let's Argue', 23; F Schimmelfennig, 'The Community Trap: Liberal Norms, Rhetorical Action, and the Eastern Enlargement of the European Union', *International Organization* 55 (2001), 47–80.

[26] See also A Hurrell, 'Conclusion: International Law and the Changing Constitution of International Society' in M Byers (ed), *The Role of Law in International Politics*, Oxford: Oxford University Press, 2000, 327–47 at 332.

[27] See Chapters 4, I and II, and 5, II; also Chapter 8, III.

[28] See Chapter 6, III.

The legal environment thus pushes the logic of action towards 'arguing' rather than 'bargaining', perhaps even towards a logic of appropriateness for some actors.[29] What weight the different logics have will depend on the particular situation: the set of relevant actors, their background cultures, and shared (or divergent) commitments. And as we have seen, the pluralist interaction can help shift the dominant logic: in the case of Security Council sanctions, the initially interest-based dynamic of bargaining provoked a stronger discourse about appropriate norms that was strengthened by the appearance of domestic courts on the scene. However, a constitutionalist framework might bring about an even stronger shift: by legalizing cooperation more tightly, it might push actors further down the argumentative road, creating awareness that there is no opportunistic escape from a legal logic by reference to competing supremacy claims—it might depoliticize relations that many regard as too politicized.[30] We will need to inquire more deeply into how constitutionalism and pluralism facilitate (or hamper) stable and fair forms of cooperation before we can form a view on their respective virtues—and vices.

II. PLURALISM, COOPERATION, AND STABILITY

Any claim that pluralism might have the potential to foster stable cooperation faces an uphill battle: it has to cope with the widespread view that undecided supremacy claims tend to breed instability and chaos. Even Neil MacCormick, a key protagonist of postnational pluralism, expressed serious doubts in this respect. Pluralism, he noted, was not 'an easy way of looking at law, or of running a society':

> The problems about societal insecurity that lie at the heart of Hobbes's vision of the human condition, and that continue to animate Bentham and Austin, are real problems. The diffusionist [pluralist] picture is a happy one from many points of view, but its proponents must show that the Hobbesian problems can be handled even without strong central authorities, last-resort sovereigns for all purposes.[31]

---

[29] See also T Risse, 'Global Governance und kommunikatives Handeln' in P Niesen & B Herborth (eds), *Anarchie der kommunikativen Freiheit: Jürgen Habermas und die Theorie der internationalen Politik*, Frankfurt am Main: Suhrkamp Verlag, 2008, 57–83 at 69–73.

[30] See, eg, A Peters, 'Conclusions' in J Klabbers, A Peters, & G Ulfstein, *The Constitutionalization of International Law*, Oxford: Oxford University Press, 2009, 342–52 at 349.

[31] N MacCormick, *Questioning Sovereignty: Law, State, and Nation in the European Commonwealth*, Oxford: Oxford University Press, 1999, 78.

Concerns of this type led MacCormick later to opt for a softer form of pluralism, as I have sketched in Chapter 3.[32] Similar issues are raised by thinkers from very different backgrounds: Carl Schmitt thought that indecision on ultimate supremacy could only work in homogeneous societies;[33] H L A Hart held that a multiplicity of rules of recognition represented a 'substandard, abnormal case containing with it the threat that the legal system will dissolve'.[34] And most pertinently perhaps, Stanley Hoffmann famously maintained that '[b]etween the cooperation of existing nations and the breaking in of a new one there is no stable middle ground.... [H]alf-way attempts like supranational functionalism must either snowball or roll back.'[35]

Hoffmann's focus, the European Community, survives even forty years later, but many believe that its continued success depends on its ability to assimilate to a statal form; the drive towards a European constitution can be seen as a step in this direction. Yet Hoffmann's main concern was less about institutional structures than about their social grounding—and loyalties in Europe still lie mostly with nation-states and are unlikely to shift any time soon.[36] Short of a wholesale transformation of such loyalties—improbable in Europe, practically impossible on a global scale—the challenge lies in devising structures most apt for stable cooperation under the circumstances, with an awareness of the potential for challenge the fragmented structure of postnational society represents.

Two Dimensions

In order to compare different structures, it is useful to characterize more precisely how they relate to forms of cooperation typically explored in the literature. The key dimension on which pluralism and constitutionalism differ is the degree of *hierarchy*: while constitutionalism presupposes a fully determined framework that sets out relationships of super- and subordination, pluralism operates with relations of sub-orders that leave ultimate hierarchies open. In that sense, on a continuum between coordination and hierarchy, constitutionalism is further to the right, while pluralism lies

---

[32] See Chapter 3, I.

[33] C Schmitt, *Verfassungslehre*, 9th edn, Berlin: Duncker & Humblot, [1928] 2003, 375–9.

[34] H L A Hart, *The Concept of Law*, 2nd edn, Oxford: Oxford University Press, 1994, 123.

[35] S Hoffmann, 'Obstinate or Obsolete? The Fate of the Nation-State and the Case of Western Europe', *Daedalus* 95 (1966), 862–915 at 910.

[36] See Chapter 2, III.2.

somewhere in the middle, and other forms, such as government networks, are positioned further left.

Secondly, constitutionalism and pluralism vary in the dimension of *integration*: both assume that the clear separation between domestic and international law—characteristic of classical, dualist international law, and underlying the operation of government networks—has faded, but they differ in the extent to which they see the two layers as connected; pluralism's heterarchy introduces an element of distance here.

This initial take on differences in institutional structures can help us connect to existing debates about forms of cooperation. At least four debates offer links: one is that over the respective benefits and costs of network and hierarchical settings, often seen as the main poles in discussions of institutional design in postnational governance.[37] The second debate, that on hard and soft law in international politics, explores similar issues with a stronger emphasis on legal forms and driven by the broader exploration of legalization beyond the state.[38] The third related debate takes into view the role of the domestic/international interface in the construction of supranational authority. It is typically focused on the role of domestic courts in the stabilization of the European Union, but has also explored other institutional settings and more broadly the 'politicization' of international institutions in domestic politics.[39] A fourth debate starts from the exploration of federal orders and uses it to illuminate postnational contexts, primarily the European Union.[40]

---

[37] See, eg, M Kahler & D A Lake, 'Economic Integration and Global Governance: Why So Little Supranationalism?' in W Mattli & N Woods (eds), *The Politics of Global Regulation*, Princeton, NJ: Princeton University Press, 2009, 242–75; M Eilstrup-Sangiovanni, 'Varieties of Cooperation: Government Networks in International Security' in M Kahler (ed), *Networked Politics: Agency, Power, and Governance*, Ithaca, NY: Cornell University Press, 2009, 194–227.

[38] See, eg, K W Abbott & D Snidal, 'Hard and Soft Law in International Governance', *International Organization* 54 (2000), 421–56; K Raustiala, 'Form and Substance in International Agreements', *American Journal of International Law* 99 (2005), 581–614; A T Guzman, 'The Design of International Agreements', *European Journal of International Law* 16 (2005), 579–612.

[39] See, eg, A-M Burley & W Mattli, 'Europe Before the Court: A Political Theory of Legal Integration', *International Organization* 47 (1993), 41–76; K J Alter, *Establishing the Supremacy of European Law*, Oxford: Oxford University Press, 2001; L R Helfer & A-M Slaughter, 'Toward a Theory of Effective Supranational Adjudication', *Yale Law Journal* 107 (1997), 273–91; Zürn et al, 'Ordnungsbildung'.

[40] See, eg, D McKay, *Designing Europe: Comparative Lessons from the Federal Experience*, Oxford: Oxford University Press, 2001; R D Kelemen, *The Rules of Federalism: Institutions and Regulatory Politics in the EU and Beyond*, Cambridge,

Most pertinently for our question, the comparison of hierarchical and network modes in global governance—like that of hard and soft law—typically identifies a number of key factors. Harder, hierarchical forms are usually seen as preferred in order to

- solve collaboration problems through credible commitments, monitoring, and enforcement,
- deal with incomplete contracting through delegation, and
- stabilize a regime over time and thereby reduce future transaction costs.

On the other hand, softer, network forms are deemed beneficial in order to

- reduce contracting costs by making initial negotiations less consequential and therefore easier and speedier,
- deal with uncertainty about future changes in the environment and own preferences, and
- limit sovereignty costs.[41]

Softer tools are often useful to accommodate compromises, but in many circumstances they may not provide for stable cooperation. They are typically better suited to coordination rather than collaboration situations because of their weaker enforcement element, and they work best in relatively small, homogeneous groups that allow for the build-up of trust.[42] Even then, as studies of EU network governance have shown, they often require a 'shadow of hierarchy' to provide incentives for actors tempted by free-riding or cheating.[43] The 'shadow of anarchy', characteristic of the global sphere, operates as a substitute only if the costs of non-cooperation for all actors are sufficiently high.[44]

MA: Harvard University Press, 2004; M Filippov, P C Ordeshook, & O Shvetsova, *Designing Federalism: A Theory of Self-sustainable Federal Institutions*, Cambridge: Cambridge University Press, 2004.

[41] Cf Abbott & Snidal, 'Hard and Soft Law'; Eilstrup-Sangiovanni, 'Varieties'; see also Kahler & Lake, 'Economic Integration', for a different emphasis.

[42] Eilstrup-Sangiovanni, 'Varieties', 205–6.

[43] See A Héritier & D Lehmkuhl, 'Introduction: The Shadow of Hierarchy and New Modes of Governance', *Journal of Public Policy* 28 (2008), 1–17; T Börzel, 'Der "Schatten der Hierarchie"–ein Governance-Paradox?' in G F Schuppert & M Zürn (eds), *Governance in einer sich wandelnden Welt*, Politische Vierteljahresschrift: Sonderheft 41/2008, 118–31.

[44] M Zürn, 'Governance in einer sich wandelnden Welt—eine Zwischenbilanz' in Schuppert & Zürn, *Governance*, 553–80 at 566–7.

Constitutionalism and Pluralism: Costs and Benefits

In this picture, hard, hierarchical modes will often be preferable because they lengthen the shadow of the future and stabilize cooperation beyond the immediate cost–benefit calculation of the actors involved. Constitutionalist structures will typically be associated with these latter benefits: they set up institutions and assign powers in a way that abstracts from immediate situational pressures and interests. Yet this abstraction only works up to a point: like other institutions, constitutions can shift some incentives in favour of cooperation, especially through the creation of focal points and enforcement mechanisms. But beyond that, they have to be self-enforcing even in the domestic context: they have to rest on matching social structures and cannot stray too far from actors' preferences.[45]

Meanwhile, tightly legalized, constitutionalized regimes are difficult to set up and create particular problems of adaptation later on. In situations of uncertainty in global politics, states will often choose to create flexible institutions to cope with future shocks.[46] The case studies are all evidence of such shocks: they reflect processes of resistance to strong institutions and especially to *change*—change in institutions' powers and the direction of their policies. Yet flexibility is not easily constitutionalized. From the study of domestic constitutions, we know only too well about the dilemmas involved: the right balance between rigidity and adaptability is often elusive and typically requires an interplay of formal amendment procedures and informal, often judicially driven processes.[47] In the postnational setting, this problem is exacerbated in two ways. First, because of contestation about the sites of decision-making, constitutional authority is not located on any one

---

[45] See R Hardin, 'Why a Constitution?' in B Grofman & D Wittman (eds), The Federalist Papers *and the New Institutionalism*, New York: Agathon Press, 1989, 100–20; J Bedner, W N Eskridge Jr, & J A Ferejohn, 'A Political Theory of Federalism' in J A Ferejohn, J N Rakove, & J Riley (eds), *Constitutional Culture and Democratic Rule*, Cambridge: Cambridge University Press, 2001, 223–70; Filippov, Ordeshook, & Shvetsova, *Designing Federalism*.

[46] B Koremenos, C Lipson, & D Snidal, 'The Rational Design of International Institutions', *International Organization* 55 (2001), 761–99 at 793; B P Rosendorff & H V Milner, 'The Optimal Design of International Trade Institutions: Uncertainty and Escape', *International Organization* 55 (2001), 829–57 at 832–5.

[47] See, eg, D S Lutz, 'Toward a Theory of Constitutional Amendment', *American Political Science Review* 88 (1994), 355–70; S Levinson (ed), *Responding to Imperfection: The Theory and Practice of Constitutional Amendment*, Princeton, NJ: Princeton University Press, 1995; R Simeon, 'Constitutional Design and Change in Federal Systems: Issues and Questions', *Publius: The Journal of Federalism* 39 (2009), 241–61.

level; as a result, change cannot be reliably steered in a commonly accepted institutional process. Secondly, because of the fluidity of postnational politics, institutional change usually comes at a rapid pace; but because of the strength of disagreement on substantive issues, it tends to imply significant costs for some states.[48] At times—as perhaps in the GMO example[49]—it may even affect absolute baselines for certain actors.

This brings us back to the difficulties of constitutionalism in multicultural settings I have discussed in Chapter 2. When acceptance of a common level of constitution-making is lacking, processes of constitutional change will often provoke serious backlash—I mentioned the example of Canada's constitutional crisis in the 1980s and 1990s.[50] In the postnational context, with loyalties further fragmented, the situation is even more difficult. Because of the distribution of costs, attempts at change will often provoke significant resistance. If change is undertaken in spite of it, it will easily overstretch the authority of the respective decision-making site, thus undermining the stability of the overall order. Decision-making rules can prevent this through high thresholds for amendments, but these also prevent adaptation to changing environments, thereby undermining the effectiveness of the institutions concerned.[51] The EU's reform difficulties of the last decades are an example. Yet as we have seen above, the soft, networked alternative is not always helpful either. It does not come with the strict authority claims of a constitutional framework and may therefore accommodate change more easily, but it can also not provide the cooperative benefits often required to provide solutions to problems of regional or global scope.

In this quandary, pluralism's virtue (as well as its vices) derives from the fact that it represents a *hybrid* between hierarchical and network forms of order. It allows for regimes with an internally hierarchical structure, but denies them ultimate supremacy, and thus navigates between routine hierarchies and exceptional disruptions, to be solved eventually only through consensual forms. This interplay has been present in all the cases we have analysed: cooperation was the norm in the European human rights regime,

---

[48] On the distributional challenges that arise even in coordination games, see S D Krasner, 'Global Communications and National Power: Life on the Pareto Frontier', *World Politics* 43 (1991), 336–66.

[49] See the discussion in Chapter 6, V.

[50] See Chapter 2, III.3.

[51] See McKay, *Designing Europe*, 150; on the federal context, B Galligan, 'Comparative Federalism' in R A W Rhodes, S A Binder, & B A Rockman, *The Oxford Handbook of Political Institutions*, Oxford: Oxford University Press, 2006, 261–80 at 269–70.

the implementation of UN sanctions as well as the regime complex around GMOs. Much of the cooperation in the latter two cases took the form of networks in which consensual decision-making was the standard mode; but these networks were embedded in a hierarchical context (of the UN Security Council and the WTO Dispute Settlement Body) that could (and did) step in to rectify failures. Yet these hierarchies themselves were not absolute: in some cases, as we have seen, resistance flared up and with it an insistence on rival supremacy norms. The conflict of principle was, of course, not solved in any of the examples; but in most of them, actors found ways to bracket it and work around it in a pragmatic, largely consensual fashion.

To some extent, pluralism thus provides a safety valve constitutionalism is lacking:[52] it creates an opening that can be used to signal a need for change as well as the point when the direction of the regime becomes unacceptable to some actors. At the same time, it allows for hierarchies and possibilities of close integration the absence of which typically places limits on network forms of coordination. Pluralism oscillates between hierarchy and network, but this also means that it shares not only in the benefits but also in the deficits of both. In particular, by opening hierarchies up, it relativizes the strength of a regime—in the worst case, rival supremacy claims can become excuses for non-compliance whenever a rule or decision goes against the interests of an actor. Here, pluralism risks creating a slippery slope.

In the case studies, this danger always lurked in the background. The refusal by national courts to follow the ECtHR in sensitive cases showed the Court's limits of authority; the ECJ's critique of UN sanctions could have led to non-compliance with the overall regime; and in the GMO example, the US certainly regarded the EU as non-compliant *tout court*, just as in other food safety-related cases. The typical pattern in those instances was, however, not that of simple disregard of a global regulatory regime for the sake of one's own interest (even if it was that too). Instead, as we have seen, resistance in both the sanctions and GMO cases followed a period in which critique of the regime had accumulated and found expression in institutional forms—resolutions by other UN bodies in the former case, the Biosafety Protocol in the latter. The pluralist opening in these cases was not exploited for individual states' pursuit of their interests alone; it was also part of a broader movement for change that could not succeed in rigid formal processes. This embeddedness may, however, be a mere coincidence that tells us little about the dangers inherent in pluralist orders. These dangers cannot be fully contained in

---

[52] See also L R Helfer, 'Regime Shifting: The TRIPs Agreement and New Dynamics of International Intellectual Property Lawmaking', *Yale Journal of International Law* 29 (2004), 1–83 at 56, on regime shifting as creating a safety valve.

institutional forms—pluralism is characterized precisely by the *absence* of a legal and institutional framework to regulate disputes between sub-orders. This is its strength, but also its weakness.

What other conditions then would need to be in place to limit the possibilities of abusing pluralism for the pursuit of opportunistic goals? From a rationalist perspective, the main deterrent for abuse would be the related costs.[53] Such costs can be material, as in the WTO with its sanctioning mechanism for non-compliance, or in a weaker form in general international law which holds states responsible for violations and requires them to provide reparation or compensation. They can also lie in reduced expectations of gains from reciprocity, if other states limit their investment in a given regime as a response; but this deterrent may be less effective in regimes not based on directly reciprocal relations, as is the case in human rights. Here, though, the interest in maintaining the regime's impact on others might provide a serious incentive.[54] Thirdly, costs can also be of a reputational character, depending on the importance a particular regime, or a general appearance as law-abiding, for a state's status. All these considerations flow from general theories of compliance with international law[55] and apply to constitutionalist and pluralist orders alike. Pluralism's openness, though, may require stronger incentives to ensure broad compliance.

The Domestic Angle

A key difference between constitutionalism and pluralism, when it comes to containing non-compliance, emerges if we focus on the domestic side of postnational regimes. Given that the idea of 'postnational law' is predicated on greater interlinkages between the different levels of politics and law, such a focus—a 'liberal' turn[56]—is called for in any case. But it is also central because studies of the creation and consolidation of supranational (and federal) authority typically find that key sources of stability lie in domestic politics and institutions.[57]

---

[53] See, eg, Rosendorff & Milner, 'Optimal Design', 845–50.

[54] See Chapter 4, III.1.

[55] See, eg, the overviews in H H Koh, 'Why Do Nations Obey International Law?', *Yale Law Journal* 106 (1997), 2599–659; Kingsbury, 'Concept of Compliance'.

[56] See A Moravcsik, 'Taking Preferences Seriously: A Liberal Theory of International Politics', *International Organization* 51 (1997), 513–53.

[57] See, eg, Filippov, Ordeshook, & Shvetsova, *Designing Federalism*, on the importance of domestic party structures for the stability of federal orders; B A Simmons, *Mobilizing for Human Rights: International Law in Domestic Politics*,

Constitutionalism and pluralism are distinguished, in large part, by the different extent to which they formally link the various spheres of law and politics. While pluralism regards them as separate in their foundations (despite tight links in practice), global constitutionalism, properly understood, is a monist conception that integrates those spheres into one.[58] As a result, rules about the relationship of national, regional, and global norms are immediately applicable in all spheres, and neither political nor judicial actors can justify non-compliance on legal grounds. In the EU, for example, this tight legal integration has helped mobilize domestic actors, especially courts, so as to bolster and stabilize the postnational regime significantly. Lower domestic courts were empowered by the direct effect of European law, stipulated by the ECJ, and enforced it in political and legal systems otherwise reluctant to respond.[59] Likewise, studies of human rights instruments in Europe and beyond suggest that their anchoring in domestic law, with the possibility of using domestic courts for enforcement, were important factors in achieving compliance.[60]

Pluralism does not automatically imply such a tight connection, and this might reduce its chances to ensure norm-compliance—and allow actors to abuse its openness for opportunistic reasons. Yet as the European example shows, pluralism also does not rule out the direct effect of regional or global norms in other orders. As we have seen in Chapter 5, the EU legal order has a pluralist character because of rival supremacy claims of the different levels, and still we can observe a tight integration and mobilization of domestic actors. Likewise, in the European human rights regime we have observed domestic courts using the European Convention of Human Rights and judgments of the ECtHR as a matter of course—despite their insistence that national constitutions remain the ultimate point of reference.[61] And the ECJ

Cambridge: Cambridge University Press, 2009, 371–3, on the effectiveness of human rights treaties.

[58] See also M Kumm, 'The Cosmopolitan Turn in Constitutionalism: On the Relationship between Constitutionalism in and beyond the State' in J L Dunoff & J P Trachtman (eds), *Ruling the World? Constitutionalism, International Law, and Global Governance*, Cambridge: Cambridge University Press, 2009, 258–324 at 279, fn 34.

[59] Weiler, 'Transformation', 2426; Burley & Mattli, 'Europe Before the Court', 62–4; Alter, *Establishing the Supremacy*.

[60] Simmons, *Mobilizing for Human Rights*, 355–63. See also H Keller & A Stone Sweet, 'Assessing the Impact of the ECHR on National Legal Systems' in H Keller & A Stone Sweet (eds), *A Europe of Rights: The Impact of the ECHR on National Legal Systems*, Oxford: Oxford University Press, 2008, 677–710 at 683–6.

[61] See Chapter 4, I and II.

may have distanced EU law from WTO law in principle, but this has not prevented it from making ample use of the latter.[62]

Even if it is a contingent, not a necessary component in pluralism, a tight integration of the different layers of law might help to keep resistance and non-compliance exceptional. On the other hand, the focus on the domestic side reveals particular benefits of pluralism's openness, its accommodation of (occasional) resistance. For it shifts our attention to the alterations in the domestic political process brought about by postnational governance. One of them is a shift towards the executive as the primary actor, partly due to the traditional executive preponderance in foreign affairs which has now gained a broader ambit; partly due to functional reasons that make it difficult to include other actors in what are typically already overloaded and cumbersome negotiation processes. Even in the relatively small and well-structured European Union, the participation of national parliaments in law-making at the Union level remains limited.[63]

The resulting 'executive multilateralism'[64] leads to a relegation of parliaments and courts in the law-making process—a relegation that is hardly remedied by requirements of ratification and implementation, which have long been of limited impact[65] and have become ever weaker as a result of delegated law-making at the global level, factual pressures to ratify, and more direct channels of implementation in which administrative and regulatory actors bypass parliaments.[66] But this relegation reduces the information of domestic actors and individuals at the law-making stage, and it limits the likelihood of signals about domestic interests and values that might be affected by new rules. What interests and values are affected, may in any event not be foreseeable at that stage; they might only crystallize later in the life of a regime when domestic actors are even further excluded from its processes.

---

[62] See Chapter 6, II.2 and IV.

[63] See P Kiiver, 'The Treaty of Lisbon, the National Parliaments and the Principle of Subsidiarity', *Maastricht Journal of European and Comparative Law* 15 (2008), 77–83.

[64] M Zürn, 'Global Governance and Legitimacy Problems', *Government & Opposition* 39 (2004), 260–87 at 264–5.

[65] See, eg, E Benvenisti, 'Exit and Voice in the Age of Globalization', *Michigan Law Review* 98 (1999), 167–213 at 184–9, 200–1.

[66] See Chapter 1, II; B Kingsbury, N Krisch, & R B Stewart, 'The Emergence of Global Administrative Law', *Law & Contemporary Problems* 68:3 (2005), 15–61 at 18–27.

The more postnational governance deals with matters of public interest, the more it comes to affect deeply held convictions and entrenched interests in domestic society. And as it acts increasingly through precise and concrete obligations—often enacted by bodies with delegated rule-making powers—it provokes stronger resistance once domestic actors become aware of the impact. International institutions become 'politicized' as a result.[67] In the context of the WTO, for example, increasing legalization has been seen to mobilize domestic interest groups in opposition to trade liberalization. This can lead to a destabilization of the regime if options to accommodate such opposition are foreclosed. As Judith Goldstein and Lisa Martin put it, '[l]egalization can increase social resistance to new cooperative agreements by reducing the number and types of instruments available to politicians to deal with a rise in antitrade sentiment'. They suggest that 'trade regimes need to incorporate some flexibility in their enforcement procedures; too little enforcement may encourage opportunism, but too much may backfire ...'.[68]

Pluralism may contribute to such flexibility by allowing for a limited escape from the regime. In the GMO case we have seen how such an escape was used to cope with strong and widespread opposition in Europe; and similarly in the sanctions example European institutions distanced their legal order from that of the UN when fundamental norms seemed to be transgressed. In this vein, pluralist structures also open up channels for signalling strong preferences of key domestic actors that otherwise would not find institutional expression.

If the domestic angle allows us to see a potential virtue in the flexibility of a pluralist order, it also suggests certain conditions that could help contain the risk of abuse of pluralism's openness. The closer analysis of the processes of mutual accommodation in the European human rights regime had suggested that the particular position of the institutions involved had a major role to play. Mutual dependence and mutual empowerment seemed key to understanding why the ECJ and the ECtHR sought to reinforce rather than weaken each other; and also why certain domestic courts—the Spanish Constitutional Court or the House of Lords in the UK—tied themselves so closely to ECtHR jurisprudence.[69] This ties in with the story of the mobilization of lower courts in the service of EU law, which gave them a new,

---

[67] Zürn et al, 'Ordnungsbildung', 149–58; W Mattli & N Woods, 'In Whose Benefit? Explaining Regulatory Change in Global Politics' in Mattli & Woods, *The Politics of Global Regulation*, 1–43 at 21–39.

[68] Goldstein & Martin, 'Legalization, Trade Liberalization, and Domestic Politics', at 631. For a similar appraisal, see Rosendorff & Milner, 'Optimal Design'.

[69] See Chapter 4, I.1, II.2, and III.2.

independent tool to review domestic institutions. On the other hand, as suggested in Chapter 5, the ECJ's strong stance against the Security Council may also be due to a dependence—a dependence not on a UN body, but on national constitutional courts which might otherwise have stepped in to defend due process rights.[70] Whether courts (and other institutions) will associate with their counterparts in other spheres of postnational governance, thus probably hinges on the extent to which they can thereby hope to raise their own authority and ward off challenges from others.

The Politics of Authority

This latter remark raises the question of how and when cooperation may be bolstered by the 'authority' of common institutions. The construction of such authority may not be necessary for institutional structures to emerge— indeed, these structures may often be based on mutual gains or coercion in the first place. But it helps them persist and be effective over time; they are more resistant to challenge when interest constellations change or coercive instruments become too costly.[71] The stability of federal orders, for example, has often been linked to loyalties that transcend the calculation of interests.[72] This is particularly so because authority facilitates processes of institutional evolution: actors will more easily accept adverse changes if an institution is based on a deeper sense of legitimacy.

This makes the creation of authority particularly relevant in our context. For as we have seen, many of the processes of resistance and accommodation we studied were triggered by prior elements of change, or at least by shifts in the information of actors about the impact and distributive consequences of the respective regimes. Moreover, some of this change accentuated the 'political' character of obligations under regimes that had previously been

---

[70] See Chapter 5, II.3.

[71] I Hurd, 'Legitimacy and Authority in International Politics', *International Organization* 53 (1999), 379–408 at 383–9. On the general importance of authority and legitimacy for broader patterns of change in world politics, see eg, J G March & J P Olsen, 'The Institutional Dynamics of International Political Orders', *International Organization* 52 (1998), 943–69; A Wendt, *Social Theory of International Politics*, Cambridge: Cambridge University Press, 1999; T J Biersteker & C Weber (eds), *State Sovereignty As Social Construct*, Cambridge: Cambridge University Press, 1996.

[72] See T M Franck, 'Why Federations Fail' in T M Franck (ed), *Why Federations Fail*, New York: New York University Press, 1968, 167–99 at 167–83; J Johnson, 'Inventing Constitutional Traditions: The Poverty of Fatalism' in Ferejohn, Rakove, & Riley, *Constitutional Culture*, 71–109. See also the emphasis on historical groundings in M Burgess, *Comparative Federalism*, London: Routledge, 2006, ch 11.

seen as largely technical in nature—this is quite obvious in the case of the WTO and its SPS Agreement, which had initially attracted little attention because of its supposedly technical character. But it may also be true for the sanctions example, in which the image of the effects of Security Council decisions in the domestic context shifted—especially for Western countries—from that of technical regulations of foreign trade to an appreciation that key values (of due process) were at stake. And in the European human rights context, national courts began to signal resistance at a point when the ECtHR had transformed the regime from one of limited checks on domestic politics on a fairly consensual basis to one resembling a constitutional framework dealing with issues of greater political salience. Such a shift from technical to political issues typically provokes fresh legitimacy demands. As Fritz Scharpf has argued with respect to the EU, common decision-making can then no longer be based solely on output considerations—the benefits accruing from the regime—but have to be grounded in a deeper sense of legitimacy.[73]

How then does the structural framework—constitutionalist or pluralist—affect the likelihood that such deeper legitimacy and authority may emerge and stabilize cooperation? A constitutionalist response would be straightforward: because rules about hierarchies and the relationships of different layers of governance flow from reasoned construction, they are more likely to generate acceptance than rules or processes flowing from political whim. This may be true, but it does not confront a main difficulty of postnational politics, namely disagreement over what a reasonable construction of such relationships might imply. For those with strong loyalties to national communities, regional or global decision-making may be anathema; for those who believe global problems need to be tackled globally, it will appear as a moral imperative.[74] In order to build a stable political order, such identifications cannot be ignored; they need to find reflection in the institutions themselves.[75]

Tackling this gap, bridging this disagreement, requires processes of social change that are largely independent from grand structural frameworks such as constitutionalism or pluralism.[76] We are only beginning to

[73] F Scharpf, *Governing in Europe: Effective and Democratic?*, Oxford: Oxford University Press, 1999, 21–8.

[74] See Chapter 3, II.3 and III.

[75] See McKay, *Designing Europe*, 145–6.

[76] On varied channels of norm diffusion, also apart from socialization-based ones, see B A Simmons, F Dobbin, & G Garrett (eds), *The Global Diffusion of Markets and Democracy*, Cambridge: Cambridge University Press, 2008.

understand socialization processes—persuasion and social influence—in the postnational realm, but it is often assumed that socialization is facilitated by deliberation in small settings, face-to-face interaction, the acculturation to norms in the surrounding culture or in attractive groups, and by processes of backpatting and opprobrium.[77] It is also linked to norm entrepreneurs that gather support and initiate norm cascades.[78] Larry Helfer and Anne-Marie Slaughter have shown how some of these tools—especially face-to-face interaction and the creation of familiarity—have been of use in the processes of authority creation for the ECJ and the ECtHR.[79] Such processes are possible in both constitutionalist and pluralist frameworks, yet pluralism seems to have an edge in one respect: the space it creates for incrementalism.

Incrementalism

Incrementalist approaches are useful for building and developing postnational institutions not only from a constructivist perspective. Moving step by step, rather than through inital grand designs or big leaps, may be helpful because it affects states' interests only to a limited extent at each turn. As a result, the costs of exit for states will often be higher than the new costs arising from a single step, and states will typically not be driven fully to reassess the costs and benefits of their participation in a regime. A similar dynamic may pertain at the level of domestic actors: those actors that stand to lose from a stronger role of regional and global governance structures are less likely to stage strong resistance if the new threat to their authority with each step is relatively small. And in a neofunctionalist vein, incrementalism reflects the gradual adjustment of interests and expectations in the process of integration.

This may go some way to explain, for example, why domestic supreme courts (and political actors) have not shown firmer, and earlier, reactions

---

[77] See A I Johnston, 'Treating International Institutions as Social Environments', *International Studies Quarterly* 45 (2001), 487–515; R Goodman & D Jinks, 'How to Influence States: Socialization and International Human Rights Law', *Duke Law Journal* 54 (2004), 621–703; also J T Checkel, 'Why Comply? Social Learning and European Identity Change', *International Organization* 55 (2001), 553–88 at 560–4.

[78] See M Finnemore & K Sikkink, 'International Norm Dynamics and Political Change', *International Organization* 52 (1998), 887–917; T Risse, S C Ropp, & K Sikkink, *The Power of Human Rights: International Norms and Domestic Change*, Cambridge: Cambridge University Press, 1999.

[79] Helfer & Slaughter, 'Effective Supranational Adjudication', 290–336.

to the gradual expansion of authority by the ECJ and the ECtHR.[80] Yet the full importance of incrementalism here, as more broadly in the construction of postnational governance, comes into view only through an appreciation of the role of ideas. First, a step-by-step approach can lead to change in the acceptance of regional or global institutions via a process of *entrapment*. For if actors fail to protest against new authority claims, they may later find themselves entrapped in this initial (if tacit) acceptance: in a context of path-dependence, a shift of the argumentation framework is difficult to undo at a later stage.[81] It is a typical strategy of courts to wrap fundamental shifts in their jurisprudence in decisions that favour those actors most affected by the shift. This softens the blow, makes strong reactions in the case at hand less likely, and makes later resistance more difficult.

A second, further-reaching advantage of incrementalism emerges when we return to processes of *socialization*. Theorists generally find that socialization is most successful when new norms resonate with existing ones or do not run up against entrenched normative convictions; unsurprisingly, actors change their minds more easily when their views on issues are not fully settled.[82] This suggests some scepticism about the potential for deep authority in postnational governance structures—its construction will typically have to confront well-established assumptions in favour of national institutions, as we have seen, for example, in domestic courts' attitudes towards the European human rights regime.[83] This may lead us to assume, in a rationalist vein, that interest- rather than authority-based forms of cooperation promise greater success in this realm.[84] But it also has implications for the conditions under which the construction of postnational authority is likely to succeed. It suggests that processes that can avoid head-on confrontations on entrenched issues hold greater promise for limiting large-scale resistance and thus for inducing change over time. The image of dialogues fits this

---

[80] On the ECJ, see Weiler, 'Transformation', 2447–8; Burley & Mattli, 'Europe Before the Court', 55–6, 67–9.

[81] See, eg, A Stone Sweet, 'Path Dependence, Precedent, and Judicial Power' in M Shapiro & A Stone Sweet, *On Law, Politics, and Judicialization*, Oxford: Oxford University Press, 2002, 112–35.

[82] Johnston, 'International Institutions as Social Environments', 496–9; Checkel, 'Why Comply?', 562–4; see also A Acharya, 'How Ideas Spread: Whose Norms Matter? Norm Localization and Institutional Change in Asian Regionalism', *International Organization* 58 (2004), 239–75.

[83] See Chapter 4, III.2 and 3.

[84] See, eg, J Kelley, 'International Actors on the Domestic Scene: Membership Conditionality and Socialization by International Institutions', *International Organization* 58 (2004), 425–57.

point.[85] Incrementalist approaches that bracket issues of principle and are able to respond to feedback and resistance run a lower risk of antagonizing key actors and may be able to shift understandings about sites of authority more effectively.

Accordingly, incrementalism is often seen as a key element in the construction of postnational authority,[86] and our case studies have confirmed this to some extent. The slow process by which the European human rights bodies came to assert their independence and expand their scope of action is probably the clearest example here: taking cues from domestic politics about potential limits, they reassured political and judicial actors that their authority was not under serious threat. And they moved to bolder assertions only once their status was more settled.[87]

In principle, incremental processes are possible in both constitutionalist and pluralist settings. But they face tighter limits in constitutionalism: an overarching framework that settles hierarchies may provide some *marge de manoeuvre* through vague norms, and it may allow for gradual reinterpretations of once-settled concepts. But the very point of the constitutionalist endeavour is to fix these relations legally: to remove them from the political process, to immunize them from constant readjustment. As mentioned above, constitutions vary in the extent to which they accommodate change; but for large-scale shifts, they typically require either formal amendments or something akin to Bruce Ackerman's 'constitutional moments'.[88] And it is very difficult for them simply to bracket issues of principle: the claim to institutionalize the forces of reason as against 'accident and force' can only be upheld if those issues are somehow settled through identifiable—reasonable—rules.

Pluralism allows for greater flexibility here. Bracketing hierarchies is its very characteristic: between the supremacy claims of competing regimes, it does not pretend to offer a resolution. In this way, as we have seen in the case studies, it allows for processes of mutual accommodation by which sub-orders react to each other's signals. Such processes are typically incremental: in the European human rights context as well as the UN sanctions regime

---

[85] For an emphasis on dialogue as a source of supranational judicial authority, see A Torres Pérez, *Conflicts of Rights in the European Union: A Theory of Supranational Adjudication*, Oxford: Oxford University Press, 2009, ch 5.

[86] eg, Helfer & Slaughter, 'Effective Supranational Adjudication', 314–17; Goodman & Jinks, 'How to Influence States', 701–2.

[87] See Chapter 4, II.3.

[88] B Ackerman, *We the People*, vol 1: *Foundations*, Cambridge, MA: Harvard University Press, 1991.

and the regime complex around GMOs, actors have taken in feedback from other sites and have adjusted their behaviour accordingly. They were not forced to confront the issues of principle—they could either maintain their own supremacy claims (as the German Constitutional Court did) or leave their views about hierarchies undefined (as the UK courts did with respect to UN sanctions). In this way, pluralism can protect itself from overreaching and can tie itself more closely to processes of social change. And it can establish an order of mutual tolerance[89] by avoiding the confrontation of deeply entrenched convictions of principle that we have seen hindering socialization processes.

We lack reliable data on whether this has in fact led to a change in beliefs about the proper sites of authority, or on whether it has indeed favoured such a change. What we can observe, though, is a significant degree of acceptance in a number of contexts: the ECtHR is broadly recognized as a decision-maker on human rights issues in Europe, as is the ECJ in matters of EU law. The authority of the Security Council and of WTO bodies is probably less stable, but in both cases, authority construction is still at a relatively early stage, and as we have seen, domestic actors have come to follow their decisions as a matter of some routine—even if they insist that such compliance is ultimately voluntary. A fair proportion of this acceptance may be reducible to the pursuit of interests by the respective actors, but some will have deeper roots—if only because it is based on an interest to tap into (or ward off challenges from) the authority of another, postnational institution. If such authority exists, it is probably due, in part, to the step-by-step, incrementalist approach a pluralist order facilitates.

III. PLURALISM AND THE PROBLEM OF POWER

Pluralism may contribute to the stability of postnational governance structures, but this alone does not make it an attractive model. In fact, much of the critique sees pluralism's main weakness not in its alleged instability, but in the unfairness of the outcomes to which it leads, in the fact that it seems open to manipulation and abuse by the powerful in a way constitutionalism is not.

The most vocal articulation of this critique stems from Eyal Benvenisti and George Downs who use political economy tools to understand the dynamics of a fragmented global legal order, and to compare it to a more integrated

---

[89] See J H H Weiler, 'In Defence of the Status Quo: Europe's Constitutional *Sonderweg*' in J H H Weiler & M Wind (eds), *European Constitutionalism Beyond the State*, Cambridge: Cambridge University Press, 2003, 7–23 at 15–23.

alternative.[90] They describe strategies of fragmentation that play into the hands of powerful states: a high differentiation of regimes which renders cross-issue coalitions and logrolling more difficult for weaker states; the choice of single-event settings that limit the coordination advantages weaker actors might have in repeat games; or the selection of alternative, often informal fora when resistance in the initial venue grows. Daniel Drezner makes a similar point, and both analyses tie in with broader accounts of the effects of forum-shopping, which typically benefits actors that have the resources to influence the choice through agenda-setting and enforcement powers, and the ability to bear greater transaction costs.[91] It also connects with comparisons of hierarchical and network settings as regards the impact of material power: informal, non-hierarchical frameworks are usually seen to be more vulnerable to capture by powerful actors.[92] Compared with more legalized, constitutionalist alternatives, pluralism thus seems hardly a goal worth striving for; quite the contrary.

A Mixed Empirical Picture

Surprisingly then, the picture that emerges from our case studies looks quite different. In the GMO case, the challenge to the WTO that resulted from the Biosafety Protocol was driven not only by the (powerful) European Union but in large part also by developing countries for whom SPS rules appeared as overly demanding and indifferent to precautionary considerations. In the sanctions case, the ECJ's test of the UN Security Council responded to a mobilization of norms that originated mainly from smaller European countries, such as Switzerland and Sweden, but also from a number of developing countries. The bigger countries in the campaign, Germany for example, were not necessarily the most influential in the area of international security. The European human rights case—like that of the EU—is more ambivalent; in both, the most articulated resistance to regional institutions came from courts in Germany, certainly one of the key actors in European politics.

---

[90] E Benvenisti & G W Downs, 'The Empire's New Clothes: Political Economy and the Fragmentation of International Law', *Stanford Law Review* 60 (2007), 595–631.

[91] See, eg, D W Drezner, 'The Power and Peril of International Regime Complexity', *Perspectives on Politics* 7 (2009), 65–70 at 66–7.

[92] See Kahler & Lake, 'Economic Integration', 259–60, 274; see also Eilstrup-Sangiovanni, 'Varieties', 226–7; N Krisch, 'International Law in Times of Hegemony: Unequal Power and the Shaping of the International Legal Order', *European Journal of International Law* 16 (2005), 369–408 at 392.

Though in both, as we have seen, courts from other countries also played a significant part.

This mixed empirical picture mirrors findings by Karen Alter and Sophie Meunier about the consequences of what they call 'regime complexity'—the 'presence of nested, partially overlapping, and parallel international regimes that are not hierarchically ordered'. These consequences 'do not point in a single direction. Sometimes complexity empowers powerful states actors, while at other times weaker actors gain from the overlap of institutions and rules.'[93] This ambiguity is borne out, for example, in Larry Helfer's study of the creation of intellectual property rules.[94] In the 1980s, powerful Western states managed to shift it from the World Intellectual Property Organization (WIPO) into the more favourable General Agreement on Tariffs and Trade (GATT) context, resulting in the TRIPS Agreement—a treaty very sympathetic to Western conceptions of intellectual property rights and through the WTO endowed with a strong enforcement machinery. After the adoption of TRIPS, though, developing countries and civil society groups made their own attempt at regime-shifting, this time into arenas such as human rights, public health, and biodiversity which, because of their institutionalization in the World Health Organization, the UN Food and Agriculture Organization (FAO), or the Convention on Biological Diversity, were more open to their concerns. This destabilized TRIPS, leading for example to the settlement on essential medicines, initiated by the Doha Declaration.[95] Yet it also led to countermoves by the US and the EU: these now sought to incorporate stricter intellectual property rules into bilateral and regional trade and investment agreements, soon labelled by critics as 'TRIPS plus' treaties.[96]

Forum-shopping and Institutionalized Power

Why is this picture so much more mixed than predicted by theorists? One reason may be that the analogy with forum-shopping only holds in part. While analyses of forum-shopping are typically concerned with a single favourable decision in an authoritative forum, choices among a multiplicity of governance sites are usually part of a broader web of decision-making

---

[93] Alter & Meunier, 'Regime Complexity', 13, 14.

[94] Helfer, 'Regime Shifting: The TRIPs Agreement and New Dynamics of International Intellectual Property Lawmaking', 'Regime Shifting in the Intellectual Property System'.

[95] See F M Abbott, 'The WTO Medicines Decision: World Pharmaceutical Trade and the Protection of Public Health', *American Journal of International Law* 99 (2005), 317–58.

[96] Helfer, 'Regime Shifting in the Intellectual Property System', 41.

instances which feed into a solution on the issue at hand as well as a longer term process defining broader rules.[97] In this context, the different fora operate in parallel and influence (reinforce, destabilize) each other. As a result, the power to shift venues is not exclusive: it may trigger countermoves, the initial choice is less consequential, and states will keep the longer term implications of engagement in different fora in mind.[98]

Another potential reason for the imprecision of the prediction emerges when we move from comparative statics to a more dynamic analysis. It is certainly true, as Benvenisti and Downs suggest, that powerful states will choose, or even create, the forum that suits them best at a given time, and that they will often have the means to make their choice prevail. But 'at a given time' is important here: what is relatively best for them at one point may differ from what was relatively best for them at an earlier stage—the range of options will have shifted, at times shrunk. This may be illustrated with John Ikenberry's influential characterization of institutions as 'locking in' victories, as allowing great powers to preserve choices made in conditions of a more favourable distribution of power.[99] At a later stage, the creation of a new forum (or choice of an existing one) might lead to a different result.

This new choice of forum will then reflect a changed power constellation, but we should be careful not to conceive of power constellations as uniform. Just as an earlier institutionalization may have resulted from the use of power *within* an existing regime, the creation of a rival venue will often flow from power within a different institution. The respective regimes can thus far be seen as 'intervening variables' in the power play of international politics, or even as more broadly constitutive of interests and power relations.[100] We have observed this in the GMO case: while the SPS Agreement emerged out of the GATT, with a particular membership and rules of interaction, the Biosafety Protocol grew out of the Convention on Biological Diversity—a setting in which power was distributed very differently. Here, developing countries had a greater say and environmental, not trade ministries took

---

[97] See also Helfer, 'Regime Shifting in the Intellectual Property System', 39.

[98] On the role of future expectations in the choice of international fora, see M L Busch, 'Overlapping Institutions, Forum Shopping, and Dispute Settlement in International Trade', *International Organization* 61 (2007), 735–61.

[99] G J Ikenberry, *After Victory: Institutions, Strategic Restraint, and the Rebuilding of Order after Major Wars*, Princeton, NJ: Princeton University Press, 2001.

[100] See S D Krasner, 'Structural Causes and Regime Consequences: Regimes as Intervening Variables' and 'Regimes and the Limits of Realism: Regimes as Autonomous Variables' in S D Krasner (ed), *International Regimes*, Ithaca, NY: Cornell University Press, 1983, 1–21, 355–68; March & Olsen, 'Institutional Dynamics'.

the lead. Likewise, in the creation of the UNESCO Convention on Cultural Diversity—yet another attempt to soften WTO rules—France and Canada made use of the much greater power they (and their cause) enjoyed within UNESCO than in the WTO.[101] However, as we can see from the intellectual property example, alternative fora can also favour the powerful: influential countries may turn to bilateral treaties, opt for informal settings, or pursue their interests by unilateral means when this option is available.[102]

When we think about power in the creation of alternative fora, we should thus think of it as differentiated over time and across institutions. The main determinant of whether the creation of a rival forum is likely to benefit powerful states is then the proximity of the existing forum to their current ideal point. Multilateral institutions will usually operate at a certain distance from that point; otherwise they could not maintain the autonomy necessary to fulfill the legitimation functions for which they are often sought.[103] Yet in many cases, such as the UN security regime, the international financial institutions, or the WTO, this distance is not great, the formal equality in them has little substance, and organizational as well as substantive rules project earlier (more favourable) power constellations into the future.[104] In these circumstances, and unless powerful states retain a credible outside option to counteract the shift,[105] the creation of alternative fora—or the assertion of rival supremacy claims—is likely to lead to resistance to power, rather

---

[101]   See, eg, J Pauwelyn, 'The UNESCO Convention on Cultural Diversity, and the WTO: Diversity in International Law-Making?', *ASIL Insight*, 15 November 2005, <http://www.asil.org/insights051115.cfm#_edn4>.

[102]   See Benvenisti & Downs, 'Empire's New Clothes', 614–19.

[103]   See K W Abbott & D Snidal, 'Why States Act through Formal International Organizations', *Journal of Conflict Resolution* 42 (1998), 3–32 at 18–19.

[104]   See, eg, N Woods, 'The United States and the International Financial Institutions: Power and Influence within the World Bank and the IMF' in R Foot, S N MacFarlane, & M Mastanduno (eds), *US Hegemony and International Organizations*, Oxford: Oxford University Press, 2003, 92–114; R H Steinberg, 'In the Shadow of Law or Power? Consensus-Based Bargaining and Outcomes in the GATT/WTO', *International Organization* 56 (2002), 339–74.

[105]   See Benvenisti & Downs, 'Empire's New Clothes', 614–19. On limits to the availability of outside options, see D W Drezner, *All Politics is Global: Explaining International Regulatory Regimes*, Princeton, NJ: Princeton University Press, 2007, 211–12. For an illuminating discussion of outside options in the case of the UN Security Council, see E Voeten, 'Outside Options and the Logic of Security Council Action', *American Political Science Review* 95 (2001), 845–58. For a discussion of alternative options of powerful states more broadly, see Krisch, 'International Law in Times of Hegemony'.

than in its reinforcement. The resulting picture is far more complex than the more unidirectional predictions of Benvenisti and Downs and Drezner. It shows that under certain, not unlikely conditions, fragmentation and pluralism may benefit rather than harm weaker actors.

Capture, Information, and the Demand for Change

We can theorize those conditions with greater specificity when we look at the microprocesses of institutional design, and especially when we draw upon insights about regulatory capture in domestic contexts. Walter Mattli and Ngaire Woods have used this body of scholarship to theorize the conditions under which global regulatory bodies are likely to follow the interests of powerful actors (states or economic actors) or respond to broader publics.[106]

For them, the key factor is the *demand* for accountability—unless there is strong demand, regulatory institutions will be set up and continue to operate in the interest of the powerful. This is largely because of the interest structure, asymmetrical information, and capacities for collective action. Strong corporate actors are usually affected by regulation more directly and are thus ready (and because of their organizational structure also able) to invest the resources necessary for information-gathering and interest representation. In contrast, broader publics will typically even lack the knowledge about regulatory regimes that would allow them to assess to what extent their interests are affected and to respond. In Mattli and Woods's account, this typically changes in situations of crisis: when the negative impact of regulatory policies becomes visible, civil society groups will begin to gather information and translate a demand for change more effectively.[107]

Much of this picture applies also to the role of strong and weak states in postnational governance; information and resources are distributed between them just as unevenly.[108] And it resonates with the account in our case studies: in all three of them, domestic publics and institutions as well as weaker states only came to realize the impact of global institutions over time. This was partly due to an expansion of the institutions' scope of action, as I have discussed above; but it was also due to a delay in the appreciation of the extent and shape of the institutions' powers. Thus, in the GMO case, the implications of the SPS Agreement were initially not

---

[106] Mattli & Woods, 'In Whose Benefit?'.

[107] Mattli & Woods, 'In Whose Benefit?', 21–6.

[108] For an analysis of the Codex Alimentarius Commission along those lines, see B S Chimni, 'Co-option and Resistance: Two Faces of Global Administrative Law', *NYU Journal of International Law and Politics* 37 (2005), 799–827.

fully understood because it was seen as too technical to warrant a greater investment of resources. It only attracted broader attention once it came to impact on key domestic policy choices.[109] Likewise, the UN Security Council had already begun targeting individuals in the mid-1990s,[110] but the human rights sensitivity of the issue did not come to the foreground until the early 2000s when problematic individual cases were picked up by the media.[111] And the expansion of the ECtHR's powers did not become an issue for domestic supreme and constitutional courts until the European Court specifically stepped on their toes.[112] The creation and change of post-national governance structures went unobserved and unresisted as long as they operated below the surface; only once a crisis broke out did domestic institutions and governments muster the strength for greater exploration and challenge.

This analysis has important implications for understanding the creation of alternative regimes and the assertion of rival supremacy claims. For it shows how the constellation of *mobilized* power can differ between the creation or change of a regime and the point where rival claims emerge. And it makes it likely that at this later point, if it follows a crisis and greater awareness, previously excluded actors with less organizational capacity can have greater influence on institutional design.

Trajectories of Normative Change

If the power constellation can change through new *information*, it can also change through the emergence of new *norms*. The case study of the sanctions regime was instructive on this point: change occurred here not only because of greater awareness of the expanded scope of Security Council action, but also because this awareness led to a reconsideration of the appropriate norms governing its action. Up until the 1990s, the Security Council had been seen as an intergovernmental body, subject to the organizational

---

[109] See Chapter 6, I.

[110] See, eg, SC Res 917 (1994), 6 May 1994, on Haiti; J A Frowein & N Krisch, 'Introduction to Chapter VII' in B Simma et al (eds), *The Charter of the United Nations: A Commentary*, 2nd edn, Oxford: Oxford University Press, 2002, 701–16 at 715–16.

[111] See, eg, P Cramér, 'Recent Swedish Experiences with Targeted UN Sanctions: The Erosion of Trust in the Security Council' in E de Wet & A Nollkaemper (eds), *Review of the Security Council by Member States*, Antwerp: Intersentia, 2003, 85–106.

[112] See Chapter 4, I and II.

and substantive norms of the UN Charter (at best).[113] The increasing impact it had on individuals came to challenge this frame, and from the late 1990s onwards, a discussion emerged on whether it was, or should be, bound by human rights norms.[114] It took a while for this discourse to take hold: it became mainstream only in the mid-2000s, when it entered the institutional practice of other UN bodies and was even recognized—in a limited way—by the Security Council itself.[115] It was at this point in the norm trajectory that the ECJ drew upon (European) human rights norms to challenge Security Council practices.

This process is illuminating for the power implications of a pluralist, relatively fragmented order. For if we think that norms matter in international politics, this normative shift towards human rights has altered what states and institutions could or could not do, and at what cost. A forum created (or chosen) at the end of this period is then more likely to reflect a human rights orientiation than at its beginning.

This does not imply, of course, that reflecting a changed normative understanding will always be normatively preferable, or that it will typically favour weaker actors. Norms can change in all kinds of directions. But in the construction of postnational governance, we can observe certain patterns that might indicate a dynamic of empowerment. Norm change in international affairs is not very well understood, but certain elements stand out from the existing studies on the topic. Key to any process of norm change, especially in its early stages, is the challenge of existing normative convictions, largely through reframing issues in a new light.[116] New norms do not emerge in a vacuum, they have to compete with previous understandings.[117] In order to be successful, they have to find support from actors such as 'norm entrepreneurs', but they also depend on further favourable conditions, such as resonance with broader meta-norms and triggering events that unsettle

---

[113] On growing problems with this paradigm, see M Koskenniemi, 'The Police in the Temple: Order, Justice and the UN: A Dialectical View', *European Journal of International Law* 6 (1995), 1–25.

[114] See, eg, W M Reisman & D L Stevick, 'The Applicability of International Law Standards to United Nations Economic Sanctions Programmes', *European Journal of International Law* 9 (1998), 86–141.

[115] See Chapter 5, I. On the state of the debate in the mid-2000s, see, eg, E de Wet, *The Chapter VII Powers of the United Nations Security Council*, Oxford: Hart Publishing, 2004.

[116] Finnemore & Sikkink, 'International Norm Dynamics', 897.

[117] See the emphasis in W Sandholtz, 'Dynamics of International Norm Change: Rules against Wartime Plunder', *European Journal of International Relations* 14 (2008), 101–31 at 103–7.

old structures. Such triggering events, sometimes also broader processes of environmental—technological or political—change, lead to disputes, then to rival arguments, and thereby shift the argumentative space step by step.[118]

In the construction of postnational governance, triggering events are usually brought about by particularly salient exercises of a regime's power; and challenges to such exercises can often have recourse to alternative (meta-) frameworks borrowed from the domestic context. Concepts such as the rule of law, democracy, or rights—traditionally not seen as applying to international institutions—then come to the fore and destabilize classical, intergovernmental understandings. Over time, new understandings emerge; when they find sufficient support, they might spread through 'norm cascades' or 'spirals' and then harden into more stable norms, of a legal as well as non-legal character.[119]

If this is a typical trajectory, it suggests that exercising power *through* institutions becomes more difficult over time as normative expectations adjust. This adjustment needs time: triggering events, norm entrepreneurs, and the destabilization of previous frames come about only once institutions have already gained and exercised their (new) powers—and brought about some kind of crisis or contestation.[120] In this sociological sense, Thomas Nagel may be right to think that only through strong, illegitimate institutions can new norms of justice on the global scale emerge.[121] This lag between institutionalization and normative response, however, should let us assume that an alternative forum created at a later point in time may often hold the promise to constrain the exercise of material power, rather than strengthen it.

Constitutionalism, Power, and Change

If these remarks suggest a potential for rival, pluralist assertions of supremacy to *contain* power, they counter the widespread claims to the contrary mentioned at the beginning of this section. They should, however, not give rise to excessive optimism: the conditions of postnational governance may come to empower weaker actors over time—because of greater information

---

[118] W Sandholtz & K Stiles, *International Norms and Cycles of Change*, Oxford: Oxford University Press, 2008, chs 1 and 12.

[119] See Finnemore & Sikkink, 'International Norm Dynamics'; Risse, Ropp, & Sikkink, *The Power of Human Rights*.

[120] See also Mattli & Woods, 'In Whose Benefit?', 36–9, on the production of new ideas through crises.

[121] T Nagel, 'The Problem of Global Justice', *Philosophy & Public Affairs* 33 (2005), 113–47.

and normative change. But they empower them always only to some extent, and there is no guarantee that a rival forum will strengthen their position—many other factors may work in the opposite direction.

If pluralism thus remains vulnerable to exploitation in certain circumstances, we may ask: would not a constitutionalist model create a stronger bulwark against abuse by the powerful? Such an assumption would be in line with the widespread view that power- and rule-based forms of politics are somewhat antithetical—that the creation of rules limits the impact of power because of a stronger role of publicity and argument; and that rules contain power in their application because they treat all actors alike. These beliefs are a key element of the rule-of-law ideal to which I will return in the next chapter. In this light, the tighter legalization in a constitutionalist framework promises to restrain power better than the more open, flexible structure of a pluralist order.

Yet already doubts arise from our consideration of constitutionalist practice in diverse societies in Chapter 2. Rather than being instruments of moderation and balance, constitutions often appeared as tools for powerful groups to protect their vision of society from challenge.[122] These visions may be economic, social, or institutional, and have often included the shape of the nation; from the angle of minority groups, they have thus often appeared as an imposition rather than a fair accommodation of different views.[123]

The situation is unlikely to be different in international politics. The more rules and institutions matter, the more powerful states will invest in their design and seek to shape them according to their preferences. Rules are then likely to stabilize, rather than challenge, their position—Ikenberry's analysis of international institutions as tools to lock in beneficial power constellations, already mentioned above, is a graphic illustration of this point.[124] Such stabilization is counteracted by the implications of formal rule-making—equal participation as well as publicity and uniformity of the resulting norms. Yet the effect of those is likely to be limited: formal equality has not been found to hamper power politics significantly;[125] formally uniform rules

---

[122] See Chapter 2, III.3.

[123] See only the critiques in J Tully, *Strange Multiplicity: Constitutionalism in an Age of Diversity*, Cambridge: Cambridge University Press, 1995; R Hirschl, *Towards Juristocracy: The Origins and Consequences of the New Constitutionalism*, Cambridge, MA: Harvard University Press, 2004.

[124] Ikenberry, *After Victory*; see also L Gruber, *Ruling the World: Power Politics and the Rise of Supranational Institutions*, Princeton, NJ: Princeton University Press, 2000.

[125] Steinberg, 'In the Shadow of Law or Power?'.

can still be skewed in substance or so indeterminate as to lose all bite;[126] and as we can see in the UN Security Council, the World Bank, and the IMF, public rule-making processes may well lead to explicit privileges for certain powerful actors. Even in the widely praised 'convention' that produced the draft European constitution, the dominance of bargaining and power politics were not challenged decisively.[127] Acting through law imposes some constraints on the powerful—constraints they may at times seek to evade, especially when they see themselves on the rise. But typically, these constraints are weak compared to the benefits that accrue from the stabilization and legitimation of power through law.[128]

A second caveat to constitutionalism's supposedly beneficial effects stems from the element of change. Change has been a persistent theme throughout this chapter: it has been found to explain the drive towards pluralism as well as many of its benefits. Pluralism seemed to facilitate cooperation particularly through its responsiveness to new circumstances, and also its potential in containing power has been seen to lie especially in its nexus with processes of informational and normative change.

Constitutionalism is typically more resistant to change. One reason is its very ambition: as mentioned above, if constitutionalism seeks to frame politics through law, it cannot follow political changes at every junction. Instead, it needs to contain change through substantive limits as well as procedural rules, but already on the domestic level, such amendment rules with their balance of rigidity and adaptability are difficult to design.[129] In the postnational context, this difficulty increases exponentially. The persisting strength of national loyalties typically requires a strong consensus orientation in the making and modification of fundamental rules.[130] And while a

---

[126] See M Koskenniemi, *From Apology to Utopia: The Structure of International Legal Argument*, 2nd edn, Cambridge: Cambridge University Press, 2006.

[127] See P Magnette & K Nicolaïdis, 'The European Convention: Bargaining in the Shadow of Rhetoric', *West European Politics* 27 (2004), 381–404; J E Fossum & A J Menéndez, 'The Constitution's Gift? A Deliberative Democratic Analysis of Constitution Making in the European Union', *European Law Journal* 11 (2005), 380–410. But see also T Risse & M Kleine, 'Assessing the Legitimacy of the EU's Treaty Revision Methods', *Journal of Common Market Studies* 45 (2007), 69–80, for a more benign interpretation of the convention's work.

[128] Cf Krisch, 'International Law in Times of Hegemony', 376–80; see also W Sandholtz & A Stone Sweet, 'Law, Politics, and International Governance' in C Reus-Smit (ed), *The Politics of International Law*, Cambridge: Cambridge University Press, 2004, 238–71.

[129] See text at n 47 above.

[130] See McKay, *Designing Europe*, 150.

consensus requirement makes initial decisions difficult, it often renders later changes impossible. Fritz Scharpf has described the problem in the context of federal states and the EU as the 'joint-decision trap'—once a consensual decision is made, states are later trapped in it as a wide range of veto players will usually prevent changes.[131]

Constitutional change in the postnational space is thus difficult to institutionalize: unless one risks friction through the alienation of key actors, amendment rules have to contain a great number of veto rights—thus setting the threshold so high as to make change practically impossible. This is a general problem in a context as fluid as the postnational one, which requires adaptation at a relatively rapid pace. But it is a particular problem for resistance to institutionalized power: if indeed the promise of such resistance lies in greater information and normative shifts triggered through institutional crises, constitutionalism with its bias towards the status quo is likely to have negative rather than positive effects. It may fare better if the status quo is on the side of the weak, as when an existing regime is closer to the ideal point of weaker actors, or when alternative fora would clearly benefit the powerful. But given that institutions and law on the postnational level tend to follow power more than resist it, constitutionalism's promise in that respect is rather slim.

IV. CONCLUSION

This chapter has sought to shed light on two of the main challenges for a pluralist postnational order: its supposed instability, and its vulnerability to power. Whatever other strengths people have associated with pluralism, on these two issues it has often been seen as weak. Yet with such weaknesses, it would hardly be of much appeal as a framework for postnational governance.

The picture that has emerged in this chapter is, however, much less gloomy. Certain weaknesses remain: pluralism's openness may allow for more opportunistic behaviour of states, and it may fail to stabilize beneficial regimes in the same way against later attacks as tight, constitutionalist structures. Yet pluralism, being a hybrid between hierarchical and network forms of order, has also been found to have important strengths. It allows for signals from (especially domestic) actors otherwise left out of decision-making structures and prevents backlashes against excessive legalization

---

[131] F Scharpf, 'Die Politikverflechtungsfalle: Europäische Integration und deutscher Föderalismus im Vergleich', *Politische Vierteljahresschrift* 26 (1985), 323–56; F Scharpf, 'The Joint-Decision Trap Revisited', *Journal of Common Market Studies* 44 (2006), 845–64.

unsupported by societal structures. It facilitates socialization processes that proceed incrementally and bracket issues of principle the resolution of which would trigger resistance. It assists the revision of regimes in response to crises that have left a broader public better informed (and mobilized) about them. And it helps tracing changes in social norms that may come about as a result of greater awareness about the operation and implications of postnational governance.

Many of pluralism's strengths are linked to the management of change—to the processes of mutual accommodation that become easier if actors are thrown back to consensual processes when they have overstretched their hierarchical tools. This does not imply that pluralism is always beneficial: with its lesser rigidity, it may also fail to tame adverse processes of change. To a significant extent then, our comparison of pluralist and constitutionalist models hinges on the direction and desirability of change in postnational politics. If we think change will mainly benefit the strong, we may prefer to freeze institutions—to immunize them against revision—through a constitutionalist framework. If we think change will, on balance, have beneficial effects for the weak, we may prefer a pluralist order that holds a greater potential for challenge.

As we have seen, a number of factors make institutional change not only inevitable in the fast-moving environment of postnational politics but also likely to assist regime stability and empower disadvantaged actors. This is in part because weaker players have fewer resources to gain information and participate in formal processes of regime design; they will often become aware of a regime's implications only at the implementation stage. Responding to their interests, and to the processes of normative change triggered by greater information, requires strong adaptative capacities in a regime. Such adaptation will also help a regime's stability: it lowers resistance and helps build authority and legitimacy step by step, thus potentially distancing the regime over time from the vagaries of mere interest calculation of the participants.

Naturally, most of the obstacles to stable and fair cooperation stem from features of postnational society on which institutional structures only have a limited effect. The character of the actors, the distribution of power among them, as well as the shape of their identities and interests condition the workings of both constitutionalist and pluralist orders, even if they may themselves change under the influence of a regime over time. Formal structures and institutions may facilitate such change, and perhaps this will eventually lead to a reconfigured postnational society in which a constitutionalist framework might flourish. Until then, pluralism's openness appears to have an edge in striking the balance between rigidity and flexibility that fair and stable cooperation requires.

8

Pluralist Challenges

In the previous chapter, I examined the charge that pluralism is bound to be unstable and likely to favour the powerful over the weak. As we have seen, this charge appears to be exaggerated: under certain conditions, pluralism has a greater potential than constitutionalism to stabilize cooperation in the postnational space. It provides a safety valve when processes of change adversely affect certain actors, and it avoids antagonizing potential resisters in the incremental creation of postnational authority. And it is also not as vulnerable to exploitation by the powerful as might appear at first sight: because it accommodates change and contestation more easily, it allows actors a voice who were excluded or sidelined in the formal processes of regime creation.

Yet pluralism faces still other—potentially no less weighty—challenges. In this chapter, I take up two of them, both connected to central strands of (Western) domestic political traditions: democracy and the rule of law. We have seen in Chapter 1 why domestic concepts are increasingly invoked as guides for the political and legal order beyond the state—the growing inter-linkages between (partly even integration of) different layers of law make it impossible to confine the realization of political ideals to just one of these layers. Yet translating concepts from the national to the postnational context raises serious problems. Most pressing among them is the reconciliation of diverse political traditions, kept apart in the 'Westphalian' structure but now competing with one another for dominance in the new, more integrated postnational sphere.

This difficulty lurks in the background of any consideration of democracy and the rule of law beyond the state. I cannot address it here satisfactorily, but I also do not aim to present a fully fledged theory of either democracy or the rule of law in the postnational space. I assume that there is a legitimate demand for their realization in this context and sketch some of the parameters for such an endeavour. Yet my goal in this chapter is merely to work out how we can think about *pluralism*'s relationship with these concepts—indeed whether they pose as serious a challenge to a pluralist vision as some contend. This is the subject of Sections I and II. In

Section III, I then examine one element of a pluralist order that is central to realizing rights, democracy, and the rule of law: the construction of interface norms at the points of contact between the different sub-orders. It is here that fundamental normative conflicts find their institutional, legal, sometimes judicial reflection.

I. DEMOCRATIC ACCOUNTABILITY IN A PLURALIST POSTNATIONAL ORDER

Democracy beyond the state is one of those quandaries about which libraries have been written, with a continuously reinforced sense that the task is urgent, but also with few tangible results.[1] Given this intractability, it might be tempting to bracket the issue,[2] but for our purposes, as we seek to assess pluralism's normative credentials, this is not an option.[3]

1. The Challenge of Translating Democracy

Democracy poses a challenge for any model designed to structure the postnational space: if a grounding in democracy is a key condition for the legitimate exercise of public power, and public power has now moved into the postnational sphere, it is plausible to hold that democracy needs to follow this move.[4]

How great a challenge this represents, however, is not entirely clear. Some authors point to the flaws of domestic democracy and the restricted range of issues decided beyond the state in order to argue that the 'democratic deficit'

---

[1] For useful surveys, see D Archibugi, 'Cosmopolitan Democracy and its Critics: A Review', *European Journal of International Relations* 10 (2004), 437–73; G de Búrca, 'Developing Democracy Beyond the State', *Columbia Journal of Transnational Law* 46 (2008), 101–58.

[2] See B Kingsbury, N Krisch, & R B Stewart, 'The Emergence of Global Administrative Law', *Law & Contemporary Problems* 68:3 (2005), 15–61 at 48–51; N Krisch, 'Global Administrative Law and the Constitutional Ambition' in M Loughlin & P Dobner (eds), *The Twilight of Constitutionalism?*, Oxford: Oxford University Press, 2010, 245–66 at 255–64.

[3] See also the critique in S Marks, 'Naming Global Administrative Law', *NYU Journal of International Law and Politics* 37 (2005), 995–1001 at 998–1001; de Búrca, 'Developing Democracy', at 104–7.

[4] See the classic statement in D Held, *Democracy and the Global Order*, Cambridge: Polity Press, 1995; see also, eg, D Archibugi, *The Global Commonwealth of Citizens: Toward Cosmopolitan Democracy*, Princeton, NJ: Princeton University Press, 2008.

in postnational governance is limited.[5] They are right in stressing the fact that domestic democratic processes face certain problems, especially as regards the inclusion of affected outsiders, which regional and global decision-making remedies rather than aggravates.[6] Problems with a democratic deficit may also be alleviated because of the type of problems regional and global governance are designed to solve. The more technical these problems and the closer the solutions are to pareto-optimality, the less intense may be the need to ground decision-making in democratic procedures.[7] Likewise, we may expect gains (in terms of justice or effectiveness) from global cooperation that we would have to forego if we insisted on a strong (national) democratic grounding.[8] But even if these considerations suggest that we may accept a lower level of democratic (input) legitimacy in global governance, they do not eliminate the need for such a grounding entirely. There will always be dispute over whether a solution is indeed pareto-optimal, and over how gains ought to be distributed even if all actors are (absolutely) better off. Visions of justice simply diverge too widely for us to be able to rely on output criteria alone to legitimate governance—after all, we need fair processes of decision-making over societal goals, and these will typically have to take democratic forms.[9]

This does not necessarily imply the same in the postnational as in the classical, national context. For example, we may find that in order to cope with political diversity democratic ideals should reduce their ambition and accept compromises with other visions of political order. In addition, because

---

[5] See, eg, A Moravcsik, 'Is there a "Democratic Deficit" in World Politics? A Framework for Analysis', *Government and Opposition* 39 (2004), 336–63.

[6] See R O Keohane, S Macedo, & A Moravcsik, 'Democracy-Enhancing Multilateralism', *International Organization* 63 (2009), 1–31; S Benhabib, 'Claiming Rights across Borders: International Human Rights and Democratic Sovereignty', *American Political Science Review* 103 (2009), 691–704. But see also the balanced account in A Buchanan & R Powell, 'Survey Article: Constitutional Democracy and the Rule of International Law: Are They Compatible?', *Journal of Political Philosophy* 16 (2008), 326–49. See also the discussion in Chapter 1, III.2 and Chapter 3, II.3.

[7] F Scharpf, 'Legitimationskonzepte jenseits des Nationalstaats', *MPIfG Working Paper* 04/6, available at: <http://www.mpifg.de/pu/workpap/wp04-6/wp04-6.html>, section 4.

[8] See Buchanan & Powell, 'Constitutional Democracy', 348–9.

[9] See also Krisch, 'Constitutional Ambition', 249–51. The argument about disagreement and democracy borrows from the discussion of national political structures in J Waldron, *Law and Disagreement*, Oxford: Oxford University Press, 1999, chs 10–13.

democratic processes within and beyond the state can be seen as complementary, the burden on each of them is lighter than if they had to shoulder all of it alone. This may help postnational democracy cope with serious societal constraints—after all, access to resources is so unequal, feelings of trust and solidarity so weak, and the potential for transboundary communication still so underdeveloped that a strong form of democracy beyond the state remains hardly conceivable.[10]

Even if we thus relax expectations to some exent—how to conceptualize democratic standards in the postnational sphere, and how to realize them institutionally, has so far remained elusive. This is in part due to the difficulty of using institutional models from the domestic level. The size, scale, and structure of the global polity resist the transfer of elections and parliaments, key elements of modern national democracies. For one, the size of electoral districts that would be needed for a minimally functioning parliament would remove the institutions so far from the people that we would probably end up with a democracy only in name.[11]

This latter difficulty has led theorists to explore alternative routes. Many of them are based on forms of deliberative democracy—deliberation seems easier to take beyond borders than elections.[12] However, the quality of deliberation is likely to suffer in a vast, highly diverse setting in which not even a language is shared.[13] And in order to ground decision-making, deliberation

---

[10] On these different preconditions for strong democracy, see, eg, B R Barber, *Strong Democracy: Participatory Politics for a New Age*, Berkeley, CA: University of California Press, 1984; D Miller, *On Nationality*, Oxford: Oxford University Press, 1995, 96–8; S Marks, *The Riddle of All Constitutions: International Law, Democracy, and a Critique of Ideology*, Oxford: Oxford University Press, 2000.

[11] See, eg, R A Dahl, 'Can International Organizations be Democratic? A Skeptic's View' in I Shapiro & C Hacker-Cordón (eds), *Democracy's Edges*, Cambridge: Cambridge University Press, 1999, 19–36. For more optimistic views, see, eg, R Falk & A Strauss, 'Toward Global Parliament', *Foreign Affairs* 80 (January–February 2001), 212–20; M Koenig-Archibugi, 'Is Global Democracy Possible?', *European Journal of International Relations*, forthcoming (available at: <http://personal.lse.ac.uk/KOENIGAR/Koenig-Archibugi_Is_Global_Democracy_Possible.pdf>).

[12] J S Dryzek, *Deliberative Global Politics: Discourse and Democracy in a Divided World*, Cambridge: Polity Press, 2006, 26–8; see also J Bohman, *Democracy across Borders*, Cambridge, MA: MIT Press, 2007; S Besson, 'Institutionalising Global Demoi-cracy' in L H Meyer (ed), *Legitimacy, Justice and Public International Law*, Cambridge: Cambridge University Press, 2009, 58–91 at 74–5.

[13] See J Habermas, 'Hat die Konstitutionalisierung des Völkerrechts noch eine Chance?' in J Habermas, *Der gespaltene Westen*, Frankfurt am Main: Suhrkamp Verlag, 2004, 113–93 at 137–42, and 'Kommunikative Rationalität und grenzüber-

needs a strong link to formal processes of law-making and regulation—after all, domestic theories of deliberative democracy typically place deliberation *alongside* elections as pillars of democratic governance and thereby ensure such a link.[14] Free-standing deliberation would probably be too weak to deliver the democratic promise;[15] but linking it institutionally to formal decision-making processes may face similar difficulties as the replication of electoral processes.

Another strand of democratic thought has sought to unbundle democratic practices, on the assumption that if the domestic model cannot be translated wholesale into the global context, some of its elements may still be realized there. This is thought to include the transparency and openness of postnational institutions, individual and public participation in regulatory procedures, or guarantees for the expertise and impartiality of decision-makers.[16] Such elements may be realized more easily than grander designs, but they do, of course, run the risk of selling democracy short. As a result, a number of theorists have turned towards more dynamic visions—visions that do not define a concrete endpoint but understand democracy as a process, a process of 'democratization' or 'democratic-striving'.[17] The basic idea is that adding more and more democratic elements is the most likely route towards a reasonably democratic structure. Yet here, too, serious problems arise. Most crucially, without defining an endpoint we may be unable to define what is 'more' democratic at any point in the process. For example, the idea of focusing on 'the fullest public participation

---

schreitende Politik' in P Niesen & B Herbort (eds), *Anarchie der kommunikativen Freiheit*, Frankfurt am Main: Suhrkamp Verlag, 2007, 406–59 at 435–8, for a discussion of the preconditions of democracy and deliberation at the global level.

[14] See J Bohman, 'The Coming of Age of Deliberative Democracy', *Journal of Political Philosophy* 6 (1998), 400–25 at 412–15; I M Young, *Inclusion and Democracy*, Oxford: Oxford University Press, 2000, 128–33; Habermas, 'Kommunikative Rationalität', 435.

[15] Bohman, *Democracy across Borders*, 42–5; A Peters, 'Dual Democracy' in J Klabbers, A Peters, & G Ulfstein, *The Constitutionalization of International Law*, Oxford: Oxford University Press, 2009, 263–341 at 270–1. But see also H Brunkhorst, *Solidarity: From Civic Friendship to a Global Legal Community* (J Flynn, trans), Cambridge, MA: MIT Press, 2005, 137–42; Dryzek, *Deliberative Global Politics*, ch 3, for different degrees of hope in non-institutionalized, 'weak' publics.

[16] For an overview (and critique) of this 'compensatory approach', see de Búrca, 'Developing Democracy', 121–8.

[17] Bohman, *Democracy across Borders*, 36; de Búrca, 'Developing Democracy', 130.

possible' at a given time[18] underrates the trade-offs involved: 'fullest' may not necessarily be 'fairest' unless we have a clear idea of how equality in participation can be ensured institutionally and what 'fair' procedures might look like in the end.

2. Three Parameters

As stated at the outset, I do not propose here to formulate an own way out of these difficulties. If I tried, I would have to build on the foundation in private and public autonomy outlined in Chapter 3. It is not clear that this could solve the conundrum—the preconditions for meaningful democracy on the postnational level may simply not exist, or only exist in some contexts and not in others.[19] Just as with the argument about constitutionalism in Chapter 2, it would then be preferable to name the deficit rather than water down our normative standards.

In contrast, my aim here is quite limited. I seek only to elucidate how the two structural visions of the postnational order at the centre of this book's inquiry—pluralism and constitutionalism—*compare* as regards democratic prospects. For this endeavour, I will try to define a number of parameters any successful approach to postnational democracy will have to work with, and indicate how constitutionalist and pluralist structures would relate to them. Three key parameters stand out: institutionally, the plurality of governance sites; socially, the multiplicity of *demoi*; and conceptually, the multi-dimensional character of democracy.

Institutions: The Plurality of Governance Sites

Postnational governance is made up of a multitude of institutions, regimes, and layers of governance, interwoven sometimes through formal frameworks but more often in informal ways. We have seen examples of this in Chapters 4 to 6. The institutional networks that emerge from this maze pose a serious challenge for democratic practices in two dimensions.[20] First, accountability structures typically rely on a clear identification of an institution or actor answerable for a given action. As responsibility is shared among various institutions, this identification becomes increasingly difficult, and the resulting 'problem of many hands' often prevents the imposition of

---

[18] de Búrca, 'Developing Democracy', 133–4.

[19] See, eg, the differentiated forms of legitimation envisaged in Habermas, 'Kommunikative Rationalität', 447–59.

[20] See also T Macdonald & K Macdonald, 'Non-Electoral Accountability in Global Politics: Strengthening Democratic Control within the Global Garment Industry', *European Journal of International Law* 17 (2006), 89–119 at 98–9.

negative consequences for undesired behaviour.[21] Secondly, a plurality of sites typically leads to a dispersal of public attention. Unable to concentrate on a single locus of decision-making, public participation becomes diluted and ever more virtual. This may be remedied by refocusing citizen input through central sites of accountability, perhaps of a quasi-parliamentary character.[22] But such centralization faces obstacles stemming not only from the practicalities of implementation, but also from the conditions that underlie the pluralization of governance sites. These reflect not simply the vagaries of institutional creation and path-dependence, but often follow radically divergent views on the right framework of decision-making. The institutional setting of the dispute over genetically modified organisms (GMO) analysed in Chapter 6 is a good example here. Streamlining decision-making and public participation, perhaps in a constititutionalist fashion, thus has to overcome high structural hurdles. Most probably, some of the plurality of decision-making institutions would have to be replicated in the structures designed to hold them accountable.

Society: The Multiplicity of Demoi

One of the key factors behind the pluralization of institutions is the multiplicity of collectives (*demoi*) claiming ultimate decision-making power in postnational governance. This theme has already been the focus of Chapter 3. My argument for pluralism in that chapter relied primarily on the autonomy of citizens to define the collective in which they are governed. As individuals' choices and allegiances diverge, competing (and equally legitimate) frameworks arise, but the relationship between them remains unsettled.[23] As we have seen in Chapter 2, a multiplicity of *demoi* is not only characteristic of regional or global settings; we observe it in multinational federations as well. However, traditional constitutional responses to such diversity are unattractive in postnational society. Federal approaches typically need to define some form of hierarchy among layers of governance and *demoi*, if only by distributing powers and defining rules for amending a common constitution, which is bound to create tensions with the socially unsettled character of these questions. Consociational approaches, on the other hand, usually become unworkable with large numbers of participants, and they

---

[21] M Bovens, *The Quest for Responsibility: Accountability and Citizenship in Complex Organisations*, Cambridge: Cambridge University Press, 1998, 45–52; see also Y Papadopoulos, 'Problems of Democratic Accountability in Network and Multilevel Governance', *European Law Journal* 13 (2007), 469–86 at 473–6.

[22] Falk & Strauss, 'Toward Global Parliament'; Papadopoulos, 'Problems of Democratic Accountability', 485.

[23] See Chapter 3, III.

also operate with a relative insulation of decision-makers from participation in the respective collectives.[24]

Taking the multiplicity of *demoi* seriously in the postnational context requires us to explore alternative paths. It implies at a minimum the opening of a plurality of democratic channels by which the different collectives can make their voices heard.[25] Yet unless these are to remain 'weak publics' with merely informal influence, they require formalized opportunities for impact. We may build linkages with quasi-federal decision-making processes, as James Bohman proposes with a view to the European Union.[26] But beyond this particular—institutionally highly integrated—setting, this option is problematic. For other spaces, Bohman tellingly returns to the stipulation of a mere 'democratic minimum'. Relativizing borders in the name of justice and pointing to the potential of the international sphere in terms of democratic checks and balances, as he suggests, may be a step in the right direction, but it leaves most institutional questions open. However, recreating quasi-federal structures in the global context—for example by concentrating supranational powers in one world organization, as Jürgen Habermas proposes[27]—sits uneasily with the factors driving institutional pluralization in the first place.

Concepts: Multidimensional Democracy

Recent theorizing has increasingly come to recognize pillars of democratic practice that operate alongside, or independently of, electoral mechanisms. One of these pillars is, as already mentioned, deliberation—the existence of a discursive basis of a democratic polity in which elections are not merely procedures for aggregating interests, but connect to processes of communication about the direction of the polity.[28] Another such pillar, which has gained theoretical prominence recently, is that of contestation. Philip Pettit and Pierre Rosanvallon have, from different starting points, emphasized the dependence of democratic orders on strong forms of contestation and

---

[24] See Chapter 2, III.3.

[25] See K Nicolaïdis, 'We, the Peoples of Europe …', *Foreign Affairs* 83:6 (2004), 97–110; Bohman, *Democracy across Borders*, 28–36; Besson, 'Global *Demoi*-cracy', 66–75.

[26] Bohman, *Democracy across Borders*, ch 4. A similar focus on the EU is apparent in Besson, 'Global *Demoi*-cracy'.

[27] Habermas, 'Kommunikative Rationalität', 449–55.

[28] See, eg, Bohman, 'Coming of Age'; Young, *Inclusion and Democracy*; J S Dryzek, *Deliberative Democracy and Beyond*, Oxford: Oxford University Press, 2000.

'counter-democracy'.[29] Such forms complement electoral processes, which are always deficient instruments of popular control—elections aggregate a large number of value judgements and operate at long intervals, and they can thus control actual, individual decisions only in a very indirect way. Popular influence then also has to rely on retrospective mechanisms of account-ability, of a formal or informal kind, through plebiscites as well as demon-strations, court action as well as non-governmental organization (NGO) activism, oversight instruments as well as the vigilance of citizens.[30] Such mechanisms alone will not suffice to make a polity democratic, but without them democracy remains a formality.

This emphasis on the multidimensional character of democracy should help us situate the democratic challenge in postnational governance better. It helps relativize the place of electoral mechanisms in democratic theory and shifts our focus to the elements of popular control possible without elections—or with the very limited input from elections at a national (some-times also regional) level. Elections will probably remain central to any conceptualization of democracy, but some of the weight they carry domes-tically might, in the postnational sphere, be borne by other, contestatory mechanisms.[31]

3. Democracy and Pluralist Contestation

These parameters point to directions for the further theorization of post-national democracy, including for its prospective, authorial, election side. Taking account of the plurality of sites and the multiplicity of *demoi* sug-gests an exploration of linkages between elected (or otherwise representa-tive) institutions at different levels. And the point about multidimensionality indicates a need to investigate contestatory mechanisms in the postnational space more broadly—something a number of scholars have already begun to do, though so far with excessive emphasis on judicial checks and little

---

[29] P Pettit, *Republicanism: A Theory of Freedom and Government*, Oxford: Oxford University Press, 1997, 183–205; P Pettit, 'Democracy, Electoral and Contestatory', *NOMOS* 42 (2002), 105–44; P Rosanvallon, *Counter-Democracy: Politics in an Age of Distrust* (A Goldhammer, trans), Cambridge: Cambridge University Press, 2008.

[30] Pettit, 'Democracy, Electoral and Contestatory'; Rosanvallon, *Counter-Democracy*, 12–18 and passim.

[31] P Pettit, 'Democracy, National and International', *The Monist* 89 (2006), 301–24 at 315–22 (though with an overestimation of the potential of contestatory mecha-nisms in the international sphere).

attention to the actual workings of the mechanisms under analysis.[32] Taken together, these parameters help us assess the democratic promise (and problems) of a pluralist vision of postnational order—even if, for lack of a full conception of postnational democracy, in a necessarily provisional form.

Accountability, Revisability, and Contestation

Some of this promise comes into view if we understand the interplay of different layers of law in a pluralist order as an accountability mechanism itself. In the GMO dispute, for example, the Biosafety Protocol and EU limitations on the direct effect of World Trade Organization (WTO) norms in EU law have accountability functions vis-à-vis the WTO: as we have seen in Chapter 6, they make the WTO dispute settlement system answerable to a broader range of actors (states, domestic actors) than represented in its formal organs. Likewise, the resistance of the European Court of Justice (ECJ) to UN Security Council decisions, the subject of Chapter 5, introduces a new channel for accountability in the global security regime. In both cases, these are not classical accountability mechanisms as we know them from domestic settings; they do not operate inside a given regime, as participation or review mechanisms, but outside, seeking to influence the regime through different, partly political means. Yet they fulfil functions very similar to those classical mechanisms, as they make regulatory processes respond to particular concerns and constituencies and provide checks against regulatory excesses.[33] They are 'non-institutionalized' accountability mechanisms,[34] and represent a further layer of contestatory devices in postnational politics.

Such channels of contestation are particularly called for in the postnational sphere. As we have seen above, in the picture of multidimensional democracy, contestation has to bear a heavy load due to the dearth of electoral mechanisms beyond the state—even if it cannot fully replace the latter.[35] Contestation is also central to ensuring the revisability of decisions. As we have seen in the previous chapter, administering change represents a particular difficulty in the postnational space because of the large number

---

[32] See, eg, A Kuper, *Democracy Beyond Borders: Justice and Representation in Global Institutions*, Oxford: Oxford University Press, 2004, ch 4. But see also the discussion in Macdonald & Macdonald, 'Non-Electoral Accountability', 105–17.

[33] See also N Krisch, 'The Pluralism of Global Administrative Law', *European Journal of International Law* 17 (2006), 247–78 at 249–63, for discussion.

[34] See R O Keohane, 'Global Governance and Democratic Accountability' in D Held & M Koenig-Archibugi (eds), *Taming Globalization: Frontiers of Governance*, Cambridge: Polity Press, 2003, 130–59 at 139–40.

[35] Pettit, 'Democracy, National and International', 314–16; see also Macdonald & Macdonald, 'Non-Electoral Accountability', 92–9.

of participants and veto players. The 'joint-decision trap' is a common problem here—once agreement has been found on a set of rules, amendments become exceptionally difficult.[36] This causes problems not only for the stability of a regime, but also (and perhaps greater ones) for its democratic credentials. Revisability is commonly seen as a key element of democratic orders, and its limitation (for example through constitutional norms with higher thresholds for amendment) is often seen as democratically suspect.[37] It may be justified to protect a higher law through which 'the people' has exercised its powers as a *pouvoir constituant* and also set rules to ensure the democratic quality of day-to-day decision-making.[38] Yet such a justification has a limited reach—it would hardly provide the basis for far-reaching substantive settlements on trade liberalization, anti-terrorism policies, or other domains of postnational governance. And it could hardly ground broad delegations of law-making authority to a host of institutions, political or judicial, as in the cases of the WTO, the UN Security Council, or the European Court of Human Rights (ECtHR).

As Rosanvallon notes, contestability is key to countering the lack of trust that follows from an increasing temporal distance of decisions from initial elections or appointments.[39] In postnational politics, this problem of trust is even greater, given the weakness of electoral, prospective channels of accountability, and the distance between governance structures and governed individuals. Ensuring the revisability of norms and decisions then becomes a key democratic demand, and pluralism's legal and institutional openness facilitates it.

Representing Multiple Demoi

If pluralism introduces a contestatory element, does it introduce the right one? Does it allow stronger input for the constituencies that deserve it? As is the case in discussions of accountability, all too often *more* contestation is automatically seen as *better*. Yet what matters is *who* is empowered by such mechanisms, *to whom* greater accountability is ensured.[40] In the examples we have studied in Chapters 4 to 6, pluralist contestation has given a greater

---

[36] See Chapter 7, III.

[37] For a recent argument, see R Bellamy, *Political Constitutionalism: A Republican Defence of the Constitutionality of Democracy*, Cambridge: Cambridge University Press, 2007.

[38] See, eg, B Ackerman, *We the People*, vol 1: *Foundations*, Cambridge, MA: Harvard University Press, 1991, and the discussion in Chapter 2, II.

[39] Rosanvallon, *Counter-Democracy*, 3–24.

[40] C Scott, 'Accountability in the Regulatory State', *Journal of Law and Society* 27 (2000), 38–60 at 41; R W Grant & R O Keohane, 'Accountability and Abuses of

voice to a number of constituencies that were less influential in formal procedures, as for example developing countries and NGOs in the WTO. By
creating an alternative regulatory site, the Biosafety Protocol provided an
external challenge to such exclusion, which may over time lead to changes
in WTO mechanisms and a reinterpretation of WTO norms.

In a pluralist regime complex, rather than in a single regime, a multiplicity of voices can find institutional homes.[41] This not only holds for a broader
range of states; it also applies to sub-state actors. As we have seen throughout
the case studies and in the more detailed analysis in the previous chapter,
many of the benefits of pluralist orders stem from the fact that they open up
space for input by domestic actors. By keeping the layers of law at a distance
from one another, it allows for a dominant voice of different collectives—different *demoi*—in those different contexts. In the GMO example, it provides
checks on an *international* constituency (in the WTO) by empowering (1) a
broader, *global* one through the Biosafety Protocol, (2) a narrower, *European*
one through the reservations on direct effect in EU law, and (3) a yet narrower, *national* one through the potential for resistance of the national level
in the pluralist setting of the EU itself. The channels by which these different
collectives are brought into play are partly political, partly judicial—with
the latter ones often serving to reinforce, or open up spaces for, the former.

Pluralism thus facilitates contestation by a number of different collectives
and therefore responds to one of the parameters discussed above—the multiplicity of *demoi* at the basis of postnational democracy. Still, it hardly seems
to provide guidance on *which* collectives are entitled to input—its openness,
beneficial for contestation, leads to an underdetermination, with the potential result that any group may make use of the openness if only it can muster
sufficient power.

In practice, as we have seen in the previous chapter, this risk has largely
been contained by the fact that rival supremacy claims were typically embedded in political movements with broad support in postnational society. But
pluralism is unable to guarantee this *institutionally*—it is based on the openness of the links of the different layers of governance. This openness is its virtue as well as its vice. But in a pluralist order too, we can formulate demands
on eligible polities, as I have sketched in Chapter 3. There I argued that col-
lectives/polities/*demoi* should find recognition and consideration by others

---

Power in World Politics', *American Political Science Review* 99 (2005), 29–43 at 42; see
also Krisch, 'Pluralism of Global Administrative Law', 249–51.

[41] For a similar argument, see M Koskenniemi & P Leino, 'Fragmentation of
International Law? Postmodern Anxieties', *Leiden Journal of International Law* 15
(2002), 553–79. On the notion of a 'regime complex', see Chapter 6, II.1.

only if they have a sufficient basis in the public autonomy of citizens—both in terms of links to citizens within the respective polity and of inclusiveness towards affected outsiders.[42] Such criteria may not be institutionalized or centrally enforced, but they can serve as guidance in the decisions each polity has to make on how to take account of the perspective of others.

4. Democracy: Pluralist or Constitutionalist?

If pluralism's weakness stems from its institutional openness, a more clearly defined, constitutionalist model might represent a better, more democratic option. It would provide a structured framework for, and assign decision-making rights to, the different collectives that deserve input. Just as in a federal polity, this might bring into balance the competing visions and ensure their common participation in a joint endeavour.[43]

As attractive as this might seem, it conceals a number of democratic difficulties raised by the institutional determination of the different polities. First, as we have seen in the discussion of the parameters above (and more extensively in Chapters 2 and 3), a constitutionalist setting needs to define hierarchies between the polities if it seeks to integrate them into a common whole. It needs to make choices of which governance layer has powers in one respect, which in another. And it has to set rules for the amendment of the overall constitution and assign the different polities their place in this regard. Such hierarchies, however, clash with the *parallel* groundings of rival supremacy claims in postnational society. If polities derive these claims from individual loyalties and choices, none of them can *a priori* claim supremacy over the others.

Secondly, the institutional determination of the respective places of the different polities would provide closure where responsiveness might be more appropriate. The determination of the relevant polities through individual allegiances is hardly fixed—in the current, fluid setting of postnational politics it is subject to constant fluctuation and revision. What polity is relevant in what respect is determined in an iterative process in which old understandings are continuously reinterpreted and may change radically

---

[42] Chapter 3, III.3.

[43] For such proposals see Held, *Democracy in the Global Order*, ch 10; Archibugi, 'Cosmopolitan Democracy', 452–3, and *Global Commonwealth*, ch 4; Habermas, 'Konstitutionalisierung des Völkerrechts', 133–42, and 'Kommunikative Rationalität', 443–6, 449–55. See also the proposal of a 'cosmo-federalism' in R Marchetti, *Global Democracy: For and Against*, Abingdon: Routledge, 2008, ch 7.

over time.[44] Fixing them through a distribution of powers in a quasi-federal style will hamper this process of change—and later produce friction when formal rules and factual allegiances diverge.

None of this allows for ultimate conclusions about pluralism's and constitutionalism's respective virtues when it comes to democratic governance. After all, the potential shape of postnational democracy is too unclear, and too many uncertainties are at play when it comes to the definition of input channels for citizens at all levels of governance. Yet as we have seen, pluralism's openness responds in important ways to the structural features of postnational society. It reflects the societally open relationships between the different *demoi* involved, it allows for their iterative redefinition over time, and it provides for channels of contestation that can help complement the weak forms of electoral input that will probably continue to characterize the postnational space.

II. PLURALISM VS THE RULE OF LAW?

If considerations from democracy cautiously support a pluralist vision, another key value of the Western liberal tradition may create more serious problems: the rule of law. Concerns about the rule of law are particularly weighty as the concept has—even more than that of democratic governance—found a strong anchor in the global context. Seen as more neutral and less associated with thick, particularistic conceptions of political order, it has found reflection in countless international documents, including the UN Millennium Declaration.[45] Brian Tamanaha may thus be right when he observes a 'unanimity in support of the rule of law [that] is a feat unprecedented in history'.[46]

The Rule of Law and Integrity in a Pluralist Order

The rule-of-law critique of pluralism is relatively straightforward. Julio Baquero Cruz, for example, notes:

> [In a pluralist order] the rule of law, legal certainty and the effective protection of individual rights may be endangered by the lack of clear relationships among judicial institutions. 'Heterarchical' and 'horizontal' are instinctively appealing notions, while 'hierarchy' and 'vertical' sound old-fashioned,

---

[44] On such iterative redefinitions, see S Benhabib, *The Rights of Others*, Cambridge: Cambridge University Press, 2004, ch 5.

[45] UN Doc A/RES/55/2, 18 September 2000.

[46] B Z Tamanaha, *On the Rule of Law—History, Politics, Theory*, Cambridge: Cambridge University Press, 2004, 3.

'anti-modern', almost reactionary, but any legal order may decay and collapse sooner or later without a minimum degree of predictability with regard to its application.[47]

I have discussed the issue of stability in the previous chapter; here I am more concerned with Baquero Cruz's comments about the protection of the individual and its relation with the rule of law. Pluralism seems to leave individuals in limbo: their rights and duties are not ultimately defined by law but remain open to political determination. This can indeed lead to significant uncertainty, as we have seen, for example, in the chapter on UN sanctions.[48] Individuals were faced with an unresolved parallelism of UN sanctions, their implementation in European and domestic law as well as potentially diverging rights guarantees of international, EU, and national constitutional provenance. Confronted with such contradictions, they had serious difficulties in assessing what law to take into account when adjusting their behaviour. The stabilization of expectations, the predictability that we expect from an order governed by the rule of law,[49] was thus seriously challenged. And this was not accidental: in a pluralist setting, predictability is *bound* to be challenged by the degree of indecision that characterizes the relationship of the different parts of the legal order.

This may be 'practically embarrassing' for defenders of strong pluralism, as Neil MacCormick noted when he turned away from his earlier 'radical pluralism' to the softer 'pluralism under international law'.[50] It also connects with other lines of critique. Pavlos Eleftheriadis, for example, has challenged pluralism on the basis of the ideal of 'integrity', a key element of the idea of law in Ronald Dworkin's theory.[51] This ideal requires 'government to speak with one voice, to act in a principled and coherent manner toward all its citizens, to extend to everyone the same substantive standards of justice

---

[47] J Baquero Cruz, 'The Legacy of the Maastricht-Urteil and the Pluralist Movement', *European Law Journal* 14 (2008), 389–422 at 414.

[48] Chapter 5, II.

[49] On the concept of the rule of law (and different conceptions of it), see J Raz, 'The Rule of Law and its Virtue' in J Raz, *The Authority of Law*, Oxford: Oxford University Press, 2nd edn, 2009, 210–29; J Waldron, 'The Concept and the Rule of Law', *Georgia Law Review* 43 (2008), 1–61.

[50] N MacCormick, 'Risking Constitutional Collision in Europe?', *Oxford Journal of Legal Studies* 18 (1998), 517–32 at 530; see also Chapter 3, I.

[51] P Eleftheriadis, 'Pluralism and Integrity' in M Avbelj & J Komárek (eds), *Constitutional Pluralism in the European Union and Beyond*, forthcoming, 2010.

or fairness it uses for some'.[52] And it implies that courts should 'identify legal rights and duties, so far as possible, on the assumption that they were all created by a single author—the community personified—expressing a coherent conception of justice and fairness'.[53] Indeed, a pluralist order does not place emphasis on integrity thus understood; it allows for disjunctions and contradictions and it abandons the hope of constructing one coherent legal order to which the individual is subject. As we have seen, in pluralism one might be subject to a multiplicity of legal orders, and even if courts try to reconcile them as best they can, such reconciliation has limits and will always be undertaken from the vantage point of one of the competing systemic perspectives. Pluralism and integrity are at odds, and Eleftheriadis concludes that pluralism cannot be justified. In his view, we should return to a dualist model—one in which the individual is directly subject only to domestic law and all other layers of law would be relegated to the outside.[54]

Fact and Fiction in the Rule of Law

The critique from the rule of law and integrity draws a stark line between unitary and pluralist orders, but this contrast may be overstated. To some extent all legal orders—constitutional, unitary ones, too—lack legal certainty. One does not have to share the views of critical legal scholars to appreciate the fact that even for the legal expert, let alone for the average citizen, the law necessarily appears indeterminate in many respects. In the face of unclear language or competing principles, we cannot know what the law is until a final court judgment tells us, and then it is too late to adjust the behaviour that has triggered the judgment in the first place. Legal certainty then seems to be just as elusive as it is in pluralism.

Yet such similarities could also turn out to be superficial. For even if the overarching norms in a unitary order are vague and the outcome of court proceedings difficult to predict, legal reasoning and judicial proceedings may be subject to constraints, and reflective of a particular rationality, that the openness of the pluralist order is not. Accordingly, most contemporary accounts conceive of the rule of law not as precise predictability but as rule on the basis of a particular form of argument or set of institutions that condition the open pursuit of self-interest or negotiating power.[55] Pluralism seems

---

[52] R Dworkin, *Law's Empire*, Cambridge, MA: Harvard University Press, 1986, 165.

[53] ibid, 225.

[54] Eleftheriadis, 'Pluralism and Integrity'.

[55] See, eg, J Habermas, *Between Facts and Norms*, Cambridge, MA: MIT Press, 1996, ch 5; Waldron, 'The Concept and the Rule of Law', 19–35.

to allow precisely for the opposite: in the determination of the relationship between different layers of law, legal method cedes the ground to whatever political means are available. Argumentative rationality is not *necessarily* absent here, as we have seen in the courts' dialogues in the European human rights context in Chapter 4. But it is contingent—a fortunate occurrence, not structurally secured through overarching norms and institutions that enforce them.

Yet this contrast, too, attaches too much importance to form and fiction and too little to fact. As much as we may hope that legal argument is distinct from political and strategic considerations and instills a particular rationality into decision-making, the empirical record in this respect is not overly strong. Studies of the US Supreme Court find an influence of legal factors (precedent, argument),[56] but in many contested cases decisions appear to be driven by attitudinal or strategic factors.[57] In an experiment in 2002, legal scholars were less successful in predicting the outcome of cases before the court than was a statistical model that relied on general case characteristics without information about the specific laws or facts of the cases.[58] Findings from other courts confirm the limited role of narrow legal factors in judicial decision-making on high-profile issues.[59] Which laws govern those issues may then be less important than who decides, in which procedures, and in which broader political constellation. In this case, however, the categorical difference between law-governed/unitary and open/pluralist orders collapses and gives way to gradual distinctions, conditioned by the particular institutions at play and the strength of the social (not necessarily legal)

[56] T M Keck, 'Party, Policy, or Duty: Why Does the Supreme Court Invalidate Federal Statutes?', *American Political Science Review* 101 (2007), 321–38; M A Bailey & F Maltzmann, 'Does Legal Doctrine Matter? Unpacking Law and Policy Preferences on the Supreme Court', *American Political Science Review* 102 (2008), 369–84.

[57] See J A Segal & H J Spaeth, *The Supreme Court and the Attitudinal Model*, New York: Cambridge University Press, 1992; L Epstein, J Knight, & A D Martin, 'Review Essay: The Supreme Court as a Strategic National Policy-Maker', *Emory Law Journal* 50 (2001), 583–611. See also the overview in J L Gibson, 'Judicial Institutions' in R A W Rhodes, S A Binder, & B A Rockman (eds), *The Oxford Handbook of Political Institutions*, Oxford: Oxford University Press, 2006, 515–34; and the discussion in Chapter 4, III.2.

[58] T W Ruger et al, 'The Supreme Court Forecasting Project: Legal and Political Science Approaches to Predicting Supreme Court Decisionmaking', *Columbia Law Review* 104 (2004), 1150–210.

[59] See, eg, G Vanberg, *The Politics of Constitutional Review in Germany*, Cambridge: Cambridge University Press, 2005.

norms actors can appeal to for justification.[60] As regards predictability and argumentative rationality then, pluralism does not necessarily fare worse than constitutionalism.

An Absolute Rule of Law?

The critique of pluralism is also misguided insofar as it takes the rule of law and integrity to be absolute values. Even Dworkin concedes that integrity, though important, is not an absolute condition for a political and legal order: '[i]ntegrity ... is a virtue beside justice and fairness and due process, but that does not mean that ... integrity is necessarily or always sovereign over the other virtues'.[61] He goes on to explain circumstances in which the pursuit of justice clashes with integrity—for example when it requires a break with previous policies and thus creates incoherence in the law as a whole—but in which justice should nevertheless prevail.[62] Contrary to what critics such as Eleftheriadis suggest, violations of integrity are not always inadmissible, although they do require a cogent justification on the basis of other political values.

This argument mirrors one more commonly found in discussions of the rule of law, and especially of claims to give it overriding importance. The most prominent of such claims has been advanced by Friedrich von Hayek, for whom legal certainty and predictability as protections of individual liberty trumped the pursuit of other social goals.[63] But this result is only plausible on a libertarian background. As Joseph Raz has argued, the rule of law is not itself an ultimate goal even if it serves to protect individual rights; it has a subservient role, 'designed to minimize the harm to freedom and dignity which the law may cause in the pursuit of its goals'.[64] In a political order not characterized by the absolute dominance of a conception of negative freedom, this has important implications:

> Since the rule of law is just one of the virtues the law should possess, it is to be expected that it possesses no more than prima facie force. It has always to be balanced against competing claims of other values.... A lesser degree of

[60] See T Risse, 'Global Governance und kommunikatives Handeln' in Niesen & Herborth, *Anarchie der kommunikativen Freiheit*, 57–83 at 69–73, on findings concerning the institutional preconditions for arguing in international politics.

[61] Dworkin, *Law's Empire*, 217.

[62] ibid, 217–24.

[63] F A Hayek, *The Constitution of Liberty*, London: Routledge, [1960] 2006, chs 14 and 15.

[64] Raz, 'Rule of Law', 228.

conformity is often to be preferred because it helps the realization of other goals.[65]

This diagnosis is linked to Raz's relatively restrictive, formal definition of what the rule of law implies. If one defines its scope more broadly, by including in it substantive values, one will describe such tensions as internal rather than external to the concept. But then its formal elements have an even weaker claim to absolute respect.[66] Jeremy Waldron, for instance, highlights the tensions between elements of the rule of law that stress the clarity and predictability of norms and those that place greater emphasis on non-arbitrary procedures for legal decision-making. The latter, argumentative as they are, may often undercut the determinacy and settled character of the rules in question. From the perspective of individual freedom, this unsettling effect can be desirable:

> To say that we should value aspects of governance that promote the clarity and determinacy of rules for the sake of individual freedom, but not the opportunities for argumentation that a free and selfpossessed individual is likely to demand, is to truncate what the Rule of Law rests upon: respect for the freedom and dignity of each person as an active center of intelligence.[67]

What matters, then, is whether individual freedom is best promoted by subjection to clear rules or by participation and deliberation over the content of the law. For Waldron, the balance may easily tip in favour of the latter, especially when issues of central societal importance are at stake. When it comes to constitutional matters, above all the interpretation of rights constraints on legislation, he believes deliberation—political, not legal deliberation—is preferable to judicial decision-making. A court, in his view, would cut off, rather than enhance, the possibility for individuals to participate in shaping their political order.[68]

This aligns directly with broader accounts of the tensions and trade-offs between democratic practices and the rule of law.[69] And it is sensible if the

---

[65] ibid.

[66] See, eg, G Palombella, 'The Rule of Law Beyond the State: Failures, Promises, and Theory', *International Journal of Constitutional Law* 7 (2009), 442–67.

[67] Waldron, 'The Concept and the Rule of Law', 60.

[68] J Waldron, *Law and Disagreement*, ch 11.

[69] See, eg, J Ferejohn & P Pasquino, 'Rule of Democracy and Rule of Law' in A Przeworski & J M Maravall (eds), *Democracy and the Rule of Law*, Cambridge: Cambridge University Press, 2003, 242–60. For a broader critique of rule-of-law ideals, see D Kennedy, *A Critique of Adjudication (fin de siècle)*, Cambridge, MA: Harvard University Press, 1999.

rule of law is regarded as one among many dimensions of realizing individual freedom, rather than as a good in itself. If different dimensions of individual freedom clash, we cannot simply point to one of them to resolve the contest.

Competing Values in the Postnational Order

In our context, too, the rule of law conflicts with values related to democratic decision-making. Legal certainty and predictability in the postnational order could better be achieved through an overarching normative framework that would assign the different sub-orders their place and provide resources for resolving conflicts among them. Yet as we have seen throughout this book, such a constitutionalist framework would not allow us to reflect the multiplicity of *demoi* legitimately competing for control. And it would weaken the element of contestation, through which a pluralist order promises to enhance the democratic character of the postnational order.

My main argument for pluralism—in Chapter 3 and again in the section on democracy in the present chapter—has been based on its potential to reflect the diverging views on the right polity that characterize postnational governance. Different collectives—local, national, regional, global, etc—compete for influence, and this competition reflects diverging choices and allegiances of the individuals entitled to define the polity in which they want to be governed. These choices and allegiances are exercises of individual autonomy and deserve respect, and their divergence also reflects different legitimate interpretations of how the balance between inclusiveness and self-determination in global governance ought to be struck.[70] Settling relations between the different collectives through law—in a way that would satisfy demands of legal certainty and predictability—would require adopting one of the competing views and would thus ignore those normatively relevant (and relevantly diverging) loyalties. In the GMO case, for example, fixing conflict rules between WTO law, the Biosafety Protocol, EU law, and national legal orders would have privileged one of these sites quite in contrast with the conflicting allegiances and choices we observed in postnational society.

This is merely a reflection of the fact that the rule of law, after all, is not only about law, impartiality, and predictability, but also about *rule*. Accepting the rule of law means accepting the rule of the authors of the law—if the law rules, somebody rules through it. Critics of an international rule of law emphasize this point by equating it with the rule of *international law* and probing its compatibility with (national) democratic processes.[71] Indeed,

---

[70] See Chapter 3, III.

[71] See, eg, Buchanan & Powell, 'Constitutional Democracy'.

constructing a *global* constitutionalist order would downplay the normative importance of national allegiances, as it would have to define areas in which ultimate control lies with a regional or global constituency. On the other hand, a return to a classical dualist order in which the rule of law is ensured because the individual is subject to one legal order alone—as Eleftheriadis suggests[72]—does not provide an escape route either. Such a national (or perhaps European) constitutionalism would also define *who rules*, only in a different way. It would accord primacy to the *national* collective—the relevance of regional or global norms would be subject to a decision in the state setting, thus easily excluding affected outsiders.[73]

Creating a coherent order in which legal relationships are settled along the lines of the rule-of-law model would thus imply taking sides in a social struggle with good arguments on all sides. This might, after all, create greater friction and instability than would the openness of a pluralist order, and it would fail to reflect the equally respectable claims to decision-making power of different collectives in postnational governance. Institutionalizing the tension between universality and particularity in a pluralist order may then be preferable.[74]

A departure from the ideal of a unitary, coherent legal order may also be warranted for the sake of contestation. This is again a democratic argument, as we have seen in the previous section: an argument based on the need to counterbalance the lack of authorial, electoral forms of democratic participation in postnational politics by establishing stronger editorial, contestatory forms in global politics.[75] This need will remain as long as we cannot imagine—and establish—better equivalents to elections in the postnational context, and it is difficult to satisfy in more tightly institutionalized structures which would approximate the rule of law more closely. Contestation, to be meaningful, has to be able to attack fundamental choices, not only minor decisions; at the same time, the range of those potentially entitled to contestation is virtually unlimited. How such contestation can be made institutionally effective but at the same time channelled in order to reduce risks to stability is not obvious. The less formal nature of pluralist contestation may erect a useful threshold but also allow for a

---

[72] Eleftheriadis, 'Pluralism and Integrity'.

[73] See also Chapter 1, III.2.

[74] See, in the UN sanctions context, D Halberstam & E Stein, 'The United Nations, the European Union, and the King of Sweden: Economic Sanctions and Individual Rights in a Plural World Order', *Common Market Law Review* 46 (2009), 13–72 at 61.

[75] See text at Section I.3 above.

safety valve if the threshold turns out to be too high in the fluid context of postnational governance.

Contestation is particuarly important in our context because many of the current structures of global governance entrench, rather than remedy, the inequalities of world politics, as we have seen in the previous chapter.[76] In these circumstances, contestation and change are more likely to further fairness and justice than efforts at stabilization through stronger legalization. Take as an example the debate surrounding the UN Security Council.[77] The global security architecture not only accords little importance to rights concerns, it is also institutionally underinclusive by relying on a largely unaccountable, partly even unelected body (the Security Council) to take decisions with a major, worldwide impact and binding force. This structure is almost impossible to change through ordinary procedures; amendments of the UN Charter require large majorities and the assent of those most privileged by the current system, the Security Council's permanent members.[78] The failure of the Security Council reform process, underway since the 1990s and without even modest success, is evidence of the difficulties involved.[79] Significant obstacles also lie in the way of procedural change in sanctions administration; too keen are the Council's permanent members to guard their autonomy in decision-making.[80] As the 1267 Committee's monitoring team noted, '[i]t is difficult to imagine that the Security Council could accept any review panel that appeared to erode its absolute authority to take action on matters affecting international peace and security'.[81] Change is thus likely to be brought about mainly outside formal channels, and it may be facilitated by the openness of a pluralist order. The ECJ's assertion of authority

---

[76] See Chapter 7, III.

[77] See also Chapter 5, I and III.3.

[78] UN Charter Arts 108, 109.

[79] See B Fassbender, 'All Illusions Shattered? Looking Back on a Decade of Failed Attempts to Reform the UN Security Council', *Max Planck Yearbook of United Nations Law* 7 (2003), 183–218. For a broader historical perspective on the difficulties, see D Bourantonis, *The History and Politics of UN Security Council Reform*, London: Routledge, 2005.

[80] See M Heupel, 'Multilateral Sanctions against Terror Suspects and the Violation of Due Process Standards', *International Affairs* 85 (2009), 307–21 at 313–14; P Gutherie, 'Security Council Sanctions and the Protection of Individual Rights', *NYU Annual Survey of American Law* 60 (2004), 491–541 at 530–5.

[81] Eighth report of the Monitoring Team, UN Doc S/2008/324, 14 May 2008, para 41.

has certainly left an impression—as the same monitoring team put it, the *Kadi* judgment 'has changed the terms of debate'.[82]

In an order that is largely immune to attempts at large-scale revision, the contestatory elements of a pluralist structure may thus help to further values that are otherwise neglected.[83] This is not to say that a constitutionalist order, based on a firm formal rule of law, could not achieve the same goal. But for this to happen, it would have to embody transformative values that are unlikely to find their way into a positive constitution in the circumstances of global politics at any time soon.

The Place of the Rule of Law

The rule-of-law critique of pluralism in the postnational order is thus ultimately unconvincing. It overstates the degree to which law typically achieves certainty and predictability, and it exaggerates the place of the rule of law and integrity relative to other political values. As we have seen, important values in postnational politics—the need to reflect multiple competing polities and to enable strong contestation—can serve to justify compromises with rule-of-law ideals.

This does not make the rule of law meaningless in the postnational order: it continues to represent an important political ideal, only one that does not find an *institutional* home in the macro-structure of the legal order. It does not lead to an integrated legal order that defines which law rules when, but exerts its influence in a more context-dependent way.[84] Alongside democracy and other political virtues, it continues to provide guidance for institutional design and decision-making in all parts of the political and legal system, and especially in the construction of the interface norms at the heart of the pluralist postnational order. Reducing arbitrariness and achieving certainty and predictability are important (though not all-important) ends here.

III. THE CONSTRUCTION OF INTERFACE NORMS

In a pluralist order, much depends on the norms (and institutions) at the interfaces of the different sub-orders. They regulate to what extent norms and decisions in one sub-order have effect in another; they are the main legal

---

[82] Ninth Report of the 1267 Committee's monitoring team, UN Doc S/2009/245, 13 May 2009, para 27.

[83] See also Palombella, 'Rule of Law', 461–4.

[84] See also Palombella, 'Rule of Law'; M Kumm, 'International Law in National Courts: The International Rule of Law and the Limits of the Internationalist Model', *Virginia Journal of International Law* 44 (2003), 19–32.

expression of openness and closure, friendliness or hostility among the different parts.

Constructing them, however, presents a particular challenge. Unlike in a constitutionalist order, there are no overarching rules that would—as in a federal system—define the relationships of the different layers. In a pluralist setting, the rules are set by each sub-order for itself, with a constant risk of conflict when different sub-orders produce diverging norms. Yet the sub-orders cannot evade this risk by returning to the classical framework with its monist and dualist approaches, which had provided for relatively clear and stable rules. In the classical situation, national and international law were far enough apart to allow for a clear separation in a dualist framework; the limited degree of their interaction did not necessitate further engagement. Likewise, international law was innocuous enough to allow states to opt for monist orders—because it was thin und largely underspecified, even a connection as tight as monism did not constrain national decision-making too much. On the other hand, international law's ambit was limited enough not to have to pay much regard to domestic law and its contents.

1. Structures

In the postnational setting, the different layers of law have come closer together: as we have seen in the introductory chapter, they are now closely linked, and this requires a more finely tuned legal and doctrinal instrumentarium than before. The interaction between courts has been central to these relations, but the doctrinal tools in which this interaction has been framed remain largely unsettled. In the European human rights context, central instruments were the margin-of-appreciation doctrine and the evolutive approach to interpretation, granting the ECtHR great flexibility in responding to outside influences from political or judicial bodies.[85] In the chapter on UN sanctions, I discussed the *Solange* doctrine and the UK courts' conciliation approach,[86] and in the study of the GMO dispute we saw how similar mechanisms operate in the horizontal relationship of WTO law with general international law—WTO panels have carved out a doctrinal basis that allows them to take the latter into account but does not tie them to it.[87]

Taking into Account

'Taking into account' could more broadly be described as the most typical tool of courts to manoeuvre their distance from the rules and policies of

[85] Chapter 4, II.3.

[86] Chapter 5, II.

[87] Chapter 6, II.1.

other orders; we also encountered it in the approach of national courts in the UK, Germany, and Spain as well as the ECJ to the jurisprudence of the ECtHR. Its beauty lies in its flexibility: 'taking into account' signals an opening, perhaps some kind of 'sympathetic consideration', as Neil Walker has termed this broad bag of relations between orders.[88] But in and of itself, it does not imply any such sympathy; it mainly confers discretion on courts to situate themselves towards other orders as they please. This will work best when courts act in a thick context of normative expectations that constrains their *marge de manoeuvre* and leads to relatively predictable results, as is the case in the example of the European Convention on Human Rights. And just as the margin-of-appreciation doctrine, it might also stabilize itself over time because of an accretion of jurisprudence which, if not specifying the terms of the relationship with great precision, at least provides indications of what to expect and thus allows other institutions to calibrate their posture.

Varieties of Conditional Recognition

The *Solange* doctrine is emblematic of a more substantive approach, 'conditional recognition', in which norms and decisions from another order have to meet certain substantive requirements before being granted respect. Setting such conditions still leaves sufficient discretion to protect the courts' flexibility, but it sends clearer signals about the framework in which cooperation can develop and mutual accommodation is possible. Unlike the 'taking into account' language, such conditionality can also provide guidance. It formulates the desired standards in such a way that the target context can take them into consideration for future shifts. And it spells out rules that can be applied by actors in one's own context—which may be useful for the legislature to control the executive and judiciary, and for high courts to keep a check on lower ones. The more intertwined different layers of law become, the more their application will be a matter for all institutions in a jurisdiction; forging a common, coordinated approach will then require the development of a rule-guided, rather than merely discretionary, framework.

Conditional recognition may thus well become paradigmatic for interactions in pluralist orders, but it does not itself define the content of the relationships. It can be filled by a whole spectrum of substantive positions, ranging from checks for extreme excesses to requirements of value identity. The former, more superficial check bears resemblance to doctrines of the conflict of laws, with their reliance on *ordre public* reservations to ensure extreme content of other orders does not enter one's own. The similarity has

[88] N Walker, 'Beyond Boundary Disputes and Basic Grids: Mapping the Global Disorder of Normative Orders', *International Journal of Constitutional Law* 6 (2008), 373–96 at 383–5.

led various commentators to draw analogies for the study of global law, and especially for pluralist orders.[89] Yet these analogies should be approached with caution. In the conflict-of-laws approach the guiding idea is to distribute jurisdictional powers among *a priori* unconnected orders with parallel claims to autonomy, whereas the pluralist setting is concerned with orders that have established firm linkages and accepted forms of common decision-making. This level of interconnectedness requires more careful calibrations, which should also find reflection in the terminology: the vocabulary of 'collision' norms seems less appropriate than other terms—such as 'interface norms'—to signal enmeshment and joint engagement in a common space.

If conditional recognition in this variant would merely test for excesses, it can also occupy the other end of the spectrum. In *Kadi*, the Advocate-General (and to a lesser extent, or at least less explicitly, also the ECJ) insisted on value identity as a basis for deference, on a 'shared understanding of values' and a 'mutual commitment to protect them'.[90] In his extrajudicial writings, the Advocate-General in this case, Miguel Poiares Maduro, has developed this position further and has posited 'systemic compatibility' and 'an identity as to the essential values' as a basis for systematic deference of one order to another.[91] In his view, these conditions are fulfilled within Europe where they are based on an underlying, common political community; here they sustain intensive exchange and deference as part of the 'internal' pluralism that bridges EU law and domestic constitutional orders. But none of this applies in the external dimension, which radically reduces the potential for interaction. More than 'taking into account' (or perhaps some weak form of

---

[89] See C Joerges, 'Conflict of Laws as Constitutional Form: Reflections on International Trade Law and the *Biotech* Panel Report', RECON Online Working Paper 2007/03, at: <http://www.reconproject.eu/projectweb/portalproject/RECONWorkingPapers.html>; also A Fischer-Lescano & G Teubner, *Regime-Kollisionen: Zur Fragmentierung des globalen Rechts*, Frankfurt am Main: Suhrkamp Verlag, 2006; P Schiff Berman, 'Global Legal Pluralism', *Southern California Law Review* 80 (2007), 1155–237 at 1228–34; K Knop, R Michaels, & A Riles, 'International Law in Domestic Courts: A Conflict of Laws Approach', *American Society of International Law Proceedings* 103 (2009), forthcoming, at <http://scholarship.law.duke.edu/faculty_scholarship/1998/>.

[90] See ECJ, Opinion of Advocate-General Poiares Maduro, 16 January 2008, C-402/05, *Kadi and Al-Barakaat*, para 44; and the discussion in Chapter 5, II.2.

[91] M Poiares Maduro, 'Courts and Pluralism: Essay on a Theory of Judicial Adjudication in the Context of Legal and Constitutional Pluralism' in J L Dunoff & J P Trachtman (eds), *Ruling the World? Constitutionalism, International Law, and Global Governance*, Cambridge: Cambridge University Press, 2009, 356–79 at 378–9.

persuasion when solutions are 'functionally equivalent' in a given case) is accordingly ruled out in this dimension.[92]

More towards the middle of the spectrum lies the 'equivalence' approach of the ECtHR, which is similar to the *Solange* approach of the *Bundesverfassungsgericht*, as I have pointed out in Chapter 5.[93] It acknowledges the need for a certain humility in the insistence on one's own values. In the words of the ECtHR,

> State action taken in compliance with [international] legal obligations is justified as long as the relevant [international] organisation is considered to protect fundamental rights, as regards both the substantive guarantees offered and the mechanisms controlling their observance, in a manner which can be considered at least equivalent to that for which the Convention provides ... By 'equivalent' the Court means 'comparable'; any requirement that the organisation's protection be 'identical' could run counter to the interest of international cooperation pursued ... However, any such finding of equivalence could not be final and would be susceptible to review in the light of any relevant change in fundamental rights protection....

> If such equivalent protection is considered to be provided by the organisation, the presumption will be that a State has not departed from the requirements of the Convention when it does no more than implement legal obligations flowing from its membership of the organisation. However, any such presumption can be rebutted if, in the circumstances of a particular case, it is considered that the protection of Convention rights was manifestly deficient. In such cases, the interest of international cooperation would be outweighed by the Convention's role as a 'constitutional instrument of European public order' in the field of human rights ...[94]

As we can see in this approach, the degree of deference to other orders—itself steered by the equivalence criterion—is reflected in the default rule courts apply. Once general equivalence has been ascertained, courts take a step back and only intervene in the case of manifest violations. This mechanism differs from the other two variants of the conditional recognition approach: in the one testing only for excessive content, checks would be limited to special and manifest problems from the beginning; there would be no first hurdle to overcome. In the more stringent, *Kadi*-style variant, courts would never take the step back and would apply full scrutiny to all external norm and decisions.

---

[92] Poiares Maduro, 'Courts and Pluralism', 371–9.

[93] Chapter 5, II.2 and III.

[94] ECtHR, Judgment of 30 June 2005, *Bosphorus Hava Yolları Turizm v Ireland*, paras 155–6.

Minimalism

The degree of scrutiny under a *Solange* approach is linked with, though not identical to, the degree of activism in a court. In *Kadi*, the ECJ went far in scrutinizing the procedure of the UN Security Council, but this intensity has not been on display in all, or even most, of the cases analysed in this book. The ECtHR has at times shown a robust approach towards the ECJ, as have some domestic courts vis-à-vis European courts. However, the overall picture is one of relative reluctance—a few warning shots coupled with a general hesitancy to step on each other's toes, and a readiness to grant space to political actors. Domestic courts have typically refrained from non-compliance with European or international norms and decisions; the ECtHR has been careful not to antagonize its political counterparts. Beyond Europe, the ECJ has in principle stepped aside as regards WTO law, leaving its implementation to the political organs of the EU.

The openness of the postnational constellation has produced significant new challenges for courts, as it has left central parts of the law—the relation between the different legal orders—unsettled. Courts could have used this situation to engage in far-reaching activism in filling the gap.[95] By and large, they have not done so; they have refrained from overly intrusive action or very broad, principled statements. Much of the court action we have witnessed in this book could indeed be described as 'minimalist' in the understanding put forward by Cass Sunstein: as narrow in the sense that courts restrict themselves to the circumstances of the particular case, and as shallow in the sense that they do not develop a deep theory of the law on the issue.[96] We have found examples of this in the WTO Panel's *Biotech* report, in the stance of UK courts on UN sanctions, and in the ECtHR's evolutive, but highly case-specific application of the margin of appreciation.

We should not generalize this result: not all the instances we have looked at are minimalist in this sense (think of *Kadi* or the *Bundesverfassungsgericht*'s stance towards the ECJ), and we have only studied a limited array of cases. Still, the finding contrasts with what Maduro, for example, suggests should be the preferred strategy for courts in a pluralist order. In his view, courts should rely on a 'reinforced' teleological approach to confront the challenge of a pluralist order. Such an approach would 'force courts to articulate the

---

[95] See also Poiares Maduro, 'Courts and Pluralism', 365–7.

[96] C Sunstein, *Legal Theory and Political Conflict*, Oxford: Oxford University Press, 1996; C Sunstein, *One Case at a Time: Judicial Minimalism on the Supreme Court*, Cambridge, MA: Harvard University Press, 2001; but see also the more nuanced stance on the uses of minimalism in C Sunstein, 'Beyond Judicial Minimalism', *Harvard University Public Law and Legal Theory Working Paper* no 08-40, <http://ssrn.com/abstract=1274200>.

normative preferences they attribute to particular rules and to relate them to the normative preferences of the overall legal order'.[97] By laying bare such fundamental choices it would, in Maduro's view, enhance judicial accountability and pave the way for a discursive engagement with other institutions. Mattias Kumm's proposal to construct postnational legal practice as part of a common 'constitutional cognitive frame' similarly reflects an aspiration to reach coherence as part of a broad teleology, as does Samantha Besson's insistence on integrity as a guiding value in the adjudicative practice within the EU and beyond.[98]

The problems with such proposals are closely linked to those of the teleological method in constitutional interpretation generally—a debate I do not intend to enter here. Yet it raises particular difficulties in the highly diverse setting of postnational pluralist adjudication in which, as Maduro rightly stresses, dialogues between judicial and political institutions from different backgrounds are key. Institutions with such different backgrounds will often be unable to reach a shared understanding of the 'normative preferences of the overall order' that could provide the basis for future convergence. Instead, agreement is more likely on a lower level of abstraction, as in the 'incompletely theorised agreements' Sunstein sees as the foundation of much of constitutional law and adjudication.[99] Under these circumstances, broad teleological reasoning is likely to emphasize difference, to increase conflict and take it to a more fundamental level. Minimalist reasoning, in contrast, may help shape a common path even if disagreement over fundamental issues remains.[100] And as we have seen in the case of the European human rights regime, an under-theorized, incremental approach can foster convergence of normative expectations over time.[101]

2. Courts' Multiple Identities

The approaches discussed so far have in common that they rely on a constitutive distinction between inside and outside—between one legal order and the rest. Law is always thought primarily from the perspective of one's

---

[97] Poiares Maduro, 'Courts and Pluralism', 368.

[98] M Kumm, 'The Cosmopolitan Turn in Constitutionalism: On the Relationship between Constitutionalism in and beyond the State' in Dunoff & Trachtman, *Ruling the World?*, 258–324 at 321–3; S Besson, 'From European Integration to European Integrity: Should European Law Speak with Just One Voice?', *European Law Journal* 10 (2004), 257–81; Besson, 'Global *Demoi*-cracy', 78.

[99] Sunstein, *Legal Reasoning*, ch 2; Sunstein, *One Case at a Time*, ch 1.

[100] Sunstein, 'Beyond Judicial Minimalism', 9–11.

[101] See Chapter 4, III.3.

own legal and constitutional framework, and courts often see themselves as guardians of that framework. The ECJ in *Kadi* was particularly vocal about that role. Yet the progressing interlinkages between orders undermine the clear inside/outside distinction, and this also begins to be reflected in judicial pronouncements.[102] In the EU, enmeshment has gone so far as to challenge the identity of domestic courts and push them towards a self-understanding as both national and European courts, as guardians of both bodies of law—courts with two hats, so to speak.[103] This has been triggered by the direct effect of EU law in member states' legal orders: a direct effect which, though regarded with sceptical eyes by the highest national courts, was often greeted by lower courts as it extended their options and gave them more power in the judicial hierarchy and vis-à-vis political actors.[104] Thus being mobilized in the service of EU law, and being pushed towards a uniform interpretation throughout the Union by the ECJ,[105] their character and self-understanding may have slowly shifted.

In contrast, analyses of domestic courts' decision-making on international law matters rarely reveal such a transcendence of the national frame of reference; in fact, the interpretation of international law by national courts often has a nationalizing tendency.[106] This may begin to change as courts engage in stronger transboundary communication and see themselves as united in a particular role faced with executive branches that cooperate with one another.[107] In the example of the UK courts discussed in Chapters 4 and 5, we can observe an attempt to take seriously their role as interpreters of international law as such. They could have opted for a 'domestic' reading of the rights under the Human Rights Act—one in which the interpretation of these rights was a largely internal matter. Instead, they came to see them as international in origin and thus assumed, to some extent, the perspective

---

[102] See also Chapter 1, II.

[103] Poiares Maduro, 'Courts and Pluralism', 375; see also N W Barber, 'Legal Pluralism and the European Union', *European Law Journal* 12 (2006), 306–29 at 326–7, for an emphasis on the inconsistencies arising from this duplication.

[104] See Chapter 4, III.2; also Chapter 5, II.3.

[105] ECJ, Judgment of 6 October 1982, 283/81, *CILFIT*, ECR 1982, 03415.

[106] See E Benvenisti, 'Judicial Misgivings Regarding the Application of International Law: An Analysis of Attitudes of National Courts', *European Journal of International Law* 4 (1993), 159–83; K Knop, 'Here and There: International Law in Domestic Courts', *NYU Journal of International Law and Politics* 32 (2000), 501–35.

[107] See E Benvenisti, 'Reclaiming Democracy: The Strategic Uses of Foreign and International Law by National Courts', *American Journal of International Law* 102 (2008), 241–74.

of the ECtHR.[108] In attempting to reconcile sanctions decisions and human rights, the lower UK courts showed less deference to the UN than the ECtHR has displayed in recent decisions,[109] but their argument was one from international, not domestic law.[110]

This did not lead to the construction of an integrated, constitutionalized global legal order on a domestic, federal model; international influences remained punctual and under the (potential) control of British law and the British parliament. Yet the self-understanding of UK judges still appears as more open than that of the EU courts, and perhaps this is not entirely accidental, given their common law background. For the common law has always subverted the systematic, hierarchical aspirations of the civil law and has resisted being reduced to a single source. Drawing on social customs, it is inevitably closer to actual practices than legal systems with an exclusive focus on texts, and this might give common law courts greater sensitivity for changes in their practical context. Moreover, the inductive nature of much of legal reasoning makes it easier to avoid questions of principle and hierarchy than is the case when legal argument relies on deduction and has to identify ultimate sources.[111] And the graduated forms of authority—especially the concept of 'persuasive' authority—help steer a course through a variety of judicial practices, just as they have allowed common law courts to borrow from other jurisdictions more freely than civil law courts.[112] In this way, a court's identity is less fixed and less tied to a particular authority with law-making power. Wearing more than one hat becomes easier for a court in this context.

When courts begin to take on such multiple identities, the institutional framework of a pluralist order undergoes a transformation. Instead of pitting courts against one another as guardians of different orders, the rationalities of those orders flow together (and potentially conflict) within a single body. Reconciliation may then be attempted but not always achieved, and the continuing pluralist character of the order is reflected in the absence of ultimate conflict norms. For courts, this is a far messier situation than that

---

[108] See Chapter 4, II.2.

[109] eg, ECtHR, Decision of 2 May 2007, *Behrami and Saramati v France, Germany and Norway*.

[110] See Chapter 5, II.1.

[111] See, in general, H P Glenn, *Legal Traditions of the World*, 3rd edn, Oxford: Oxford University Press, 2007, ch 7.

[112] See H P Glenn, 'Persuasive Authority', *McGill Law Journal* 32 (1987), 261–98; H P Glenn, 'Transnational Common Laws', *Fordham International Law Journal* 29 (2006), 457–71.

of the typical single perspective and not easy to cope with through the typical tools of legal reasoning. But it also allows them to assume a coordinating role—that of an arbiter or mediator between orders, rather than an advocate for one of them.

3. Interface Rules and their Substance

Notwithstanding the variations across countries, the approaches sketched in the previous sections signal a noteworthy shift in the way different layers of law position themselves vis-à-vis one another. The classical stance on the relationship between domestic and international law had been characterized by formality; countries were regarded as either monist or dualist, but they typically did not differentiate a great deal in their reception of international law. They often distinguished the effects of treaties and customary law, but did not introduce distinctions as to areas of international law, its substance, or the processes of its creation.

As we have seen throughout the case studies in this book, this approach has changed significantly. EU law, the European Convention on Human Rights, UN law, and WTO law are all treated differently by domestic courts, and these regimes have developed their own, particular responses and have in some cases established special relations with each other. The change is most visible in conditional-recognition approaches which reveal a shift from the formal appreciation of a norm's source to a more substantive evaluation of its content and context. A norm's democratic and human rights credentials have come to the foreground here and help determine whether, and with that strength, it enters another layer of law. In the UN context, the weight of global security concerns affects domestic proportionality analyses when it comes to the interference with fundamental rights.[113] And in the WTO context, reciprocity expectations influence the domestic effect of international norms.[114] Today, not all international law is equal before domestic courts, and this parallels a turn to a more gradated, or 'relative', normativity within the international legal order itself.[115] Authority structures have become far more complex than the classical binary law/non-law and inside/outside dichotomies suggest.[116]

---

[113] See V Gowlland-Debbas (ed), *National Implementation of United Nations Sanctions: A Comparative Study*, Leiden: Martinus Nijhoff, 2004.

[114] See Chapter 6, II.2.

[115] See the classic treatment in P Weil, 'Towards Relative Normativity in International Law', *American Journal of International Law* 77 (1983), 413–42.

[116] See Walker, 'Beyond Boundary Disputes', 376–85.

This shift responds to the factual and normative pressures I have sketched in Chapter 1 and taken up in the previous sections of the present chapter. As interlinkages between the layers of law grow and the idea of their formal separation becomes increasingly untenable, claims arise to extend thick domestic political values—democracy, the rule of law, individual rights—into the postnational sphere. They enter this sphere especially at the interfaces of the different layers: in the rules that guide the reception of outside norms in a given legal order.

In the development of these interface norms, the emphasis in practice and theory has so far been on individual rights—here, the immediate pressure has been greatest, and courts have also presented themselves as adequate institutions for their protection. The *Solange*, *Bosphorus*, and *Kadi* decisions are the prime examples here, and a huge scholarly literature has developed on the protection of human rights against European and international institutions. Much of it is based on the assumption that European and global governance needs to comply with rights standards identical, or at least equivalent, to those prevailing in the domestic (or regional) sphere.

The focus on rights and substantive equivalence, however, risks neglecting other normative demands on the regulation of the interface between layers of law—those of a more jurisdictional nature. As we have seen in Chapter 3, different polities—national, regional, international, global, etc—owe each other respect not simply on the basis of an identity of values (which would be a weak basis for genuine respect).[117] Instead, the requirement of respect stems from the extent to which a polity is a valid expression of the public autonomy of individuals. This emphasis on autonomy includes a concern for *rights* but also connects with *democratic* demands on postnational governance. If—and to the extent that—a polity can make a claim to strike a reasonable balance between the depth of self-government of its members and the inclusiveness of its scope, other polities ought to respect its norms as a matter of principle and not just on a case-by-case basis.

This interplay between self-government and inclusiveness also implies that there is no *a priori* superiority of the national level in the interplay of polities. In many areas, broader, more inclusive polities may have a stronger claim to recognition, and their norms ought to be be given weight even if they diverge from the normative understandings of the 'importing' polity. Narrower polities, on the other hand, may deserve respect insofar as they allow for deep participation and self-government as well as rights protection, but their claims suffer if they cannot provide a convincing account of

---

[117] Chapter 3, III.3.

why potentially affected outsiders should not be included in decision-making—also on the definition of the rights themselves. It is thus the autonomy pedigrees of the different polities that ought to determine their weight in the pluralist interplay of legal layers and shape the default rules on the recognition of external norms.

Such interface norms will also reflect other factors, such as the degree of prior formal acceptance of other norms (for example, through ratification), the proximity of values (for example, equivalence or identity in the interpretation of rights), or functional considerations, such as the utility of cooperation in a regime. Yet these should be secondary factors, operating *within* the autonomy-based framework I have just outlined. If a polity has a strong autonomy pedigree, its norms are due respect even if they are based on distinct values or compliance with them does not have immediate benefits.

Unlike in a constitutionalist structure, the strength of the respective claims in a pluralist order is not assessed by a single decision-maker or from a central vantage point. The pluralist setting distinguishes itself precisely by the fact that the conflict rules do *not* have an overarching legal character; they are normative, moral demands that find (potentially diverging) legal expressions only within the various sub-orders.[118] This can lead to incoherences in the overall order, as we have seen in the discussion of the rule of law earlier in this chapter. Yet the rule of law also poses demands on decision-makers in a pluralist setting: its asks legislators and judges to pursue the values of legal certainty and predictability by striving for consistency in the overall order. At times this goal may be trumped by other values—autonomy, democracy, and rights among them. If another order does not deserve respect on the basis of its autonomy pedigree, overall consistency need not be ensured. Yet in the case of competing autonomy claims of various orders, political and judicial decision-makers should try to reconcile their norms as best they can and thus also provide a degree of certainty and predictability for the individuals subject to legal multiplicity.

As we have seen earlier, courts may best pursue this aim of consistency in a minimalist fashion: not by seeking (unrealistically and perhaps counterproductively) to forge a grand *telos* of the overall system, but rather by formulating the *teloi* of different sub-orders in a way that is responsive to, and accommodates as far as possible, those of other orders. In this cautious sense, the quest for coherence—as compatibility, rather than deep uniformity[119]—is part and parcel of the broader quest for a just postnational order.

---

[118] See Chapter 3, I. For an elaboration of the contrasting constitutionalist vision see Kumm, 'Cosmopolitan Turn', 311–13, 320–3.

[119] See also Fischer-Lescano & Teubner, *Regime-Kollisionen*, 62.

ᗏ 9 ᗍ

Conclusion: Postnational Pluralism and Beyond

Globalization and the rise of global governance have long left lawyers quite indifferent. 'Plus ça change, plus c'est la même chose' seemed to be their axiom, and uncomfortable insights were brushed aside as long as possible.[1] This stance is slowly giving way to the realization that the classical structure of the legal order beyond the state, based on a neat distinction between the domestic and the international level, is disappearing. Yet what precisely this means, and what consequences it entails, remains uncertain and highly contested.

I. PLURALISM IN POSTNATIONAL LAW AND POLITICS

In this book, I have made a case for the recognition of this fundamental change in the legal order, a turn towards 'postnational law'. And I have tried to elucidate some of the key structural choices that follow from this turn— choices resulting from the fact that the different layers of law in the postnational order no longer operate in separate spheres but are deeply intertwined. This development puts pressure on the guiding principles and forms of legitimation of those orders. In the classical picture, thick (but diverse) sources of domestic legitimacy (liberal democracy, people's democracy, theocracy, etc) could coexist and find coordination in an international legal order based on the thin ground of consent. As the line of separation between the layers fades away, this division of labour no longer holds. Central elements of domestic political and legal orders move into the international sphere and clash with one another and with the classical international commitment to accommodate diversity.

In Chapter 1, I trace this process and the main responses to it in theory and practice. 'Containment', the attempt to limit the shift and re-domesticate global governance in national constitutional frameworks, appears as impractical in the absence of a return to less dense forms of transboundary cooperation. It also turns out to be normatively problematic as it privileges

---

[1] See P Alston, 'The Myopia of the Handmaidens: International Lawyers and Globalization', *European Journal of International Law* 3 (1997), 435–48.

decision-making in national communities over more inclusive fora which often correspond more closely with the range of those affected.

Among the other responses to the postnationalization of law, two stand out—constitutionalism and pluralism—and they form the focus of this book. Both take the increasing enmeshment of national, regional, and international law seriously but follow very different inspirations. While constitutionalism seeks to transfer domestic models of order to the postnational sphere, pluralism sees the need for a break with those models and proposes to develop fresh alternatives. In the first part of this book, I dissect both approaches and inquire into their normative grounding. Chapter 2 analyses the legacy of constitutionalism for politics and law beyond the state. It retraces the different modes in which constitutionalism has been conceptualized in regional and global contexts, asks what it means to 'translate' such a concept into another sphere, and investigates the historical and normative pedigree of its main strands—power-limiting and foundational constitutionalism. Foundational constitutionalism has been the dominant tradition in Western politics over the last two centuries, but if we take the experience of divided societies as a measure, it is unlikely fully to redeem its promise of framing (and taming) politics through law in the highly diverse and contested postnational space. Yet lowering ambitions and retreating to a power-limiting form of constitutionalism—a frequent move in current debates—would sell the constitutionalist project short: it would fail to connect with the more radical promise connected with it historically.

Against the background of these difficulties with postnational constitutionalism, Chapter 3 develops a pluralist alternative. Postnational pluralism recognizes the blurred separation of layers of law but does not seek to reorganize them in an overarching legal framework, as does constitutionalism. It envisages a heterarchical structure in which the interaction of different layers is not ultimately determined by one legal rule but influenced by a variety of (potentially conflicting) norms emanating from each of the layers. Between the different layers, there is no common point of reference in law; their relationship is fundamentally open and depends, in large part, on political factors.

Pluralism has been increasingly used as a prism for understanding the structure of law beyond the state, yet it has gained less attention as a normative vision. While a number of arguments have been advanced in its favour by commentators, none of them turns out to be fully convincing. In this chapter, I develop an alternative defence, based on the private and public autonomy of individuals. If public autonomy is to redeem its promise, it has to extend to the definition of the scope of the polity itself; individuals' choices, loyalties, and allegiances to particular polities thus demand respect in the construction of an institutional and jurisdictional framework. Individuals' attitudes on this point diverge widely, with many favouring a primacy of the national (or subnational) collective, others preferring regional or global polities. Most of these positions have a sound normative grounding, and the structure of postnational governance should accommodate their multiplicity rather than settle in favour of one of them. Pluralism, I argue, better reflects this need than constitutionalist models.

The discussion in the first three chapters operates on an abstract level, and it leaves open a number of questions about the current shape of postnational governance as well as the actual functioning of (and dangers linked to) pluralist orders. The second part of the book addresses these issues more concretely, using three case studies of particular contexts of postnational politics and law. Chapter 4 analyses the European human rights regime, often regarded as a prime example of constitutionalization beyond the state because of its development towards an integrated order with the European Convention of Human Rights as its 'constitutional instrument' at the top. On closer inspection, however, this description turns out to be misguided—the regime is better regarded as pluralist, as characterized by a heterarchical relationship between its constituent parts that is ultimately defined politically and not legally. In this chapter, I trace the emergence and workings of this pluralist order through the interaction of the European Court of Human Rights with courts in Spain, France, the European Union, and the United Kingdom. All these cases not only show conflicts over questions of ultimate supremacy but also significant convergence and harmony in day-to-day practice. I begin to identify factors that have led to this convergence and conclude that central characteristics of pluralism—incrementalism and the openness of ultimate authority—seem to have contributed to the generally smooth evolution of the European human rights regime in a significant way.

This finding suggests a broader appeal of pluralist models as alternatives to constitutionalism in the construction of postnational authority and law, but it also comes with a number of caveats. After all, the European human rights regime has developed in circumstances far more favourable than those existing in most other contexts of postnational governance. Chapter 5 analyses a harder case, that of the dispute over rights protection in UN sanctions. This dispute, which pitches high politics—security—against diverse interpretations of fundamental rights, brings out the increasing enmeshment of layers of law in a particularly pointed way, exemplified here in UK and EU law and jurisprudence. Courts in these jurisdictions have developed very different approaches to the broader challenge this enmeshment represents, ranging from monist/constitutionalist to pluralist visions, and from clear assertions of supremacy of the international, regional, and national levels to more accommodating attitudes. The overall picture here is again pluralist but, despite the high stakes and the substantial diversity in approaches, has not proved to be unstable. Challenges to the UN regime have failed to produce serious non-compliance, and the pluralist contestation over fundamentals has generally been buffered by an accommodating, pragmatic mode of cooperation on most issues. The UN Security Council has deliberately chosen this accommodating stance over the more hierarchical tools at its disposal, and this choice alone signals awareness that hierarchical forms do not sit well with the structure of postnational society and politics.

Chapter 6 focuses on a central area of global governance that is often regarded as an example of *failed* cooperation—the regime complex around trade, food safety, and the environment, exemplified in the dispute over trade in genetically modified organisms (GMOs). The chapter analyses the different institutions and their modes of interaction in this area, and it shows how their competing authority claims relate to broader claims by various collectives striving for control in the construction of global governance. It also continues the investigation into the charge that pluralist orders create instability. As in previous chapters, the analysis of the GMO dispute does not confirm this view: it reveals limits to what global risk regulation can achieve in the face of highly politicized conflicts, but it also shows significant cooperation successes. Moreover, it suggests that the limits of cooperation are due less to institutional than to societal structures, and that by leaving issues of principle open, a pluralist order may provide a safety valve for issues of high salience, thus avoiding frictions a constitutionalist order might produce.

The third part of the book draws the insights of the more abstract argument and the specific case studies together to inquire in greater depth into some of the most trenchant critiques levelled at a pluralist vision. Chapter 7 focuses on prospects of cooperation and problems of power. It begins by sketching the contours of the trajectories of postnational governance that have emerged from the case studies, arguing that in most of them the assertion of competing supremacy claims is part of processes of change in the respective regimes. More specifically, such claims can be understood as a reaction to an increasing legalization and strengthening of postnational institutions over time.

This element of change is also crucial for the assessment of pluralism's promise as regards the stability of cooperation. Pluralism occupies a middle ground between hard, legalized and softer network forms of cooperation and thus combines the virtues of greater flexibility with those of (limited) hierarchical instruments. Yet compared with constitutionalism's emphasis on hard law, it also opens up space for opportunistic behaviour and non-compliance, thus potentially undermining common regimes. This ambiguity flows from the diversity of postnational society, which resists hard legalization but also limits the prospects of softer regulation. Pluralism's benefits emerge more clearly from the presence of two other factors in the postnational context: a strong role of domestic publics and institutions and a large extent of institutional change. Domestic actors typically only play a marginal role in formal processes of regime design on the global level, but they have the potential to destabilize a regime later on. Moreover, when institutions change rapidly (and radically), with substantially increased costs for some players, resistance becomes more likely—again, most fundamentally among those actors not implicated in formal processes. Competing supremacy claims can give expression to—and buffer—such resistance. Leaving ultimate supremacy open and working around competing claims in an incrementalist fashion, as pluralism does, may then increase the prospects of stabilizing cooperation and constructing postnational authority over time.

As regards problems of power, the element of change turns out to be central too. A common charge against pluralism is that it favours the powerful over the weak by allowing for the political (not legal) determination of the relation between sub-orders. Interestingly, the case studies do not confirm this, presenting instead a more complex picture. This is in part because of the element of time: as postnational governance evolves, its effects on societal actors become more visible, thus triggering engagement, demand for institutional transformation, and processes of normative change. At a later point in time, the actor constellation will thus often be more inclusive and favourable to fair solutions than at the initial stage of regime design, which is typically dominated by arcane forms of negotiation among (select) governments, often enough driven by well-organized interest groups. It is this initial design that a constitutionalist framework is likely to stabilize whereas pluralism introduces an element of challenge and potentially gives initially excluded actors greater influence.

Chapter 8 inquires into pluralism's implications for democracy and the rule of law. It does not develop a theory of postnational democracy, but analyses the ways in which a pluralist order relates to three key parameters of any such theory—the plurality of governance sites, the multiplicity of *demoi*, and the multidimensional nature of democracy. It takes up the argument developed in Chapter 3 that much of pluralism's virtue lies precisely in situating the institutions of postnational governance at a distance from the competing visions of the right locus of authority. The chapter also sees a key advantage in the destabilization of the institutional order pluralism brings about—in the element of revisability and contestation that flows from the coexistence of different sub-orders in a heterarchical setting. The checks so introduced resonate well with contemporary emphases on contestation in democratic theory.

The rule of law, even more than democracy, is often seen as a particular problem for a pluralist vision, because of pluralism's emphasis on openness rather than legal determination. Legal certainty and consistency are indeed not central to the pluralist imagination. However, also in a domestic context, predictability is not assured when it comes to particularly salient issues, and the rule of law is usually not seen as absolute (except perhaps in a libertarian approach). This should caution us against seeing it as a key obstacle for pluralism: as long as there are strong normative arguments for a departure from a unitary legal setting—as is the case here with respect especially to the multiplicity of *demoi* and the need to allow for effective contestation—formal rule-of-law values may not be ultimately controlling.

Democracy and the rule of law should, however, influence the construction of the interface norms through which much of the institutional structure in a pluralist postnational order is determined. These norms are produced in the various sub-orders themselves—and may thus come into conflict, without a common constitutional frame that could provide resolution among them. Yet the interface norms should follow a normatively defensible vision of when one sub-order needs to show respect for norms emanating from another. In the conception put forward in this book, such a vision should be based on the private and public autonomy of individuals—sub-orders are due respect when they have a sufficient autonomy pedigree; when they are linked to the self-government of individuals and are sufficiently inclusive. This does not settle their ultimate weight: there may well be many situations in which norms from national, regional, and global contexts can all be seen to further an autonomy-based vision of postnational politics. If this is the case, they should strive to achieve consistency or at least compatibility with the other sub-orders, rather than trying to impose themselves on them.

II. PLURALISM IN THE POSTNATIONAL
SPHERE AND BEYOND

As I have pointed out at various junctures, the argument presented here is provisional—not all theoretical arguments are pursued in sufficient depth, nor are the empirical findings sufficiently robust to ground ultimate conclusions. More work will be necessary, both theoretically and empirically, and some of it is likely to raise doubts over my findings. Until this happens, though, there appears to be a relatively strong case for the pluralist vision set out here.

The argument in this book has implications for a number of current debates. The turn towards a 'postnational' law challenges the *distinction between domestic and international law*, so constitutive for both, and leaves both layers of law radically transformed and exposed to demands that they realize the guiding principles of the respective other. The argument for pluralism as not only a useful analytical prism but also a normative vision questions the *predominance of holistic, unitary frames* as a model for postnational politics and law. The emphasis on the parallel grounding of competing polities in individual autonomy brings out the problematic nature of both *cosmopolitan and nationalist visions* of institutional development, which all too easily brush over actual societal contestation in favour of substantive considerations in the determination of the preferred scope of the polity.[2] By stressing the value of fluidity and openness, the book also calls into doubt the virtues of the widely hailed *legalization* of international politics—a legalization which, if taken too far, may well provoke a backlash and weaken rather than stabilize cooperation. Its insights into the mobilization of actors and normative resources as well as shifts in power constellations in the development of regimes may help us better understand processes of *normative change* in international politics. More broadly, the book suggests that the widespread hope of constructing the postnational space on the basis of *domestic models* runs into serious obstacles, and that alternative approaches may fare better in the highly diverse and contested society that characterizes the world beyond the state.

We have encountered more detailed discussions of these and other points throughout the previous chapters. They have focused on the domain of the postnational, but the argument in this book may also lead us to question some traditional understandings of the domestic context, and of the phenomenon of law as such. The focus on diversity as the driving force behind postnational pluralism indicates that a pluralist order may be attractive also in other highly diverse settings, such as multinational federations. Where the locus of ultimate authority is similarly contested as in the postnational space, pragmatic accommodation and institutional equidistance may be preferable to constitutional settlement, both on moral and prudential grounds. Fixing the relationships between the different polities would potentially disregard well-founded claims of some polities, and overcoming the ensuing resistance may overstretch existing normative resources, thus destabilizing the overall order.[3] Pluralism might then provide a better fit. In these circumstances, it may also be advisable to shift our *interpretation* of existing constitutional settlements—instead of regarding them as ultimate frames of reference, we may see them as compromises on circumscribed issues, leaving fundamental questions undecided except where explicitly agreed. We might then interpret these polities as pluralist—in the sense that

---

[2] For a related critique, see N Torbisco Casals, 'Beyond Unity and Coherence: The Challenge of Legal Pluralism in a Post-National World', *Revista Jurídica de la Universidad de Puerto Rico* 77 (2008), 531–51 at 541–9.

[3] I have discussed related studies in Chapter 2, III, Chapter 3, III, and Chapter 7, II.

the locus of ultimate supremacy is left open and subject to political dispute rather than legal determination. James Tully's vision of a 'common constitutionalism', which interprets constitutions as treaties, would be close to that vision.[4] Olivier Beaud's reconstruction of federalism as involving multiple levels of sovereignty—evoking an older line of federalism that also inspired Carl Schmitt—points in a similar direction.[5]

A rethinking might also be in order in less fundamentally contested settings. Even when there is little or no contestation over the right *polity*, there may still be sufficient diversity in society to warrant a re-examination of the character of constitutional frameworks. We commonly interpret them as holistic settlements, which comprehensively establish and regulate the exercise of public power and thereby allow for the joint exercise of private and public autonomy. We have seen in Chapter 2 how this vision of foundational constitutionalism has become dominant over the last two centuries. Among other things, this frame makes us understand constitutions as crucial elements in the integration of diverse societies—as steps on the way from a *modus vivendi* to an overlapping consensus, as John Rawls puts it.[6] And it makes it possible to interpret vague constitutional norms (especially rights provisions) in a principled fashion, as expressions of a shared moral understanding in an abstract form.[7]

Yet such a reading conceals historical processes of constitution-making, in which conflict and compromise, rather than general agreement, often explain the vagueness of the resulting norms—unclear norms may just as well point to disagreement as to agreement. If we emphasize (as I have done in this book) the public autonomy of individuals, which extends to the definition of their constitutional framework, we will give weight to, and respect, such disagreement. This may lead us to understand constitutions as contracts or compromises,[8] interpret vague provisions as open, and counsel constitutional courts against filling them.[9] It may also lead us to emphasize

---

[4] J Tully, *Strange Multiplicity: Constitutionalism in an Age of Diversity*, Cambridge: Cambridge University Press, 1995.

[5] O Beaud, *Théorie de la Fédération*, Paris: Presses Universitaire de France, 2007. See also Chapter 3, I.

[6] J Rawls, *Political Liberalism*, New York: Columbia University Press, 1996, 158–68.

[7] See R Dworkin, *Law's Empire*, Cambridge, MA: Harvard University Press, 1986, ch 10; R Dworkin, *Freedom's Law: The Moral Reading of the American Constitution*, Cambridge, MA: Harvard University Press, 1996.

[8] See, eg, G Frankenberg, 'The Return of the Contract: Problems and Pitfalls of European Constitutionalism', *European Law Journal* 6 (2002), 257–76; R Bellamy, *Liberalism and Pluralism: Towards a Politics of Compromise*, London: Routledge, 1999.

[9] See, eg, J Waldron, *Law and Disagreement*, Oxford: Oxford University Press, 1999.

the extent to which constitutions leave inter-institutional relations unde-fined.[10] More generally, such a reading will promote investigations into the history of constitutional settlements and encourage us not to assume prin-cipled agreement when the societal constellation is characterized by deep-seated difference. Of course, such openness seems to pose problems for a constitution's role in integrating and stabilizing society—aims so closely linked to the modern constitutionalist project. Yet it appears as less prob-lematic if we acknowledge the stabilizing potential for political orders that may lie in the *absence* of constitutional settlement, which we have witnessed throughout this book. Accepting such openness will seem desirable if we regard constitutions—and law more generally—as (at least in part) instru-ments of control of one group over others. The more diverse a society is perceived to be, the more such a reading suggests itself: presumably neutral rules then often appear as biased and discriminatory in effect.[11]

The turn towards postnational pluralism indicates that we should rethink law and politics in yet other, perhaps even more fundamental respects. On the one hand, this is because of the shift away from binary conceptions of law I have sketched already in Chapter 1.[12] With the turn to postnational law, norms 'foreign' to one of the sub-orders often escape the binding/non-binding dichotomy that is so characteristic of the legal system.[13] Instead, they acquire a form of gradated authority: they are not entirely ignored but also not regarded as controlling—they are only 'taken into account'. The resulting picure resembles the common law's use of 'persuasive authority', quite distinct from classical civil law categories and from categorical distinc-tions between inside and outside and law and non-law.

Another central element of legal thought comes under pressure in the post-national order. As we have seen, constitutions are only pieces in a broader puzzle; they can no longer redeem their holistic ambition and have therefore lost some of their allure. They have also lost their ability to ensure the *unity* of the law, so central to contemporary theories of law which hold the legal

[10] See D Halberstam, 'Constitutional Heterarchy: The Centrality of Conflict in the European Union and the United States' in J L Dunoff & J P Trachtman (eds), *Ruling the World? Constitutionalism, International Law and Global Government*, Cambridge: Cambridge University Press, 326–55.

[11] See, eg, I M Young, *Justice and the Politics of Difference*, Princeton, NJ: Princeton University Press, 1990; N Torbisco Casals, *Group Rights as Human Rights: A Liberal Approach to Multiculturalism*, Dordrecht: Springer Verlag, 2006, ch 4. See also Chapter 2, III.3 and Chapter 7, III.

[12] See Chapter 1, II.

[13] On the centrality of this dichotomy for law, see N Luhmann, *Das Recht der Gesellschaft*, Frankfurt am Main: Suhrkamp Verlag, 1993, 60.

order together by means of a *Grundnorm* or rule of recognition.[14] Pluralism radically undermines ideas of unity: without a common point of reference, different parts of the legal order lead distinct, formally unconnected lives.[15] They may produce *internal* unity—national law continues to accept the supremacy of the national constitution, international law continues to ignore the latter and deduce its validity from independent sources. Between them, though, there is no arbiter—neither in the form of an institution nor through a norm valid for all. This does not imply that between the layers no communication takes place; as we have seen in our case studies, interaction is often constant and intense. Yet the different parts are not formally integrated. This is perhaps not news to those, especially sociologically minded, voices who have for long sought to unmask the hierarchy and unity of law as a fiction. By bringing the different layers of law closer together, postnational governance—perhaps paradoxically—highlights the distance between them and brings out the lack of a common frame; it has perhaps become the most potent force in undermining law's hierarchy and unity.[16]

The turn towards postnational governance is thus bound to have a subversive effect. It unsettles traditional understandings of the structure of both domestic and international law and in the process reshapes the respective roles of law and politics. Amongst the many laws in a pluralist order, law can no longer decide; recourse must be had to other, often political means, and pluralism brings this fact out into the open. It also helps to make visible another consequence of the multiplicity of laws—the loss of universality, and with it the loss of neutrality. More clearly than in the unitary conception, law becomes *particular*—the reflection of particular values and particular projects of individuals and groups, in competition with the values and projects of others. The legal form may mitigate the partiality of these endeavours but it can neither eliminate nor conceal it effectively. Amid the multiplicity of laws, the law exposes itself as deeply implicated in this partiality.

This partiality is not as such negative; it is merely a consequence of the diverse character of modern societies. It is also not novel: the space for

---

[14] H Kelsen, *Reine Rechtslehre*, Leipzig/Vienna: Deuticke, 1934; H L A Hart, *The Concept of Law*, 2nd edn, Oxford: Oxford University Press, 1994.

[15] See Torbisco Casals, 'Beyond Unity', 538–40.

[16] See G Teubner, 'The King's Many Bodies: The Self-Deconstruction of Law's Hierarchy', *Law & Society Review* 31 (1997), 763–88 at 768–9, with a focus on globalization and the production of non-state forms of law, especially the *lex mercatoria*. See also P Zumbansen, 'Transnational Legal Pluralism', *Comparative Research in Law & Political Economy Research Paper* 01/2010, <http://ssrn.com/abstract=1542907>.

politics in the face of legal indeterminacy as well as the law's partial character have long been highlighted by critical scholars.[17] Yet the postnational context accentuates these traits—the more contested politics becomes, the less the law is able to maintain a neutral appearance. This is, in part, the dilemma of postnational constitutionalism—insisting on the rule of law in the postnational context means (more obviously than in the domestic realm) insisting on the rule of *one* law, *one* polity, *one* project over others. In a space in which material power relations are so central and governance arrangements so fluid, legalizing/constitutionalizing relations always runs the risk of unduly preferring one perspective over others, of locking in domination.

In this light, pluralism's openness comes to appear as a chance more than as a menace: as a chance to contest, destabilize, delegitimize entrenched power positions—and to pursue progressive causes by other means than constitutional settlements. This chance comes with a greater burden for everyday political action: if the realization of crucial values cannot be left to institutional structures, it depends on continuous engagement and struggle. This implies greater fluidity and also risk: but as we have seen, the hope of eliminating this risk in postnational society is in any case slim and burdened by high costs. In the fluid, divided, and highly contested space of the postnational, easy solutions are elusive—and pluralism, for all its complexity, may allow us to realize central political values better than more clearly structured, constitutional frames.

---

[17] On international law, see M Koskenniemi, *From Apology to Utopia: The Structure of International Legal Argument*, 2nd edn, Cambridge: Cambridge University Press, 2006.

References

'Das tut mir weh' (interview with L Wildhaber), *Der Spiegel* 47/2004, 15 November 2004

'Im Ausland mißverständlich', Frankfurter Allgemeine Zeitung, 23 October 2004

'Straßburg ist kein oberstes Rechtsmittelgericht' (interview with H-J Papier), Frankfurter Allgemeine Zeitung, 9 December 2004

'Welches Gericht hat das letzte Wort?', Frankfurter Allgemeine Zeitung, 10 December 2004

Abbott, F M, 'The WTO Medicines Decision: World Pharmaceutical Trade and the Protection of Public Health', *American Journal of International Law* 99 (2005), 317–18

Abbott, K W & Snidal, D, 'Why States Act through Formal International Organizations', *Journal of Conflict Resolution* 42 (1998), 3–32

—— & —— 'Hard and Soft Law in International Governance', *International Organization* 54 (2000), 421–56

Abraham, R, 'Le juge administratif français et la cour de Strasbourg' in P Tavernier (ed), *Quelle Europe pour les droits de l'homme?*, Brussels: Emile Bruylant, 1996, 235–47

Acharya, A, 'How Ideas Spread: Whose Norms Matter? Norm Localization and Institutional Change in Asian Regionalism', *International Organization* 58 (2004), 239–75

Ackerman, B, *We the People*, vol 1, Cambridge, MA: Harvard University Press, 1991

Alemanno, A, *Trade in Food: Regulatory and Judicial Approaches in the EC and the WTO*, London: Cameron May, 2007

Alexander, L (ed), *Constitutionalism: Philosophical Foundations*, Cambridge: Cambridge University Press, 2001

Allott, P, 'Epilogue: Europe and the Dream of Reason' in J H H Weiler & M Wind (eds), *European Constitutionalism Beyond the State*, Cambridge: Cambridge University Press, 2003, 202–25

Almqvist, J, 'A Human Rights Critique of European Judicial Review: Counter-Terrorism Sanctions', *International and Comparative Law Quarterly* 57 (2008), 303–31

Alston, P, 'The Myopia of the Handmaidens: International Lawyers and Globalization', *European Journal of International Law* 3 (1997), 435–48

—— (ed), *The EU and Human Rights*, Oxford, New York: Oxford University Press, 1999

Alter, K J, *Establishing the Supremacy of European Law: The Making of an International Rule of Law in Europe*, Oxford: Oxford University Press, 2001

—— & Meunier, S, 'The Politics of International Regime Complexity', *Perspectives on Politics* 7 (2009), 13–24

Alvarez, J E, 'Hegemonic International Law Revisited', *American Journal of International Law* 97 (2003), 873–88

—— 'The Security Council's War on Terrorism: Problems and Policy Options' in E de Wet & A Nollkaemper (eds), *Review of the Security Council by Member States*, Antwerp: Intersentia, 2003, 119–45

—— 'International Organizations: Then and Now', *American Journal of International Law* 100 (2006), 324–47

Amar, A R, 'Of Sovereignty and Federalism', *Yale Law Journal* 96 (1987), 1425–520

Anderson, B, *Imagined Communities: Reflections on the Origin and Spread of Nationalism*, London: Verso, 1983

Anderson, G W (ed), *Rights and Democracy: Essays in UK-Canadian Constitutionalism*, London: Blackstone Press, 1999

Andriantsimbazovina, J, *L'autorité des décisions de justice constitutionnelles et européennes sur le juge administratif français*, Paris: LGDJ, 1998

—— '"Savoir n'est rien, imaginer est tout": libre conversation autour de l'arrêt Kress de la Cour européenne des droit de l'homme', *Recueil Dalloz* 2001, 2611–18

Ansell, C & Vogel, D (eds), *What's the Beef? The Contested Governance of European Food Safety*, Cambridge, MA: MIT Press, 2006

—— & —— 'The Contested Governance of European Food Safety Regulation' in C Ansell & D Vogel (eds), *What's the Beef? The Contested Governance of European Food Safety*, Cambridge, MA: MIT Press, 2006, 3–32

Antoniadis, A, 'The European Union and WTO Law: A Nexus of Reactive, Coactive, and Proactive Approaches', *World Trade Review* 6 (2007), 45–87

Arai-Takahashi, Y, *The Margin of Appreciation Doctrine and the Principle of Proportionality in the Jurisprudence of the ECHR*, Antwerp: Intersentia, 2002

Arangio-Ruiz, G, 'International Law and Interindividual Law' in J Nijman & A Nollkaemper, *New Perspectives on the Divide Between National and International Law*, Oxford: Oxford University Press, 2007, 15–51

Archibugi, D, 'Cosmopolitan Democracy and its Critics: A Review', *European Journal of International Relations* 10 (2004), 437–73

—— *The Global Commonwealth of Citizens: Toward Cosmopolitan Democracy*, Princeton, NJ: Princeton University Press, 2008

Arendt, H, *On Revolution*, London: Penguin Books, [1963] 1990

Avbelj, M & Komárek, J (eds), *Constitutional Pluralism in the European Union and Beyond*, Oxford: Hart Publishing, forthcoming, 2010

Baczko, B, 'The Social Contract of the French: Sieyes and Rousseau', *Journal of Modern History* 60 (1988), S98–S125

Bail, C, Falkner, R, & Marquard, H (eds), *The Cartagena Protocol on Biosafety: Reconciling Trade in Biotechnology with Environment and Development*, London: Earthscan, 2002

Bailey, M A & Maltzman, F, 'Does Legal Doctrine Matter? Unpacking Law and Policy Preferences on the US Supreme Court', *American Political Science Review* 102 (2008), 369–84

Bamforth, N, 'Understanding the Impact and Status of the Human Rights Act 1998 within English Law', *NYU Global Law Working Paper* 10/2004

Baquero Cruz, J, 'The Legacy of the Maastricht-Urteil and the Pluralist Movement', *European Law Journal* 14 (2008), 389–422

Barber, B R, *Strong Democracy: Participatory Politics for a New Age*, Berkeley, CA: University of California Press, 1984

Barber, N W, 'Legal Pluralism and the European Union', *European Law Journal* 12 (2006), 306–29

Barr, M S & Miller, G P, 'Global Administrative Law: The View from Basel', *European Journal of International Law* 17 (2006), 15–46

Barrett, R, 'Al-Qaeda and Taliban Sanctions Threatened', *PolicyWatch* 1409, <http://www.washingtoninstitute.org/templateC05.php?CID=2935>

Barry, B, 'Political Accommodation and Consociational Democracy', *British Journal of Political Science* 5 (1975), 477–505

—— *Culture and Equality: An Egalitarian Critique of Multiculturalism*, Cambridge, MA: Harvard University Press, 2002

Barton, J H, Goldstein, J L, Josling, T E, & Steinberg, R H, *The Evolution of the Trade Regime: Politics, Law, and Economics of the GATT and the WTO*, Princeton, NJ: Princeton University Press, 2006, 62–7

BBC Online, 'GM Potato Cleared for EU Farming', 2 March 2010, <http://news.bbc.co.uk/2/hi/8545503.stm>

Beaud, O, *Théorie de la Fédération*, Paris: Presses Universitaires de France, 2007

Beck, G, 'The Problem of *Kompetenz-Kompetenz*: A Conflict Between Right and Right in Which There Is No *Praetor*', *European Law Review* 30 (2005), 42–67

Bedner, J, Eskridge Jr, W N, & Ferejohn, J A, 'A Political Theory of Federalism' in J A Ferejohn, J N Rakove, & J Riley (eds), *Constitutional Culture and Democratic Rule*, Cambridge: Cambridge University Press, 2001, 223–70

Bellamy, R, *Liberalism and Pluralism: Towards a Politics of Compromise*, London: Routledge, 1999

—— *Political Constitutionalism*, Cambridge: Cambridge University Press, 2007

Benhabib, S, *The Rights of Others*, Cambridge: Cambridge University Press, 2004

—— 'Reclaiming Universalism: Negotiating Republican Self-Determination and Cosmopolitan Norms', *The Tanner Lectures on Human Values* 25 (2005), 113–66

—— 'Claiming Rights across Borders: International Human Rights and Democratic Sovereignty', *American Political Science Review* 103 (2009), 691–704

Benvenisti, E, 'Judicial Misgivings Regarding the Application of International Law: An Analysis of Attitudes of National Courts', *European Journal of International Law* 4 (1993), 159–83

—— 'Exit and Voice in the Age of Globalization', *Michigan Law Review* 98 (1999), 167–213

—— 'Reclaiming Democracy: The Strategic Uses of Foreign and International Law by Domestic Courts', *American Journal of International Law* 102 (2008), 241–74

—— & Downs, G W, 'The Empire's New Clothes: Political Economy and the Fragmentation of International Law', *Stanford Law Review* 60 (2007), 595–631

Berman, H J, *Law and Revolution: The Formation of the Western Legal Tradition*, Cambridge: MA: Harvard University Press, 1983

Berman, P S, 'From International Law to Law and Globalization', *Columbia Journal of Transnational Law* 43 (2005), 485–556

—— 'Global Legal Pluralism', *Southern California Law Review* 80 (2007), 1155–237

Bernhardt, R, 'Commentary: The European System', *Connecticut Journal of International Law* 2 (1987), 299–301

Besson, S, 'From European Integration to European Integrity: Should European Law Speak with Just One Voice?', *European Law Journal* 10 (2004), 257–81

—— 'Institutionalising Global *Demoi*-cracy' in L H Meyer (ed), *Legitimacy, Justice and Public International Law*, Cambridge: Cambridge University Press, 2009, 58–91

—— 'Whose Constitution(s)? International Law, Constitutionalism, and Democracy' in J L Dunoff & J P Trachtman (eds), *Ruling the World? Constitutionalism, International Law, and Global Governance*, Cambridge: Cambridge University Press, 2009, 381–407

Bethlehem, D, 'The European Union' in V Gowlland-Debbas (ed), *National Implementation of United Nations Sanctions: A Comparative Study*, The Hague: Martinus Nijhoff, 2004, 123–65

Biersteker, T J & Weber C (eds), *State Sovereignty As Social Construct*, Cambridge: Cambridge University Press, 1996

Blackburn, R, 'The United Kingdom' in R Blackburn & J Polakiewicz (eds), *Fundamental Rights in Europe: The European Convention on Human Rights and its Member States, 1950–2000*, Oxford: Oxford University Press, 2001, 935–1008

—— & Polakiewicz, J (eds), *Fundamental Rights in Europe: The European Convention on Human Rights and its Member States, 1950–2000*, Oxford: Oxford University Press, 2001

Böckenförde, E-W, *Recht, Staat, Freiheit*, Frankfurt am Main: Suhrkamp Verlag, 1991

—— *Staat, Verfassung, Demokratie*, Frankfurt am Main: Suhrkamp Verlag, 1991

—— 'Der deutsche Typ der konstitutionellen Monarchie im 19. Jahrhundert' in E-W Böckenförde, *Recht, Staat, Freiheit*, Frankfurt am Main: Suhrkamp Verlag, 1991, 273–305

—— 'Geschichtliche Entwicklung und Bedeutungswandel der Verfassung' in E-W Böckenförde, *Staat, Verfassung, Demokratie*, Frankfurt am Main: Suhrkamp Verlag, 1991, 29–52

—— *Staat, Nation, Europa*, Frankfurt am Main: Suhrkamp Verlag, 1999

—— 'Die Zukunft politischer Autonomie' in E-W Böckenförde, *Staat, Nation, Europa*, Frankfurt am Main: Suhrkamp Verlag, 1999, 103–26

Böckenförde, M, *Grüne Gentechnik und Welthandel: Das Biosafety-Protokoll und seine Auswirkungen auf das Regime der WTO*, Heidelberg: Springer, 2004

Bogdandy, A von, 'Constitutionalism in International Law: Comments on a Proposal from Germany', *Harvard International Law Journal* 47 (2006), 223–42

—— & Bast, J (eds), *Europäisches Verfassungsrecht*, 2nd edn, Berlin: Springer Verlag, 2009

Bohman, J, 'The Coming of Age of Deliberative Democracy', *Journal of Political Philosophy* 6 (1998), 400–25

—— *Democracy across Borders*, Cambridge, MA: MIT Press, 2007

Boisson de Chazournes, L & Mbengue, M M, 'GMOs and Trade: Issues at Stake in the EC Biotech Dispute', *Review of European Community and International Environmental Law* 13 (2004), 289–305

Börzel, T, 'Der "Schatten der Hierarchie"—ein Governance-Paradox?' in G F Schuppert & M Zürn (eds), *Governance in einer sich wandelnden Welt*, Politische Vierteljahresschrift: Sonderheft 41/2008, 118–31

Bourantonis, D, *The History and Politics of UN Security Council Reform*, London: Routledge, 2005

Bovens, M, *The Quest for Responsibility: Accountability and Citizenship in Complex Organisations*, Cambridge: Cambridge University Press, 1998

Brauch, J A, 'The Margin of Appreciation and the Jurisprudence of the European Court of Human Rights', *Columbia Journal of European Law* 11 (2004), 113–50

Bröhmer, J et al (eds), *Internationale Gemeinschaft und Menschenrechte: Festschrift für Georg Ress*, Cologne: Heymanns, 2005

Bronckers, M, 'From "Direct Effect" to "Muted Dialogue": Recent Developments in the European Courts' Case Law on the WTO and Beyond', *Journal of International Economic Law* 11 (2008), 885–98

Brunkhorst, H, *Solidarity: From Civic Friendship to a Global Legal Community* (J Flynn, trans), Cambridge, MA: MIT Press, 2005

Buchanan, A & Powell, R, 'Survey Article: Constitutional Democracy and the Rule of International Law: Are They Compatible?', *Journal of Political Philosophy* 16 (2008), 326–49

Büthe, T, 'The Globalization of Health and Safety Standards: Delegation of Regulatory Authority in the SPS Agreement of the 1994 Agreement Establishing the World Trade Organization', *Law & Contemporary Problems* 71 (Winter 2008), 219–55

Bull, H, *The Anarchical Society*, London: Macmillan, 1977

Burgess, M, *Comparative Federalism*, London: Routledge, 2006

Burley, A-M & Mattli, W, 'Europe Before the Court: A Political Theory of Legal Integration', *International Organization* 47 (1993), 41–76

Busch, M L, 'Overlapping Institutions, Forum Shopping, and Dispute Settlement in International Trade', *International Organization* 61 (2007), 735–61

Byers, M (ed), *The Role of Law in International Politics*, Oxford: Oxford University Press, 2000

Callewaert, J, 'The European Convention on Human Rights and European Union Law: A Long Way to Harmony', *European Human Rights Law Review* (2009), 768–83

Canivet, G, Andenas, M, & Fairgrieve, D (eds), *Comparative Law Before the Courts*, London: BIICL, 2004

Canor, I, 'Primus Inter Pares. Who is the Ultimate Guardian of Fundamental Rights in Europe?', *European Law Review* 25 (2000), 3–21

Caporaso, J A & Kim, M, 'The Dual Nature of European Identity: Subjective Awareness and Coherence', *Journal of European Public Policy* 16 (2009), 19–42

Carrillo Salcedo, J A, 'España y la protección de los derechos humanos: el papel del Tribunal Europeo de Derechos Humanos y del Tribunal constitucional español', *Archiv des Völkerrechts* 32 (1994), 187–201

Casanovas, O, *Unity and Pluralism in Public International Law*, Leiden: Martinus Nijhoff, 2001

Chalmers, D & Tomkins, A, *European Union Public Law*, Cambridge: Cambridge University Press, 2007

Checkel, J T, 'Why Comply? Social Learning and European Identity Change', *International Organization* 55 (2001), 553–88

—— & Katzenstein, P J (eds), *European Identity*, Cambridge, Cambridge University Press, 2009

Chimni, B S, 'Co-option and Resistance: Two Faces of Global Administrative Law', *NYU Journal of International Law and Politics* 37 (2005), 799–827

Choudhry, S (ed), *The Migration of Constitutional Ideas*, Cambridge: Cambridge University Press, 2007

—— (ed), *Constitutional Design for Divided Societies: Integration or Accommodation?*, Oxford: Oxford University Press, 2008

—— 'Does the World Need more Canada? The Politics of the Canadian Model in Constitutional Politics and Political Theory' in S Choudhry (ed), *Constitutional Design for Divided Societies: Integration or Accommodation?*, Oxford: Oxford University Press, 2008, 141–72

Chryssogonos, K, 'Zur Inkorporation der Europäischen Menschenrechtskonvention in den nationalen Rechtsordnungen der Mitgliedstaaten', *Europarecht* 36 (2001), 49–61

Colandrea, V, 'On the Power of the European Court of Human Rights to Order Specific Non-monetary Measures: Some Remarks in Light of the Assanidze, Broniowski and Sejdovic Cases', *Human Rights Law Review* 7 (2007), 396–411

Comanducci, P, 'Ordre ou norme? Quelques idées de constitution au XVIIIe siècle' in M Troper & L Jaume (eds), *1789 et l'invention de la Constitution*, Paris: LGDJ-Bruylant, 1994, 23–43

Connor, W, 'Nation-Building or Nation-Destroying?', *World Politics* 24 (1972), 319–55

Cortell, A P & Peterson, S, 'Dutiful Agents, Rogue Actors, or Both? Staffing, Voting, Rules and Slack in the WHO and WTO' in D G Hawkins et al (eds), *Delegation and Agency in International Organizations*, Cambridge: Cambridge University Press, 2006, 255–80

Cortright, D & Lopez, G A, *The Sanctions Decade: Assessing UN Strategies in the 1990s*, Boulder, CO: Lynne Rienner, 2000

—— & —— (eds), *Smart Sanctions: Targeting Economic Statecraft*, Lanham, MD: Rowman & Littlefield, 2002

—— & —— (eds), *Uniting Against Terror: Cooperative Nonmilitary Responses to the Global Terrorist Threat*, Cambridge, MA: MIT Press, 2007

——, ——, & Gerber-Stellingwerf, L, 'The Sanctions Era: Themes and Trends in UN Security Council Sanctions since 1990' in V Lowe et al (eds), *The United Nations Security Council and War*, Oxford: Oxford University Press, 2008, 205–25

—— et al, 'Global Cooperation Against Terrorism: Evaluating the Counter-Terrorism Committee' in D Cortright & G A Lopez (eds), *Uniting Against Terror: Cooperative Nonmilitary Responses to the Global Terrorist Threat*, Cambridge, MA: MIT Press, 2007, 23–50

Costello, C, 'The Bosphorus Ruling of the European Court of Human Rights: Fundamental Rights and Blurred Boundaries in Europe', *Human Rights Law Review* 6 (2006), 87–130

—— & Browne, E, 'ECHR and the European Union' in U Kilkelly (ed), *ECHR and Irish Law*, Bristol: Jordan Publishing, 2004, 35–80

Craig, P P, 'Constitutions, Constitutionalism, and the European Union', *European Law Journal* 7 (2001), 125–50

—— & de Búrca, G, *EU Law: Text, Cases, and Materials*, 4th edn, Oxford: Oxford University Press, 2008

Cramér, P, 'Recent Swedish Experiences with Targeted UN Sanctions: The Erosion of Trust in the Security Council' in E de Wet & A Nollkaemper (eds), *Review of the Security Council by Member States*, Antwerp: Intersentia, 2003, 85–106

Craven, M, 'Unity, Diversity and the Fragmentation of International Law', *Finnish Yearbook of International Law* 14 (2003), 3–34

Cronin, B & Hurd, I (eds), *The UN Security Council and the Politics of International Authority*, London: Routledge, 2008

Dahl, R A, 'Decision-Making in a Democracy: The Supreme Court as a National Policy-Maker', *Journal of Public Law* 6 (1957), 279–95

—— 'Federalism and the Democratic Process' in J R Pennock and J W Chapman (eds), *NOMOS XXV: Liberal Democracy*, New York: New York University Press, 1983, 95–108

—— 'Can International Organizations be Democratic? A Skeptic's View' in I Shapiro & C Hacker-Cordón (eds), *Democracy's Edges*, Cambridge: Cambridge University Press, 1999, 19–36

Davies, A, 'Connecting or Compartmentalizing the WTO and United States Legal Systems? The Role of the *Charming Betsy* Canon', *Journal of International Economic Law* 10 (2007), 117–49

de Búrca, G, 'Developing Democracy Beyond the State', *Columbia Journal of Transnational Law* 46 (2008), 101–58

—— 'The European Court of Justice and the International Legal Order after *Kadi*', *Jean Monnet Working Paper* 01/09, <http://www.jeanmonnetprogram.org/papers/09/090101.html>

—— & Gerstenberg, O, 'The Denationalization of Constitutional Law', *Harvard International Law Journal* 47 (2006), 243–62

—— & Scott, J (eds), *Law and New Governance in the EU and the US*, Oxford: Hart Publishing, 2006

de Gouttes, R, 'Le juge judiciaire français et la Convention européenne des droits de l'homme: avancées et reticences' in P Tavernier (ed), *Quelle Europe pour les droits de l'homme?*, Brussels: Emile Bruylant, 1996, 217–34

—— 'La Convention Européenne des Droits de l'Homme et le juge français', *Revue Internationale de Droit Comparé* 51 (1999), 294–8

—— 'L'intervention du Ministère public au cours de la phase d'instruction: La situation à la Cour de cassation' in I Pingel & F Sudre (eds), *Le ministère public et les exigences du procès équitable*, Brussels: Bruylant, 2003, 63–80

de Schutter, O, 'L'influence de la Cour européenne des droits de l'homme sur la Cour de justice des Communautés européennes', *CRIDHO Working Paper* 2005/07

de Sousa Santos, B, *Toward a New Legal Common Sense*, London: Butterworths, 2002

—— 'Beyond Neoliberal Governance: The World Social Forum as Subaltern Cosmopolitan Politics and Legality' in B de S Santos & C A Rodríguez-Garavito (eds), *Law and Globalization from Below*, Cambridge: Cambridge University Press, 2005, 29–63

—— & Rodríguez-Garavito, C A (eds), *Law and Globalization from Below*, Cambridge: Cambridge University Press, 2005

de Wet, E, *The Chapter VII Powers of the United Nations Security Council*, Oxford: Hart Publishing, 2004

—— 'The Emergence of International and Regional Value Systems as a Manifestation of the Emerging International Constitutional Order', *Leiden Journal of International Law* 19 (2006), 611–32

—— 'The International Constitutional Order', *International & Comparative Law Quarterly* 55 (2006), 51–76

—— & Nollkaemper, A, 'Review of Security Council Decisions by National Courts', *German Yearbook of International Law* 45 (2002), 166–202

—— & —— (eds), *Review of the Security Council by Member States*, Antwerp: Intersentia, 2003

de Witte, B, 'Community Law and National Constitutional Values', *Legal Issues of European Integration* 1991:2, 1–22

Delgado Barrio, J, 'Proyección de las decisiones del Tribunal Europeo de Derechos Humanos en la jurisprudencia española', *Revista de Administración Publica* 119 (1989), 233–52

Delmas-Marty, M, *Towards a Truly Common Law: Europe as a Laboratory for Legal Pluralism* (N Norberg, trans), Cambridge: Cambridge University Press, 2002

—— *Ordering Pluralism: A Conceptual Framework for Understanding the Transnational Legal World* (N Norberg, trans), Oxford: Hart Publishing, 2009

Deutsche Welle, 'Germany to Ban US Biotech Giant's Genetically Modified Corn Strain', 14 April 2009, <http://www.dw-world.de/dw/article/0,,4176790,00. html>

Douglas-Scott, S, 'A Tale of Two Courts: Luxembourg, Strasbourg and the Growing European Human Rights *Acquis*', *Common Market Law Review* 43 (2006), 629–65

Drago, R, Case note, *Recueil Dalloz* 2001, 2624–7

Drezner, D W, *All Politics is Global: Explaining International Regulatory Regimes*, Princeton, NJ: Princeton University Press, 2007

—— 'The Power and Peril of International Regime Complexity', *Perspectives on Politics* 7 (2009), 65–70

Dryzek, J S, *Deliberative Democracy and Beyond*, Oxford: Oxford University Press, 2000

—— *Deliberative Global Politics: Discourse and Democracy in a Divided World*, Cambridge: Polity Press, 2006

Dunoff, J L, 'Constitutional Conceits: The WTO's "Constitution" and the Discipline of International Law', *European Journal of International Law* 17 (2006), 647–75

—— & Trachtman, J P (eds), *Ruling the World? Constitutionalism, International Law, and Global Governance*, Cambridge: Cambridge University Press, 2009

—— & —— 'A Functional Approach to International Constitutionalization' in J L Dunoff & J P Trachtman (eds), *Ruling the World? Constitutionalism, International Law, and Global Governance*, Cambridge: Cambridge University Press, 2009, 3–35

Dupré, C, 'France' in R Blackburn & J Polakiewicz (eds), *Fundamental Rights in Europe: The European Convention on Human Rights and its Member States, 1950–2000*, Oxford: Oxford University Press, 2001, 313–33

Dupuy, P-M, 'L'unité de l'ordre juridique international', *Recueil des cours de l'Académie du droit international* 297 (2003), 9–489

Dutheillet de Lamothe, O, 'European Law and the French Constitutional Council' in G Canivet, M Andenas, & D Fairgrieve (eds), *Comparative Law Before the Courts*, London: BIICL, 2004, 91–8

Dworkin, R, *Law's Empire*, Cambridge, MA: Harvard University Press, 1986

—— *Freedom's Law: The Moral Reading of the American Constitution*, Cambridge, MA: Harvard University Press, 1996

Eeckhout, P, 'Community Terrorism Listings, Fundamental Rights, and UN Security Council Resolutions: In Search of the Right Fit', *European Constitutional Law Review* 3 (2007), 183–206

—— 'Kadi and Al Barakaat: Luxembourg is not Texas—or Washington DC', *EJIL:Talk!*, 25 February 2009, at: <http://www.ejiltalk.org/kadi-and-al-barakaat-luxembourg-is-not-texas-or-washington-dc/>

Eilstrup-Sangiovanni, M, 'Varieties of Cooperation: Government Networks in International Security' in M Kahler (ed), *Networked Politics: Agency, Power, and Governance*, Ithaca, NY: Cornell University Press, 2009, 194–227

Eissen, M-A, 'L'interaction des jurisprudences constitutionnelles nationales et de la jurisprudence de la Cour européenne des Droits de l'homme' in D Rousseau & F Sudre (eds), *Conseil constitutionnel et Cour européenne des droits de l'homme: Droits et libertés en Europe*, Paris: Editions STH, 1990, 137–215

Eleftheriadis, P, 'Pluralism and Integrity' in M Avbelj & J Komárek (eds), *Constitutional Pluralism in the European Union and Beyond*, Oxford: Hart Publishing, forthcoming, 2010

Elster, J (ed), *Deliberative Democracy*, Cambridge: Cambridge University Press, 1998

—— 'Deliberation and Constitution Making' in J Elster (ed), *Deliberative Democracy*, Cambridge: Cambridge University Press, 1998, 97–122

Epstein, L & Knight, J, 'Toward a Strategic Revolution in Judicial Politics', *Political Research Quarterly* 53 (2000), 625–61

——, ——, & Martin, A D, 'Review Essay: The Supreme Court as a Strategic National Policy-Maker', *Emory Law Journal* 50 (2001), 583–611

Escobar Roca, G, 'Spain' in R Blackburn & J Polakiewicz (eds), *Fundamental Rights in Europe: The European Convention on Human Rights and its Member States, 1950–2000*, Oxford: Oxford University Press, 2001, 809–31

Falk, R & Strauss, A, 'Toward Global Parliament', *Foreign Affairs* 80 (January–February 2001), 212–20

Falkner, R, 'Regulating Biotech Trade: the Cartagena Protocol on Biosafety', *International Affairs* 76 (2000), 299–313

Farrall, J M, *United Nations Sanctions and the Rule of Law*, Cambridge: Cambridge University Press, 2007

—— & Rubenstein, K (eds), *Sanctions, Accountability and Governance in a Globalised World*, Cambridge: Cambridge University Press, 2009

Fassbender, B, 'The United Nations Charter as Constitution of the International Community', *Columbia Journal of Transnational Law* 36 (1998), 529–619

—— 'All Illusions Shattered? Looking Back on a Decade of Failed Attempts to Reform the UN Security Council', *Max Planck Yearbook of United Nations Law* 7 (2003), 183–218

Fenwick, H, Masterman, R, & Phillipson, G (eds), *Judicial Reasoning under the UK Human Rights Act*, Cambridge: Cambridge University Press, 2007

——, ——, & —— 'The Human Rights Act in Contemporary Context' in H Fenwick, R Masterman, & G Phillipson, *Judicial Reasoning under the UK Human Rights Act*, Cambridge: Cambridge University Press, 2007, 1–21

Ferejohn, J & Pasquino, P, 'Rule of Democracy and Rule of Law' in A Przeworski & J M Maravall (eds), *Democracy and the Rule of Law*, Cambridge: Cambridge University Press, 2003, 242–60

—— & —— 'The Law of the Exception: A Typology of Emergency Powers', *International Journal of Constitutional Law* 2 (2004), 210–39

——, Rakove, J N, & Riley, J (eds), *Constitutional Culture and Democratic Rule*, Cambridge: Cambridge University Press, 2001

Ferreres Comella, V, 'El juez nacional ante los derechos fundamentales europeos. Algunas reflexiones en torno a la idea de diálogo', in *Integración europea y poder judicial*, Bilbao: Instituto Vasco de Administración Publica, 2006, 227–65

Filippov, M, Ordeshook, P C, & Shvetsova, O, *Designing Federalism: A Theory of Self-sustainable Federal Institutions*, Cambridge: Cambridge University Press, 2004

Finnemore, M & Sikkink, K, 'International Norm Dynamics and Political Change', *International Organization* 52 (1998), 887–917

Fischer-Lescano, A & Teubner, G, *Regime-Kollisionen: Zur Fragmentierung des globalen Rechts*, Frankfurt am Main: Suhrkamp Verlag, 2006

Fish, M S & Brooks, R S, 'Does Diversity Hurt Democracy?', *Journal of Democracy* 15 (2004), 154–66

Flauss, J-F, 'La Cour européenne des droits de l'homme est-elle une Cour constitutionnelle?', *Revue française de droit constitutionnel* 36 (1998), 711–28

Fligstein, N, *Euroclash: The EU, European Identity, and the Future of Europe*, Oxford: Oxford University Press, 2008

Foot, R, 'The United Nations, Counter Terrorism, and Human Rights: Institutional Adaptation and Embedded Ideas', *Human Rights Quarterly* 29 (2007), 489–514

——, MacFarlane, S N, & Mastanduno, M (eds), *US Hegemony and International Organizations*, Oxford: Oxford University Press, 2003

Fossum, J E & Menéndez, A J, 'The Constitution's Gift? A Deliberative Democratic Analysis of Constitution Making in the European Union', *European Law Journal* 11 (2005), 380–410

Franck, T M (ed), *Why Federations Fail*, New York: New York University Press, 1968

—— 'Why Federations Fail' in T M Franck (ed), *Why Federations Fail*, New York: New York University Press, 1968, 167–99

Frankenberg, G, 'The Return of the Contract', *European Law Journal* 6 (2000), 257–76

Fromont, M, 'Die Bedeutung der Europäischen Menschenrechtskonvention in der französischen Rechtsordnung', *Die Öffentliche Verwaltung* 58 (2005), 1–10

—— 'Le juge français et la Cour européenne des droits de l'homme' in J Bröhmer et al (eds), *Internationale Gemeinschaft und Menschenrechte: Festschrift für Georg Ress*, Cologne: Heymanns, 2005, 965–77

Frowein, J A, 'The European Convention on Human Rights as the Public Order of Europe', *Collected Courses of the Academy of European Law*, 1:2 (1992), 267–358

—— 'Der europäische Grundrechtsschutz und die deutsche Rechtsprechung', *Neue Zeitschrift für Verwaltungsrecht* 21 (2002), 29–33

—— & Krisch, N, 'Introduction to Chapter VII' in B Simma et al (eds), *The Charter of the United Nations*, 2nd edn, Oxford: Oxford University Press, 2002, 701–16

—— & —— 'Article 41' in B Simma et al (eds), *The United Nations Charter: A Commentary*, 2nd edn, Oxford: Oxford University Press, 2002, 735–49

—— & —— 'Germany' in V Gowlland-Debbas (ed), *National Implementation of United Nations Sanctions: A Comparative Study*, The Hague: Martinus Nijhoff, 2004, 233–64

Galligan, B, 'Comparative Federalism' in R A W Rhodes, S A Binder, & B A Rockman, *The Oxford Handbook of Political Institutions*, Oxford: Oxford University Press, 2006, 261–80

Galston, W A, *Liberal Pluralism*, Cambridge: Cambridge University Press, 2002

García de Enterría, E, 'Valeur de la jurisprudence de la Cour européenne des Droits de l'Homme en droit espagnol' in F Matscher & H Petzold (eds), *Protecting Human Rights: The European Dimension: Studies in Honour of G J Wiarda*, Cologne: Heymanns, 1988, 221–30

Gattini, A, Note on *Kadi and Al Barakaat*, *Common Market Law Review* 46 (2009), 213–39

Gearty, C A (ed), *European Civil Liberties and the European Convention on Human Rights*, The Hague: Kluwer Law International, 1997

Genevois, B, 'L'intervention du Ministère public au cours de la phase d'instruction: La situation au Conseil d'Etat' in I Pingel & F Sudre (eds), *Le ministère public et les exigences du procès équitable*, Brussels: Bruylant, 2003, 81–93

—— 'L'intervention du Ministère public au cours du délibéré: La situation au Conseil d'Etat' in I Pingel & F Sudre (eds), *Le ministère public et les exigences du procès équitable*, Brussels: Bruylant, 2003, 189–97

Gibson, J L, 'Judicial Institutions' in R A W Rhodes, S A Binder, & B A Rockman (eds), *The Oxford Handbook of Political Institutions*, Oxford: Oxford University Press, 2006, 515–34

Ginsburg, T, 'The Global Spread of Constitutional Review' in K Whittington, R D Keleman, & G A Caldera (eds), *The Oxford Handbook of Law and Politics*, Oxford: Oxford University Press, 2008, 81–98

Glenn, H P, 'Persuasive Authority', *McGill Law Journal* 32 (1987), 261–98

—— 'Transnational Common Laws', *Fordham International Law Journal* 29 (2006), 457–71

—— *Legal Traditions of the World*, 3rd edn, Oxford: Oxford University Press, 2007

GMO Compass, 'Italian Court Gives GM Go-ahead', 5 February 2010, <http://www.gmo-compAorg/eng/news/487.docu.html>

Goldsmith, J & Levinson, D, 'Law for States: International Law, Constitutional Law, Public Law', *Harvard Law Review* 122 (2009), 1791–868

Goldstein, J & Martin, L L, 'Legalization, Trade Liberalization and Domestic Politics: A Cautionary Note', *International Organization* 54 (2000), 603–32

—— et al (eds), *Legalization and World Politics*, Cambridge, MA: MIT Press, 2001

Goodman, R & Jinks, D, 'How to Influence States: Socialization and International Human Rights Law', *Duke Law Journal* 54 (2004), 621–703

Goold, B J & Lazarus, L (eds), *Security and Human Rights*, Oxford: Hart Publishing, 2007

Gowlland-Debbas, V (ed), *National Implementation of United Nations Sanctions*, The Hague: Martinus Nijhoff, 2004

—— 'Concluding Remarks' in V Gowlland-Debbas (ed), *National Implementation of United Nations Sanctions*, The Hague: Martinus Nijhoff, 2004, 643–58

—— 'Implementing Sanctions Resolutions in Domestic Law' in V Gowlland-Debbas (ed), *National Implementation of United Nations Sanctions: A Comparative Study*, The Hague: Martinus Nijhoff, 2004, 33–78

Graber, C B, 'The New UNESCO Convention on Cultural Diversity: A Counterbalance to the WTO?', *Journal of International Economic Law* 9 (2006), 553–74

Grant, R W & Keohane, R O, 'Accountability and Abuses of Power in World Politics', *American Political Science Review* 99 (2005), 29–43

Greenwood, C, 'United Kingdom' in V Gowlland-Debbas (ed), *National Implementation of United Nations Sanctions: A Comparative Study*, The Hague: Martinus Nijhoff, 2004, 581–604

Greer, S, *The European Convention on Human Rights: Achievements, Problems and Prospects*, Cambridge: Cambridge University Press, 2006

Grewe, C & Gusy, C (eds), *Menschenrechte in der Bewährung: Die Rezeption der Europäischen Menschenrechtskonvention in Frankreich und Deutschland im Vergleich*, Baden-Baden: Nomos, 2005

Griffiths, J, 'What is Legal Pluralism?', *Journal of Legal Pluralism* 24 (1986), 1–55

Griffith, J A G, 'The Brave New World of Sir John Laws', *Modern Law Review* 63 (2000), 159–76

—— 'The Common Law and the Political Constitution', *Law Quarterly Review* 117 (2001), 42–67

Griller, S, 'Is this a Constitution? Remarks on a Contested Concept' in S Griller & J Ziller (eds), *The Lisbon Treaty: EU Constitutionalism without a Constitutional Treaty?*, Vienna: Springer Verlag, 2008, 21–56

—— & Ziller, J (eds), *The Lisbon Treaty: EU Constitutionalism without a Constitutional Treaty?*, Vienna: Springer Verlag, 2008

Grimm, D, *Deutsche Verfassungsgeschichte 1776–1866*, Frankfurt am Main: Suhrkamp Verlag, 1988

—— *Die Zukunft der Verfassung*, Frankfurt am Main: Suhrkamp Verlag, 1994

—— 'Der Verfassungsbegriff in historischer Entwicklung' in D Grimm, *Die Zukunft der Verfassung*, Frankfurt am Main: Suhrkamp Verlag, 1994, 101–55

—— 'Die Zukunft der Verfassung' in D Grimm, *Die Zukunft der Verfassung*, Frankfurt am Main: Suhrkamp Verlag, 1994, 399–439

—— 'Entstehungs- und Wirkungsbedingungen des modernen Konstitutionalismus' in D Grimm, *Die Zukunft der Verfassung*, Frankfurt am Main: Suhrkamp Verlag, 1994, 31–66

—— 'Integration by Constitution', *International Journal of Constitutional Law* 3 (2005), 193–208

—— 'The Constitution in the Process of Denationalization', *Constellations* 12 (2005), 447–63

—— 'The Achievement of Constitutionalism and its Prospects in a Changed World' in Loughlin, M & Dobner, P (eds), *The Twilight of Constitutionalism?*, Oxford: Oxford University Press, 2010, 3–22

Grofman, B & Wittman, D (eds), The Federalist Papers *and the New Institutionalism*, New York: Agathon Press, 1989

Groh, K et al (eds), *Die Europäische Verfassung—Verfassungen in Europa*, Baden-Baden: Nomos Verlag, 2005

Gross, O, 'The Normless and Exceptionless Exception: Carl Schmitt's Theory of Emergency Powers and the "Norm-Exception" Dichotomy', *Cardozo Law Review* 21 (2000), 1825–68

—— 'Chaos and Rules: Should Responses to Violent Crises Always be Constitutional?', *Yale Law Journal* 112 (2003), 1011–34

—— & Aolain, F Ni, *Law in Times of Crisis: Emergency Powers in Theory and Practice*, Cambridge: Cambridge University Press, 2006

Gruber, L, *Ruling the World: Power Politics and the Rise of Supranational Institutions*, Princeton, NJ: Princeton University Press, 2000

Gusy, C, 'Die Rezeption der EMRK in Deutschland' in C Grewe & C Gusy (eds), *Menschenrechte in der Bewährung: Die Rezeption der Europäischen Menschenrechtskonvention in Frankreich und Deutschland im Vergleich*, Baden-Baden: Nomos, 2005, 129–58

Gutherie, P, 'Security Council Sanctions and the Protection of Individual Rights', *NYU Annual Survey of American Law* 60 (2004), 491–541

Guzman, A T, 'The Design of International Agreements', *European Journal of International Law* 16 (2005), 579–612

Habermas, J, 'Reconciliation through the Public Use of Reason: Remarks on John Rawls's Political Liberalism', *Journal of Philosophy* 92 (1995), 109–31

—— *Between Facts and Norms* (W Rehg, trans), Cambridge: Polity Press, 1996

—— 'Citizenship and National Identity' in J Habermas, *Between Facts and Norms* (W Rehg, trans), Cambridge: Polity Press, 1996, 491–515

—— *Die postnationale Konstellation*, Frankfurt am Main: Suhrkamp Verlag, 1998

—— *The Postnational Constellation* (M Pensky, trans), Cambridge, MA: MIT Press, 2001

—— 'Why Europe Needs a Constitution', *New Left Review* 11 (September–October 2001), 5–26

—— 'Constitutional Democracy: A Paradoxical Union of Contradictory Principles?', *Political Theory* 29 (2001), 766–81

—— *Der gespaltene Westen*, Frankfurt am Main: Suhrkamp Verlag, 2004

—— 'Hat die Konstitutionalisierung des Völkerrechts noch eine Chance?' in J Habermas, *Der gespaltene Westen*, Frankfurt am Main: Suhrkamp Verlag, 2004, 113–93

—— 'Kommunikative Rationalität und grenzüberschreitende Politik: eine Replik' in P Niesen & B Herborth (eds), *Anarchie der kommunikativen Freiheit: Jürgen Habermas und die Theorie der internationalen Politik*, Frankfurt am Main: Suhrkamp Verlag, 2007, 406–59

Haïm, V, 'Faut-il supprimer la Cour européenne des droits de l'homme', *Recueil Dalloz* 2001, 2988–94

Halberstam, D, 'Constitutional Heterarchy: The Centrality of Conflict in the European Union and the United States' in J L Dunoff & J P Trachtman (eds), *Ruling the World? Constitutionalism, International Law and Global Government*, Cambridge: Cambridge University Press, 2009, 326–55

—— & Stein, E, 'The United Nations, the European Union, and the King of Sweden: Economic Sanctions and Individual Rights in a Plural World Order', *Common Market Law Review* 46 (2009), 13–72

Haltern, U, 'Internationales Verfassungsrecht? Anmerkungen zu einer kopernika-nischen Wende', *Archiv des öffentlichen Rechts* 128 (2003), 511–57

Hamilton, A, Madison, J, & Jay, J, *The Federalist Papers* (L Goldman, ed), Oxford: Oxford University Press, 2008

Hardin, R, 'Why a Constitution?' in B Grofman & D Wittman (eds), The Federalist Papers *and the New Institutionalism*, New York: Agathon Press, 1989, 100–20

Harrison, P, 'EU Meeting on GM Maize Ends in Deadlock', Reuters, 25 February 2009, <http://uk.reuters.com/article/behindTheScenes/idUK-TRE51O57320090225>

—— 'EU Upholds Austria, Hungary Right to Ban GM Crops', Reuters, 2 March 2009, <http://uk.reuters.com/article/environmentNews/idUK-TRE5212OL20090302>

Hart, H L A, *The Concept of Law*, 2nd edn, Oxford: Oxford University Press, 1994

Harvey, C, Morison, J, & Shaw, J, 'Voices, Spaces, and Processes in Constitutionalism', *Journal of Law and Society* 27 (2000), 1–3

Hawkins, D G et al (eds), *Delegation and Agency in International Organizations*, Cambridge: Cambridge University Press, 2006

Hayek, F A, *The Constitution of Liberty*, Abingdon: Routledge, [1960] 2006

Hedetoft, U & Hjort, M (eds), *The Postnational Self: Belonging and Identity*, Minneapolis, MN: University of Minnesota Press, 2002, iii–xxxii

—— & —— 'Introduction' in U Hedetoft & M Hjort (eds), *The Postnational Self: Belonging and Identity*, Minneapolis, MN: University of Minnesota Press, 2002

Hegel, G W F, *The Philosophy of History* (J Sibree, trans), Buffalo, NY: Prometheus Books, 1991

Held, D, *Democracy and the Global Order: From the Modern State to Cosmopolitan Governance*, Cambridge: Polity Press, 1995

—— & Koenig-Archibugi, M (eds), *Taming Globalization: Frontiers of Governance*, Cambridge: Polity Press, 2003

—— 'Democratic Accountability and Effectiveness from a Cosmopolitan Perspective', *Government & Opposition* 39 (2004), 365–91

Helfer, L R, 'Regime Shifting: The TRIPs Agreement and New Dynamics of International Intellectual Property Lawmaking', *Yale Journal of International Law* 29 (2004), 1–83

—— 'Regime Shifting in the International Intellectual Property System', *Perspectives on Politics* 7 (2009), 39–44

—— & Slaughter, A-M, 'Toward A Theory of Effective Supranational Adjudication', *Yale Law Journal* 107 (1997), 273–91

Héritier, A & Lehmkuhl, D, 'Introduction: The Shadow of Hierarchy and New Modes of Governance', *Journal of Public Policy* 28 (2008), 1–17

Heupel, M, 'Combining Hierarchical and Soft Modes of Governance: The UN Security Council's Approach to Terrorism and Weapons of Mass Destruction Proliferation after 9/11', *Cooperation and Conflict* 43 (2008), 7–29

—— 'Multilateral Sanctions against Terror Suspects and the Violation of Due Process Standards', *International Affairs* 85 (2009), 307–21

Heuschling, L, 'Comparative Law and the European Convention on Human Rights in French Human Rights Cases' in E Örücü (ed) *Judicial Comparativism in Human Rights Cases*, London: UKNCCL and BIICL, 2003, 23–47

Hirschl, R, *Towards Juristocracy: The Origins and Consequences of the New Constitutionalism*, Cambridge, MA: Harvard University Press, 2004

Hirst, P Q (ed), *The Pluralist Theory of the State*, London: Routledge, 1989

—— 'Introduction' in P Q Hirst (ed), *The Pluralist Theory of the State*, London: Routledge, 1989, 1–4

—— *Associative Democracy*, Cambridge: Polity Press, 1994

Hoffmann, S, 'Obstinate or Obsolete? The Fate of the Nation-State and the Case of Western Europe', *Daedalus* 95 (1966), 862–915

Hoffmeister, F, 'Die Europäische Menschenrechtskonvention als Grundrechtsverfassung und ihre Bedeutung in Deutschland', *Der Staat* 40 (2001), 349–81

—— 'Germany: Status of European Convention on Human Rights in Domestic Law', *International Journal of Constitutional Law* 4 (2006), 722–31

Hooper, J, 'Human Rights Ruling Against Classroom Crucifixes Angers Italy', *Guardian Online*, 3 November 2009, <http://www.guardian.co.uk/world/2009/nov/03/italy-classroom-crucifixes-human-rights>

Horowitz, D, 'Constitutional Design: Proposals Versus Processes' in A Reynolds (ed), *The Architecture of Democracy: Constitutional Design, Conflict Management, and Democracy*, Oxford: Oxford University Press, 2002, 15–36

Hovell, D, 'A House of Kadis? Recent Challenges to the UN Sanctions Regime and the Continuing Response to the ECJ Decision in Kadi', *EJIL:Talk!*, 7 July 2009, <http://www.ejiltalk.org/a-house-of-kadis-recent-challenges-to-the-un-sanctions-regime-and-the-continuing-response-to-the-ecj-decision-in-kadi/>

—— 'The Deliberative Deficit: Transparency, Access to Information and UN Sanctions' in J Farrall & K Rubenstein (eds), *Sanctions, Accountability and Governance in a Globalised World*, Cambridge: Cambridge University Press, 2009, 92–122

Howse, R, 'The WHO/WTO Study on Trade and Public Health: A Critical Assessment', *Risk Analysis* 24 (2004), 501–7

—— & Mavroidis, P C, 'Europe's Evolving Regulatory Strategy for GMOs—The Issue of Consistency with WTO Law: Of Kine and Brine', *Fordham International Law Journal* 24 (2000), 317–70

—— & Horn, H, 'European Communities—Measures Affecting the Approval and Marketing of Biotech Products', *World Trade Review* 8 (2009), 49–83

Hülsse, R, 'Even Clubs Can't do Without Legitimacy: Why the Anti-money Laundering Blacklist was Suspended', *Regulation & Governance* (2008), 459–79

Hunt, M, *Using Human Rights Law in English Courts*, Oxford: Hart Publishing, 1997

Hurd, I, 'Legitimacy and Authority in International Politics', *International Organization* 53 (1999), 379–408

—— *After Anarchy: Legitimacy and Power in the United Nations Security Council*, Princeton, NJ: Princeton University Press, 2007

Hurrell, A, 'Conclusion: International Law and the Changing Constitution of International Society' in M Byers (ed), *The Role of Law in International Politics*, Oxford: Oxford University Press, 2000, 327–47

—— *On Global Order*, Oxford: Oxford University Press, 2007

Hutchinson, M R, 'The Margin of Appreciation Doctrine in the European Court of Human Rights', *ICLQ* 48 (1999), 638–50

Hutter, F-J, 'Die Erfolgsgeschichte der EMRK—Vom Nachkrieg zur europäischen Friedensordnung' in C Grewe & C Gusy (eds), *Menschenrechte in der Bewährung: Die Rezeption der Europäischen Menschenrechtskonvention in Frankreich und Deutschland im Vergleich*, Baden-Baden: Nomos, 2005, 36–54

ICTSD, 'Luxembourg to Ban GM Maize Cultivation', Bridges Trade BioRes 9:6, 3 April 2009, <http://ictsd.net/i/news/biores/44622/>

Ikenberry, G J, *After Victory: Institutions, Strategic Restraint, and the Rebuilding of Order After Major Wars*, Princeton, NJ: Princeton University Press, 2001

Isensee, J & Kirchhof, P (eds), *Handbuch des Staatsrechts der Bundesrepublik Deutschland*, vol II, 3rd edn, Heidelberg: C F Müller Verlag, 2004; vol VII, Heidelberg: C F Müller Verlag, 1992

Jaume, L, 'Constituent Power in France: The Revolution and its Consequences' in M Loughlin & N Walker (eds), *The Paradox of Constitutionalism: Constituent Power and Constitutional Form*, Oxford: Oxford University Press, 2007, 67–85

Joerges, C, 'Rethinking the Supremacy of European Law', *EUI Working Paper Law* 2005/12

—— 'Conflict of Laws as Constitutional Form: Reflections on International Trade Law and the *Biotech* Panel Report', *RECON Online Working Paper* 2007/39-13, at: <http://www.reconproject.eu/main.php/RECON_wp_0703.pdf?fileitem=5456959>

Johnson, J, 'Inventing Constitutional Traditions: The Poverty of Fatalism' in J A Ferejohn, J N Rakove, & J Riley (eds), *Constitutional Culture and Democratic Rule*, Cambridge: Cambridge University Press, 2001, 71–109

Johnston, A I, 'Treating International Institutions as Social Environments', *International Studies Quarterly* 45 (2001), 487–515

Johnstone, I, 'Security Council Deliberations: The Power of the Better Argument', *European Journal of International Law* 14 (2003), 437–80

—— 'The Security Council as Legislature' in B Cronin & I Hurd (eds), *The UN Security Council and the Politics of International Authority*, London: Routledge, 2008, 80–104

Jordan, A & Schout, A (eds), *The Coordination of the European Union*, Oxford: Oxford University Press, 2006

Jupille, J & Caporaso, J A, 'Domesticating Discourses: European Law, English Judges, and Political Institutions', *European Political Science Review* 1 (2009) 205–28

Kahler, M (ed), *Networked Politics: Agency, Power, and Governance*, Ithaca, NY: Cornell University Press, 2009

—— & Lake, D A, 'Economic Integration and Global Governance: Why So Little Supranationalism?, in W Mattli & N Woods (eds), *The Politics of Global Regulation*, Princeton, NY: Princeton University Press, 2009, 242–75

Kalyvas, A, 'Popular Sovereignty, Democracy, and the Constituent Power', *Constellations* 12 (2005), 223–44

Kanetake, M, 'Enhancing Community Accountability of the Security Council through Pluralistic Structure: The Case of the 1267 Committee', *Max Planck Yearbook of United Nations Law* 12 (2008), 113–75

Kant, I, 'Zum ewigen Frieden: Ein philosophischer Entwurf' in I Kant, *Schriften zur Anthropologie, Geschichtsphilosophie, Politik und Pädagogik I* (Werkausgabe, vol XI; W Weischedel, ed), Frankfurt am Main: Suhrkamp Verlag, 1993, 191–251

—— *Schriften zur Anthropologie, Geschichtsphilosophie, Politik und Pädagogik I* (Werkausgabe, vol XI; W Weischedel, ed), Frankfurt am Main: Suhrkamp Verlag, 1993

Karl, W & Schöpfer, E C, 'Österreichische Rechtsprechung zur Europäischen Menschenrechtskonvention im Jahr 2004', *Zeitschrift für öffentliches Recht* 61 (2006), 151–200

Karlsson, C, 'Deliberation at the Convention: The Final Verdict', *European Law Journal* 14 (2008), 604–19

Katzenstein, P J & Checkel, J T, 'Conclusion—European Identity in Context' in J T Checkel & P J Katzenstein (eds), *European Identity*, Cambridge, Cambridge University Press, 2009, 213–27

Keck, T M, 'Party, Policy, or Duty: Why Does the Supreme Court Invalidate Federal Statutes', *American Political Science Review* 101 (2007), 321–38

Kelemen, R D, *The Rules of Federalism: Institutions and Regulatory Politics in the EU and Beyond*, Cambridge, MA: Harvard University Press, 2004

Keller, H, 'Reception of the European Convention for the Protection of Human Rights and Fundamental Freedoms (ECHR) in Poland and Switzerland', *Zeitschrift für ausländisches öffentliches Recht und Völkerrecht* 65 (2005), 283–349

—— & Stone Sweet, A (eds), *A Europe of Rights: The Impact of the ECHR on National Legal Systems*, Oxford: Oxford University Press, 2008

—— & —— 'Assessing the Impact of the ECHR on National Legal Systems' in H Keller & A Stone Sweet (eds), *A Europe of Rights: The Impact of the ECHR on National Legal Systems*, Oxford: Oxford University Press, 2008, 677–712

—— & —— 'The Reception of the ECHR in National Legal Orders' in H Keller & A Stone Sweet (eds), *A Europe of Rights: The Impact of the ECHR on National Legal Systems*, Oxford: Oxford University Press, 2008, 3–28

Kelley, J, 'International Actors on the Domestic Scene: Membership Conditionality and Socialization by International Institutions', *International Organization* 58 (2004), 425–57

Kelsen, H, *Reine Rechtslehre*, Leipzig/Vienna: Deuticke, 1934

—— *The Law of the United Nations*, London: Stevens & Sons, 1950

Kennedy, D, *A Critique of Adjudication (fin de siècle)*, Cambridge, MA: Harvard University Press, 1999

Kennedy, D, 'The Mystery of Global Governance' in J L Dunoff & J P Trachtman (eds), *Ruling the World? Constitutionalism, International Law, and Global Governance*, Cambridge: Cambridge University Press, 2009, 37–68

Keohane, R O, 'The Demand for International Regimes', *International Organization* 36 (1982), 325–55

—— *After Hegemony: Cooperation and Discord in the World Political Economy*, Princeton, NJ: Princeton University Press, 1984

—— 'Governance in a Partially Globalized World', *American Political Science Review* 95 (2001), 1–13

—— 'Global Governance and Democratic Accountability' in D Held & M Koenig-Archibugi (eds), *Taming Globalization: Frontiers of Governance*, Cambridge: Polity Press, 2003, 130–59

——, Macedo, S, & Moravcsik, A, 'Democracy-Enhancing Multilateralism', *International Organization* 63 (2009), 1–31

——, Moravcsik, A, & Slaughter, A-M, 'Legalized Dispute Resolution: Interstate and Transnational', *International Organization* 54 (2000), 457–88

Kiiver, P, 'The Treaty of Lisbon, the National Parliaments and the Principle of Subsidiarity', *Maastricht Journal of European and Comparative Law* 15 (2008), 77–83

Kilkelly, U (ed), *ECHR and Irish Law*, Bristol: Jordan Publishing, 2004

Kingsbury, B, 'Sovereignty and Inequality', *European Journal of International Law* 9 (1998), 599–625

—— 'The Concept of "Law" in Global Administrative Law', *European Journal of International Law* 20 (2009), 23–57

—— 'Weighing Global Regulatory Rules and Decisions in National Courts', *Acta Juridica* (2009), 90–119

——, Krisch, N, & Stewart, R B, 'The Emergence of Global Administrative Law', *Law & Contemporary Problems* 68:3 (2005), 15–61

Kirchhof, P, 'Der deutsche Staat im Prozeß der europäischen Integration' in J Isensee & P Kirchhof (eds), *Handbuch des Staatsrechts der Bundesrepublik Deutschland*, vol VII, Heidelberg: C F Müller Verlag, 1992, 855–87

—— 'Die Identität der Verfassung' in J Isensee & P Kirchhof (eds), *Handbuch des Staatsrechts der Bundesrepublik Deutschland*, vol II, 3rd edn, Heidelberg: C F Müller Verlag, 2004, 261–316

Klabbers, J, *An Introduction to International Institutional Law*, Cambridge: Cambridge University Press, 2002

——'Constitutionalism Lite', *International Organizations Law Review* 1 (2004), 31–58

—— 'Setting the Scene' in J Klabbers, A Peters, & G Ulfstein, *The Constitutionalization of International Law*, Oxford: Oxford University Press, 2009, 1–44

——, Peters, A, & Ulfstein, G, *The Constitutionalization of International Law*, Oxford: Oxford University Press, 2009

Klein, C, 'Pourquoi écrit-on une constitution?' in M Troper & L Jaume (eds), *1789 et l'invention de la Constitution*, Paris: LGDJ-Bruylant, 1994, 89–99

Knop, K, 'Here and There: International Law in Domestic Courts', *NYU Journal of International Law and Politics* 32 (2000), 501–35

——, Michaels, R, & Riles, A, 'International Law in Domestic Courts: A Conflict of Laws Approach', *American Society of International Law Proceedings* 103 (2009), forthcoming, <http://scholarship.law.duke.edu/faculty_scholarship/1998/>.

Koenig-Archibugi, M, 'Is Global Democracy Possible?', *European Journal of International Relations*, forthcoming, <http://personal.lse.ac.uk/KOENIGAR/Koenig-Archibugi_Is_Global_Democracy_Possible.pdf>

Koh, H H, 'Why Do Nations Obey International Law?', *Yale Law Journal* 106 (1997), 2599–659

Komárek, J, 'European Constitutionalism and the European Arrest Warrant: In Search of the Limits of "Contrapunctual Principles"', *Common Market Law Review* 44 (2007), 9–40

Koremenos, B, Lipson, C, & Snidal, D, 'The Rational Design of International Institutions', *International Organization* 55 (2001), 761–99

——, ——, & —— (eds), *The Rational Design of International Institutions*, Cambridge, MA: MIT Press, 2004

Koskenniemi, M, 'The Police in the Temple: Order, Justice and the UN: A Dialectical View', *European Journal of International Law* 6 (1995), 1–25

—— *From Apology to Utopia: The Structure of International Legal Argument*, 2nd edn, Cambridge: Cambridge University Press, 2006

—— 'Constitutionalism as Mindset: Reflections on Kantian Themes about Law and Globalization', *Theoretical Inquiries in Law* 8 (2007), 9–36

—— 'The Fate of Public International Law: Between Technique and Politics', *Modern Law Review* 70 (2007), 1–30

—— & Leino, P, 'Fragmentation of International Law? Postmodern Anxieties', *Leiden Journal of International Law* 15 (2002), 553–79

——, Kaukoranta, P, & Björklund, M, 'Finland' in V Gowlland-Debbas (ed), *National Implementation of United Nations Sanctions: A Comparative Study*, The Hague: Martinus Nijhoff, 2004, 167–94

Krasner, S D (ed), *International Regimes*, Ithaca, NY: Cornell University Press, 1983

—— 'Regimes and the Limits of Realism: Regimes as Autonomous Variables' in S D Krasner (ed), *International Regimes*, Ithaca, NY: Cornell University Press, 1983, 355–68

—— 'Structural Causes and Regime Consequences: Regimes as Intervening Variables' in S D Krasner (ed), *International Regimes*, Ithaca, NY: Cornell University Press, 1983, 1–21

—— 'Global Communications and National Power: Life on the Pareto Frontier', *World Politics* 43 (1991), 336–66

Krisch, N, 'Amerikanische Hegemonie und liberale Revolution im Völkerrecht', *Der Staat* 43 (2004), 267–97

—— 'The Rise and Fall of Collective Security: Terrorism, US Hegemony, and the Plight of the Security Council' in C Walter et al (eds), *Terrorism as a Challenge for National and International Law*, Berlin/Heidelberg: Springer Verlag, 2004, 879–908

—— 'International Law in Times of Hegemony: Unequal Power and the Shaping of the International Legal Order', *European Journal of International Law* 16 (2005), 369–408

—— 'Die Vielheit der europäischen Verfassung' in K Groh et al (eds), *Die Europäische Verfassung—Verfassungen in Europa*, Baden-Baden: Nomos Verlag, 2005, 61–90

—— 'The Pluralism of Global Administrative Law', *European Journal of International Law* 17 (2006), 247–78

—— 'The Security Council and the Great Powers' in V Lowe et al (eds), *The Security Council and War*, Oxford: Oxford University Press, 2008, 133–53

—— 'Global Administrative Law and the Constitutional Ambition' in M Loughlin & P Dobner (eds), *The Twilight of Constitutionalism?*, Oxford: Oxford University Press, 2010, 245–66

Krzyżanowska-Mierzewska, M, 'The Reception Process in Poland and Slovakia' in H Keller & A Stone Sweet (eds), *A Europe of Rights: The Impact of the ECHR on National Legal Systems*, Oxford: Oxford University Press, 2008, 531–602

Kuijper, P J & Bronckers, M, 'WTO Law in the European Court of Justice', *Common Market Law Review* 42 (2005), 1313–55

Kukathas, C, *The Liberal Archipelago*, Oxford: Oxford University Press, 2003

Kumm, M, 'International Law in National Courts: The International Rule of Law and the Limits of the Internationalist Model', *Virginia Journal of International Law* 44 (2003), 19–32

—— 'The Legitimacy of International Law: A Constitutionalist Framework of Analysis', *European Journal of International Law* 15 (2004), 907–31

—— 'Constitutional Democracy Encounters International Law: Terms of Engagement' in S Choudhry (ed), *The Migration of Constitutional Ideas*, Cambridge: Cambridge University Press, 2007, 256–93

—— 'The Cosmopolitan Turn in Constitutionalism: On the Relationship between Constitutionalism in and beyond the State' in J L Dunoff & J P Trachtman (eds), *Ruling the World? Constitutionalism, International Law, and Global Governance*, Cambridge: Cambridge University Press, 2009, 258–324

—— & Ferreres Comella, V, 'The Primacy Clause of the Constitutional Treaty and the Future of Constitutional Conflict in the European Union' in J H H Weiler & C Eisgruber (eds), *Altneuland: The EU Constitution in a Contextual Perspective*, *Jean Monnet Working Paper* 5/04, at: <http://www.jeanmonnetprogram.org/papers/04/040501-15.html>

Kuper, A, *Democracy Beyond Borders: Justice and Representation in Global Institutions*, Oxford: Oxford University Press, 2004

Kymlicka, W, *Multicultural Citizenship*, Oxford: Clarendon Press, 1995

Ladeur, K-H, 'Postmoderne Verfassungstheorie' in U K Preuß (ed), *Zum Begriff der Verfassung: Die Ordnung des Politischen*, Frankfurt am Main: Fischer, 1994, 304–31

Lake, D A & McCubbins, M D, 'The Logic of Delegation to International Organizations' in D G Hawkins et al (eds), *Delegation and Agency in International Organizations*, Cambridge: Cambridge University Press, 2006, 341–68

Lambert, E, *Les effets des arrêts de la Cour européenne des droits de l'homme: Contribution à une approche pluraliste du droit européen des droits de l'homme*, Brussels: Emile Bruylant, 1999

Lambert Abdelgawad, E & Weber, A, 'The Reception Process in France and Germany' in H Keller & A Stone Sweet (eds), *A Europe of Rights: The Impact of the ECHR on National Legal Systems*, Oxford: Oxford University Press, 2008, 107–59

Landfried, C, *Bundesverfassungsgericht und Gesetzgeber*, Baden-Baden: Nomos Verlag, 1984

—— (ed), *Constitutional Review and Legislation: An International Comparison*, Baden-Baden: Nomos Verlag, 1988

Lane, J-E, *Constitutions and Political Theory*, Manchester: Manchester University Press, 1996

Lang, A & Scott, J, 'The Hidden World of WTO Governance', *European Journal of International Law* 20 (2009), 575–614

Laski, H J, 'The Problem of Administrative Areas' in P Q Hirst (ed), *The Pluralist Theory of the State*, London: Routledge, 1989, 131–63

—— 'Law and the State' in P Q Hirst (ed), *The Pluralist Theory of the State*, London: Routledge, 1989, 197–227

Lasser, M, 'The European Pasteurization of French Law', *Cornell Law Review* 90 (2005), 995–1083

Lemmens, P, 'The Relation between the Charter of Fundamental Rights of the European Union and the European Convention on Human Rights—Substantive Aspects', *Maastricht Journal of European and Comparative Law* 8 (2001), 49–67

Lessig, L, 'Fidelity in Translation', *Texas Law Review* 71 (1993), 1165–268

—— 'Fidelity and Constraint', *Fordham Law Review* 65 (1997), 1365–433

Levinson, S (ed), *Responding to Imperfection: The Theory and Practice of Constitutional Amendment*, Princeton, NJ: Princeton University Press, 1995

Ley, I, 'Kant versus Locke: Europarechtlicher und völkerrechtlicher Konstitutionalismus im Vergleich', *Zeitschrift für ausländisches öffentliches Recht und Völkerrecht* 69 (2009), 317–45

Liisberg, J B, 'Does the EU Charter of Fundamental Rights Threaten the Supremacy of Community Law?', *Jean Monnet Working Paper* 4/01

Lijphart, A, *Democracy in Plural Societies*, New Haven, CT: Yale University Press, 1978

—— *Thinking About Democracy: Power Sharing and Majority Rule in Theory and Practice*, London: Routledge, 2008

Lindahl, H, 'Constituent Power and Reflexive Identity: Towards an Ontology of Collective Selfhood' in M Loughlin & N Walker, *Paradox of Constitutionalism: Constituent Power and Constitutional Form*, Oxford: Oxford University Press, 2007, 9–24

—— 'A-Legality: Postnationalism and the Question of Legal Boundaries', *Modern Law Review* 73 (2010) 30–56

Loughlin, M, 'Rights Discourse and Public Law Thought in the United Kingdom' in G W Anderson (ed), *Rights and Democracy: Essays in UK-Canadian Constitutionalism*, London: Blackstone Press, 1999, 435–54

—— 'Constituent Power Subverted: From English Constitutional Argument to British Constitutional Practice' in M Loughlin & N Walker (eds), *The Paradox of Constitutionalism: Constituent Power and Constitutional Form*, Oxford: Oxford University Press, 2007, 27–48

—— 'What is Constitutionalisation?' in M Loughlin & P Dobner (eds), *The Twilight of Constitutionalism?*, Oxford: Oxford University Press, 2010, 47–69

—— & Walker, N (eds), *The Paradox of Constitutionalism: Constituent Power and Constitutional Form*, Oxford: Oxford University Press, 2007

—— & Dobner, P (eds), *The Twilight of Constitutionalism?*, Oxford: Oxford University Press, 2010

Loveland, I, 'Does Homelessness Decision-Making Engage Article 6(1) of the European Convention on Human Rights?', *European Human Rights Law Review* 2003, 176–204

Lowe, V et al (eds), *The United Nations Security Council and War*, Oxford: Oxford University Press, 2008

Luhmann, N, 'Verfassung als evolutionäre Errungenschaft', *Rechtshistorisches Journal* 9 (1990), 176–220

—— *Das Recht der Gesellschaft*, Frankfurt am Main: Suhrkamp Verlag, 1993

Lutz, D S, 'Toward a Theory of Constitutional Amendment', *American Political Science Review* 88 (1994), 355–70

MacCormick, N, 'Beyond the Sovereign State', *Modern Law Review* 56 (1993), 1–18

—— 'The Maastricht-Urteil: Sovereignty Now', *European Law Journal* 1 (1995), 259–66

—— 'Risking Constitutional Collision in Europe?', *Oxford Journal of Legal Studies* 18 (1998), 517–32

—— *Questioning Sovereignty: Law, State, and Nation in the European Commonwealth*, Oxford: Oxford University Press, 1999

Macdonald, R S J, 'The Margin of Appreciation' in R S J Macdonald, F Matscher, & H Petzold (eds), *The European System for the Protection of Human Rights*, Dordrecht: Martinus Nijhoff, 1993, 83–124

—— (ed), *Towards World Constitutionalism*, Leiden: Martinus Nijhoff, 2005

——, Matscher, F, & Petzold, H (eds), *The European System for the Protection of Human Rights*, Dordrecht: Martinus Nijhoff, 1993

Macdonald, T & Macdonald, K, 'Non-Electoral Accountability in Global Politics: Strengthening Democratic Control within the Global Garment Industry', *European Journal of International Law* 17 (2006), 89–119

Magalhães, P C, *The Limits to Judicialization: Legislative Politics and Constitutional Review in the Iberian Democracies*, PhD Diss, University of Ohio, 2003, <http://www.ohiolink.edu/etd/send-pdf.cgi?osu1046117531>

Magnette, P & Nicolaïdis, K, 'The European Convention: Bargaining in the Shadow of Rhetoric', *West European Politics* 27 (2004), 381–404

Mancini, G F, 'The Making of a Constitution for Europe', *Common Market Law Review* 26 (1989), 595–614

March, J G & Olsen, J P, 'The Institutional Dynamics of International Political Orders', *International Organization* 52 (1998), 943–69

Marchetti, R, *Global Democracy: For and Against*, Abingdon: Routledge, 2008

Marks, S, *The Riddle of All Constitutions: International Law, Democracy, and a Critique of Ideology*, Oxford: Oxford University Press, 2000

—— 'Naming Global Administrative Law', *NYU Journal of International Law and Politics* 37 (2005), 995–1001

Marmo, M, 'The Execution of Judgments of the European Court of Human Rights—A Political Battle', *Maastricht Journal of European and Comparative Law* 15 (2008), 235–58

Martín-Retortillo Baquer, L, 'La recepción por el Tribunal Constitucional de la jurisprudencia del Tribunal Europeo de Derechos Humanos', *Revista de Administración Publica* 137 (1995), 7–29

—— *La Europa de los derechos humanos*, Madrid: Centro de estudios políticos y constitucionales, 1998

—— 'Notas para la historia del apartado segundo del artículo 10 de la Constitución' in L Martín-Retortillo Baquer, *La Europa de los derechos humanos*, Madrid: Centro de estudios políticos y constitucionales, 1998, 177–92

Masterman, R, 'Taking the Strasbourg Jurisprudence into Account: Developing a "Municipal Law of Human Rights" under the Human Rights Act', *International and Comparative Law Quarterly* 54 (2005), 907–32

—— 'Aspiration or Foundation? The Status of the Strasbourg Jurisprudence and the "Convention Rights" in Domestic Law' in H Fenwick, R Masterman, & G Phillipson (eds), *Judicial Reasoning under the UK Human Rights Act*, Cambridge: Cambridge University Press, 2007, 57–86

Mathieu, B, 'De quelques examples récents de l'influence des droits européens sur le juge constitutionnel français', *Dalloz* 2002, no 18, 1439–41

Matscher, F, 'Methods of Interpretation of the Convention' in R S J Macdonald, F Matscher, & H Petzold (eds), *The European System for the Protection of Human Rights*, Dordrecht: Martinus Nijhoff, 1993, 63–81

—— & H Petzold (eds), *Protecting Human Rights: The European Dimension: Studies in honour of G J Wiarda*, Cologne: Heymanns, 1988

Mattli, W & Slaughter, A-M, 'Revisiting the European Court of Justice', *International Organization* 52 (1998), 177–210

—— & Woods, N (eds), *The Politics of Global Regulation*, Princeton, NJ: Princeton University Press, 2009

—— & —— 'In Whose Benefit? Explaining Regulatory Change in Global Politics' in W Mattli & N Woods (eds), *The Politics of Global Regulation*, Princeton, NJ: Princeton University Press, 2009, 1–43

Matz, N, *Wege zur Koordinierung völkerrechtlicher Verträge*, Heidelberg: Springer Verlag, 2005

Maus, I, 'Verfassung oder Vertrag: Zur Verrechtlichung globaler Politik' in P Niesen & B Herborth (eds), *Anarchie der kommunikativen Freiheit*, Frankfurt am Main: Suhrkamp Verlag, 2007, 350–82

Mayer, F C, *Kompetenzüberschreitung und Letztentscheidung*, Munich: C H Beck, 2000

—— 'Europarecht als französisches Verfassungsrecht', *Europarecht* 39 (2004), 925–36

McCormick, J P, 'People and Elites in Republican Constitutions, Traditional and Modern' in M Loughlin & N Walker (eds), *The Paradox of Constitutionalism: Constituent Power and Constitutional Form*, Oxford: Oxford University Press, 2007, 107–25

McCrudden, C, 'A Common Law of Human Rights? Transnational Judicial Conversations on Constitutional Rights', *Oxford Journal of Legal Studies* 20 (2000), 499–532

McGarry, J, O'Leary, B, & Simeon, R, 'Integration or Accommodation? The Enduring Debate in Conflict Regulation' in S Choudhry (ed), *Constitutional Design for Divided Societies: Integration or Accommodation?*, Oxford: Oxford University Press, 2008, 41–88

McIlwain, C H, *Constitutionalism: Ancient and Modern*, Ithaca, NY: Cornell University Press, 1940 (reprint: Clark: Lawbook Exchange, 2005)

McKay, D, *Designing Europe: Comparative Lessons from the Federal Experience*, Oxford: Oxford University Press, 2001

Meidinger, E, 'The Administrative Law of Global Private-Public Regulation: The Case of Forestry', *European Journal of International Law* 17 (2006), 47–87

Melchior, M & Courtoy, C, 'The Relations between the Constitutional Courts and the Other National Courts, Including the Interference in this Area of the Action of European Courts: Part III', *Human Rights Law Journal* 23 (2002), 327–30

Melissaris, E, *Ubiquitous Law: Legal Theory and the Space for Legal Pluralism*, Farnham: Ashgate, 2009

Merry, S E, 'Legal Pluralism', *Law & Society Review* 22 (1988), 869–96

Meyer, L H (ed), *Legitimacy, Justice and Public International Law*, Cambridge: Cambridge University Press, 2009

Michaels, R, 'Global Legal Pluralism', *Annual Review of Law and Social Science* 5 (2009), 243–62

Michelman, F, 'Law's Republic', *Yale Law Journal* 97 (1998), 1493–537

Miller, D, *On Nationality*, Oxford: Oxford University Press, 1995

—— *National Responsibility and Global Justice*, Oxford: Oxford University Press, 2007

Möllers, C, *Staat als Argument*, Munich: C H Beck, 1999

—— 'Verfassunggebende Gewalt—Verfassung—Konstitutionalisierung' in A v Bogdandy & J Bast (eds), *Europäisches Verfassungsrecht*, 2nd edn, Berlin: Springer Verlag, 2009, 227–78

——, Vosskuhle, A, & Walter, C (eds), *Internationales Verwaltungsrecht*, Tübingen: Mohr Siebeck, 2007

Moore, S F, 'Law and Social Change: the Semi-Autonomous Social Field as an Appropriate Subject of Study', *Law & Society Review* 7 (1973), 719–46

Moran, M, 'Shifting Boundaries: The Authority of International Law' in J Nijman & A Nollkaemper (eds), *New Perspectives on the Divide Between National and International Law*, Oxford: Oxford University Press, 2007, 163–90

Moravcsik, A, 'Taking Preferences Seriously: A Liberal Theory of International Politics', *International Organization* 51 (1997), 513–53

—— *The Choice for Europe: Social Purpose and State Power from Messina to Maastricht*, London: UCL Press, 1998

—— 'The Origins of Human Rights Regimes: Democratic Delegation in Postwar Europe', *International Organization* 54 (2000), 217–52

—— 'Why Is US Human Rights Policy So Unilateralist?' in S Patrick & S Forman (eds), *Multilateralism and US Foreign Policy*, Boulder, CO: Lynne Rienner, 2002, 345–76

—— 'Is there a 'Democratic Deficit' in World Politics? A Framework for Analysis', *Government and Opposition* 39 (2004), 336–63

Mouffe, C, *The Democratic Paradox*, London: Verso, 2000

—— *On the Political*, Abingdon: Routledge, 2005

Mowbray, A, 'The Creativity of the European Court of Human Rights', *Human Rights Law Review* 5 (2005), 57–79

Müller, H, 'Arguing, Bargaining and All That: Communicative Action, Rationalist Theory and the Logic of Appropriateness in International Relations', *European Journal of International Relations* 10 (2004), 395–435

Müller, R, 'Das letzte Wort', *Frankfurter Allgemeine Zeitung*, 23 October 2004

Mulheron, R, 'A Potential Framework for Privacy? A Reply to *Hello!*', *Modern Law Review* 69 (2006), 679–713

Murkens, J, 'Countering Anti-Constitutional Argument: The Reasons for the European Court of Justice's Decision in *Kadi and Al Barakaat*', *Cambridge Yearbook of European Legal Studies* 11 (2009), 15–51

Nagel, T, 'The Problem of Global Justice', *Philosophy & Public Affairs* 33 (2005), 113–47

Nicholls, D, *The Pluralist State: The Political Ideas of J N Figgis and his Contemporaries*, 2nd edn, Basingstoke: Macmillan, 1994

Nicol, D, 'Original Intent and the European Convention on Human Rights', *Public Law* (2005), 152–72

Nicolaïdis, K, 'We, the Peoples of Europe . . .', *Foreign Affairs* 83:6 (2004), 97–110

Niesen, P & Herborth, B (eds), *Anarchie der kommunikativen Freiheit*, Frankfurt am Main: Suhrkamp Verlag, 2007

Nijman, J & Nollkaemper, A (eds), *New Perspectives on the Divide Between National and International Law*, Oxford: Oxford University Press, 2007

—— & —— 'Beyond the Divide' in J Nijman & A Nollkaemper (eds), *New Perspectives on the Divide Between National and International Law*, Oxford: Oxford University Press, 2007, 341–60

Nußberger, A, 'The Reception Process in Russia and Ukraine' in H Keller & A Stone Sweet (eds), *A Europe of Rights: The Impact of the ECHR on National Legal Systems*, Oxford: Oxford University Press, 2008, 603–74

O'Brien, C & Klug, F, 'The First Two Years of the Human Rights Act', *Public Law* (2002), 649–62

Oestreich, G, 'Vom Herrschaftsvertrag zur Verfassungsurkunde' in R Vierhaus (ed), *Herrschaftsverträge, Wahlkapitulationen, Fundamentalgesetze*, Göttingen: Vandenhoeck & Ruprecht, 1977, 45–67

Oeter, S, 'Souveränität und Demokratie als Probleme in der "Verfassungsentwicklung" der Europäischen Union', *Zeitschrift für ausländisches öffentliches Recht und Völkerrecht* 55 (1995), 659–707

—— 'Rechtsprechungskonkurrenz zwischen nationalen Verfassungsgerichten, Europäischem Gerichtshof und Europäischem Gerichtshof für Menschenrechte', *Veröffentlichungen der Vereinigung deutscher Staatsrechtslehrer* 66 (2007), 361–91

Örücü, E (ed), *Judicial Comparativism in Human Rights Cases*, London: UKNCCL and BIICL, 2003

Ostrovsky, A A, 'The New Codex Alimentarius Commission Standards for Food Created with Modern Biotechnology: Implications for the EC GMO Framework's Compliance with the SPS Agreement', *Michigan Journal of International Law* 25 (2004), 813–43

Paine, T, *Rights of Man*, Mineola, NY: Dover Thrift Editions, 1999

Palombella, G, 'The Rule of Law Beyond the State: Failures, Promises, and Theory', *International Journal of Constitutional Law* 7 (2009), 442–67

Papadopoulos, Y, 'Problems of Democratic Accountability in Network and Multilevel Governance', *European Law Journal* 13 (2007), 469–86

Papier, H-J, 'Koordination des Grundrechtsschutzes in Europa—die Sicht des Bundesverfassungsgerichts', *Zeitschrift für Schweizerisches Recht* 124 (2005) II, 113–27

Pasquino, P, *Sieyès et l'invention de la constitution en France*, Paris: Odile Jacob, 1998

Patrick, S & Forman, S (eds), *Multilateralism and US Foreign Policy*, Boulder, CO: Lynne Rienner, 2002

Paulus, A, *Die internationale Gemeinschaft im Völkerrecht*, Munich: C H Beck, 2001

Pauwelyn, J, *Conflict of Norms in Public International Law: How WTO Law Relates to Other Rules of International Law*, Cambridge: Cambridge University Press, 2003

—— 'The UNESCO Convention on Cultural Diversity, and the WTO: Diversity in International Law-Making?', *ASIL Insight*, 15 November 2005, <http://www.asil. org/insights051115.cfm#_edn4>

Peel, J, 'Risk Regulation under the WTO SPS Agreement: Science as an International Normative Yardstick?', *Jean Monnet Working Paper* 02/04, available at: <http://www.jeanmonnetprogram.org/papers/04/040201.html>

—— 'A GMO by Any Other Name ... Might be an SPS Risk!: Implications of Expanding the Scope of the WTO *Sanitary and Phytosanitary Measures Agreement*', *European Journal of International Law* 17 (2006), 1009–31

Pennock, J R and Chapman, J W (eds), *NOMOS XXV: Liberal Democracy*, New York: New York University Press, 1983

Peters, A, 'Compensatory Constitutionalism: The Function and Potential of Fundamental International Norms and Structures', *Leiden Journal of International Law* 19 (2006), 579–610

—— 'The Globalization of State Constitutions' in J Nijman & A Nollkaemper (eds), *New Perspectives on the Divide Between National and International Law*, Oxford: Oxford University Press, 2007, 251–308

—— 'Conclusions' in J Klabbers, A Peters, & G Ulfstein, *The Constitutionalization of International Law*, Oxford: Oxford University Press, 2009, 342–52

—— 'Dual Democracy' in J Klabbers, A Peters, & G Ulfstein (eds), *The Constitutionalization of International Law*, Oxford: Oxford University Press, 2009, 263–341

Petersmann, E-U, 'Human Rights, Constitutionalism and the World Trade Organization: Challenges for World Trade Organization Jurisprudence and Civil Society', *Leiden Journal of International Law* 19 (2006), 633–67

Pettit, P, *Republicanism: A Theory of Freedom and Government*, Oxford: Oxford University Press, 1997

—— 'Democracy, Electoral and Contestatory', *NOMOS* 42 (2002), 105–44

—— 'Democracy, National and International', *The Monist* 89 (2006), 301–24

Phillipson, G, 'Transforming Breach of Confidence? Towards a Common Law Right of Privacy under the Human Rights Act', *Modern Law Review* 66 (2003), 726–58

Pildes, R H, 'Ethnic Identity and Democratic Institutions: A Dynamic Perspective' in S Choudhry (ed), *Constitutional Design for Divided Societies: Integration or Accommodation?*, Oxford: Oxford University Press, 2008, 173–201

Pingel, I & Sudre, F (eds), *Le ministère public et les exigences du procès équitable*, Brussels: Bruylant, 2003

Poiares Maduro, M, 'Contrapunctual Law: Europe's Constitutional Pluralism in Action' in N Walker (ed), *Sovereignty in Transition*, Oxford: Hart Publishing, 2003, 501–38

—— 'Europe and the Constitution: What if This is as Good as it Gets?' in J H H Weiler & M Wind (eds), *European Constitutionalism Beyond the State*, Cambridge: Cambridge University Press, 2003, 74–102

—— 'The Importance of Being Called a Constitution: Constitutional Authority and the Authority of Constitutionalism', *International Journal of Constitutional Law* 3 (2005), 332–56

—— 'Courts and Pluralism: Essay on a Theory of Adjudication in the Context of Legal and Constitutional Pluralism' in J L Dunoff & J P Trachtman (eds), *Ruling the World? Constitutionalism, International Law and Global Government*, Cambridge: Cambridge University Press, 2009, 356–79

Polakiewicz, J, *Die Verpflichtungen der Staaten aus den Urteilen des Europäischen Gerichtshofs für Menschenrechte*, Berlin, Heidelberg: Springer Verlag, 1993

Poli, S, 'The European Community and the Adoption of International Food Standards within the Codex Alimentarius Commission', *European Law Journal* 10 (2004), 613–30

Pollack, M A & Shaffer, G C, *When Cooperation Fails: The International Law and Politics of Genetically Modified Foods*, Oxford: Oxford University Press, 2009

Poole, T, 'Back to the Future? Unearthing the Theory of Common Law Constitutionalism', *Oxford Journal of Legal Studies* 23 (2003), 435–54

—— 'Harnessing the Power of the Past? Lord Hoffmann and the *Belmarsh Detainees* Case', *Journal of Law and Society* 32 (2005), 534–61

Posner, E A & Yoo, J C, 'Judicial Independence in International Tribunals', *California Law Review* 93 (2005), 1–74

Prantl, H, 'Juristisches Röhren', *Süddeutsche Zeitung*, 20 October 2004

Preuß, U K (ed), *Zum Begriff der Verfassung: Die Ordnung des Politischen*, Frankfurt am Main: Fischer, 1994

—— 'The Constitution of a European Democracy and the Role of the Nation State', *Ratio Juris* 12 (1999), 417–28

—— 'Disconnecting Constitutions from Statehood: Is Global Constitutionalism a Viable Concept?' in M Loughlin & P Dobner (eds), *The Twilight of Constitutionalism?*, Oxford: Oxford University Press, 2010, 23–46

Princen, S, 'EC Compliance with WTO Law: the Interplay of Law and Politics', *European Journal of International Law* 15 (2004), 555–74

Przeworski, A & Maravall, J M (eds), *Democracy and the Rule of Law*, Cambridge: Cambridge University Press, 2003

Queralt Jiménez, A, *La interpretación de los derechos: del Tribunal de Estrasburgo al Tribunal Constitucional*, Madrid: Centro de Estudios Políticos y Constitucionales, 2008

Rajagopal, B, 'Limits of Law in Counter-hegemonic Globalization: The Indian Supreme Court and the Narmada Valley Struggle' in B de S Santos & C A Rodríguez-Garavito (eds), *Law and Globalization from Below*, Cambridge: Cambridge University Press, 2005, 183–217

Rakove, J N, *Original Meanings: Politics and Ideas in the Making of the Constitution*, New York: Knopf, 1996

Raustiala, K, 'The Architecture of International Cooperation: Transgovernmental Networks and the Future of International Law', *Virginia Journal of International Law* 43 (2002), 1–92

—— 'Form and Substance in International Agreements', *American Journal of International Law* 99 (2005), 581–614

—— & Victor, D G, 'The Regime Complex for Plant Genetic Resources', *International Organization* 58 (2004), 277–309

Rawls, J, *Political Liberalism*, New York: Columbia University Press, 1996

—— 'Reply to Habermas' in J Rawls, *Political Liberalism*, New York: Columbia University Press, 1996, 372–434

Raz, J, 'On the Authority and Interpretation of Constitutions: Some Preliminaries' in L Alexander (ed), *Constitutionalism: Philosophical Foundations*, Cambridge: Cambridge University Press, 2001, 152–93

—— *The Authority of Law*, 2nd edn, Oxford: Oxford University Press, 2009

—— 'The Rule of Law and its Virtue' in J Raz, *The Authority of Law*, 2nd edn, Oxford: Oxford University Press, 2009, 210–29

Reinisch, A (ed), *Challenging Acts of International Organizations Before National Courts*, Oxford: Oxford University Press, 2010, forthcoming

Reisman, W M & Stenvick, D L, 'The Applicability of International Law Standards to United Nations Economic Sanctions Programmes', *European Journal of International Law* 9 (1998), 86–141

Requejo Pagés, J L, 'La articulación de las jurisdicciones internacional, constitucional y ordinaria en la defensa de los derechos fundamentales', *Revista Española de Derecho Constitucional* 12 (1992) 35, 179–99

Reus-Smit, C (ed), *The Politics of International Law*, Cambridge: Cambridge University Press, 2004

Reuters, 'EU Approves Genetically Modified Soybean for Import', 4 December 2008, <http://uk.reuters.com/article/environmentNews/idUK-TRE4B33GO20081204>

Revenga Sánchez M, 'En torno a la eficacia de las Sentencias del TEDH: Amparo de ejecución o afianzamiento de doctrina? Una propuesta de reforma', *Revista española de Derecho Europeo* 2004, 521–38

Reynolds, A (ed), *The Architecture of Democracy: Constitutional Design, Conflict Management, and Democracy*, Oxford: Oxford University Press, 2002

Rhodes, R A W, Binder, S A, & Rockman, B A (eds), *The Oxford Handbook of Political Institutions*, Oxford: Oxford University Press, 2006, 261–80

Richardson, H S, *Democratic Autonomy*, Oxford: Oxford University Press, 2002

Richmond, C, 'Preserving the Identity Crisis: Autonomy, System and Sovereignty in European Law', *Law and Philosophy* 16 (1997), 377–420

Risse, T, '"Let's Argue!" Communicative Action in World Politics', *International Organization* 54 (2000), 1–39

—— 'Global Governance und kommunikatives Handeln' in P Niesen & B Herborth (eds), *Anarchie der kommunikativen Freiheit: Jürgen Habermas und die Theorie der internationalen Politik*, Frankfurt am Main: Suhrkamp Verlag, 2008, 57–83

—— & Kleine, M, 'Assessing the Legitimacy of the EU's Treaty Revision Methods', *Journal of Common Market Studies* 45 (2007), 69–80

—— & Ropp, S C, 'International human rights norms and domestic change: conclusions', in T Risse, S C Ropp & K Sikkink (eds), *The Power of Human Rights: International Norms and Domestic Change*, Cambridge: Cambridge University Press, 1999, 234–78

——, ——, & Sikkink, K (eds), *The Power of Human Rights: International Norms and Domestic Change*, Cambridge: Cambridge University Press, 1999

Röben, V, 'Constitutionalism of the European Union after the Draft Constitutional Treaty: How Much Hierarchy?', *Columbia Journal of European Law* 10 (2004), S339–S377

Roberts, D, 'Preliminary Assessment of the Effects of the WTO Agreement on Sanitary and Phytosanitary Measures', *Journal of International Economic Law* 1 (1998), 377–405

—— & Unnevehr, L, 'Resolving Trade Disputes Arising from Trends in Food Safety Regulation: The Role of the Multilateral Governance Framework', *World Trade Review* 4 (2005), 469–97

Roberts, J M, *The French Revolution*, 2nd edn, Oxford: Oxford University Press, 1997

Rosand, E, 'Security Council Resolution 1373, the Counter-Terrorism Committee, and the Fight against Terrorism', *American Journal of International Law* 97 (2003), 333–41

—— 'The Security Council's Efforts to Monitor the Implementation of Al Qaeda / Taliban Sanctions', *American Journal of International Law* 98 (2004), 745–63

—— & Millar, A, 'Strengthening International Law and Global Cooperation' in D Cortright & G A Lopez (eds), *Uniting Against Terror: Cooperative Nonmilitary Responses to the Global Terrorist Threat*, Cambridge, MA: MIT Press, 2007, 51–82

Rosanvallon, P, *Counter-Democracy: Politics in an Age of Distrust* (A Goldhammer, trans), Cambridge: Cambridge University Press, 2008

Rosenau, J N, *Along the Domestic-Foreign Frontier: Exploring Governance in a Turbulent World*, Cambridge: Cambridge University Press, 1997

Rosendorff, B P & Milner, H V, 'The Optimal Design of International Trade Institutions: Uncertainty and Escape', *International Organization* 55 (2001), 829–57

Rousseau, D & Sudre, F (eds), *Conseil constitutionnel et Cour européenne des droits de l'homme: Droits et libertés en Europe*, Paris: Editions STH, 1990

Ruiz Miguel, C, *La ejecución de las sentencias del Tribunal Europeo de Derechos Humanos*, Madrid: tecnos, 1997

Ruiz-Fabri, H, 'Jeux dans la fragmentation: La Convention sur la promotion et la protection de la diversité des expressions culturelles', *Revue générale de droit international public* 111 (2007), 43–87

Runciman, D, *Pluralism and the Personality of the State*, Cambridge: Cambridge University Press, 1997

Sabel, C F & Zeitlin, J, 'Learning from Difference: The New Architecture of Experimentalist Governance in the EU', *European Law Journal* 14 (2008), 271–327

—— & —— (eds), *Experimentalist Governance in the European Union: Towards a New Architecture*, Oxford: Oxford University Press, 2010

Sadurski, W, '"Solange, Chapter 3": Constitutional Courts in Central Europe—Democracy—European Union', *European Law Journal* 14 (2008), 1–35

Safrin, S, 'Treaties in Collision? The Biosafety Protocol and the World Trade Organization Agreements', *American Journal of International Law* 96 (2002), 606–28

Sáiz Arnaiz, A, *La apertura constitucional al derecho internacional y europeo de los derechos humanos. El artículo 10.2 de la Constitucion Española*, Madrid: Consejo General del Poder Judicial, 1999

Salzman, J, 'Labor Rights, Globalization and Institutions: The Role and Influence of the Organization for Economic Cooperation and Development', *Michigan Journal of International Law* 21 (2000), 769–848

Sandel, M J, 'The Procedural Republic and the Unencumbered Self', *Political Theory* 12 (1984), 81–96

—— *Democracy's Discontent*, Cambridge, MA: Harvard University Press, 1996

Sandholtz, W, 'Dynamics of International Norm Change: Rules against Wartime Plunder', *European Journal of International Relations* 14 (2008), 101–31

—— & Stiles, K, *International Norms and Cycles of Change*, Oxford: Oxford University Press, 2008

—— & Stone Sweet, A, 'Law, Politics, and International Governance' in C Reus-Smit (ed), *The Politics of International Law*, Cambridge: Cambridge University Press, 2004, 238–71

Scharpf, F, 'Die Politikverflechtungsfalle: Europäische Integration und deutscher Föderalismus im Vergleich', *Politische Vierteljahresschrift* 26 (1985), 323–56

—— *Governing in Europe: Effective and Democratic?*, Oxford: Oxford University Press, 1999

—— 'Legitimationskonzepte jenseits des Nationalstaats', *MPIfG Working Paper* 04/6, available at: <http://www.mpifg.de/pu/workpap/wp04-6/wp04-6.html>

—— 'The Joint-Decision Trap Revisited', *Journal of Common Market Studies* 44 (2006), 845–64

—— 'Legitimacy in the Multilevel European Polity', *MPIfG Working Paper* 09/1 (2009), <http://www.mpifg.de/pu/workpap/wp09-1.pdf>

Schauer, F, 'Amending the Presuppositions of a Constitution' in S Levinson (ed), *Responding to Imperfection: The Theory and Practice of Constitutional Amendment*, Princeton, NJ: Princeton University Press, 1995, 145–61

Scheeck, L, 'The Relationship between the European Courts and Integration through Human Rights', *Zeitschrift für ausländisches öffentliches Recht und Völkerrecht* 65 (2005), 837–85

Schimmelfennig, F, 'The Community Trap: Liberal Norms, Rhetorical Action, and the Eastern Enlargement of the European Union', *International Organization* 55 (2001), 47–80

Schmidt-Aßmann, E, 'The Internationalization of Administrative Relations as a Challenge for Administrative Law Scholarship', *German Law Journal* 9 (2008), 2061–80

Schmitt, C, *Verfassungslehre*, 9th edn, Berlin: Duncker & Humblot, [1928] 2003

—— *Political Theology: Four Chapters on the Concept of Sovereignty* (G Schwab, trans), Chicago, IL: Chicago University Press, 2005

Schönberger, C, *Unionsbürger: Europas föderales Bürgerrecht in vergleichender Sicht*, Tübingen: Mohr Siebeck, 2005

Schütze, R, *From Dual to Cooperative Federalism: The Changing Structure of European Law*, Oxford: Oxford University Press, 2009

—— 'On "Federal" Ground: The European Union as an (Inter)national Phenomenon', *Common Market Law Review* 46 (2009), 1069–105

—— 'Federalism as Constitutional Pluralism: "Letter from America"' in M Avbelj & J Komárek (eds), *Constitutional Pluralism in the European Union and Beyond*, Oxford: Hart Publishing, forthcoming, 2010

Schuppert, G F & Zürn, M (eds), *Governance in einer sich wandelnden Welt*, Politische Vierteljahresschrift: Sonderheft 41/2008

Scott, C, 'Accountability in the Regulatory State', *Journal of Law and Society* 27 (2000), 38–60

Scott, J, 'European Regulation of GMOs and the WTO', *Columbia Journal of European Law* 9 (2003), 213–39

—— *The WTO Agreement on Sanitary and Phytosanitary Measures*, Oxford: Oxford University Press, 2007

Segal, J A, 'Judicial Behavior' in K E Whittington, R D Kelemen, & G A Caldeira (eds), *The Oxford Handbook of Law and Politics*, Oxford: Oxford University Press, 2008, 19–33

—— & Spaeth, H J, *The Supreme Court and the Attitudinal Model*, New York: Cambridge University Press, 1992

Shany, Y, *Regulating Jurisdictional Relations Between National and International Courts*, Oxford: Oxford University Press, 2007

Shapiro, I & Hacker-Cordón, C (eds), *Democracy's Edges*, Cambridge: Cambridge University Press, 1999

—— —— 'Outer Edges and Inner Edges' in I Shapiro & C Hacker-Cordón (eds), *Democracy's Edges*, Cambridge: Cambridge University Press, 1999, 1–16

Shapiro, M, 'Political Jurisprudence' in M Shapiro & A Stone Sweet, *On Law, Politics, and Judicialization*, Oxford: Oxford University Press, 2002, 19–54

—— 'The Success of Judicial Review and Democracy' in M Shapiro & A Stone Sweet, *On Law, Politics, and Judicialization*, Oxford: Oxford University Press, 2002, 149–83

—— & Stone Sweet, A, *On Law, Politics, and Judicialization*, Oxford: Oxford University Press, 2002

Shaw, J, 'Postnational Constitutionalism in the European Union', *Journal of European Public Policy* 6 (1999), 579–97

Sieyès, E-J, *Qu'est-ce que le Tiers Etat?*, Paris: Alexandre Correard, 1822

Simeon, R, 'Constitutional Design and Change in Federal Systems: Issues and Questions', *Publius: The Journal of Federalism* 39 (2009), 241–61

Simma, B, 'From Bilateralism to Community Interest in International Law', *Recueil des Cours de l'Academie de Droit International* 250 (1994-VI), 217–384

—— & Pulkowski, D, 'Of Planets and the Universe: Self-contained Regimes in International Law', *European Journal of International Law* 17 (2006), 483–529

—— et al (eds), *The Charter of the United Nations*, 2nd edn, Oxford: Oxford University Press, 2002

Simmons, B A, *Mobilizing for Human Rights: International Law in Domestic Politics*, Cambridge: Cambridge University Press, 2009

——, Dobbin, F, & Garrett, G (eds), *The Global Diffusion of Markets and Democracy*, Cambridge: Cambridge University Press, 2008

Simon, D, 'Des influences réciproques entre CJCE et CEDH: 'Je t'aime, moi non plus?'', *Pouvoirs* 2001, no 96, 31–49

Simpson, A W B, 'Britain and the European Convention', *Cornell International Law Journal* 34 (2001), 523–54

Skogstad, G, 'The WTO and Food Safety Regulatory Policy Innovation in the European Union', *Journal of Common Market Studies* 39 (2001), 485–505

—— 'Regulating Food Safety Risks in the European Union: A Comparative Perspective' in C Ansell & D Vogel (eds), *What's the Beef? The Contested Governance of European Food Safety*, Cambridge, MA: MIT Press, 2006, 213–36

Slaughter, A-M, 'A Typology of Transjudicial Communication', *University of Richmond Law Review* 29 (1994), 99–137

—— *A New World Order*, Princeton, NJ: Princeton University Press, 2004

—— & Burke-White, W, 'The Future of International Law is Domestic (or, The European Way of Law)', *Harvard International Law Journal* 47 (2006), 327–52

——, Stone Sweet, A, & Weiler, J H H (eds), *The European Courts and National Courts*, Oxford: Hart Publishing, 1997

Slotboom, M, 'Do Public Health Measures Receive Similar Treatment in European Community and World Trade Organization Law?', *Journal of World Trade* 37 (2003), 553–96

Smith, J, 'EU Clashes on Authorizing Monsanto GM Soybean', Reuters, 19 November 2008, <http://uk.reuters.com/article/environmentNews/idUK-TRE4AI71C20081119>

Snyder, F, 'Governing Economic Globalisation: Global Legal Pluralism and European Law', *European Law Journal* 5 (1999), 334–74

—— 'The Gatekeepers: The European Courts and WTO Law', *Common Market Law Review* 40 (2003), 313–67

Société française pour le droit international (ed), *La juridictionnalisation du droit international*, Paris: Pedone, 2003

Soriano, M C, 'The Reception Process in Spain and Italy' in H Keller & A Stone Sweet (eds), *A Europe of Rights: The Impact of the ECHR on National Legal Systems*, Oxford: Oxford University Press, 2008, 393–450

Soysal, Y N, *Limits of Citizenship: Migrants and Postnational Membership in Europe*, Chicago, IL: University of Chicago Press, 1994

Spielmann, D, 'Human Rights Case Law in the Strasbourg and Luxembourg Courts: Conflicts, Inconsistencies, and Complementarities' in P Alston (ed), *The EU and Human Rights*, Oxford/New York: Oxford University Press, 1999, 757–80

Starmer, K & Klug, F, 'Incorporation through the Back Door?', *Public Law* (1997), 223–33

—— & —— 'Incorporation through the "Front Door": The First Year of the Human Rights Act', *Public Law* (2001), 645–65

Stein, A A, 'Coordination and Collaboration: Regimes in an Anarchic World', *International Organization 36* (1982), 299–324

Stein, E, 'Lawyers, Judges, and the Making of a Transnational Constitution', *American Journal of International Law 75* (1981), 1–27

Steinberg, R H, 'In the Shadow of Law or Power? Consensus-Based Bargaining and Outcomes in the GATT/WTO', *International Organization 56* (2002), 339–74

Steiner, E, 'France' in C A Gearty (ed), *European Civil Liberties and the European Convention on Human Rights*, The Hague: Kluwer Law International, 1997

Steiner, H J, Alston, P, & Goodman, R, *International Human Rights in Context*, 3rd edn, Oxford: Oxford University Press, 2007

Stewart, R B, 'The Global Regulatory Challenge to US Administrative Law', *NYU Journal of International Law and Politics 37* (2005), 695–762

Steyn, L, '2000–2005: Laying the Foundations of Human Rights Law in the United Kingdom', *European Human Rights Law Review 2005*, 349–62

Stolleis, M, *Geschichte des öffentlichen Rechts in Deutschland*, vol II, Munich: C H Beck, 1992

Stone Sweet, A, *The Birth of Judicial Politics in France: The Constitutional Court in Comparative Perspective*, Oxford: Oxford University Press, 1992

—— 'Constitutional Dialogues in the European Community' in A-M Slaughter, A Stone Sweet, & J H H Weiler (eds), *The European Courts and National Courts*, Oxford: Hart Publishing, 1997, 305–30

—— *Governing with Judges: Constitutional Politics in Europe*, Oxford: Oxford University Press, 2000

—— 'Path Dependence, Precedent, and Judicial Power' in M Shapiro & A Stone Sweet, *On Law, Politics, and Judicialization*, Oxford: Oxford University Press, 2002, 112–35

—— *The Judicial Construction of Europe*, Oxford: Oxford University Press, 2004

Stourzh, G, 'Staatsformenlehre und Fundamentalgesetze in England und Nordamerika im 17. und 18. Jahrhundert' in R Vierhaus (ed), *Herrschaftsverträge, Wahlkapitulationen, Fundamentalgesetze*, Göttingen: Vandenhoeck & Ruprecht, 1977, 294–327

Strange, S, *The Retreat of the State: The Diffusion of Power in the World Economy*, Cambridge: Cambridge University Press, 1996

Sudre, F, 'Vers la normalisation des relations entre le Conseil d'Etat et la Cour européenne des droits de l'homme', *Revue française de droit administratif 2006*, 286–98

Suganami, H, *The Domestic Analogy and World Order Proposals*, Cambridge: Cambridge University Press, 1989

Sunstein, C R, *Legal Reasoning and Political Conflict*, Oxford: Oxford University Press, 1996

—— *One Case at a Time: Judicial Minimalism on the Supreme Court*, Cambridge, MA: Harvard University Press, 1999

—— 'Beyond Judicial Minimalism', *Harvard Public Law Working Paper* 08-40, <http://ssrn.com/abstract=1274200>

Szasz, P C, 'The Security Council Starts Legislating', *American Journal of International Law* 96 (2002), 901–5

Tamanaha, B Z, *On the Rule of Law—History, Politics, Theory*, Cambridge: Cambridge University Press, 2004

Tavernier, P (ed), *Quelle Europe pour les droits de l'homme?*, Brussels: Emile Bruylant, 1996

Taylor, C, *Philosophical Arguments*, Cambridge, MA: Harvard University Press, 1995

—— 'The Politics of Recognition' in C Taylor, *Philosophical Arguments*, Cambridge, MA: Harvard University Press, 1995, 225–56

Teubner, G (ed), *Global Law Without a State*, Dartmouth: Aldershot, 1997

—— 'Global Bukowina: Legal Pluralism in the World Society' in G Teubner (ed), *Global Law Without a State*, Dartmouth: Aldershot, 1997, 3–28

—— 'The King's Many Bodies: The Self-Deconstruction of Law's Hierarchy', *Law & Society Review* 31 (1997), 763–88

—— 'Globale Zivilverfassungen: Alternativen zur staatszentrierten Verfassungstheorie', *Zeitschrift für ausländisches öffentliches Recht und Völkerrecht* 63 (2003), 1–28

—— 'Fragmented Foundations: Societal Constitutionalism beyond the Nation State' in M Loughlin & P Dobner (eds), *The Twilight of Constitutionalism?*, Oxford: Oxford University Press, 2010, 327–41

Thierry, J, Case note, *Recueil Dalloz* 2000, Commentaires, 653–4

Thies, A, 'Biret and Beyond: The Status of WTO Rulings in EC Law', *Common Market Law Review* 41 (2004), 1661–82

Thurnherr, D, 'The Reception Process in Austria and Switzerland' in H Keller & A Stone Sweet (eds), *A Europe of Rights: The Impact of the ECHR on National Legal Systems*, Oxford: Oxford University Press, 2008, 311–91

Tierney, S, *Constitutional Law and National Pluralism*, Oxford: Oxford University Press, 2004

Tomkins, A, *Public Law*, Oxford: Oxford University Press, 2003

Tomuschat, C, 'International Law: Ensuring the Survival of Mankind on the Eve of a New Century', *Recueil des Cours de l'Académie de Droit International* 281 (1999), 9–438

—— Note on *Kadi*, *Common Market Law Review* 43 (2006), 537–51

Torbisco Casals, N, *Group Rights as Human Rights: A Liberal Approach to Multiculturalism*, Dordrecht: Springer Verlag, 2006

—— 'Beyond Unity and Coherence: The Challenge of Legal Pluralism in a Post-National World', *Revista Jurídica de la Universidad de Puerto Rico* 77 (2008), 531–51

Torres Pérez, A, *Conflicts of Rights in the European Union: A Theory of Supranational Adjudication*, Oxford: Oxford University Press, 2009

Tretter, H, 'Austria' in R Blackburn & J Polakiewicz (eds), *Fundamental Rights in Europe: The European Convention on Human Rights and its Member States, 1950–2000*, Oxford: Oxford University Press, 2001, 103–65

Troper, M & Jaume, L (eds), *1789 et l'invention de la Constitution*, Paris: LGDJ-Bruylant, 1994

Trubek, D M & Trubek, L G, 'Hard and Soft Law in the Construction of Social Europe: The Role of the Open Method of Coordination', *European Law Journal* 11 (2005), 343–64

Tsagourias, N (ed), *Transnational Constitutionalism: International and European Models*, Cambridge: Cambridge University Press, 2007

—— 'Introduction—Constitutionalism: A Theoretical Roadmap' in N Tsagourias (ed), *Transnational Constitutionalism: International and European Models*, Cambridge: Cambridge University Press, 2007, 1–13

Tully, J, *Strange Multiplicity: Constitutionalism in an Age of Diversity*, Cambridge: Cambridge University Press, 1995

Tushnet, M (ed), *The Constitution in Wartime: Beyond Alarmism and Complacency*, Durham, NC: Duke University Press, 2005

—— 'Emergencies and the Idea of Constitutionalism' in M Tushnet (ed), *The Constitution in Wartime: Beyond Alarmism and Complacency*, Durham, NC: Duke University Press, 2005, 39–54

Tzanakopoulos, A, 'Domestic Court Reactions to UN Security Council Sanctions' in A Reinisch (ed), *Challenging Acts of International Organizations Before National Courts*, Oxford: Oxford University Press, 2010, forthcoming, available at: <http://ssrn.com/abstract=1480184>

van Aaken, A, 'Transnationales Kooperationsrecht nationaler Aufsichtsbehörden als Antwort auf die Herausforderung globalisierter Finanzmärkte' in C Möllers, A Vosskuhle, & C Walter (eds), *Internationales Verwaltungsrecht*, Tübingen: Mohr Siebeck, 2007, 219–57

van Dijk, P & van Hoof, G J H, *Theory and Practice of the European Convention on Human Rights*, 3rd edn, The Hague: Kluwer Law International, 1998

Vanberg, G, *The Politics of Constitutional Review in Germany*, Cambridge: Cambridge University Press, 2005

Veggeland, F & Borgen, S O, 'Negotiating International Food Standards: The World Trade Organization's Impact on the Codex Alimentarius Commission', *Governance* 18 (2005), 675–708

Verdross, A, *Die Verfassung der Völkerrechtsgemeinschaft*, Vienna: Springer Verlag, 1926

Victor, D G, 'The Sanitary and Phytosanitary Agreement of the World Trade Organization: An Assessment After Five Years', 32 *NYU Journal of International Law and Politics* (2000), 865–937

Vierhaus, R (ed), *Herrschaftsverträge, Wahlkapitulationen, Fundamentalgesetze*, Göttingen: Vandenhoeck & Ruprecht, 1977

Voeten, E, 'Outside Options and the Logic of Security Council Action', *American Political Science Review* 95 (2001), 845–58

—— 'The Political Origins of the UN Security Council's Ability to Legitimize the Use of Force', *International Organization* 59 (2005), 527–57

—— 'The Politics of International Judicial Appointments: Evidence from the European Court of Human Rights', *International Organization* 61 (2007), 669–701

Vogel, D, 'The Politics of Risk Regulation in Europe and the United States', *Yearbook of European Environmental Law* 3 (2003), 1–43

Wahl, R, 'Verfassungsstaatlichkeit im Konstitutionalismus und in der Weimarer Zeit' in R Wahl, *Verfassungsstaat, Europäisierung, Internationalisierung*, Frankfurt am Main: Suhrkamp Verlag, 2003, 331–7

—— *Verfassungsstaat, Europäisierung, Internationalisierung*, Frankfurt am Main: Suhrkamp Verlag, 2003

Waldron, J, *Law and Disagreement*, Oxford: Clarendon Press, 1999

—— 'The Concept and the Rule of Law', *Georgia Law Review* 43 (2008), 1–61

Walker, N, 'The Idea of Constitutional Pluralism', *Modern Law Review* 65 (2002), 317–59

—— 'Postnational Constitutionalism and the Problem of Translation' in J H H Weiler & M Wind (eds), *European Constitutionalism Beyond the State*, Cambridge: Cambridge University Press, 2003, 27–54

—— 'European Constitutionalism in the State Constitutional Tradition', *Current Legal Problems* 59 (2006), 51–89

—— 'Beyond Boundary Disputes and Basic Grids: Mapping the Global Disorder of Normative Orders', *International Journal of Constitutional Law* 6 (2008), 373–96

—— 'Taking Constitutionalism Beyond the State', *Political Studies* 56 (2008), 519–43

—— 'Beyond the Holistic Constitution?' in M Loughlin & P Dobner (eds), *The Twilight of Constitutionalism?*, Oxford: Oxford University Press, 2010, 291–308

Walter, C, 'Die Europäische Menschenrechtskonvention als Konstitutionalisierungsprozeß', *Zeitschrift für ausländisches öffentliches Recht und Völkerrecht* 59 (1999), 961–83

—— 'International Law in a Process of Constitutionalization' in J Nijman & A Nollkaemper (eds), *New Perspectives on the Divide Between National and International Law*, Oxford: Oxford University Press, 2007, 191–215

—— et al (eds), *Terrorism as a Challenge for National and International Law*, Berlin/ Heidelberg: Springer Verlag, 2004

Waters, M, 'Creeping Monism: The Judicial Trend toward Interpretive Incorporation of Human Rights Treaties', *Columbia Law Review* 107 (2007), 628–705

Weber, A, 'Zur föderalen Struktur der Europäischen Union im Entwurf des Europäischen Verfassungsvertrags', *Europarecht* 39 (2004), 841–56

Weil, P, 'Towards Relative Normativity in International Law', *American Journal of International Law* 77 (1983), 413–42

Weiler, J H H, 'The Transformation of Europe', *Yale Law Journal* 100 (1991), 2403–83

—— 'A Quiet Revolution: The European Court of Justice and its Interlocutors', *Comparative Political Studies* 26 (1994), 510–34

—— 'The State 'über alles': Demos, Telos and the German Maastricht Decision', *Jean Monnet Working Papers* 6/95

—— *The Constitution of Europe*, Cambridge: Cambridge University Press, 1999

—— 'In Defence of the Status Quo: Europe's Constitutional *Sonderweg*' in J H H Weiler & M Wind (eds), *European Constitutionalism Beyond the State*, Cambridge: Cambridge University Press, 2003, 7–23

—— 'The Geology of International Law—Governance, Democracy and Legitimacy', *Zeitschrift für ausländisches öffentliches Recht und Völkerrecht* 64 (2004), 547–62

—— 'On the Power of the Word: Europe's Constitutional Iconography', *International Journal of Constitutional Law* 3 (2005), 173–90

—— 'Editorial', *European Journal of International Law* 19 (2008), 895–9

—— & Eisgruber, C (eds), *Altneuland: The EU Constitution in a Contextual Perspective*, *Jean Monnet Working Paper* 5/04, at: <http://www.jeanmonnetprogram.org/papers/04/040501-15.html>

—— & Lockhart, N S, '"Taking Rights Seriously" Seriously: The European Court and its Fundamental Rights Jurisprudence', *Common Market Law Review* 32 (1995), 51–94, 579–627

—— & Wind, M (eds), *European Constitutionalism Beyond the State*, Cambridge: Cambridge University Press, 2003

Wendt, A, *Social Theory of International Politics*, Cambridge: Cambridge University Press, 1999

—— 'Comment on Held's Cosmopolitanism' in I Shapiro & C Hacker-Cordón (eds), *Democracy's Edges*, Cambridge: Cambridge University Press, 1999, 127–33

—— 'Why a World State is Inevitable', *European Journal of International Relations* 9 (2003), 491–542

Whitlock, C, 'Terrorism Financing Blacklist at Risk', *Washington Post*, 2 November 2008, <http://globalpolicy.org/component/content/article/178/33243.html>

Whittington, K, Keleman, R D, & Caldera, G A (eds), *The Oxford Handbook of Law and Politics*, Oxford: Oxford University Press, 2008

Whytock, C A, 'Thinking Beyond the Domestic–International Divide: Toward a Unified Concept of Public Law', *Georgetown Journal of International Law* 36 (2004), 155–93

Wicks, E, 'Taking Account of Strasbourg? The British Judiciary's Approach to Interpreting Convention Rights', *European Public Law* 11 (2005), 907–32

Wiener, J B & Rogers, M D, 'Comparing Precaution in the United States and Europe', *Journal of Risk Research* 5 (2002), 317–49

Wildhaber, L, 'Ein Überdenken des Zustands und der Zukunft des Europäischen Gerichtshofs für Menschenrechte', *Europäische Grundrechte-Zeitschrift* 36 (2009), 549–53

Wood, G, *The Creation of the American Republic, 1776–1787*, Chapel Hill, NC: University of North Carolina Press

Woods, N, 'The United States and the International Financial Institutions: Power and Influence within the World Bank and the IMF' in R Foot, S N MacFarlane, & M Mastanduno (eds), *US Hegemony and International Organizations*, Oxford: Oxford University Press, 2003, 92–114

Young, A R & Holmes, P, 'Protection or Protectionism? EU Food Safety and the WTO' in C Ansell & D Vogel (eds), *What's the Beef? The Contested Governance of European Food Safety*, Cambridge, MA: MIT Press, 2006, 281–305

Young, I M, *Justice and the Politics of Difference*, Princeton, NJ: Princeton University Press, 1990

—— *Inclusion and Democracy*, Oxford: Oxford University Press, 2000

Young, M A, 'The WTO's Use of Relevant Rules of International Law: An Analysis of the *Biotech* Case', *International and Comparative Law Quarterly* 56 (2007), 907–30

Yourow, H C, *The Margin of Appreciation Doctrine in the Dynamics of European Human Rights Jurisprudence*, The Hague: Kluwer Law International, 1996

Zimmermann, A, 'Germany' in R Blackburn & J Polakiewicz (eds), *Fundamental Rights in Europe: The European Convention on Human Rights and its Member States, 1950–2000*, Oxford: Oxford University Press, 2001, 335–54

Zumbansen, P, 'Transnational Legal Pluralism', *Comparative Research in Law & Political Economy Research Paper* 01/2010, at: <http://ssrn.com/abstract=1542907>

Zürn, M, *Regieren jenseits des Nationalstaats*, Frankfurt am Main: Suhrkamp Verlag, 1998

—— 'The State in the Postnational Constellation—Societal Denationalization and Multi-Level Governance', *ARENA Working Papers*, WP 99/35, at: <http://www.arena.uio.no/publications/working-papers1999/papers/wp99_35.htm>

—— 'Global Governance and Legitimacy Problems', *Government & Opposition* 39 (2004), 260–87

—— 'Governance in einer sich wandelnden Welt—eine Zwischenbilanz' in G F Schuppert & M Zürn (eds), *Governance in einer sich wandelnden Welt*, Politische Vierteljahresschrift: Sonderheft 41/2008, 553–80

—— et al, 'Politische Ordnungsbildung wider Willen', *Zeitschrift für internationale Beziehungen* 14 (2007), 129–64

Index